OIL AND THE INTERNATIONAL ECONOMY

OIL AND THE
INTERNATIONAL ECONOMY

Lessons from Two Price Shocks

**Georg Koopmann, Klaus Matthies,
and Beate Reszat**

Transaction Publishers
New Brunswick (U.S.A.) and Oxford (U.K.)

Library of Congress Catalog Number: 88-27133
ISBN: 0-88738-616-4
Printed in the United States of America

Library of Congress Cataloging-in-Publication Data

Koopmann, Georg.
  Oil and the international economy: lessons from two price shocks / Georg Koopmann, Klaus Matthies, Beate Reszat.
    Reprint. Originally published: Hamburg: Verlag Weltarchiv, 1984.
    Bibliography: p.
    ISBN 0-88738-616-4
    1. Petroleum industry and trade. 2. International economic relations. 3. International finance. I. Matthies, Klaus.
    II. Reszat, Beate. III. Title.
[HD9560.5.K685 1989]
332'.042--dc19   88-27133
                                                                        CIP

PREFACE

The two sharp oil price increases in 1973/74 and 1979-81
exposed the world economy to its most severe real shocks
in the entire postwar-period. The HWWA-Institut für Wirt-
schaftsforschung-Hamburg, an independent research institute with particular interest in the empirical policy-
oriented analysis of international economic issues, has
dealt with the implications of these processes in various
studies. This volume provides a comprehensive analysis of
the patterns of international economic response to the two
price shocks, with special regard to the Federal Republic
of Germany. It traces the intertemporal similarities as
well as differences in reaction and attempts to draw lessons for coping with potential future disturbances.

The study was conducted by the Department of International
Finance, Economic Relations between Industrial Countries
of the HWWA-Institut in cooperation with experts from other
institute departments. It was directed by Georg Koopmann,
who was also in charge of writing Chapters 4, 5 and 6, the
introduction and the summary. Dr. Beate Reszat wrote the
monetary and financial parts (Chapters 2, 3 and 4.3) and
Klaus Matthies is the author of the first chapter.

The members of the project team have greatly benefitted from the ideas of, and discussion with, many experts in the academic and administrative worlds. Rather than give prominence to a few individuals or institutions only, we would like to express our sincere gratitude and appreciation to them all in this non-discriminatory way.

The book is based on a report prepared for the Federal Ministry of Economics, Bonn, to whom the HWWA is much obliged for financing the project and granting permission to publish its findings.

Hans-Eckart Scharrer
Department Head

C O N T E N T S

8

10

L I S T   O F   T A B L E S

Table

12

15

LIST OF CHARTS

INTRODUCTION

The oil price increases of the past decade left deep marks on the world economy. Not only did they lead to a massive redistribution of income in favour of the oil-producing countries, but they also caused serious disruption of growth, imbalances in foreign trade and problems of stability in oil-importing countries. The difficulties that arose can partly be explained by the fact that oil had to be replaced by relatively expensive substitutes, but they also reflect mistakes in economic policy.

Meanwhile, crude oil prices have fallen substantially in both real and nominal terms since reaching a peak in the second quarter of 1981 (see Chart 1; for real oil prices see Tables 1.1 and A-2), but in the long run real oil prices can be expected to rise once again. The long-term influences on oil prices and the probable trend are analysed in the first chapter of this study. However, the main purpose of the work is to examine the chief external and domestic consequences of rising oil prices and to identify ways of overcoming the financial and adjustment problems that are arising.

Chapter 2 analyses the links between real oil price increases and exchange rate movements. It shows that traditional adjustment mechanisms cannot restore global equilibrium but mainly affect the distribution of deficits between oil-importing countries. Hence the question arises as to how oil-induced balance-of-payments deficits can be financed without delaying the inevitable real adjustment process.

Chart 1:   PRICES OF CRUDE OIL, OTHER RAW MATERIALS AND
           INDUSTRIAL GOODS, 1972-1982

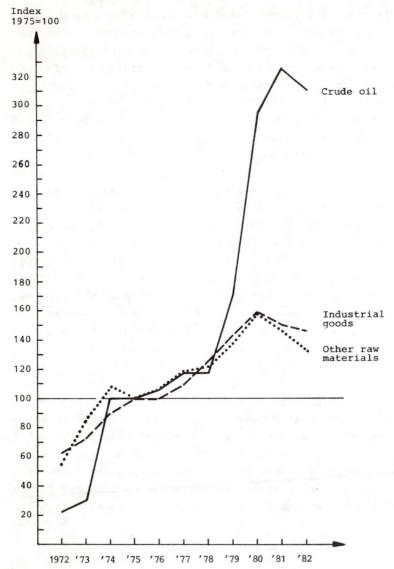

Index
1975=100

Crude oil

Industrial
goods

Other raw
materials

1972 '73 '74 '75 '76 '77 '78 '79 '80 '81 '82

Source: See Table A-1.

The third chapter describes first the manner in which the oil-exporting countries' surpluses have been recycled hitherto, the special problems this caused for the international financial markets and the importance of international institutions in this process. Finally, proposals for resolving the financial problems will be discussed.

The following chapters deal with various aspects of internal and external adjustment to dearer oil. First of all, rising oil prices pose a challenge to stabilisation policies. Chapter 4 analyses the impact of price increases for crude oil on oil product and energy prices as well as on the general price level. On this basis the internal and external pressures which stabilisation policies are facing in times of rising oil prices are examined, taking Germany as a case in point.

A consistant stabilisation policy and price relationships in line with scarcity conditions are essential requirements for successful structural adjustment to oil price shocks. This process of adjustment is analysed from various angles: in Chapter 5, after having shown the consequences of real oil price increases for overall economic growth. The main question to be asked is how structural adjustment can be encouraged by means of economic policy.

The sixth and final chapter examines the influences of real oil price rises on the conditions governing competition in international trade. These can change over the long term as oil-producing countries emerge as significant competitors in certain industrial sectors. In the short and medium term there may be an intensification of competition among enterprises from oil-importing countries. The ensuing trade conflicts can endanger the close link between financing and adjustment.

Chapter 1: The longer-term trend in real oil prices

1. The world oil market after the oil price shocks

a. History of oil prices to date

During the fifties and sixties the price of crude oil showed
very little nominal change, so that in real terms it fell considerably. The posted price[1] for Arabian Light, the reference
or "marker" crude, was at US$ 1.80 a barrel in 1970 and the aver-
age export price for crude slightly less, at $1.73. In 1971
oil prices began to rise (see Table 1.1). The rise was quite
in line with long-term demand and supply trends - the shortening
lifetime of world oil reserves and a rapid increase in US import
demand, among other things - but it was institutional changes
and political factors that determined the strength of the rise
and its timing.

The rise came in two large jumps. After a moderate increase in
the average export price between February 1972 and September
1973 to $ 3, the first oil price explosion in 1973-74 in the
wake of the Yom Kippur War led to a quadrupling of the price
to more than $ 11. During the second oil price explosion the
price tripled again from almost $ 13 a barrel in December 1978
to more than $ 35 in January 1981.

The price of oil remained largely unchanged in nominal terms
for five years after the first massive increase in 1973-74, so
that in real terms it declined considerably. This was due partly to the dampening of oil consumption in industrial countries
and partly to the moderating influence of Saudi Arabia, the
dominant oil supplier. The period of stable oil prices was brought
to an end in late 1978 by OPEC's decision to raise the price by
a total of 15 % in several stages within the space of one year
against the background of a cyclical revival in the demand for

25

Table 1.1:   CRUDE OIL PRICES, 1970-83
               (AVERAGE OFFICIAL EXPORT PRICE OF OPEC OIL)

| Years | US dollars per barrel | Indices, 1972 = 100 | |
		nominal	real[a]
1970	1.73	71	82
1971	2.14	87	95
1972	2.45	100	100
1973	3.37	138	117
1974	11.25	459	319
1975	11.02	450	278
1976	11.89	485	296
1977	12.95	529	299
1978	12.98	530	261
1979	19.00	776	333
1980	31.51	1,286	502
1981	35.01	1,429	586
1982	33.39	1,363	578
1983	29.33	1,197	530

a Deflated by the unit value indices in US dollars of the world exports
of manufactured goods.

Sources: OECD: Economic Outlook, various years; UN: Monthly
           Bulletin of Statistics, various years.

oil. However, the loss of output in Iran and the consequent precautionary buying by oil consumers in fact caused Saudi Arabia to lose control over the common price, so that oil prices were raised at a much faster rate. The posted price for Saudi oil became the minimum price for OPEC oil.

The tide turned in the first half of 1981 as a result of the onset of recession in Western industrial countries in 1980, increasing success in energy conservation and oil substitution and the high level of production maintained over a long period by Saudi Arabia. Oversupply on the world market persisted, despite the continued losses of production in Iran and Iraq and a restriction on liftings in the other OPEC countries that remains in force. A few oil-exporting countries reduced their export prices during 1982, and by the spring of 1983 it was inevitable that the OPEC reference price would have to be reduced substantially for the first time in view of the continued contraction in oil demand; accordingly, the price was cut from $ 34 to 29 a barrel.

The OPEC countries had clearly underestimated the reaction of oil consumers to the price rises, for despite continued slow economic growth world petroleum consumption steadily declined from the peak of 1979; by 1983 it had fallen by a total of 11 %. This decline will, of course, come to an end with the resumption of stronger growth; world oil consumption declined for two years after the first price jump, only to expand again until 1979, albeit at only half the rate recorded in the time of cheap oil and faster economic growth. However, the adjustments made by oil consumers as a result of the further dramatic increase in oil prices after 1979 is probably largely permanent.

The deciding factor in the sharp contraction in oil demand was the development in the Western industrial countries. They account for more than half the world consumption of oil, with the

USA alone taking more than a quarter. The centrally planned
economies consume one-fifth; within this group, the USSR is
the largest oil consumer after the USA. Around half the oil
consumed in the world is traded on the international markets.
The main suppliers of crude to the world market are still the
OPEC countries, although their market share contracted from
87 % in 1973 to less than two-thirds in 1983. As production
in other countries was not reduced or was even increased -
as in the new production areas in the North Sea, Mexico and
Alaska - OPEC bore the full brunt of the fall in demand and its
members' export earnings also declined appreciably again. Between 1978 and 1980 they had more than doubled from US$ 133
to 279 billion, but by 1983 they had fallen back to an estimated $ 160 billion owing to falling prices and deliveries (see
Table 1.2).

b.   Present projections of oil prices

The considerable raising of oil prices from the end of 1973
onwards was possible because the OPEC countries had taken over
control of their output from the foreign oil companies and ensured that the higher price would hold by restricting production. Nevertheless, the change in supply policy within OPEC
brought about by the nationalisation of oil reserves was aided
by events in the world oil market. Even before 1973 it became
clear that proven oil reserves were declining in relation to
pruduction in several important producing countries, so that
constraints on a continued rapid expansion in production were
becoming discernible and in some cases were already being felt.
In the USA, for example, oil production had peaked in 1970 and
had steadily declined thereafter, with the result that purchases from abroad increased rapidly and the USA once again became
the largest oil importer in 1973, as it had been until 1966.

After taking control of the oil supply, the producing countries

Table 1.2: OIL EXPORTS OF THE OPEC COUNTRIES, 1960-1983

Years	Exports of crude oil		Exports of crude oil and oil products	
	Mn barrels per day	As % of world exports	Mn barrels per day	US$ bn (year)
1960	6.7	92.0	7.9	5.4
1970	20.2	86.3	22.2	14.8
1971	22.0	86.3	23.8	19.6
1972	24.1	86.1	25.9	22.1
1973	27.5	87.3	29.5	34.6
1974	27.3	87.0	29.1	113.5
1975	24.1	84.4	25.6	106.7
1976	27.5	84.9	29.3	129.1
1977	27.6	84.0	29.4	141.4
1978	26.1	82.2	28.0	133.2
1979	26.8	80.2	28.9	197.1
1980	22.9	76.6	24.9	278.6
1981	18.5	71.6	20.1	255.6
1982	14.3	63.9	16.4	200.8
1983[a]	13.2	62.0	15.4	160.4

a Estimate.

Sources: OPEC: Annual Statistical Bulletin, 1979 and 1981;
          Oil & Gas Journal 21.11.1983; Shell Briefing Service,
          May 1984 (German edition).

sought to bring oil prices closer to those of other forms of energy in order to increase their receipts. This goal had both short-term and long-term connotations, for the expected dampening of demand would extend the lifetime of oil reserves. Even if OPEC had not existed, the common interest of the main oil-producing countries to restrict supply in order to support the price would probably have triggered oil market developments similar to those that occurred, at least in the long run. The second price surge, which extended over a period of two years and raised prices by much more than the first in absolute terms, sprang from the combination of two political events which had nothing to do with the existence of OPEC - the revolution in Iran and the war between Iraq and Iran. Without these two occurrences, which triggered precautionary buying by oil consumers, the rise in prices would undoubtedly have been much more moderate.

In retrospect, those critics of OPEC's pricing policy who said that the reference price of $ 34 (and occasionally far higher prices for certain African grades) was excessive and untenable have therefore been proved correct. Prices came increasingly under pressure after the supply situation had eased in 1981 and in spite of large production cuts, particularly by Saudi Arabia. OPEC finally had to fall in line with the market and to reduce its reference price by $ 5 a barrel in March 1983.

Even though the situation on the oil market was temporarily distorted to the detriment of the oil producers by destocking on the part of traders, refiners and consumers, the outlook for the next few years at least is differnt to what it was before the recent "oil glut". The unexpectedly sharp reduction in the demand for oil has seen to that; it has been caused not only by the long period of weak growth in the industrial countries that began in 1981 but also largely by the strong reaction of oil consumption to the rise in oil prices since 1973.

In addition, the supply of oil from sources outside the OECD
area has risen by more than had earlier been assumed. Whereas
most of the forecasts published before 1981 were still predicting further real price rises, now the predominant view
is that real oil prices will not rise further in the next
few years at least.

Looking further into the future, but at any event into the
nineties, opinions are divided as to the likely real oil price
trend. Those representing "conventional wisdom" expect a
renewed increase in real oil prices in the nineties, a view
that has now found "official" acceptance. For example, in
its second World Energy Outlook published in 1982 (IEA 1982a)
the International Energy Agency warns against the view that
the present glut on the world oil market reflects the underlying medium and long-term trend. Instead, the demand and
supply developments that are to be expected are likely to
lead to a renewed tightening of supply in the late eighties.
These expectations have been quantified in two scenarios.
Assuming in both cases a fall in real oil prices until the
mid-eighties, the low energy demand scenario foresees an
annual rise of 3 % in real oil prices until the end of the
nineties and a rate of growth of 2.7 % in real GNP. By way
of comparison the IEA draws a high demand scenario, in which
a constant real oil price and more rapid economic growth of
3.2 % lead to a steeper increase in energy consumption. In
1983 the IEA adjusted its growth expectations further downwards, so that its calculations are now based on an annual
rate of growth of 1.5 % until 1985 and then one of 2.5 % until the year 2000 (Die Welt, 14.4.1983). According to the
IEA, its calculations show the present favourable market situation for consumers to be "deceptive", as it overlays
longer-term developments that entail the danger of further
jumps in the price of oil at the end of the eighties.

The expectation that oil prices will again rise over the long term is not universally accepted. Critics[2] describe the conventional wisdom about events in the international oil market since 1973 as a misinterpretation. The oil price increase between 1973 and 1981 "reflected a virulent new strain of oligopolistic pricing in the context of short-term supply constraints by producers exercising a temporary control over output levels, and with the effects seriously exacerbated by inappropriate user responses caused by the industrialised countries' misinterpretations of the developing market situation" (Odell 1983, p. 393). In the meantime, high oil prices have provoked a reaction away from oil that has shown up to only a small extent so far in oil consumption. In the light of stagnating demand for OPEC oil, OPEC's influence over the oil price is fading and it is becoming increasingly difficult to exercise the necessary discipline over production (Griffin, Teece 1982, p. 215).

The new element in the "unconventional" view is the stronger confidence in adjustment reactions, for a steady decline in oil prices depends crucially on there being a lasting stagnation in the demand for OPEC oil. This seems unlikely to happen, however, if there is a resumption of lasting, albeit moderate growth in the world economy. The objection that the conventional interpretation underestimates consumers' reactions to increased oil prices could be countered with the argument that its critics might not have paid sufficient regard to the reaction to falling prices.

2. Future trends in the demand for oil

The demand for oil is determined by the interaction of a whole range of factors. Besides the price of oil, these include economic growth, advances in energy technology, the prices and availability of other energy sources and the conditions underlying energy policy.

a. The energy policy of oil-importing countries

The energy policy pursed by oil-importing countries is an important determinant of future world oil consumption. As in the past, the non-oil developing countries will be able to exert little influence on the world energy markets in spite of their rising oil requirement and will have to adjust to the situation. The Western industrial countries will continue to be the main protagonists. They co-ordinate their long-term energy policies through the International Energy Agency, which was set up within the OECD in 1974 mainly for short-term crisis management. The common objective of permanently reducing their reliance on imported oil is to be achieved by means of oil substitution, a more rational use of energy and the development of member countries' own sources of energy[3]. Similar intentions have been expressed repeatedly by the EC[4]. Most industrial countries have now adopted national energy programmes based on these concepts.

The pace at which dependence on oil imports is reduced will depend partly on how conscientiously the declarations of energy policy intent are translated into action. A determined attack on the obstacles still remaining in many countries to the more efficient use of energy and the development of new sources of energy could lead to a marked reduction in oil consumption, at least in the industrial countries.[5]

The industrial countries consider the removal of price distortions, and in particular the freeing of artificially low energy prices, to be especially important if energy consumption is to be curbed. In reality, however, there are still wide divergences from this goal (Matthies 1983). In Canada, for example, crude oil and natural gas prices are kept well below the world market level and in the USA too the prices of a substantial proportion of natural gas sales are still regulated. In many countries government regulations prevent the prices of petroleum products from adjusting to world market trends; the exceptions are the Federal Republic of Germany, the United Kingdom, Norway, Sweden, Switzerland, Australia, Japan und the USA. In addition, some electricity tariffs continue to encourage consumption. On the other hand, however, taxes and duties are also levied on energy products on the pretext of curbing consumption whereas the main motive is generally to increase government revenue.

The main thrust of government promotion efforts is concentrated on increasing the supply of energy and in particular expanding nuclear energy; in most countries, however, supply still falls far short of the plan targets. Moreover, it is primarily the production of coal, petroleum and natural gas that is being promoted, whereas the development of renewable sources of energy is receiving little financial support. Government measures to reduce the demand for energy are of minor significance by comparison with those to boost supplies.

It is almost impossible to predict how quickly the energy policy objectives can be realised. In some cases the present cost and price relationships between oil and other energy products are clearly an obstacle; for example, it is for this reason that in many countries, but in particular in Italy and Japan, heating oil is still used in large quantities for electricity generation. There are similar barriers to

34

the expansion of the power and heat combination and district heating. Progress in energy conservation and oil substitution in general is being checked by the weakness of investment, which is keeping the proportion of modern plant employing modern energy technology lower than if growth were faster.

Future developments on the world oil market will depend essentially on the vigour with which the industrial countries, the most important consumer group, pursue a consistent energy policy in line with their own declared aims.

b.   Economic growth and increasing energy consumption

Primary energy consumption in the world as a whole fluctuated very erratically from one year to the next between 1973 and 1983 but on average it rose by 1.6 % a year, while in the Western industial countries it actually declined (BP 1984, p. 28). Hence the overall rise was considerably slower than in the years before the first oil price explosion, when the rate of incrase was around 5 %. A crucial factor in the slowdown was the weakening of economic growth in the OECD countries. The average annual increase in gross domestic product after 1973 was about half the rate recorded in previous years and at the beginning of the eighties growth came practically to a standstill. Over the same period there was a steady decline in energy intensity, which measures the quantity of primary energy consumed to produce one unit of GDP (see Table 1.3). In fact, energy intensity has been falling since 1970, when energy price rises were hardly a factor.

A comparison of the rates of growth in primary energy consumption and real GDP of the kind usually carried out to illustrate the decreasing correlation between the two shows that they moved more or less in parallel in the OECD countries between 1965 and 1973; between 1973 and 1983, by contrast, energy consumption declined despite a rise in GDP. The average for a fairly long period conceals wide fluctuations from year to year and differences between member countries. In fact, the

Table 1.3:   ENERGY INTENSITY AND THE CONSUMPTION OF OIL
             AS A PROPORTION OF TOTAL PRIMARY ENERGY
             REQUIREMENTS (TPE) IN THE OECD, 1970-1982

Years	Energy intensity[a]		Share of oil in TPE (%)
	Total	Oil	
1970	89	44	50
1971	88	44	50
1972	88	45	51
1973	87	46	52
1974	86	44	51
1975	84	42	51
1976	84	43	51
1977	83	43	52
1978	83	43	52
1979	82	41	50
1980	79	37	47
1981	75	34	45
1982	73	32	44

a   TPE and oil consumption respectively in tonnes oil equivalent per
    US$ 100,000 of GDP at 1975 prices and exchange rates.

Sources: Energy Balances of OECD Countries 1970/1982;
         National Accounts of OECD Countries, 1953-1982,
         Volume I; calculations by the authors.

relationship between economic growth and the use of energy
is so complex that measurements of this kind cannot properly
be used as a basis for reliable forecasts of future trends.
Although in the past the growth in national product was broadly matched by an approximately equal increase in energy consumption, this relationship was never so close that their
parallel movement up to 1973 should be regarded as a datum
that was subsequently invalidated by the oil price explosion.
It has not yet been possible to formulate a satisfactory
theoretical explanation of the interdependent relationship
that exists between the macroeconomic aggregates.

It is an undisputed fact that since the phenomenal rise in
energy prices energy consumption per unit of GDP has steadily
decreased. Accordingly, all the energy forecasts of recent
date come to the conclusion that the rise in energy consumption in the world as a whole, and particularly in the industrial countries, will continue to lag noticeably behind the
growth in GDP. The main reasons for this assessment are the
dramatic inreases in the cost of energy in relation to the
prices of other factors of production and the adjustment
process this has set in motion. Up to now, energy price
increases have had only a partial effect on energy consumption because of the time required to develop new techniques
and implement investment projects. This process is therefore
continuing. Even with declining energy intensity, the IEA
nevertheless expects primary energy consumption in the OECD
to continue to grow and by the year 2000 to be between a good
quarter and one-half more than in 1980, depending on the rate
of economic growth assumed   (between 2.5 and 3.2 % per annum).
The slower increase in energy consumption than had been
predicted previously is attributable mainly to the assumption
of a lower rate of economic growth.

The increase in energy consumption has also slowed down in the developing countries, although not as markedly as in the industrial countries, for at their low level of consumption (more than half of the world population shares one-seventh of the energy consumed globally) the scope for energy saving is limited. Energy consumption per unit of gross national product in the developing countries undergoing industrialisation will probably decline more slowly than in the industrial countries. One factor in this will be the exhaustion of traditional fuels such as wood and agricultural waste, which are not reflected in the statistics and are mostly not used "commercially" but which account for a considerable share of the energy supply in underdeveloped regions. According to World Bank estimates (World Bank 1983 b) commercial energy consumption in the developing countries[6] will almost double between 1980 and 1995[7] on the assumption of an annual rate of growth of 4.8 % in GNP and thus increase faster than in the rest of the world, where the energy consumption is expected to increase by more than one-quarter. This implies that almost half of the projected increase in global energy consumption of about 40 %[8] will take place in the developing countries. In spite of the high rates of increase in other regions, the Western industrial countries are expected still to account for almost half of world consumption of primary energy in 1995, compared with 53 % in 1980.

c. Oil's contribution towards covering energy requirements

Since the Second World War the demand for energy has concentrated increasingly on oil and, to a lesser extent, natural gas. Low relative prices, which reflected a great expansion in the supply of oil, and advantages in transportation and use meant that oil displaced coal as the main source of energy. Between 1960 and 1983 oil's share of world primary energy consumption rose from one-third to 40 %. The trend

38

has clearly been reversed in recent years, however, as a result of the two oil price explosions.

Oil reached its highest share of energy consumption (47 %) in 1973. After the first oil price rise oil consumption fell in both absolute and relative terms for two years. It then rose again in volume, so that a share of 46 % had been reached by 1978. Since that date the proportion has been falling and since 1979 oil consumption has also declined in absolute terms.

After the second oil shock in only a few years the shifts in energy use away from oil are probably now permanent; in view of the continuing process of adjustment, its share of consumption is even likely to decrease further. A clear "decoupling" between the use of oil and economic growth can be expected, at least in the industrial countries. OECD projections for 1995 predict a resumption of real GNP growth in member countries but an absolute fall in oil consumption by comparison with 1980. In the OPEC countries and other developing countries, by contrast, a further increase in oil consumption is to be expected owing to industrialisation and their often more restricted scope for oil substitution. The net result is likely to be an increase in consumption for the world as a whole.

The pace at which oil is replaced by other sources of energy depends mainly on the trend of relative prices. The rise in the prices of oil products as a result of the first oil shock caused a delayed but substantial sympathetic rise in the prices of other sources of energy owing to low supply and demand elasticity in the short term, particularly as the price of alternative energy then acted as a spur to production; this was probably not the least of the reasons why the adjustment in their prices in the aftermath of the second oil shock has been less pronounced, at least up to now.

The slow progress being made with oil substitution is partly
due to the fact that the decision to seek alternative sources
of energy is not determined solely by the trend of relative
prices. Differences in the environmental acceptability and
user convenience of energy sources have a lasting effect on
the preparedness to substitute oil and the pace of substitution. A further requirement is that the shift in relative
prices be regarded as durable. Besides these demand factors
limitations on the supply of energy are also an important
reason why the reliance on oil is decreasing only slowly.
Many oil-importing countries have few or no competitive
sources of energy of their own that can help them avoid the
effects of the increase in oil prices. On the world market,
however, the supply of primary energy products other than
oil is limited for various reasons and cannot be expected
to increase rapidly in the foreseeable future.

Leaving aside political problems such as those in Iran, the
main obstacle to a faster increase in the supply of natural
gas is the fact that producers must increasingly exploit
deposits which entail extraordinarily high investment in
extraction and/or transport; in other words, costs and risks
are increasing. For some time, suppliers have been trying
to match natural gas prices to those for oil on the basis
of heat energy content; this demand was taken up by OPEC
in June 1980. However, such a development would increasingly
curb the potential of natural gas as a substitute for oil.
Some suppliers of natural gas are already making much more
sober estimates of worthwhile sales opportunities. For
example, Algeria no longer expects to expand its exports
of liquefied gas and Nigeria has decided to shelve similar
projects for several years. An IEA study on the prospects
for the use of natural gas in the industrialised countries
of the West comes to the conclusion that the share of natural
gas in energy consumption - which is currently about 20 %

40

- will have declined slightly by the end of the century (IEA 1982b, p. 37).

Many countries, by contrast, are banking on the greater use of coal as an alternative to oil. Even when transport costs are taken into consideration, coal has proved cheap so far, although it does have serious inconveniences in use. But it is doubtful whether the use of coal will undergo the considerable expansion that the world coal study (Wilson 1980) predicts will occur mainly in the nineties. Up to now the expected substitution of oil by coal in industrial countries has occurred on only a small scale and cannot be expected to intensify until the price advantage of coal grows substantially larger. Moreover, an increase in the use of coal on the scale forecast in the study presupposes the surmounting of considerable environmental obstacles. Finally, the opening-up of new coal deposits to meet a steep rise in demand often entails a long period of preparation involving not only the excavation of new mines but the construction or improvement of infrastructure for the transportation of coal, such as harbour facilities, railway lines and pipelines.

Coal is to be used as a substitue for oil not only directly but also indirectly in the form of processed products. However, synthetic fuels obtained from coal cannot be expected to replace oil products on a significant scale, at least during this century; not only must it still be proved that the products are competitive, but the planning and construction of the necessary plant require considerable time. Almost all the coal conversion projects begun since 1981, most of which are in the USA but some of which are in Europe, have been abandoned or shelved indefinitely in view of falling oil prices and an abundant supply of oil. According to the IEA, by the end of the century there will prob-

ably be only between four and six commercial sized coal
gasification plant in operation "if current plans material-
ise" and three coal liquefaction plant "to demonstrate the
new technology" (IEA 1982a, pp. 417-418). These projects
would be only marginally significant in 1990 and by the
year 2000 they might be producing 50 million tonnes oil
equivalent - about 3 % of OECD oil requirements - with an
energy input in the form of coal of between two and three
times this amount.

In the seventies most governments saw nuclear power generation as the best possibility of reducing the reliance on
imported oil. Government aid was therefore concentrated on
the development of nuclear energy. In the IEA member countries 64 % of state subsidies for energy research was still
going into nuclear research in 1982. Nonetheless, ambitious
plans for the construction of nuclear power stations had to
be scaled down repeatedly in almost all countries as time
went on and electricity demand growth slackened. What is
more, safety measures were tightened and approval procedures
were prolonged in many countries, not least because of the
implacable opposition of parts of the population to nuclear
power stations. The only Western country to build nuclear
power stations largely unimpeded so far is France. But even
there generating capacity is growing more slowly than originally planned due to a stagnating electricity demand.

In spite of the problems described above, a large overall
increase in nuclear energy production can confidently be
expected to occur in the industrial countries in the eighties,
given the nuclear plant that are already under construction.
What will happen in the nineties is largely open to conjec-
ture, however. According to present information, the pace
of expansion will slow down appreciably after 1990, as only
a few countries currently expect to place further orders for

power stations. The IEA puts the share of nuclear fuels in overall energy supplies (expressed in units of oil equivalent) at 11 % in the OECD countries in the year 2000, as against 4 % in 1980. The contribution of nuclear power to electricity generation is expected to rise from 12 to 25 % by the end of the century (IEA 1982a, p. 436).

The development of renewable sources of energy has been much discussed in recent years, but apart from the use of water-power to generate electricity their contribution to energy supplies has remained minimal and to all appearances will remain so. Their total contribution to energy supplies in the OECD is likely to rise from 3 million tonnes of oil equivalent in 1980 to 60 million tonnes in the year 2000; this would represent 1 % of total needs (IEA 1982a, p. 420).

To sum up, energy consumption can be expected to increase more slowly than overall demand for goods and services and energy sources other than oil will also gain further ground, for the processes of energy conservation and oil substitution induced by the sharp increase in relative energy prices and by the shift in price relations among the various energy sources will continue, even though they will receive only limited support from energy policy. However, it is unlikely that world oil consumption will show a lasting absolute decrease in the eighties and nineties; with the present depressed level as a starting point, a marked recovery can even be foreseen. According to the trend, a stagnation or even a further reduction in oil consumption in the OECD countries is probable, but this will be outweighted by rising demand in the Third World, since the developing countries cannot save energy and replace oil by other energy sources to the same extent as the industrial countries.

3. Future trends in the supply of oil

Until the first oil price explosion the supply of oil grew
flexibly in line with the increase in demand. Abundant reserves, low production costs and the expansionary production
policies of the private oil companies gave the impression
that practically limitless supplies of oil could be had at
low prices.

With the progressive nationalisation of oil deposits, the
production policies of the traditional oil-producing countries became the primary determinants of the oil supply from
1973 onwards. That does not mean that the oil states agreed
with each other on supply policy. There are differences from
one country to another in the level of oil reserves in relation to production, in their absorptive capacity and in the
economic, social and political aims that strongly affect the
volume and price targets they set for oil exports.

a. The supply policies of oil-exporting countries

The OPEC countries have lost considerable influence as suppliers of oil since 1973. Nonetheless, in 1983 they still
accounted for one-third of world production, 62 % of world exports and two thirds of economically recoverable reserves
of crude oil (see Tables 1.2 and 1.4). As the supply from
most other countries continues to grow largely oblivious
to fluctuations in demand or in some cases, such as that
of Mexico, was even still being expanded in spite of falling world demand, OPEC's policy as the supplier of the
"residue" continues to play an important part in determining
the relation between supply and demand in the oil market.
All the same, the events of 1983 show that the OPEC countries
are no longer in the position where they can at any time
dictate the world market price for crude oil by adjusting
production.

44

Table 1.4:   ECONOMICALLY RECOVERABLE WORLD OIL RESERVES
AND WORLD OIL PRODUCTION IN 1983

Regions/ Countries	Reserves (31.12.1983) Mn tonnes	Production Mn tonnes	Lifetime[a] Years
OPEC COUNTRIES	60,144	898[b]	67
Saudi Arabia[c]	22,710	246	92
Kuwait[c]	8,814	54	163
Iran	6,892	124	56
Iraq	5,733	46	125
UAE	4,262	55	78
Venezuela	3,550	98	36
Libya	2,828	52	54
Nigeria	2,236	60	37
Algeria	1,175	32	37
Indonesia	1,205	63	19
Others	739	34	22
REST OF THE WORLD	30,993	1,862	17
USSR	8,630	618	14
Mexico	6,760	149	45
USA	3,680	487	8
China	2,610	105	25
United Kingdom	1,760	115	15
Others	7,553	388	19
WORLD	91,137	2,760	33

a   Assuming unchanged production levels.
b   Including 34 mn tonnes of natural gas liquids not included
    in figures for individual member countries.
c   Including 50 % from the Neutral Zone.

Source: Esso: Oeldorado 83.

All member countries of OPEC are united in their desire to derive the highest possible earnings from oil exports, an objective that is pursued by adjusting export prices on the one hand and production volumes on the other. There is also fundamental agreement that oil revenues should be used to create sources of income that will continue after depletion of the oil, which is often these countries' only earner of foreign exchange. However, despite agreement in principle, there have been differences of opinion within the organisation on several occasions over the setting of production volumes and export prices. These disagreements can be attributed to divergences in the economic situation of the various countries. The two criteria that determine differences in the desired supply policy are the level of oil reserves and the size of the population. At one extreme there are densely populated countries with small oil reserves such as Nigeria and Algeria, which have an interest in maximum price increases so that they can earn the large amounts of foreign exchange needed to perform the feat of rapid industrialisation. Owing to the relatively short lifetime of their oil reserves they have less to fear from crash programmes in industrial countries to develop alternative sources of energy.

By contrast, the Arabian Gulf states with large oil reserves and a low population density are more interested in safeguarding their oil revenues over the long term. They fear - with reason, as the present situation has proved - that excessive price increases induce the consuming countries to save oil on such a scale that foreign exchange earnings from oil exports are no longer sufficient to finance their economic development projects.

The different economic parameters of the various countries and the political and ideological contrasts, some of which are clearly insuperable, have always prevented agreement on a common supply policy up to now. Saudi Arabia has failed in its repeated attempts to bring about a common policy on prices and volumes. The draft long-term strategy dating from 1980,[9] which provided for the real price of oil to be raised continuously in line with economic growth in the industrial countries, had to be shelved for lack of agreement. As several countries wanted to maintain production at past levels at the expense of other members and were not prepared to make substantial cuts in the common interest of high oil revenues, OPEC has not managed to create a fully functional cartel. Instead, the OPEC countries have taken advantage of favourable market conditions to raise prices without the need for a co-ordinated production policy. There was no planned shortage of supply in either 1974 or 1979; "the shortage was only in the eye of the panicked purchaser" (Stewart-Gordon 1983, p. 30). Nonetheless, some OPEC countries with a high output, in particular Saudi Arabia, have used their production policy to ensure that high oil prices could be sustained over a relatively long period. However, the OPEC countries were finally obliged to follow market signals and reduce official selling prices across the board in the spring of 1983 because it was unable to reduce production sufficiently.

b.   Oil supplies from OPEC countries

In 1983 OPEC oil production stood at an average 17.5 million barrels per day (864 million tonnes a year, see Tables 1.4 and 1.5), down 1.5 million barrels from 1982. These figures take account of the squeeze on oil demand as a result of slow growth and are undoubtedly far below the level member countries would consider desirable. An indication of what that level would be can be gained from their earlier production targets; addition of the volumes stated by the various countries for the period before the restrictions

Table 1.5:   OIL PRODUCTION OF OPEC COUNTRIES, 1979-1983[a]

- millions of barrels per day -

Countries	1979	1980	1981	1982	1983
Saudi Arabia[b]	9.5	9.9	9.8	6.5	5.1
Iran	3.2	1.5	1.3	2.4	2.4
Kuwait[b]	2.5	1.7	1.1	0.8	1.1
Iraq	3.5	2.6	0.9	1.0	1.0
UAE	1.8	1.7	1.5	1.2	1.1
Qatar	0.5	0.5	0.4	0.3	0.3
Libya	2.1	1.8	1.1	1.1	1.1
Algeria	1.2	1.0	0.8	0.7	0.6
Nigeria	2.3	2.1	1.4	1.3	1.2
Gabon	0.2	0.2	0.2	0.2	0.2
Ecuador	0.2	0.2	0.2	0.2	0.2
Venezuela	2.4	2.2	2.1	1.9	1.8
Indonesia	1.6	1.6	1.6	1.3	1.3
OPEC	30.9	26.9	22.5	19.0	17.5

a Excluding natural gas liquids.
b Including 50 % share from the Neutral Zone.

Source: Petroleum Economist, April 1984.

were agreed in May 1981 gives a daily output of about 27
million barrels, which corresponds to the production volume
in 1980. For the purposes of this calculation it is assumed
that Iran and Iraq together again produce 6.5 million barrels as in 1979 (the actual figure for 1983 was 3.4 million)
and that Saudi Arabia produces 8.5 million barrels, its
declared production ceiling [10] ever since 1978.

Only a few Gulf states are in a position to make large variations in production without also affecting their financial
and economic planning. The foremost of these is Saudi Arabia,
which stepped up production to about 10 million barrels for
several months in 1981. By contrast, the country's average
daily production of 5.1 million barrels in 1983 was clearly
well below the level that could be maintained for long without curbing expenditure. With oil priced at $ 29 a barrel,
exports of oil need to exceed 7 million barrels a day if
the annual government expenditure of about $ 75 billion is
to be financed from current oil receipts. [11] The dependence
of government expenditure on current oil receipts is eased,
however, by the substantial income from investments abroad,
so that even over the longer run, the minimum level for Saudi
Arabian production may be lower.

c.   Oil supplies from other producing countries

Oil production outside OPEC increased greatly in importance
in the seventies. Exploration work forged ahead after the
first oil price rise and deposits that had not been viable
previously were now exploited.

In 1983 the OECD countries produced almost 750 million tonnes
of oil, i.e. 13 % more than in 1973. Virtually the entire amount
is extracted by five countries - the USA, Canada, the United
Kingdom, Norway and Australia. About three-quarters of production are still in North America, chiefly the USA, although that
country's output was in decline when viewed over the entire

period. This reduction was outweighed by increases elsewhere, especially in the United Kingdom and Norway, which
raised their output from 0.1 to 145 million tonnes.

A further increase in oil production in the OECD countries
is unlikely to occur in future, however. The IEA assumes
that the volume of production will change little between
now and the end of the century (IEA 1982a, p. 26). In the
case of the USA it even predicts a further decline in production after the temporary stabilisation resulting from
the exploitation of deposits in Alaska. The deregulation
of oil prices brought a substantial increase in exploration at first, but activity was concentrated on regions
that had already been exploited to a high degree and offered
little prospect of major finds. The Federal Government's
National Energy Plan of 1981 was therefore already predicting a decline of more than 10 % in daily production in the
eighties. Not until the nineties would production again
approach the level of 1980 (DOE 1981, p. 22). Since then,
the outlook has grown worse rather than better. The decline
this decade might be less marked if drilling were concentrated on greater depths, the outer continental shelf and Alaska,
which are thought still to contain substantial deposits,
but then costs would be considerably higher. However, some
other forecasts are less optimistic than the Government's;
for example, at the end of 1980 Exxon was already predicting
a 30 % decline in US production by 1990 and only a slight
rise between then and the year 2000 (Exxon 1980, p. 22). In
1982 the IEA no longer expected production to increase in
the nineties; according to its forecasts, the decline in
extraction in the USA will have largely occurred by 1990
and will total between 10 % and a third of the 1980 production figure, depending on the assumptions adopted.

In Canada, too, oil production will continue to fall in the
next few years, although towards the end of the eighties the
opening-up of new fields off the Atlantic coast and in the
Beaufort Sea should halt the decline. Whether production will
again be rising in 1990, as the IEA assumes, is questionable,
however, because great depths of sea and extreme climatic
conditions make exploitation difficult in the new production
areas. In this connection Exxon speaks of lead times of between six and thirteen years before production begins. On the
other hand, the gradual raising of Canadian oil prices, which
have been held artificially low by the Government up to now,
might stimulate production in other regions. Unlike North America, Europe can initially expect a further rise in production
owing to the continued development of the North Sea oil fields.
Nevertheless, the prevailing opinion is that output will reach
a peak as early as the second half of the eighties and will
probably fall slowly thereafter.

The non-OPEC developing countries together produced about 365
million tonnes of crude in 1983. Thirteen of them, which account for about three-quarters of the entire oil output of developing countries, were already net oil exporters in 1980.
Nevertheless, oil exploration in developing countries has
still been seriously neglected up to now (World Bank 1980,
p. 5). In view of the long exploration and development time,
it is unlikely that an expansion in production in the oil-importing developing countries will bring about a noticeable
increase in the world supply of oil in the foreseeable future.

The largest producer among the oil-exporting (non-OPEC) developing countries is currently Mexico, with an annual production of 149 million tonnes and the fifth largest proven reserves. Mexican output more than quadrupled during the seventies. The country's high debts and large capital require-

ment for development projects make further increases
in oil production and exports likely in the next few years,
in spite of the Government's declared intention to expand
production only slowly. The Mexican energy programme from the
end of 1980 provided for limiting exports to 1.5 million barrels per day. But exports in the first half of 1983 were already slightly over this self-imposed limit (Business Week,
15.8.1983). Nevertheless, the anticipated rise in domestic
demand might eventuelly curb further export growth.

The total output of non-OPEC developing countries is unlikely to rise significantly above 600 million tonnes by the year
2000, despite the increases expected to occur in various countries such as India, Malaysia, Egypt and several countries in
West Africa. The bulk of the total will be used to meet domestic requirements.

In 1983 the centrally planned economies lifted about 750 million tonnes of oil as against 500 million in 1973. The group's
net exports came to more than 70 million tonnes. The main producer and exporter in the Soviet Union, with production of
618 million tonnes in 1983, making it the largest oil producer in the world.

As in the past, production trends in the USSR will determine
whether the centrally planned economies as a group are suppliers or purchasers of oil in the world market. Since 1977
it has been predicted repeatedly that Soviet oil production
would reach its peak at the beginning of the eighties and decline thereafter (CIA 1979), but up to now output growth only slowed down. The expected decline in production despite
the availability of abundant resources is attributed to increasing difficulties in extraction. It is uncertain whether
Soviet production together with increases in output from

other members of the group will be sufficient to meet the group's rising energy requirements in the future. According to some estimates, the centrally planned economies will need to import between 50 and 100 million tonnes of oil a year net from the mid-eighties onwards (Rahmer 1981, p. 293). On the other hand, it must be doubted that the USSR will wish to forego oil exports, its main source of foreign exchange - in 1983 the OECD countries purchased Soviet oil to the value of about US $ 15 billion (Jestin-Fleury 1984, p. 4). This seems to be confirmed by the Soviet decision to freeze oil supplies to CMEA partners at the existing level until 1985; several countries even had to accept a 10 % cut in 1982. By contrast, Soviet deliveries to Western countries rose substantially after 1981. In future, oil exports are likely to be overtaken increasingly by gas exports. All that can be foreseen with any certainty is that the volume of Soviet oil available for export to the West will not increase. The question is whether the other CMEA countries will raise their demand for oil on the world market by the amount of the restrictions on Soviet deliveries. In view of their balance of payments problems, it is more likely that they will devote greater effort to conserving energy and especially oil, where the potential is thought to be relatively large.

To sum up, the exploitation of sources of oil outside the OPEC countries has increased markedly after the jump in oil prices, but overall success has been fairly modest so far. Nonetheless, the rise in production in developing countries should more than offset the decline to be expected in industrial countries. Prospective trends in these two groups of countries leave no doubt that oil production in OPEC countries will continue to determine supply conditions on the world market for the foreseeable future.

4. Conclusions with regard to the trend of oil prices

(i)   World oil consumption is depressed by recessionary influences at present and will initially rise noticeably when economic activity recovers. Subsequently, however,
it is likely to increase only very slowly, even if economic
growth continues at a moderate pace, owing to the sharp increase in the level of oil prices since 1973. This expectation is based on the assumption that the oil-importing countries have made great strides in their structural adjustment
to higher oil prices and will continue to do so. In the longer term, perhaps over the eighties and nineties, an absolute reduction in oil consumption in the industrial countries
will be outweighed by the rise in the requirement of developing countries.

(ii)   On the supply side there is substantial idle production capacity in the OPEC countries at present, even if the
production peak of 1979 is no longer regarded as a yardstick.
For example, the production limit agreed in March 1983, which
was still well above actual production owing to destocking by
traders, refiners and consumers, was almost 10 million barrels a day less than the volume calculated from the production targets published by the OPEC countries in 1981. This
corresponds to a possible rise in world oil consumption of
about one-fifth. Outside OPEC, oil production in the rest of
the developing world will probably be expanded sufficiently
to outweigh a probable medium-term decline in OECD production.

(iii)   The prospects for economic growth in the industrial countries - and hence in the developing countries as
well - have improved again as a result of the broadly based
reduction in oil prices in the spring of 1983. At the same
time, however, the cut that has already been made and a possible further reduction mean that efforts to improve the ef-

ficiency of energy use and to substitute oil will falter and
projects in hand to expand the supply of oil will be supend-
ed, with the result that the scope for future oil price rises
will again increase. With oil prices at their present level,
it is unlikely that the more energy-efficient production processes and products introduced in recent years will be abandoned in favour of less efficient methods and products under
the impact of falling oil prices, but it must be expected,
for example, that the exploitation of oil deposits with high
production costs will slow down, thereby restricting the future oil supply. The strength of these various effects will
depend on the size and duration of the fall in price. The
larger the present price cut, the greater can the future
rise be expected to be.

(iv)   Even when the demand for oil picks up after the
end of the recession, it will be some time before the OPEC
countries, which will continue to be by far the most important suppliers in the world market, will regain the ability
to make fairly large increases in selling prices; moreover,
it is unclear at present where the starting level will be.
Barring unforeseeable political events, real oil prices seem
unlikely to rise before the end of the eighties. The opportunity to raise prices will probably not come about until the
OPEC countries' total daily production - and demand - pass
the 20 million barrels mark. Then Saudi Arabia would presumably once again have the necessary scope to act as "swing
producer" in both directions, as it did in the past. This
is based on the assumption that the OPEC countries remain
able to agree on the joint production volume over a fairly
long period. Whether the draft OPEC long-term strategy of
1980, which was drawn up largely under the influence of
Saudi Arabia and which provided for real oil prices to be
raised more or less in line with the rate of growth in industrial countries, will still be relevant must be doubted,

even though the committee dealing with it was reconvened in
mid 1983.

(v)   The expectation of a moderately rising oil
price trend poses the question as to how oil prices will
fluctuate about this trend. But even detailed analysis of
the market situation and an examination of supply policies
permit only limited conclusions to be drawn, as experience
since 1973 has shown. Both oil crises were triggered by
the climax of political circumstances and overreaction on
the part of consumers, not by an actual lasting supply
shortage. There are no grounds for believing that market
reactions will be different and price changes more smoothly in future. At best, this might be the case if the political situation in the Middle East remained quiet, if the
OPEC countries sacrificed their economic self-interest for
the sake of a joint, long-term policy on prices and volumes
and if the oil-importing countries could stabilize oil demand, primarily by avoiding sharp pro-cyclical fluctuations
of stocks. On past experience, however, these requirements
are unlikely to be fulfilled.

Footnotes to Chapter 1

1 The price used for calculating taxes and royalties due from foreign oil companies. The official selling price introduced subsequently was 7 % below the posted price.

2 A bibliography is to be found in Weyant, Kline 1982, p. 333. They do not themselves subscribe to the opinion that oil prices will not rise further.

3 The objectives and measures of IEA member countries for long-term co-operation in the energy field are laid down in Section 7 of the Agreement on an International Energy Program of 18.11.1974.

4 Such as in the communiqué of the Council of Ministers of 13.5.1980, Community Energy Objectives for 1990 and Convergence of the Policies of the Member States, press release 691/80.

5 In a "reference scenario" the IEA describes how the consistent pursuit of the energy policy objectives agreed by the member states could significantly reduce oil imports, even with more rapid economic growth. See IEA 1982a, pp. 34-37.

6 The World Bank definition of developing countries here includes China and excludes the high income oil exporters Bahrain, Brunei, Kuwait, Libya, Oman, Saudi Arabia, and UAE.

7 From 1345 million tonnes of oil equivalent (mtoe) in 1980 to 2594 mtoe in 1995. Oil importing developing countries account for 670 mtoe in 1980 and 1399 mtoe in 1995.

8 From 6744 mtoe in 1980 to 9529 mtoe in 1995.

9 The almost complete text of the draft strategy is reproduced in: International Currency Review, Vol. 12 (1980), No. 3

10 Excluding the 50 % share of the Neutral Zone.

11 Instead of expected oil receipts of more than $ 80 billion, less than $ 65 billion was recorded in the 1982-83 fiscal year (April-April). See Financial Times, 11.4.1983.

PART I THE EFFECTS OF RISING OIL PRICES ON THE INTERNATIONAL
        FINANCIAL SYSTEM

Over the medium term, in particular, rising oil prices present a challenge to the ability of real economic adjustment in
oil-exporting and consuming countries to correct the resultant current account imbalances. According to traditional
thinking, this process is initiated by exchange rate and balance-of-payments reactions. Having indicated the scale of
current account disequilibria, Chapter 2 will examine the importance of adjustment via exchange rate movements in the
event of an oil price rise.

In the short term, in other words until adjustment measures
begin to bite, "unavoidable" current account deficits have
to be financed. In the aftermath of the first oil price explosion in 1973-74 the international financial system was
therefore faced with unprecedented demands. However, the
problems that this can cause did not emerge clearly until
the second oil crisis in 1979-80, when the economic climate
was less auspicious. In both instances the oil-exporting
countries with a low absorption capacity rapidly accumulated large cash surpluses that were matched by a borrowing requirement to cover current account deficits in the oil-consuming countries. It was this juxtaposition that gave rise
to the recycling function, which consisted in channelling
the surplus funds of oil-exporting countries as rapidly and
smoothly as possible to those places where they were needed
to finance the higher oil import bill. Chapter 3 examines
how this task was accomplished.

Chapter 2: Balance-of-payments and exchange-rate adjust-
          ment

The first step will be to show the development of current
account balances in oil-exporting and oil-consuming countries after the first oil price increase. The chapter then
goes on to examine the extent to which the traditional exchange rate and balance-of-payments adjustment mechanism is
applicable in this situation. Finally, the causes of oil-
related exchange rate movements will be discussed.

1. Current account developments in times of rising oil
   prices

As Table 2 shows, after both oil price explosions the aggregate current accounts of oil-consuming countries initially recorded very large deficits, which were matched by corresponding surpluses in the oil-exporting countries.[1] After
the first oil crisis the surpluses were absorbed relatively
quickly, as were the current account deficits of the oil-
consuming industrial countries. In the group of developing
countries, by contrast, the deficits remained at a comparatively high level.

By comparison with the first oil crisis, the oil price increase in 1979-80 led to much higher current account surpluses in the oil-exporting countries and correspondingly larger
deficits in consuming countries (see also Chart 2). The
situation was particularly difficult for developing countries, which began with higher deficits remaining from the
first oil crisis and whose existing problems were severely
accentuated by the second wave of price increases.

Table 2:   CURRENT ACCOUNT BALANCES, 1973 - 1982[a]

- in billions of US $ -

	1973	1974	1975	1976	1977	1978	1979	1980	1981	1982
Industrial countries	13.4	-23.0	8.9	-10.5	-15.4	16.2	-25.3	-62.7	-21.2	-24.6
OPEC[b]	4.2	65.4	31.7	36.8	25.8	- 2.5	64.5	109.4	60.0	n.a.
Developing countries of which:	- 5.8	-28.3	-39.2	-25.1	-20.7	-33.1	-49.4	-76.5	-93.9	-73.6
- net oil exporters	- 1.4	- 3.5	- 8.0	- 6.4	- 4.5	- 6.4	- 6.3	-10.2	-21.0	-13.5
- net oil importers	- 4.5	-24.7	-31.2	-18.7	-17.2	-25.9	-41.5	-63.8	-75.1	-65.2
of which:										
. major exporters of manufac.	- 2.4	-17.6	-17.9	-10.3	- 6.5	- 8.2	-19.7	-30.2	-35.2	-31.6
. low-income countries	- 1.9	- 2.6	- 5.1	- 1.8	- 0.8	- 5.0	- 6.3	- 9.8	-11.1	-11.3
. other net oil importers	- 0.2	- 4.5	- 8.2	- 6.4	- 9.8	-12.6	-15.6	-23.8	-28.8	-22.3

a Including official transfers.

b Excluding Ecuador and Gabon, including Oman.

Source: International Monetary Fund: World Economic Outlook, Washington, D.C. 1983, Balance of Payments Statistics, Yearbook, various years; calculations by the authors.

Chart 2 : BALANCES ON CURRENT ACCOUNT, 1973-1982

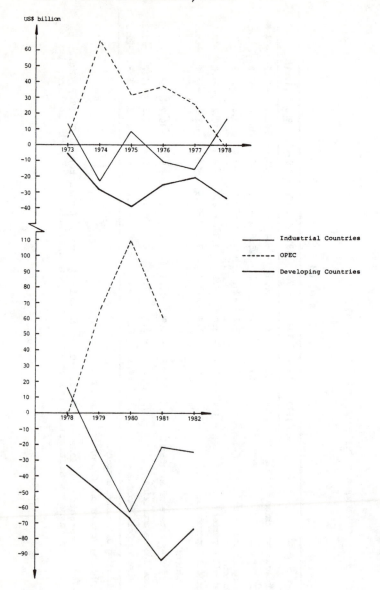

Source: See Table 2.

It can be seen from Chart 3, however, that the situation differed markedly for the various groups of developing countries in both oil crises. For example, after the first increase low-income countries and the group of "other" net oil-importers recorded relatively low current account deficits but the newly industrialising countries in particular, most of which come into the category of exporters of manufactured goods, were in a far more unfavourable situation. These countries were also the worst affected by the second oil crisis. On this occasion, however, the other groups of developing countries were also confronted with larger and more persistent deficits.

The abrupt appearance of very large current account imbalances that are reduced only gradually is characteristic of instances in which oil prices jump sharply, as we have witnessed so far. Steady and moderate price increases should produce a more even current account trend and the problems described below should be less serious. The question is whether it is possible or desirable in times of rising oil prices to achieve a reduction in current account disequilibria via adjustment to the accompanying exchange rate changes and how the consuming countries' increased oil import bill can be financed while adjustment is less than complete.

2. Effects on exchange rates

The first step will be to examine which currencies are actually affected by real oil price increases and the extent to which traditional notions of exchange rate and balance-of-payments adjustment to current account disequilibria are valid in this particular situation.

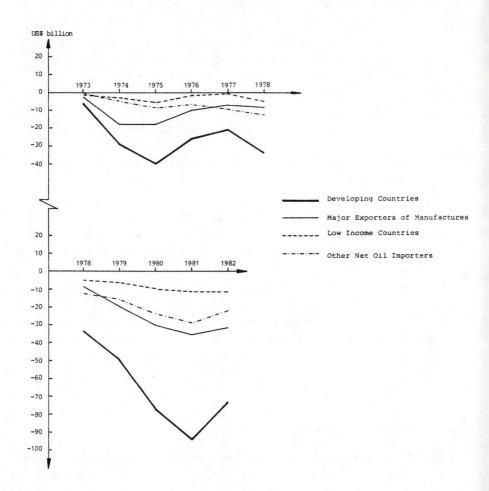

Chart 3: DEVELOPING COUNTRIES: BALANCES ON CURRENT ACCOUNT, 1973-1982

Legend:
— Developing Countries
— Major Exporters of Manufactures
---- Low Income Countries
—·—·— Other Net Oil Importers

Source: See Table 2.

a. Exchange-rate and balance-of-payments adjustment
    mechanisms

Since 1973 most Western countries have gone over to a system
of floating exchange rates. It is generally assumed that under such a system an increase in the price of a country's exports will initially lead to a rise in national income owing
to an expansion in nominal exports, thus generating growing
demand for goods in the country in question. This causes domestic output to expand and, depending on the capacity utilisation rate, the prices of domestic goods to increase. The
rise in exports is accompanied by increasing demand for the
country's currency. The combination of higher exchange rates
and increased national income lead to greater demand for imports, whereas exports fall back owing to a decline in foreign demand as a result of the original increase in prices
reinforced by the upward pressure on the exchange rate. In
this way current account balance is restored over the long
term and the currency depreciates.

In the process described here the exchange rate therefore
serves as an instrument of adjustment that brings about a
long-term reduction in current account disequilibria. When
oil prices are rising, however, this mechanism can scarcely come into operation, first because the price elasticity
of oil demand is low in the consuming countries and secondly because most oil-exporting countries have pegged their
currencies to the dollar or a basket of currencies. Under
fixed exchange rates, the adjustment process that theoret-
icians traditionally assume to apply operates broadly as
follows. The increase in export prices again leads to a
rise in the demand for the currency of the country in question, but this does not manifest itself in a rise in the
exchange rate, as in this case the central bank holds the

rate steady by purchasing foreign exchange. Instead, the domestic money supply expands and interest rates tend to fall.
Together with the original growth in nominal exports, these
developments induce an increase in national income and prices,
causing import demand to rise. At the same time, foreign demand declines as a reaction to the increase in export prices,
so that here too there is a tendency for a restoration of
current account balance over the long term. In this instance
adjustment occurs more via domestic factors such as domestic
prices and employment.

This is a highly simplified portrayal of the possible course
of events, but it does show that some of these concepts are
not applicable to the relationships between industrial and
oil-exporting countries. First, in the oil-importing countries there is only limited scope for import demand to adjust in response to rising oil prices owing to its low price
elasticity. Secondly, in some important oil-exporting countries with only a low absorption capacity an increase in oil
prices and the accompanying balance-of-payments developments
do not lead to domestic economic adjustment via prices, interest rates and changes in the money supply in the conventional sense (cf. also Dunn 1979, pp. 2 ff). In the "high
absorbers" the receipts from oil sales flow into the domestic economy, but this does not happen to the same extent in
the "low absorbers", which are chiefly the Gulf states. Here
the oil sector generally produces the predominant share of
gross national product and the level of oil production and
prices are decided autonomously by the state. As the oil
revenues accrue to state agencies that re-invest a large
proportion abroad, there is no direct relation between cur-

rent account developments and the liquidity of the private sector. The oil sector in these states should therefore be regarded as an enclave within the economy.[2]

As the low absorbers account for a considerable share of the total oil production of oil-exporting countries, this has important implications for the international monetary system. These countries' export receipts are denominated mainly in dollars and accrue to state institutions that convert only a small part into national currency. Their import demand is determined principally by official development strategies and cannot increase as rapidly as the surpluses owing to a lack of suitable investment projects and political restrictions, which, in the light of the events in Iran, permit only a very cautious expansion of the economy. Hence the domestic money supply and the exchange rates of these countries' currencies against the dollar remain largely unaffected by oil price increases and an oil-related current account surplus does not automatically trigger adjustment reactions within these economies.

The burden of adjustment therefore falls mainly on the shoulders of countries that import oil or in whose currencies part of the accumulated OPEC surpluses is invested. But here too the mechanism described above is partly neutralised. Insofar as the OPEC countries deposit their surpluses with, say, commercial banks in New York or London, and hence do not convert them into claims on the central banks of oil-importing countries, the money supply does not diminish in the oil-consuming countries as a result of a contraction in monetary base and the associated adjustment process. The effects on these countries mainly take the form of a decrease in real income as a result of rising oil prices (the terms-of-trade effect) and the impact of exchange rate changes among the currencies

of non-OPEC countries on national income, prices and employment, so that absorption of the oil-related current account
deficits proceeds more slowly.

Exchange rate changes can contribute little towards eradicat-
ing the disequilibria between surplus and deficit countries
because of the low price elasticity of the demand for oil.
The exchange rate is not therefore a suitable adjustment instrument for this purpose. However, exchange rate changes are
extremely important in distributing the burden of adjustment
among oil-importing countries. It will be demonstrated below
that the distribution of the overall current account deficit
is also partly determined by the investment behaviour of the
OPEC surplus countries.

The starting point of a highly simplified example[3] is a three-
country model in which Saudi Arabia supplies the USA and Japan with oil and as a result records a current account surplus
of $ 20 billion in the period under examination, the oil bill
being both denominated and payable in dollars. It is assumed
that the countries' current accounts are in balance at the
outset, that completely flexible exchange rates exist between
the USA and Japan, that Saudi Arabia invests its entire surplus in the other two countries and that there are no capital
transactions among the countries apart from the Saudi investments. In these conditions the division of the global current
account deficit between Japan and the USA will be determined
solely by the investment decisions of Saudi Arabia, irrespective of the quantity of oil the other two countries have each
imported.

This finding, which may appear surprising at first sight, can
be explained in the following manner. Let us assume the USA

imports oil worth $ 15 billion and Japan $ 5 billion. Japan
must buy these dollars in the foreign exchange market against
yen. The dollar exchange rate rises until this extra demand is
matched by an equal supply and equilibrium is restored in the
market. Given our initial assumptions, this can only happen
if the falling yen rate generates additional American demand
for Japanese imports to the value of $ 5 billion, so that the
USA finally records a current account deficit totalling $ 20
billion, whereas the Japanese current account is in balance.
If Saudi Arabia invests its entire surplus in the USA this
has no affect on the dollar exchange rate or on the current
accounts of the countries considered (cf. Example I). However,
if half of the $ 20 billion is invested in the USA and half in
Japan, Saudi Arabia buys yen worth $ 10 billion in the foreign
exchange market and the yen/dollar rate rises until the excess
demand is matched by a corresponding supply from Japan's current account deficit vis-à-vis the USA. Japan is then left with
an overall current account deficit of $ 10 billion, the same
as that of the USA. This is illustrated in Example II in
Chart 4.

Example III demonstrates how this result can be influenced if
international capital flows are generally permitted. It begins with the same transactions as in Example II, but now it
is assumed that Saudi Arabia's investments in the USA and Japan cause a change in the currency composition of private investors' portfolios in both countries, so that their actual
asset structure is not the one they desire. There follow portfolio adjustments and net capital outflows of $ 2.5 billion
from the USA to Japan. Investors therefore buy yen and the yen
appreciates against the dollar, so that the net result is a
reduction in the US current account deficit and an increase
of the same magnitude in the Japanese deficit.

Chart 4: CURRENT ACCOUNT AND EXCHANGE RATE ADJUSTMENT TO OIL-RELATED DISEQUILIBRIA

Example	Assumptions	Saudia Arabia	Current account movements USA	Japan	Capital movements	Exchange rate changes
I	Flexible exchange rates, no capital transactions apart from Saudi investments	+$ 20 bn	- $ 15 bn vis-à-vis Saudi Arabia - $ 5 bn vis-à-vis Japan ------ - $ 20 bn	- $ 5 bn vis-à-vis Saudi Arabia + $ 5 bn vis-à-vis USA ------ -	- Saudi Arabia invest $ 20 bn in the USA	$/yen rate rises -
II	Flexible exchange rates, no capital transactions apart from Saudi investments	+$ 20 bn	- $ 15 bn vis-à-vis Saudi Arabia - $ 5 bn vis-à-vis Japan	- $ 5 bn vis-à-vis Saudi Arabia + $ 5 bn vis-à-vis USA	- Saudi Arabia invests $ 10 bn in each in the USA and Japan	$/yen rate rises $/yen rate falls
III	Flexible exchange rates with capital transactions	+ $ 20 bn	+ $ 10 bn vis-à-vis Japan - $ 10 bn - $ 10 bn from previous transactions (Example II)	- $ 10 bn vis-à-vis USA - $ 10 bn - $ 10 bn from previous transactions (Example II)	Portfolio adjustments by investors in Japan and USA; $ 2.5 bn transferred from USA to Japan	$/yen rate falls
IV	Managed float and capital transactions	+ $ 20 bn	+ $ 2.5 bn vis-à-vis Japan - $ 7.5 bn - $ 7.5 bn from previous transactions (Example III) - $ 10 bn vis-à-vis Japan ------ - $ 17.5 bn	- $ 2.5 bn vis-à-vis USA - $ 12.5 bn - $ 12.5 bn from previous transactions (Example III) + $ 10 bn vis-à-vis USA ------ - $ 2.5 bn	Central bank interventions; purchase of $ 10 bn against yen	$/yen rate rises

If central bank intervention in the foreign exchange markets
is also permitted, this too can influence the distribution of
the overall current account deficit, as Example IV shows. Here
it is assumed that either the Bank of Japan or the US Federal
Reserve buys $ 10 billion in the foreign exchange markets. The
dollar exchange rate consequently rises against the yen and in
this example the US current account deficit increases to $ 17.5
billion, while Japan's falls to $ 2.5 billion. This is based
on the further assumption that the effects of central bank intervention on the domestic money supply are completely   neutralised and can therefore be ignored.

These examples constitute a rough and ready simplification in
that differences in current account developments owing to different oil-related rates of price increase and economic trends
in individual countries are left out of account, as is the increasing import demand of oil-exporting countries as a whole
in times of growing surpluses. Lagged adjustment responses and
the effects of short-term capital movements have also been disregarded, as it is assumed that such influences   balance each
other out over time.

To sum up, it can be concluded that the exchange rate and balance-of-payments adjustment mechanism traditionally postulated
in the event of current account disequilibria has only limited
validity between oil-exporting and oil-importing countries and
that for various reasons the exchange rate is not an appropriate adjustment instrument in this context. The currencies of
oil-exporting countries are scarcely affected by rising oil
prices. Changes in exchange rates primarily alter the distribution of the global oil-related current account deficit
among oil-consuming countries, so that the currencies affected by oil price increases are not necessarily those of countries with the highest oil imports. The section that follows

examines the extent to which rising oil prices have a direct
or indirect influence on short and long-term exchange rates.

b.   Causes of oil-related movements in exchange rates

A distiction should be made between those exchange rate determinants influenced directly or indirectly by oil price
increases that have only a temporary impact on exchange rates
and those that affect the trend permanently.[4] Let us first
examine in greater detail the effect of oil-price increases
on the long-term determinants and the possibility of a consequent lasting change in the exchange rate trend.

(1)   Long-term determinants of exchange rates

Over the long term, exchange rates are influenced primarily
by two factors - the balance of payments on current account
and differences in inflation rates. They are also affected
by capital flows, as the above example showed. The current
account trend of a country is determined mainly by its competitiveness,[5] its national income and its propensity to import. Unlike current account developments, inflation differentials influence exchange rates only indirectly by causing
a gradual shift in international price relations to the benefit of countries with low inflation rates; this brings about
a change in international competitiveness and trade flows,
which in turn creates a tendency for the currencies of these
countries to appreciate. Long-term capital movements influence the exchange rate in the form of portfolio switching from one currency into another or via increased demand
for financial assets in a particular currency owing to an
increase in wealth. Long-term wealth effects of this kind
may have various causes, such as a change in the assessment of the economic and/or political stability of particular countries by private investors.

72

An increase in oil prices affects not only the real determinants of long-term exchange rate developments but also
inflation rates and - closely allied to this - the long-term
investment decisions of holders of wealth. Existing economic
disparities are accentuated by the differing ability of individual countries to bring such price increases under control. Hence it is to be expected that future increases in
oil prices will again lead to long-term changes in the exchange rates between the currencies of industrial countries,
a current account deficit essentially indicating a tendency
for the currency to depreciate and a lower rate of price increase than in other countries signalling a tendency to appreciate. If the two factors occur simultaneously, it is
not clear in advance which will predominate. In principle,
it can be assumed that if current account balances are small
the impact of inflation differentials on exchange rates will
increase, and vice versa.

In addition, oil price increases have two further medium-
term effects on exchange rates owing to the level and deployment of the OPEC surpluses. First, the investment of these
surpluses in particular currencies has a direct influence on
the long-term exchange rate trend and hence on the current
account balances of the countries concerned. Secondly, every
desire on the part of OPEC countries to switch their portfolios and broaden the currency composition of their investments means that the preferred investment currencies are
subject to upward pressure for long periods of time. Hence
permanent exchange rate effects derive not only from the investment of current increases in wealth but also from the
long-term gradual adjustment of existing assets.

The impact of long-term factors is overlaid or accentuated
by that of short-term capital flows, so that as a rule exchange rates do not adjust smoothly to long-term realities
but in great surges ("overshooting"). The following section
examines the factors that can cause such short-term movements and the effect that oil-price increases might have in
this respect.

(2)   Short-term determinants of exchange rates

Short-term international capital flows are caused by changes in interest rate differences and/or by expectations of
exchange rate movements. Although interest rates and exchange rates can be influenced in the short term by the monetary and exchange rate policies of individual countries,
exchange rate expectations hold particular significance in
connection with the effects of oil price increases to be examined here. Such expectations are often based on long-term
exchange rate determinants such as prices, national income
and current account balances in each country, but they are
also dependent on non-quantifiable variables such as political occurrences. Changed expectations with regard to future
exchange rate developments lead to international capital movements; if they prove correct they induce a more rapid adjustment of rates, but if they are wide of the mark they accentuate the divergence from a rate that accords with underlying conditions in the real economy.

An example in this connection is the trend of the Deutsche
Mark immediately after the first oil crisis. It was generally assumed that the Federal Republic of Germany would be
harder hit than most other industrial countries because of
its particularly heavy reliance on oil and petroleum products and would experience higher inflation, current account

deficits and a setback to growth; the DM accordingly showed
a strong downward tendency. When it then emerged that these
fears were not fully justified, that the current account was
in surplus and the inflation rate low, the trend was reversed (cf. Deutsche Bundesbank: Geschäftsbericht 1974). As Chart 5
shows, expectations shaped the course of other currencies in a
similar way after the first oil crisis - witness the trend of
the French franc and the Italian lira.

Chart 6 gives an impression of the extent to which oil
prices influenced the exchange rates of Western currencies during the second oil crisis. Here too the effect is
unmistakable. For example, the combination of a current account deficit in Germany and a surplus in the USA played a
decisive role in determining the DM/dollar rate; together
with political developments in the United States (the Reagan
bonus), this led the exchange markets to expect an appreciation of the dollar.

Oil price increases therefore have direct short-term effects
on exchange rates, mainly because they shape the expectations
of operators in the foreign exchange markets. A distinction
has to be drawn here between gradual price increases and abrupt price jumps, however. The effects of gradual price increases on national economies are apparent at longer term,
so that exchange rate expectations should stabilise. The dollar rate is affected particularly strongly by speculative
capital movements, for when oil price increases are expected
and, in particular, when prices rise abruptly it can be assumed that the dollar will appreciate since oil-importing
countries will seek to purchase larger amounts of dollars
to pay their increased oil bills. Another influence in this
context springs from the investment decisions of OPEC countries. These too affect mainly the dollar exchange rate.

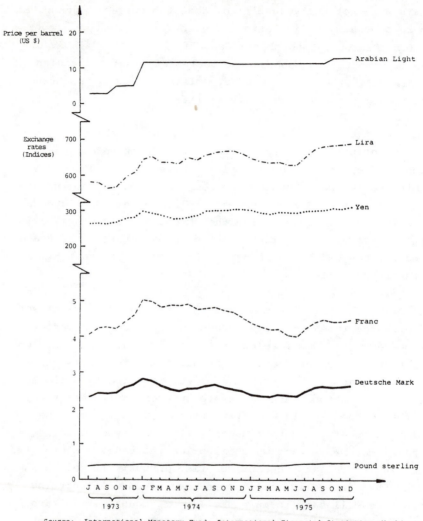

Chart 5 : NOMINAL EXCHANGE RATES OF SELECTED CURRENCIES AGAINST
THE US DOLLAR, JULY 1973 TO DECEMBER 1975

Price per barrel (US $)

Arabian Light

Exchange rates (Indices)

Lira

Yen

Franc

Deutsche Mark

Pound sterling

J A S O N D J F M A M J J A S O N D J F M A M J J A S O N D

1973   1974   1975

Source: International Monetary Fund: International Financial Statistics, Washington, D.C.,
various years; OPEC: Annual Statistical Bulletin 1981.

76

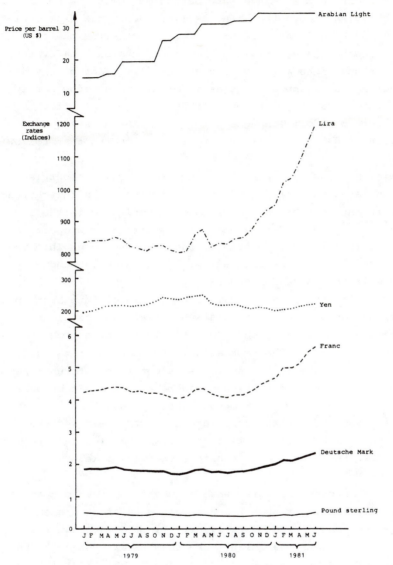

Chart 6 : NOMINAL EXCHANGE RATES OF SELECTED CURRENCIES AGAINST
THE US DOLLAR, JANUARY 1979 TO JUNE 1981

Source: International Monetary Fund: International Financial Statistics, Washington, D.C.,
various years; OPEC: Annual Statistical Bulletin 1981.

77

Past oil price increases may also be the indirect cause of large short-term exchange rate deviations owing to portfolio switching. Although the withdrawal of OPEC funds from individual banks and the switching of resources from one currency to another have no lasting impact on the banking system, such transactions may have a considerable effect on the exchange rates of the currencies involved. These stem partly from the actual flows of OPEC funds but above all from the resultant portfolio changes within the banking system (cf. Sterling 1980, p. 87 with regard to the remarks that follow).

As will be shown in Chapter 3, the Arab surplus countries hold a large part of their investments in only a few currencies in the form of short-term bank deposits, with the result that these funds account for a substantial proportion of bank liabilities. If some of these are switched into another currency the bank itself will make a corresponding change in the currency composition of its portfolio. This in turn affects other banks, and the chain of interbank operations can be such that relatively small and cautious portfolio adjustments lead cumulatively to large exchange rate fluctuations. The problem here is that the international interbank market is many times larger than international transactions between banks and non-banks. This effect possibly takes on greater importance here than in the case of transactions by conventional investors, as their individual share of bank liabilities is usually smaller, as are the repercussions of any transfers they may make.

The surplus countries are aware of these implications and generally carry out such transactions with great prudence, but situations can continually arise in the international financial markets that might make them throw caution to the wind. For example, there is the danger of political intervention, such as the temporary freezing of Iranian deposits with US banks, which can cause uncertainty among Arab investors and might lead to a flight out of a particular currency, with all that would entail.

Exchange rate fluctuations also occur as a result of the adjustment processes in the real and monetary sectors of national economies as a result of oil price increases. What is involved here is the true, conventional overshooting phenomenon, which results from the fact that money and goods markets adjust to oil price increases at different tempos. Given the more rapid adjustment of the money and foreign exchange markets, the capital flows induced under floating exchange rates to offset oil-related current account deficits require interest and exchange rate movements in the short term that exceed the rates of change resulting from the adjustment process over the long term.

To sum up, it can be concluded that oil price increases influence the long-term trend of the currencies of industrial countries through their effects on the real and monetary sectors and that they can also cause substantial short-term fluctuations in rates. In principle, the present worldwide monetary system of managed floating offers the possibility of a flexible adjustment of rates over the long term and at the same time permits erratic exchange rate fluctuations to be dampened by means of official exchange market intervention and monetary measures to soften the accompanying adverse effects on national economies.

A number of European countries have joined together to set up a system of fixed exchange rates, the European Monetary System (EMS). These countries are obliged to maintain the bilateral central rates of their currencies within margins of fluctuation of plus or minus 2.25 % by means of unlimited exchange market interventions.[6] The exceptions are the United Kingdom, which does not belong to the intervention mechanism, and Italy, which has been permitted margins of fluctuation of 6 %. Parity changes can be made only with the consent of all member countries. In practice this has led on occasion to fairly long delays in adjustment. As in every system of fixed exchange rates, it is implicitly assumed that the need for parity changes arises only in exceptional circumstances and at infrequent intervals.

The system was still in its infancy when it had to contend with the consequences of the second oil price shock. However, its operational ability was not immediately impaired; on the contrary, in the first two years it proved unexpectedly stable. Changes in central rates were rare and relatively small (cf. Deutsche Bundesbank: Geschäftsbericht 1982, p. 75). Various factors were responsible for this. From 1980 onwards the system's strongest currency measured in terms of underlying real economic variables - the Deutsche Mark - suffered a bout of weakness against the dollar that lasted until mid-1981 and caused it to depreciate against the other currencies as well (cf. Deutsche Bundesbank: Geschäftsbericht 1981, pp. 72 ff). However, this aroused no expectations of devaluation within the EMS, so that there was practically no market pressure during the first two years and the DM imposed no great strains on the system. The main cause of the Mark's weakness was the performance of the German current account, but the interest rate differential in favour of the dollar and the role of the Mark as an international reserve currency also had an adverse effect. The initial stability of the EMS can be attributed chiefly to this factor, not to a convergence in the economic development of the member countries.

This situation was not permanent, however, as can be seen from events since 1982. The frequency and size of changes in central rates have increased, an indication that the economic divergences within the system are impairing its operation. The question therefore arises whether the EMS possesses sufficient flexibility over the long run to counteract the short and long-term effects on exchange rates that would result from real oil price increases in the future.

The long-term effects of oil price increases make it fundamentally impossible to defend a constant exchange rate over a fairly long period of time. The politically motivated postponement of parity adjustments as in the EMS entails economic costs for member countries. If these costs continually increase, the countries will become less willing to uphold the system.

The continued existence of the European Monetary System in its present form is all the more threatened in the event of future oil price increases the greater the existing differences in the economic performance of member states, in other words the greater the disparities between member countries when they begin to tackle further price increases and current account shifts. However, the system is endangered not only by the long-term influences of real oil price increases but also by the short-term effects of expectations on international capital flows. With freely floating exchange rates, the ensuing temporary exchange rate movements can far exceed the limits set by the present margins of fluctuation and necessitate large-scale exchange market intervention, which may have an effect on the domestic money supply that conflicts with the domestic economic objectives. Sharper contradictions in the objectives of monetary and exchange rate policy must therefore be expected.

Not all EMS currencies are subject to short-term exchange
rate fluctuations on the same scale. The Deutsche Mark occupies a special position, as in recent years it has developed increasingly into an alternative international investment currency to the dollar and is therefore much more
strongly affected by portfolio changes than the other EMS
currencies. This not only causes considerable fluctuations
in the DM/dollar rate but also sets up strains within the
EMS.

In the light of these circumstances, it is doubtful whether
a general widening of the margins of fluctuation, which has
been frequently proposed, could improve the working of the
EMS and it might be considered whether an asymetrical arrangement would not be more appropriate, given the fact that
the special situation of the DM places a considerable extra
strain on the system. For example, like the Italian lira,
the DM might be allowed a wider margin of fluctuation than
the other member currencies in order to increase the scope
for short-term fluctuations in the DM/dollar rate. All par-
ticipants would thereby gain greater room to pursue a monetary policy directed towards domestic objectives. In addition, efforts should be directed towards developing "objective indicators" as a guide to parity changes in order to
make it easier for policy-makers to take adjustment measures and hence help avoid unnecessary delays and inadequate or excessive responses.

In conclusion, it can be seen that oil price increases can
lead to wide exchange rate fluctuations in the short term
and also influence the trend of Western currencies over the
longer term. Both effects are problematic, particularly in
a system of fixed exchange rates. In any case, the exchange
rate is not a particularly suitable instrument of adjust-

ment for reducing global disequilibria resulting from a rise in oil prices. Its principal effect is on the distribution of the overall oil-related current account deficit among the countries concerned. It is therefore all the more pertinent to inquire into the manner in which current account deficits can be financed until suitable economic strategies lead to adjustment in the domestic economy. This question will be examined in the next chapter.

Footnotes to Chapter 2

1 There is a noticeable statistical asymmetry between the aggregate current account balances of oil-exporting and oil-importing countries, which can be ascribed primarily to faulty data on some countries in these groups. Cf. also IMF 1983, pp. 161 ff.

2 This view is expressed in, for example, Crockett, Evans 1980, pp. 547 ff.

3 This example is drawn from Dunn 1979, pp. 14 ff.

4 A survey of the current state of the theoretical discussion on general short and long-term exchange rate determinants is to be found in Isard 1978 or Dornbusch 1980.

5 With regard to the influence of competitiveness on current account developments, see also Wetter et al. 1983, pp. 13 ff.

6 With regard to the working of the EMS see Gösele 1979 and Salop 1981.

Chapter 3:   The recycling of the OPEC surpluses after 1973
             and its effects on the international financial
             system

This chapter first shows the forms that recycling of the OPEC
surpluses took after the first and second oil price rises,
the importance of international institutions in this process and the challenges faced by the international financial markets. It goes on to discuss ways in which the current recycling and debt problems might be solved.

1. The recycling of the OPEC surpluses

The simplest way to finance oil-related current account deficits would be by direct recycling, whereby the oil-exporting countries reinvest their surplus funds directly in those
countries that need them to pay for increased oil imports.
As will be shown below, however, direct recycling played no
more than a minor role after 1973. Let us therefore first
examine the deployment of OPEC surpluses hitherto.

a.   The investment of OPEC surpluses

Only a small proportion of the oil-exporting countries recorded current account surpluses during all or most of the
period after 1973. These were essentially the "low absorbers" in OPEC - Qatar, Kuwait, Libya, Saudi Arabia, the United Arab Emirates and, inasfar as information is available,[1]
Iran and Iraq. In principle, their surplus funds could be
invested in a number of possible ways. However, the range
of options actually open to these countries is very much
narrower, for a number of reasons. They are subject to constraints created partly by circumstances outside their control and partly by self-imposed restrictions.

(1)   Strategies and options open to the surplus countries

From the point of view of the Arab surplus countries, three
objectives must be respected in investing resources (see
Abdullatif 1980, pp. 23 f). One is the accumulation of
foreign exchange reserves. Several reasons are given why
the oil states tend to need higher foreign currency reserves than, say, the industrial countries. First, the
liquidity of the private sector is very high in the surplus
countries, so that there is a constant danger of massive capital exports, particularly as some of the OPEC countries exercise practically no exchange control, although most of them
have pegged their currencies to the SDR, the dollar or a basket of currencies (see Table 3.1). Secondly, there are often
no financial assets in their own currency, so that the monetary instruments normally used to prevent a drain on foreign
exchange reserves in the event of capital outflows are not
available. Finally, it should be borne in mind that the budgets of these countries depend almost entirely on oil receipts, which can fluctuate widely. With government expenditure rising, substantial foreign exchange reserves ensure
greater flexibility in oil-production policies.

A second objective is the financing of future expenditure on
the economic development of the country, in other words on
the import of capital goods as part of the development process.
Thirdly and finally, the states aim to supplement or even replace the income from a non-renewable real asset, oil, by
permanent revenue from financial investments (the investment
fund principle). It is in the light of these considerations
that in some surplus countries only part of the foreign exchange reserves is held by the central bank and the remainder, in some cases the larger part, is administered by other
government institutions.

86

Table 3.1:   EXCHANGE RATE ARRANGEMENTS OF THE OPEC
              SURPLUS COUNTRIES[a]

	Currency	Fixed against	Remarks
Iran	Rial	SDR	Multiple currency practices of an un-explained nature.
Iraq	Dinar	US dollar	
Qatar	Riyal	SDR	Intervention currency is the US dollar; in principle exchange rate changes are agreed with Bahrain and UAE, but not always prac-tised.
Kuwait	Dinar	another basket of cur-cencies	
Libya	Dinar	US dollar	
Saudi Arabia	Riyal	SDR	Fixed in terms of gold from 1960 to 1975; since March 1973 the daily dollar/riyal rate is calculated on the basis of the dollar/SDR rate.
United Arab Emirates (UAE)	Dirham	SDR	In principle, exchange rate changes are agreed with Bahrain and Qatar.

a As at 31.3.1983.

Source: IMF: Annual Report on Exchange Arrangements and Ex-
          change Restrictions 1983; Le Commerce du Levant,
          15.9.1980; Arab Economic Report 1977, p. 217.

Different maturities are preferred, depending on the purpose
of the investment (see Frowen 1981, p. 126). The accumulation
of foreign exchange reserves entails short-term (revolving)
investments in Treasury bills and time deposits, mostly with
maturities of three months. The financing of future development expenditure requires a more medium-term investment;
fixed-interest securities are preferred for this and maturities are determined essentially by the development strategy.
For the generation of future income, on the other hand, investments are sought in long-term real assets such as shareholdings
in companies, real property or precious metals, with earning
power and security taking precedence over the ability to liqui-
date the assets.

The surplus countries' decisions as to the employment of their
funds are not determined solely on economic criteria, however,
but also by political factors. For example, the provision of
finance by Arab Islamic development aid funds is determined
chiefly by the objective of promoting the cohesion of the Arab
and Islamic world, although as a matter of principle almost
all developing countries have access to it.[2] The influence of
political motives was demonstrated particularly clearly in
1980 by the refusal of Saudi Arabia and Kuwait to provide
funds to the International Monetary Fund and the World Bank
under a formula that had already been agreed unless the Pal-
estine Liberation Organisation (PLO) was accorded observer
status at that year's Annual Meetings of the two institutions.[3]
As a rule, therefore, it should be assumed that the political
leverage to be gained by using the surpluses in a particular
way is as important a factor in the investment behaviour of
surplus countries as are maturity, risk and yield. This is
one characteristic that sets them apart from conventional investors.

At the forefront of all medium and long-term investment decisions by OPEC countries is the aim of maintaining the real value of their financial assets, since they consider it their duty to future generations to leave them assets comparable in value to the real resources they are depleting.[4] This explains their very high preference for security, which finds expression in very conservative investment strategies. Preference is given mainly to investment opportunities in industrial countries and financial operations with banks from industrial countries, on the assumption that in times of crisis the central banks of these countries will act as lender of last resort.

However, the surplus countries see the real value of their assets threatened by two factors - inflation and exchange rate instability. Hence on the one hand they prefer investments in the currencies of those countries that display both political stability and relative domestic price stability, but on the other they seek to diversify the currency composition of their portfolios.[5] The bulk of their export receipts are denominated initially in dollars. They can also pay for a large part of their imports in the same currency, so that the large proportion of dollars in their portfolios is not regarded as a disadvantage in principle, as long as the provision of funds for future expenditure is the prime consideration in investment decisions. On the other hand, efforts were made in the seventies to reduce the proportion of dollar investments and increase those in Deutsche Mark, Swiss francs and Yen in order to protect the value of their assets in the face of high inflation rates in the USA. The surplus countries are nevertheless aware that this can only be done gradually if they wish to avoid jeopardising the value of their own investments.[6]

Recently, there has been a general growing trend towards "off-market diversification", in other word a tendency to spread investments by reaching direct agreements with government bodies in industrial countries and with international organisations, thus circumventing the markets. Against the background of irrecoverable bank claims on developing countries and Eastern bloc states, one of the advantages from the investor's point of view is that some of the potential investment risk can be avoided. Examples in this field are Saudi Arabia's loans to the IMF since the spring of 1981,[7] the Saudi loans to the Federal German Government and Saudi Arabia's yen investments, for which the Japanese Government and central bank issued special securities (see Handelsblatt, 24./25.1.1981).

However, the surplus countries cannot be considered a homogeneous group as far as their investment strategies are concerned; there are differences even in the weight attached to the various investment objectives, which depends primarily on the long-term absorption capacity of each country, in other words on the development processes within its economy. This will be the main determinant of the distribution between medium and long-term investments. Other differences are also evident, however, such as in the countries' preparedness to co-operate with industrial countries and international institutions. Such a willingness seems to be present chiefly in the case of Saudi Arabia and Kuwait.

It is not only the countries' individual investment strategies that impose constraints on their investment opportunities. The surplus countries are often denied access to national capital markets, either through various forms of control on capital transactions or indirectly owing to the fear of foreign domination felt by national holders of capital or governments.[8] Hence in the past they could often only buy land and real

property in their chosen countries of investment. After the
second oil crisis, however, the increasing current account
deficits and growing financing problems of industrial countries brought a tendency for markets to be opened wider to
admit the surpluses of Arab states and for restrictions on
capital imports to be reduced.[9] The section that follows
examines the actual deployment of the surpluses of these
states so far.

(2)   The deployment of the surpluses after 1973

There are serious statistical problems in determining the investment behaviour of the surplus countries. Firstly, adequate information is not available on the structure of individual countries' investments and secondly the deployment
of the aggregate surpluses of the oil-exporting countries can
be identified only in broad terms. This analysis will be based on the data published by the Bank of England, some of which
are estimated.

Table 3.2 shows the distribution of the oil-exporting countries' cash surpluses among different forms of investment
from 1974 to 1982. It becomes clear that up to now deposits
with banks and particularly with Euro-banks have accounted
for the largest share but also that they are subject to wide
fluctuations depending on the level of the surpluses. They
increase dramatically immediately after an oil price increase,
but in subsequent years the rise slows down markedly. It is
also noticeable that immediately after an oil price shock
investment increases in short-term government securities but
is quickly reduced again, at least in part. In process of
time there is then a shift from short-term investments to
long-term securities.[10]

Table 3.2: DEPLOYMENT OF THE SURPLUSES OF OIL-EXPORTING COUNTRIES[a]

- in billions of US dollars -

	1974	1975	1976	1977	1978	1979	Levels end-1979	1980	1981	1982	Levels end-1982
Bank deposits	+28.6	+ 9.9	+12.0	+13.0	+ 3.9	+37.3	115.0				
in country of currency issue	+ 7.0	+ 2.0	+ 5.0	+ 2.8	+ 2.8	+ 6.3	26.0				
Euro-currency deposits	+21.6	+ 7.9	+11.5	+10.7	+ 1.1	+31.0	89.0				
Short-term government securities[b]	+ 8.0	- 0.4	- 2.2	- 1.1	- 0.8	+ 3.3	7.0				
Long-term government securities[b]	+ 1.1	+ 2.4	+ 4.4	+ 4.5	- 1.8	- 0.7	10.0				
Other capital flows[c]	+ 7.1	+12.8	+13.2	+ 9.8	+ 5.8	+ 9.0	58.0				
IMF and IBRD[d]	+ 3.5	+ 4.0	+ 2.0	+ 3.0	+ 1.0	- 2.0	46.0				
Flow of funds to developing countries[e]	+ 4.9	+ 6.5	+ 6.4	+ 7.0	+ 6.2	+ 6.9					
Total identified deployed net cash surplus	+53.3	+35.2	+35.8	+33.5	+13.4	+53.8	236.0	+126.0	+65.0	+18.0	445.0
of which:											
Investments in the USA:											
Treasury bonds and notes	+ 0.2	+ 2.0	+ 4.2	+ 4.3	- 1.5	- 1.1	8.3	+ 8.2	+10.9	+ 6.9	34.3
Treasury bills	+ 5.3	+ 0.5	- 1.0	- 0.9	- 1.0	+ 3.3	6.6	+ 1.4	- 0.5	+ 0.4	7.9
Bank deposits	+ 4.1	+ 0.6	+ 1.7	+ 0.4	+ 0.8	+ 4.9	14.3	- 1.1	- 2.0	+ 4.4	15.6
Direct investment	+ 0.1	-	-	-	+ 0.1	+ 0.1	0.3				
Other portfolio investment	+ 1.3	+ 3.2	+ 3.0	+ 3.1	+ 1.6	+ 1.0	13.5	+ 4.7	+ 4.6	- 0.4	22.4
Other	+ 0.7	+ 3.3	+ 4.4	+ 2.2	+ 1.3	+ 0.7	12.4				

Total in the USA	+11.7	+ 9.6	+12.1	+ 9.1	+ 1.3	+ 8.9	55.4	+14.1	+16.3	+13.0	98.8
Investments in the UK :											
British government stocks	+ 0.9	+ 0.4	+ 0.2	–	– 0.3	+ 0.4	1.7	+ 1.9	+ 0.9	– 0.4	4.1
Treasury bills	+ 2.7	– 0.9	– 1.2	– 0.2	+ 2.0	–	0.4	– 0.1	–	– 0.1	0.2
Sterling deposits	+ 1.7	+ 2.0	– 1.4	+ 0.3	+ 2.0	+ 1.4	4.1	+ 1.4	+ 0.4	+ 1.3	7.2
British government foreign currency bonds	–	–	–	+ 0.2	–	–	0.2	–	–	–	
Foreign currency deposits	+13.8	+ 4.1	+ 5.6	+ 3.1	– 2.0	+14.8	45.7	+14.8	+ 7.8	– 9.4	58.9
Other foreign currency borrowing	+ 1.2	+ 0.2	+ 0.8	–	–	+ 0.2	2.4	– 0.5	–	–	1.9
Direct investment	+ 0.2	–	–	–	–	–	0.2	–			
Other portfolio investment	+ 0.5	+ 0.3	+ 0.4	+ 0.4	+ 0.1	+ 0.4	2.1	–			
Other	–	–	+ 0.1	–	–	–	0.1	–			
Total in the UK	+21.0	+ 4.3	+ 4.5	+ 3.8	– 1.8	+17.2	56.9	+17.6	+ 9.3	– 9.2	74.6
Other countries and international organisations	+20.5	+21.3	+19.2	+20.6	+13.9	+27.7	123.7	+94.3	+41.4	+14.2	273.6

a   Estimated by the Bank of England, mainly on the basis of country information. The countries covered are the members of OPEC, Trinidad and Tobago, Bahrain and Oman.

b   In the USA and the United Kingdom.

c   Comprises other portfolio investment, direct investment, loans and other items.

d   Comprises investment in the IMF oil facility and complementary financing facility, the reserve position in the IMF, SDR holdings and direct purchases of IBRD bonds.

e   Comprises bilateral loans and contributions and subscriptions to regional and international development agencies other than the IMF and the IBRD.

Source: The Surpluses of the Oil Exporters, in: Bank of England, Quarterly Bulletin, June 1980, pp. 154 ff, Tables C and D; Bank of England, Quarterly Bulletin, various issues; calculations by the authors.

A considerable part of the surpluses is invested in medium
and long-term forms that cannot be identified more closely,
such as direct investment, portfolio investment or loans.
These capital flows show a more uniform increase over time
than do bank deposits. In addition, appreciable sums got to
the International Monetary Fund and the World Bank or direct
to developing countries. Lending to developing countries
holds steady even when the current account surpluses are
falling.

At the end of 1982 about 22 % of the total identified deployed surpluses were invested in the USA, about 3 % in the
domestic market in the United Kingdom and 13.2 % as foreign
currency deposits on the London Euro-Currency market. About
62 % of the surpluses accumulated by 1982 were placed in
other countries and with international organisations. The
Bank of England estimates that in 1979 the proportion of
investments in France, the Federal Republic of Germany,
Japan, the Netherlands, Belgium, Italy and Canada came to
17 %, of which about 80 % was held in the form of bank
deposits.[11]

Hence whereas about half of the accumulated surpluses was
invested in bank deposits - predominantly on the Euro-market - the OPEC share of the market is put at a constant 10 %
for the period under review. After the Herstatt crisis in
1974 deposits in this market were concentrated in a very
few large banks. Subsequently, however, the number of institutions involved has grown. Whereas in 1973 55 banks
held between 90 and 95 % of the oil-exporting countries'
deposits, after 1977 this was shared among about 90 banks.
It is almost impossible to determine the currency composition of the accumulated surpluses. The Bank of England
estimates that the dollar share has remained stable at

about three-quarters, while the sterling share has fallen
from about 10 % in 1974 to about 5 % in 1979 (see Bank of
England 1980, p. 159).

The investment of a large part of the surpluses at short
term indicates that the ability to realise the funds at
short notice was given priority in the deployment of the
funds. In recent years, however, there has been a growing
tendency to invest a larger proportion at longer term. This
can be attributed not only to the growing importance of the
aim to safeguard future income but also to the fact that
industrial countries with increasing financial problems,
for example, now offer greater incentives for the longer-
term investment of foreign capital and also that the surplus countries themselves have gained experience and are
slowly overcoming their reluctance to commit their oil funds
for long periods.

In order to give an impression of the situation of certain
important surplus countries after 1973, the main balance-of-
payments components are summarised in Tables 3.3 and 3.4.
Table 3.3 shows that the oil-exporting countries as a whole
significantly expanded their foreign currency reserves in
the period under review; this was particularly marked in the
case of Saudi Arabia and Iran. Only in 1978 and 1982 were
substantial outflows of reerves recorded by some countries.
The build-up in reserves occured mainly in 1974 and 1975
and again in 1979 and 1980, so that a close connection
with changes in the current account is evident.

Table 3.4 uses the examples of Saudi Arabia and Kuwait, by
far the largest surplus countries, to illustrate the development of short and long-term capital flows. These are contrasted with Iran, a country with much smaller surpluses.

Table 3.3: CHANGES IN THE FOREIGN EXCHANGE RESERVES OF OIL-EXPORTING COUNTRIES 1973 - 1982[a]

- in billions of US dollars -

	Level 1973	1974	1975	1976	1977	1978	1979	1980	1981	1982
All oil-export. countries	12.9	31.7	12.0	9.0	7.1	-20.0	13.0	22.3	9.2	- 4.8[b]
Iran	1.1	7.0	0.9	0.0	2.9	- 1.0	3.0	-	-	-
Kuwait	0.4	0.8	0.3	0.2	1.1	- 0.6	0.3	1.2	0.5	2.1[b]
Saudi Arabia	3.7	10.1	10.0	3.9	1.7	-12.4	- 0.1	4.9	11.0	- 1.0[b]
United Arab Emirates	0.1	0.4	0.6	0.9	1.1	0.0	0.6	0.6	1.4	-

a Excluding monetary gold.
b Fourth quarter of 1982.

Source: International Monetary Fund: International Financial Statistics, various years; calculations by the authors.

Table 3.4: NET CAPITAL TRANSACTIONS OF SELECTED OIL-EXPORTING COUNTRIES, 1973 - 1981[a]

in billions of US dollars

	1973	1974	1975	1976	1977	1978	1979	1980	1981
SAUDI ARABIA									
- Long-term capital transactions	- 0.70	- 4.51	- 5.26	- 9.18	- 9.01	- 0.82	- 4.93	- 27.80	- 22.91
Direct investment	- 0.70	- 4.47	- 1.88	- 0.37	+ 0.78	+ 0.48	- 1.17	- 3.40	+ 3.16
Portfolio investment	-	-	-	-	- 9.76	+ 0.34	- 2.70	- 23.00	- 24.74
Other[b]	- 0.00	- 0.04	- 3.38	- 8.81	- 0.03	- 1.64	- 1.06	- 0.60	- 1.33
- Short-term capital transactions	+ 0.13	- 0.62	0.06	- 0.74	- 3.11	- 4.40	- 5.97	8.37	- 10.36
Public sector	0.00	0.00	0.00	0.00	0.00	0.00	- 0.01	- 0.04	+ 1.33
Commercial banks	- 0.03	- 0.09	- 0.14	- 0.51	- 0.69	- 0.63	- 1.25	- 3.75	+ 5.87
Other sectors	+ 0.16	- 0.53	+ 0.20	- 0.23	- 2.42	- 3.77	- 4.71	- 4.58	- 5.81
KUWAIT									
- Long-term capital transactions			- 1.94	- 4.07	- 0.53	- 0.48	- 0.53	- 0.07	- 0.01
Direct investment			+ 0.04	- 1.16	- 0.12	- 0.13	+ 0.14	- 0.44	+ 0.03
Portfolio investment			+ 0.56	- 0.25	+ 0.01	- 0.00	+ 0.59	- 0.33	+ 0.27
Other[b]			- 1.42	- 2.66	- 0.40	- 0.35	- 0.08	+ 0.70	+ 0.23
- Short-term capital transactions			- 0.09	+ 0.32	- 0.06	- 0.69	+ 0.06	- 0.94	9.64
Public sector			-	-	+ 0.19	+ 0.06	+ 0.06	+ 0.38	8.17
Commercial banks			- 0.09	+ 0.32	- 0.18	- 0.76	+ 0.03	- 0.53	0.80
Other sectors			-	-	- 0.06	- 0.02	- 0.03	- 0.79	0.67
IRAN									
- Long-term capital transactions	+ 1.05	- 1.94	- 2.87	- 1.84	+ 0.36				
Direct investment	+ 0.56	+ 0.33	+ 0.14	+ 0.74	+ 0.80				
Portfolio investment	-	-	-	-	-				
Other[b]	+ 0.48	- 2.27	- 3.1	- 2.58	- 0.44				
- Short-term capital transactions	- 0.73	- 3.13	- 1.08	- 3.24	- 2.96				
Public sector	+ 0.05	+ 0.09	+ 0.02	+ 0.08	+ 0.03				
Commercial banks	- 0.03	+ 0.05	- 0.12	+ 0.45	- 0.17				
Other sectors	- 0.75	- 3.27	- 0.98	- 3.77	- 2.83				

a Capital export (-), capital import (+).
b In each case comprises other long-term transactions by the public sector, the commercial banks and other sectors.

Source: International Monetary Fund: Balance of Payments Yearbook, various years; calculations by the authors.

As was to be expected, all three countries recorded large capital exports in both areas during practically the entire period, in the case of Saudi Arabia on a much larger scale than in the other two countries (more than $ 36 billion in 1980 alone). It is striking that in Saudi Arabia and Kuwait net exports of long-term capital were often much larger than outflows of short-term funds. It may therefore be concluded that these countries lay particular emphasis on the longer-term investment objectives, although in the case of Saudi Arabia interest lies less with direct investment than with portfolio investment.

Table 3.5 shows development in the total external assets of the individual surplus countries, although these figures are not necessarily directly comparable with the data used previously as they are drawn from different sources. Here the importance of Saudi Arabia as the largest creditor by far, with a total portfolio of $ 75 billion in external claims in 1979, becomes clear. Next comes Kuwait with $ 40 billion in the same year, while the holdings of the other states were much smaller.

The figures show that particular attention should be paid to the investment behaviour of Saudi Arabia and Kuwait, which between them account for more than two-thirds of the external claims of the countries under consideration. These two countries therefore bear not inconsiderable responsibility for the working of the international financial system, for two reasons. First, in view of their financial potential they are quite able to cause considerable unrest in the international financial and monetary system. In theory, at least, there is a danger that the desire to safeguard the earning power and value of financial investments will be pushed into the background by political objectives - after a change of power in three countries, for example - and that assets will be transferred on a large

Table 3.5:   EXTERNAL CLAIMS OF ARAB SURPLUS COUNTRIES

- levels, in billions of dollar -

	1972	1977	1978	1979
Saudi-Arabia	2.3	60.0	64.0	75.0
Kuwait	2.4	22.0	28.0	40.0
United Arab Emirates	0.3	7.6	9.3	12.7
Iraq	0.7	7.0	8.6	17.5
Iran	-	n.a.	12.0	15.9
Libya	2.7	3.7	4.1	6.3
Qatar	0.4	2.6	3.0	4.3
Total	8.8	102.8	129.0	171.7

Source: Le Commerce du Levant, 23.6.1980 and 1.9.1980.

scale. The possible consequences for the international financial markets and for the monetary system must await examination elsewhere. Suffice it to say here that the high concentration of funds in the hands of only two countries means that manoeuvres in pursuit of set objectives do not require agreement among several countries that are often at odds with one another - as in the case of the price policy of the OPEC cartel. Hence their freedom of action is considerably greater in this regard.

On the other side of the coin, Saudi Arabia and Kuwait rely to a very high degree on the smooth functioning of the world economic and financial system precisely because of the large size of their financial investments. This provides some assurance that they will behave repsonsibly and may provide a starting point for resolving the recycling problem on the basis of co-operation. As these countries not only possess substantial financial resources but are also the main oil exporters, co-operation might be conceivable on two fronts simultaneously to safeguard both oil supplies and the recycling process.

The investment behaviour of the OPEC countries so far has shown that direct recycling is of no great overall significance. This raises the question of the other ways in which oil-related current account deficits are financed.

b.   Financing of current account deficits

From the point of view of financing it is appropriate to devide the oil-importing countries into two main groups - industrial countries and developing countries without adequate oil reserves - as the latter countries were already displaying much worse underlying economic conditions before the outbreak of the first oil crisis and the opportunities and conditions for financing are not the same for both groups. Particular attention should be focussed in this respect to the so-called newly industrialising countries;[12] their situation differs markedly from that of other developing countries in that their financial requirement is particularly high because of increasing industrialisation but also in that they enjoyed a better creditworthiness and had easier access to the international financial markets during the last decade owing to their growth potential.

When political discussion turns to the manner in which current account deficits are financed it is not primarily concerned with how balance-of-payments adjustment was achieved ex post: it is concerned more with the difficult problem of maintaining an ex ante ability to continue financing essential imports in the future. This point is particularly important in developing countries. In industrial countries, on the other hand, attention concentrates more on the effects that current account deficits can have on the foreign exchange reserves or the exchange rate. These are due to the fact that in principle a current account deficit will itself entail excess demand for foreign exchange at some point. If this does not happen to be matched at the prevailing exchange rate by an equally large supply of foreign currency from capital exports, the exchange rate of the country's currency will come under pressure. As a rule, such a devaluation can be an appropriate way of restoring current account equilibrium over the longer term. However, as we have shown,[13] in the event of oil price increases the exchange rate is only partly suitable as an adjustment instrument, as in these circumstances exchange rate changes only affect the relationships between oil-importing countries themselves and do not help bring about adjustment between oil-importing and oil-exporting countries. As this leads only to a redistribution of the burden of adjustment among oil-importing countries, the financing of existing current account deficits is preferable to devaluation, at least in the short term.

If the central bank does not wish to permit the exchange rate change induced by the current account deficit, it must artificially generate a coresponding supply of foreign currency, in other words it must intervene in the foreign exchange markets and accept a loss of foreign exchange reserves. This is often regarded as a disadvantage, however, and the central bank will attempt instead to create an incentive for autonomous imports of capital by altering interest rates. The government itself may also borrow abroad.

The next two subsections will examine the extent to which oil-induced current account deficits were financed by drawing on foreign exchange reserves or by importing capital and the problems that can be associated with these two methods.

(1)   Drawing on foreign exchange reserves

Table 3.6 and 3.7 show changes in the foreign exchange reserves of industrial and developing countries after 1973. Despite existing current account deficits, both groups of countries showed a tendency to add to their reserves rather than run them down in the period under review, which suggests that this form of current account financing has been of little importance up to now.

In the group of industrial countries as a whole a decline in foreign exchange reserves coincided with current account deficits only in 1979 and, albeit on a much smaller scale, in 1974. This form of financing was therefore used only as a

Table 3.6: DEVELOPMENT OF INDIVIDUAL BALANCE-OF-PAYMENTS COMPONENTS IN INDUSTRIAL COUNTRIES, 1973-1982[a]

in billions of US dollars

	1973	1974	1975	1976	1977	1978	1979	1980	1981	1982
Industrial countries as a group										
Balance on current account[b]	13.4	-23.0	8.9	-10.5	-15.4	-16.2	-25.3	-62.7	-21.2	-24.6
Long-term capital transactions[c]	-10.4	-0.6	-10.0	0.8	2.5	-19.9	-29.6	1.6	14.5	
Short-term capital transactions[c]	8.2	21.0	-8.8	13.1	31.8	-25.2	14.4	40.9	-14.8	
Change in foreign exchange reserves[d]	1.9	0.7	-5.3	-8.2	-30.8	-35.7	5.9	-28.5	-5.2	
Federal Republic of Germany										
Balance on current account[b]	4.6	10.0	4.1	3.9	4.1	9.0	6.1	-15.7	-6.5	3.3
Long-term capital transactions[c]	4.9	-2.5	-7.4	0.6	5.6	-1.5	6.5	3.4	4.0	
Short-term capital transactions[c]	-0.8	-7.0	1.8	0.5	5.2	6.8	-1.6	4.4	1.2	
Change in foreign exchange reserves[d]	-6.7	0.7	-0.1	-4.1	-3.3	-10.4	3.2	10.4	-0.9	
France										
Balance on current account[b]	1.5	-3.9	2.7	-3.4	0.4	7.0	5.2	-4.2	-4.8	-12.0
Long-term capital transactions[c]	-2.2	-0.2	1.2	1.7	0.8	3.1	-5.0	-8.4	-8.1	
Short-term capital transactions[c]	-0.3	2.8	-1.1	2.6	1.2	-0.2	3.8	17.9	15.1	
Change in foreign exchange reserves[d]	2.2	0.1	4.3	2.8	0.0	2.9	3.7	-12.5	4.5	
United Kingdom										
Balance on current account[b]	-2.2	-7.6	-3.4	-1.6	-	2.0	1.8	6.7	12.4	6.9
Long-term capital transactions[c]	0.1	3.7	0.8	1.1	6.2	5.3	3.5	8.2	-19.1	
Short-term capital transactions[c]	2.8	3.7	1.4	3.3	3.0	3.3	7.8	1.5	0.7	
Change in foreign exchange reserves[d]	-0.2	-0.4	1.2	3.1	-1.5	3.4	-4.5	-2.0	3.3	
Italy										
Balance on current account[b]	-2.6	-8.2	-0.5	-2.8	2.5	6.4	5.5	-9.7	-8.2	-5.5
Long-term capital transactions[c]	3.9	3.3	0.2	0.4	1.0	0.5	-0.3	3.6	8.7	
Short-term capital transactions[c]	-0.6	3.5	-1.0	13.4	15.7	-0.8	-1.3	7.8	0.2	
Change in foreign exchange reserves[d]	0.2	1.1	2.5	-1.9	-5.9	-6.2	-3.5	0.1	1.3	
USA										
Balance on current account[b]	7.1	2.1	18.3	4.4	-14.1	-14.8	-0.5	1.5	4.5	-8.1
Long-term capital transactions[c]	-5.6	6.5	-10.6	-6.2	-12.1	4.5	-15.2	-0.8	25.9	
Short-term capital transactions[c]	1.2	-7.4	-12.5	-6.0	-4.8	6.6	-9.7	-22.7	-51.7	
Change in foreign exchange reserves[d]	0.2	-1.4	-0.6	-2.5	-0.2	1.6	2.8	-8.1	-4.6	
Japan										
Balance on current account[b]	-0.1	-4.7	-0.7	3.3	10.9	16.5	-8.8	-10.7	4.8	6.9
Long-term capital transactions[c]	-8.4	-3.6	-0.1	0.8	-3.2	-13.2	-12.6	2.4	-6.6	
Short-term capital transactions[c]	5.0	9.6	0.6	0.7	-1.8	-5.5	5.7	16.7	4.7	
Change in foreign exchange reserves[d]	8.0	-1.1	0.1	-3.9	-5.7	8.2	13.0	-5.9	-5.7	

a Note that this is not a complete portrayal of payments balances; for example, changes in the valuation of foreign exchange reserves are not given, nor are errors and omissions.
b Including official transfer payments.
c Capital exports (-) or capital imports (+).
d Excluding valuation changes; (-) increase in foreign exchange reserves, (+) reduction in foreign exchange reserves.

Source: International Monetary Fund: Balance of Payments Statistics, various years; IMF: World Economic Outlook, Washington, C.C. 1983; calculations by the authors.

Table 3.7: CURRENT ACCOUNT FINANCING IN NON-OPEC DEVELOPING COUNTRIES,[a] 1973-1982

in billions of US dollars

	1973	1974	1975	1976	1977	1978	1979	1980	1981	1982
Current account deficit[b]	+11.3	+37.0	+46.3	+32.6	+28.9	+41.3	+61.0	+89.0	+107.7	+86.8
Use of foreign exchange reserves[c]	-10.4	- 2.7	+ 1.6	-13.0	-12.5	-17.4	-12.6	- 4.5	- 2.1	+ 7.1
Transactions not affecting net debt positions	+10.3	+14.6	+11.8	+12.6	+14.4	+17.9	+23.9	+24.1	+28.0	+25.1
- official transfers	+ 5.5	+ 8.7	+ 7.1	+ 7.5	+ 8.2	+ 8.2	+11.6	+12.5	+13.8	+13.2
- SDR allocations, valuation adjustments and monetisation of gold	+ 0.6	+ 0.6	- 0.6	+ 0.1	+ 0.8	+ 2.3	+ 3.4	+ 1.4	+ 0.3	+ 0.5
- direct investment flows, net	+ 4.2	+ 5.3	+ 5.3	+ 5.0	+ 5.4	+ 7.3	+ 8.9	+10.1	+13.9	+11.4
Net borrowing	+11.4	+25.1	+32.9	+33.0	+27.0	+40.8	+49.7	+69.3	+81.8	+54.6
- Net long-term borrowing[d]	+11.7	+18.1	+27.1	+28.0	+24.6	+37.2	+36.5	+47.2	+62.7	+41.0
. from official sources	+ 4.9	+ 6.8	+11.7	+10.5	+11.4	+13.8	+13.3	+17.6	+23.0	+19.5
. from private sources	+ 6.8	+11.3	+15.4	+17.5	+13.2	+23.4	+23.2	+29.6	+39.7	+21.5
- from financial institutions[e]	+ 6.5	+10.3	+14.2	+15.3	+ 9.4	+19.5	+21.7	+28.4	+35.7	+18.5
- from other lenders	+ 0.3	+ 1.0	+ 1.3	+ 2.2	+ 3.8	+ 3.9	+ 1.5	+ 1.2	+ 4.0	+ 3.7
- Use of reserve-related credit facilities[f]	+ 0.2	+ 1.6	+ 2.4	+ 4.6	+ 0.4	+ 0.3	+ 0.4	+ 1.8	+ 5.9	+10.7
- use of IMF credit	+ 0.1	+ 1.5	+ 2.1	+ 3.2	-	-	+ 0.2	+ 1.2	+ 5.6	+ 6.3
- Other net short-term borrowing, including residual items	- 0.5	+ 5.4	+ 3.3	- 0.4	+ 2.0	+ 3.3	+12.8	+20.4	+13.2	+ 2.9
. Special financing[e]	-	-	+ 0.1	+ 0.4	+ 2.6	+ 1.2	- 0.4	+ 4.1	+ 6.7	+14.4
- Payment arrears	-	-	-	-	+ 1.5	+ 0.4	+ 0.8	+ 1.1	+ 2.4	+ 7.1
. Other net short-term borrowing[e]	+ 3.3	+ 8.3	+ 8.9	+ 5.8	+ 2.7	+ 4.9	+14.6	+20.8	+10.1	
. Residual items	- 3.8	- 2.9	- 5.6	- 5.9	- 3.3	- 2.8	- 1.4	- 4.5	- 3.7	-11.5

a Including Ecuador and Gabon, excluding Oman.

b Excluding official transfers; (-) current account surplus, (+) current account deficit.

c (-) increase in foreign exchange reserves, (+) decrease in foreign exchange reserves.

d Calculated by the IMF on the basis of balance-of-payments statistics.

e Those items are a rough estimate of total short and long-term borrowing from commercial banks, which is broadly comparable with national balance-of-payments statistics.

f Comprises use of Fund credit and short-term borrowing from monetary authorities.

Source: International Monetary Fund: World Economic Outlook 1983.

very short-term expedient after an oil price shock, if at all. The main exception in this respect was the Federal Republic of Germany, which financed a larger part of its current account deficit after the second oil crisis by drawing on reserves.[14] In general terms, the weak relationship evident here between current account developments and foreign exchange reserves in industrial countries can be explained chiefly by the fact that movements in the exchange rates of these countries' currencies are determined in the short term primarily by international capital flows, which are subject to wide fluctuations and often induce the monetary authorities to intervene on a massive scale. Hence it is more these short-term influences that are reflected in the changes discernible in the foreign exchange reserves.

For various reasons, industrial countries often attempt to avoid reducing their foreign exchange reserves. Firstly, this is regarded as a problematic way of financing oil-induced current account deficits as the deficits are often not a temporary phenomenon but a longer-term development that might put a continuous heavy drain on the reserves. As unlimited foreign exchange reserves are not available, the authorities avoid drawing on them where possible. This argument applies equally to all deficit countries.

In addition, industrial countries usually operate on the assumption that they need fairly substantial foreign exchange reserves to prevent or dampen exchange rate fluctuations. The currencies of these countries differ from others in that they are freely convertible and widely used in international trade and capital transactions. They are therefore permanently exposed to the risk of exchange rate fluctuations, which can have an adverse effect on domestic economic developments in countries that are highly dependent on foreign

trade. It should also be borne in mind that short-term exchange rate developments are strongly influenced by the expectations of the foreign exchange markets, which might gamble
on government resistance to exchange rate changes weakening
in times of current account deficits and falling reserves and
might accentuate the pressure on a currency by speculative
transactions. For that reason too, industrial countries regard a run-down in foreign exchange reserves to finance current payments deficits as generally undesirable. This applies
even more strongly to countries belonging to a system of fixed exchange rates.

In the case of developing countries, on the other hand, another argument against reducing foreign exchange reserves
takes on particular importance. A number of them finance their
current account deficits at least partly by raising loans from
commercial banks, and for these countries the level of their
foreign exchange reserves is a factor in their credit assessment by the international financial markets. Low reserves
make access to new loans difficult or increase the cost of
borrowing. It can be seen that those groups of developing
countries with particularly large debts towards commercial
banks - primarily countries exporting industrial goods and
other middle-income oil-importing countries - are precisely the ones that have recorded substantial growth in their
foreign exchange reserves since 1973 (see Table 3.9). However, this itself further increases their borrowing requirement.

It can be concluded from the aspects described here that a
reduction in foreign exchange reserves in order to finance
oil-related current account deficits is significant only
in the short term at most. In the main, therefore, these
deficits must be financed by inflows of capital.

(2)   Inflows of capital

Table 3.6 also shows the capital transaction balances of industrial countries after 1973. As a rule, current account deficits have been financed mainly by means of imports of short-term capital. It was not until 1981 that long-term capital flows generally became an important factor. Capital account trends in individual industrial countries essentially confirm this initial impression. Germany constitutes an exception; its borrowing requirement, which did not arise until after the second oil crisis in any case, was covered mainly by means of long-term capital inflows and by drawing on foreign exchange reserves.

In comparison with other countries, Western industrial countries have little difficulty financing temporary current account deficits by means of capital imports. Their ability to induce inflows of private capital is unsurpassed. They have a relatively high credit rating and easier, cheaper access to private bank credit than many other countries. Membership of international organisations and institutions (EC, NATO, the BIS, for example) is also important in this regard; it not only enhances the creditworthiness of the industrial countries in the financial markets but also enables them to obtain additional official multilateral credit. Finally, it is easier for industrial countries to obtain official bilateral credit, even though they have made use of such facilities only on rare occasion in the past. An example in this respect is the $ 2 billion loan that the Deutsche Bundesbank granted to Italy in 1974 against the pleding of gold reserves (see Deutsche Bundesbank, Geschäftsbericht 1974, pp.55 f). Industrial countries such as Germany, France, Italy and Japan also received official loans from OPEC surplus countries, although these have been rare so far . In recent years, however,

the OPEC surplus countries have shown an increasing inclina-
tion to grant bilateral official loans to industrial countries as part of their diversification efforts and changed
currency preferences. An additional spur in this direction
came from the temporary reluctance of the international fi-
nacial markets to accept OPEC funds, so that new investment
opportunities had to be found for these resources.[15]

In principle, therefore, Western industrial countries should
have little difficulty tiding themselves over cash shortages.
The situation is different for developing countries, however.
As a rule, their credit rating is much lower and they are regarded as high-risk borrowers. This has several implications.
Private and official investors are rarely prepared to lend
to them direct. Where developing countries do have access
to the international financial markets, banks take account
of their poor creditworthiness by imposing risk surcharges,
so that the cost of borrowing is relatively high for these
countries.[16] Regardless whether they can obtain commercial
bank credit or not, developing countries therefore have to
rely to a very large extent on official transfers and the
resources of international organisations such as the IMF and
the World Bank.[17]

Table 3.7 shows clearly that official transfers, for example,
do indeed play a not inconsiderable part in financing developing countries' current account deficits. However, it also
reveals that their contribution has fallen sharply in recent
years; whereas in 1974 it accounted for 23.5 %, in 1981 it
stood at only about 12.8 %. In 1982 these countries' financial problems were exacerbated by an absolute decline in
transfers for the first time, whereas previously they had
risen steadily in nominal terms.

After both the first and second oil crises net borrowing from
private sources financed by far the largest part of the developing countries' current account deficits. It is noticeable
that short-term indebtedness increased sharply after the second oil price shock, whereas in the aftermath of the first
the decisive factor had been long-term credits. This is a serious development, as growing financial and adjustment problems make it almost impossible for certain countries to repay
maturing short-term loans and their still lower credit rating means that the fresh funds they need can be obtained only at still higher cost, if at all.

Given the financing problems of developing countries indicated above, it is surprising that the International Monetary
Fund has played such a small role in this respect. In 1973
IMF loans were used to finance only about 0.9 % of the global current account deficit of developing countries; in 1974
the figure was 4.0 %. After the second oil crisis a larger
volume of IMF resources was taken up, but it was relatively
insignificant in proportion to the deficits to be financed:
it came to about 0.3 % in 1979 and 1.3 % in 1980, but rose
nonetheless to about 7.3 % in 1982.

Chart 7 shows the different financing possibilities open
to industrial and developing countries under the auspices of
the International Monetary Fund. First, each member country
can make drawings in the tranches, that is to say it can obtain foreign currency loans from its quota paid into the
Fund. All Fund resources except drawings in the reserve
tranche are subject to conditions of differing severity.
Such drawings are usually preceded by stand-by arrangements;
these arrangements, which represent a prior commitment on
the part of the Fund to make resources available at a later
date, are often concluded by countries simply to obtain

Chart 7:   FINANCING POSSIBILITIES WITHIN THE FRAMEWORK OF THE IMF

D R A W I N G S   I N   T H E   T R A N C H E S

RESERVE TRANCHE

(Condition: Balance-of-payments need)

4 CREDIT TRANCHES

(Requirements: Pro-grammes of differ-ing severity to re-store balance-of-payments equilib-rium)

P E R M A N E N T   S P E C I A L   F A C I L I T I E S

COMPENSATORY FINANCING OF FLUCTUATIONS IN EXPORT EARN-INGS

(Requirement: Co-operation with IMF on solution to problems)

EXTENDED FUND FACILITY

(Condition: submission of an adjustment programme, credit drawn in instal-ments, performance clauses)

FINANCING OF COMMODITY BUFFER STOCKS

(Requirement: membership of a commod-ity cartel, co-operation with the IMF on solving the problems)

T E M P O R A R Y   S P E C I A L   F A C I L I T I E S

1st Oil-Facility 1974 - 1975

2nd Oil-Facility 1975 - 1976

SUPPLEMENTARY FINANCING FACILITY 1979 - 1981

(In the event of serious balance-of-payments disequilibria, requirements in accordance with operational principles. Credit drawn in instal-ments, performance clauses, limited to 2 years after first recourse)

POLICY ON ENLARGED ACCESS TO FUND RESOURCES SINCE MARCH 1981[a]

(Guidelines essentially the same as those for the Supplementary Financing Facility)

ADDITIONAL FINANCING FACILITIES FOR DEVELOPING COUNTRIES

TRUST FUND

(Loans at low rates of inter-est and on "soft" terms; re-quirement: balance-of-pay-ments adjustment programme, only certain countries eligible)

SUBSIDY ACCOUNT

(Contributions towards interest payments on 1975 Oil Facility loans are paid to the "mem-bers most seriously af-fected", only certain countries eligible)

a   Initially up to a limit of 150 % of the quota for one year or 450 % of the quota over a period of 3 years. The cumulative credits of a country may thus amount to a maximum of 600 % of its quota. See International Monetary Fund: Annual Report 1983, p. 124. Since September 1983 the upper limit has been 102 % for a single year or 306 % for three years and the limit for cumulative lending is now 408 % of the quota. See in this connection Press Communiqué of the Interim Committee of the Board of Governors of the International Monetary Fund, reprinted in: International Monetary Fund: Press Release No. 83/66, 26th September 1983.

easier access to the international financial markets. If a stand-by arrangement has been agreed with the IMF, commercial banks are more inclined to lend to the country in question. Stand-by arrangements also generally precede drawings under the Extended Fund Facility, which can be used by member countries whose borrowing requirement is higher and/or requires longer credit terms than are available in the regular tranches. However, this facility and the other two permanent special facilities established to contend with specific country problems are not intended directly for financing oil-related current account deficits.

The Fund created temporary special facilities in response to the oil price increases of recent years. The first two oil facilities, which provided finance repayable in 3 to 7 years, ran for one year each and were replaced by the Supplementary Financing Facility (the Witteveen Facility), which is supplied with funds by the central banks of individual member countries. In 1981 this facility was replaced in turn by the Policy on Enlarged Access to Fund Resources.

The IMF set up two additional financing instruments for developing countries, the Trust Fund,[18] from which loans were granted at very low interest rates until April 1981, and the Subsidy Account, from which the worst affected developing countries could obtain interest rate subsidies for drawings made under the 1975 Oil Facility. In the latter instance access was therefore restricted and the Fund announced which countries it considered fully or partially eligible.[19]

Given these many and varied possibilities and the prevailing problems of financing, the question arises as to what can explain the developing countries' modest use of Fund resources.[20] The main reason is undoubtedly that most financing facilities are tied to economic and balance-of-payments conditions of differing severity.[21] In the eyes of the governments concerned, these constitute undesirable interference in the national economic policy of the borrowing country. Hence in the past countries have drawn mainly on facilities with low conditionality, such as the reserve tranche, or on the oil facility and the facility to offset fluctuations in export earnings. The Fund is therefore in a real dilemma on this issue; if the conditions are too severe, countries will draw on its resources only in extreme emergences, by which time it is doubtful whether the conditions imposed can help solve their economic problems. On the other hand, if few restrictions are imposed, there is a great temptation for countries to use Fund resources without taking economc policy measures, thereby neglecting the adjustment of the real economy that alone can guarantee a country's creditworthiness over the long term (see Polak 1982, p. 136).

A frequent complaint levelled against the IMF is that its conditions are mainly geared to underlying economic conditions such as might be found in industrial countries and that the prescribed traditional methods of macro-economic management are not appropriate to the situation in developing countries. Critics claim that adherence to such conditions entails unacceptably high social costs, so that a country would rather take up loans at high interest rates, in the international financial markets for example, for as long as it can. However, commercial banks and bank consortia are increasingly making the granting of credit conditional on agreement between the debtor country and the IMF on a stabilisation programme.

Another reason for the small take-up of Fund credit is the
fact that the level of funds granted from the regular credit tranches and under the policy of enlarged access is related to the member country's quota. Developing countries'
quotas are still very low even after the Eighth General Review of Quotas, as Table 3.8 shows by reference to a small
selection of countries. This ultimately leads to dispropor-
tion between the conditions imposed and the amount that can
be borrowed.

However, even if the countries had wished to make full use
of the opportunities open to them and to finance a larger
part of their current account deficits via the International Monetary Fund, it is doubtful whether sufficient funds
would have been available. Until now, the Fund has created
liqudity mainly through members' quotas, which have been
raised as and when required. This has long been regarded as
inadequate, however. Even the latest increase in quotas in
February 1983,[22] which gives the Fund a maximum additional
financing capability of $ 22 billion in hard currencies,[23]
is very modest in comparison with the potential requirement.
For that reason the Fund borrowed from the central banks and
governments of wealthy member countries to finance the newly established special facilities. The tussle over the loan
from Saudi Arabia, without which the further financing of
the Witteveen Facility could not have been ensured,[24] already showed that such borrowing may not prove sufficient.
Hence member countries are now discussing whether and on
what scale the Fund should turn to the international fi-
nacial markets for resources in future. It is also being
proposed that Fund members be given greater financial scope
by creating additional special drawing rights. Both possibilities give rise to doubts about a possible worldwide acceleration in inflation as well as to fears that the Fund

Table 3.8:   IMF QUOTAS OF SELECTED COUNTRIES

in billions of US dollars

	After the Seventh[a] Review of Quotas	After the Eighth[b] Review of Quotas
Argentina	0.946	1.174
Bolivia	0.080	0.096
Brazil	1.176	1.542
Chile	0.384	0.465
India	2.025	2.329
Korea	0.302	0.488
Philippines	0.371	0.465
Thailand	0.320	0.408
By way of comparison		
Federeal Republic of Germany	3.813	5.701
France	3.394	4.729
Italy	2.193	3.069

a As at 31st December 1981.

b As at 30th November 1983.

Source: International Monetary Fund: IMF Survey, 21.2.1983;
           Hooke 1983, Appendix I, pp. 71 pp. calculations by
           the authors.

could become a development bank. This deters some countries from expanding Fund liquidity too rapidly.

Despite these funding problems and the question of conditionality, the overall data collated in Table 3.7 gloss over the importance of the Fund for financing individual countries and country groups even at a low level of resource up-take. Only a few developing countries even have the option of forgoing Fund assistance. In the past these were chiefly the newly industrialising countries,[25] whose steady economic growth gave them sufficient creditworthiness to be able to turn to the international financial markets. However, access to private-sector funds is largely closed to the majority of developing countries and they will continue to have to rely on the support of the IMF.

This state of affairs is also apparent in Table 3.9, which describes the financing of current account balances in individual country groups. Net borrowing from private sources has been of no practical significance in low-income countries, which financed their needs mainly through official transfers and loans from the IMF and other official sources. This contrasts markedly with the manner in which exporters of industrial goods and net oil exporters financed their current account deficits. Besides official transfers, borrowing from private sources played a decisive role here; at the same time, the amount of Fund resources and other reserve-related credit facilities taken up was negligible in relation to the current account balances. It must be feared, however, that some of these countries that have drawn funds largely from the private banking system up to now will have to call on the help of the Fund more than in the past as their debt burden grows and their creditworthiness diminishes.

Table 3.9: CURRENT ACCOUNT FINANCING IN INDIVIDUAL GROUPS OF NON-OPEC DEVELOPING COUNTRIES[a], 1973 - 1982

- in billions of US dollars -

	1973	1974	1975	1976	1977	1978	1979	1980	1981	1982
NET OIL EXPORTERS										
Current account deficit[b]	+ 2.6	+ 5.1	+ 9.9	+ 7.7	+ 6.4	+ 7.9	+ 8.5	+12.5	+23.5	+15.6
Use of foreign exchange reserves[c]	- 1.3	- 1.5	- 0.3	- 0.7	- 1.9	- 1.2	- 3.8	- 3.7	- 0.7	+ 2.8
Transactions not affecting net debt positions	+ 2.2	+ 3.3	+ 3.7	+ 2.7	+ 3.3	+ 3.9	+ 5.5	+ 5.6	+ 7.2	+ 5.3
Net borrowing	+ 1.6	+ 3.3	+ 6.5	+ 5.7	+ 5.0	+ 5.2	+ 6.8	+10.6	+17.0	+ 7.5
- Net long-term borrowing[d]	+ 2.2	+ 3.2	+ 7.6	+ 7.5	+ 7.5	+ 7.6	+ 7.2	+ 8.6	+15.4	+11.5
. from official sources	+ 0.8	+ 1.2	+ 3.4	+ 2.2	+ 4.2	+ 3.4	+ 2.4	+ 3.0	+ 3.5	+ 3.3
. from private sources	+ 1.4	+ 2.0	+ 4.2	+ 5.3	+ 3.4	+ 4.2	+ 4.8	+ 5.5	+11.9	+ 8.1
- Use of reserve-related credit facilities	-	-	-	+ 1.2	- 0.1	-	-	- 0.4	+ 0.1	+ 3.0
- Other net short-term borrowing	- 0.6	+ 0.1	- 1.1	- 2.9	- 2.6	- 2.4	- 0.4	+ 2.4	+ 1.5	- 6.9
MAJOR EXPOTERS OF MANUFACTURED GOOD										
Current account deficit[b]	+ 3.6	+18.8	+19.1	+12.2	+ 7.9	+ 9.8	+21.7	+32.5	+37.6	+34.3
Use of foreign exchange reserves[c]	- 5.8	+ 2.0	+ 2.0	- 7.1	- 4.4	-10.2	- 3.1	+ 2.1	- 2.3	+ 4.0
Transactions not affecting net debt positions	+ 3.8	+ 4.4	+ 2.9	+ 4.6	+ 4.5	+ 6.4	+ 7.5	+ 7.4	+ 7.9	+ 8.2
Net borrowing	+ 5.6	+12.4	+14.1	+14.7	+ 7.7	+13.7	+17.3	+23.1	+32.0	+22.0
- Net long-term borrowing[d]	+ 5.6	+ 8.6	+ 9.8	+ 9.7	+ 8.0	+15.9	+11.7	+13.2	+23.1	+ 8.4
. from official sources	+ 1.8	+ 2.1	+ 2.5	+ 2.7	+ 2.6	+ 3.7	+ 3.3	+ 3.1	+ 3.1	+ 3.5
. from private sources	+ 3.8	+ 6.5	+ 7.3	+ 7.0	+ 5.4	+12.2	+ 8.4	+10.1	+19.9	+ 4.9
- Use of reserve-related credit facilities	-	+ 0.2	+ 1.1	+ 1.9	+ 0.3	- 0.5	- 0.6	+ 0.5	+ 1.0	+ 3.3
- Other net short term borrowing	+ 0.1	+ 3.5	+ 3.2	+ 3.0	- 0.6	- 1.7	+ 6.2	+ 9.4	+ 7.9	+10.3

Table 3.9 (continued)

	1973	1974	1975	1976	1977	1978	1979	1980	1981	1982
LOW-INCOME COUNTRIES										
Current account deficits[b]	+ 3.4	+ 6.6	+ 7.3	+ 5.5	+ 5.4	+ 8.4	+ 9.9	+11.8	+12.1	+12.0
Use of foreign exchange reserves[c]	- 0.5	- 0.3	+ 0.4	- 0.7	- 1.0	+ 0.1	- 0.2	- 0.2	- 0.1	+ 0.3
Transactions not affecting net debt positions	+ 2.3	+ 3.2	+ 2.4	+ 2.3	+ 2.7	+ 3.0	+ 4.0	+ 4.3	+ 4.5	+ 4.2
Net borrowing	+ 1.6	+ 3.7	÷ 4.4	+ 3.9	+ 3.7	+ 5.3	+ 6.1	+ 7.7	+ 7.5	+ 7.6
– Net long-term borrowing[d]	+ 1.6	+ 3.0	+ 3.1	+ 2.9	+ 2.8	+ 3.9	+ 5.1	+ 5.5	+ 4.9	+ 4.7
. from official sources	+ 1.0	+ 2.1	+ 2.8	+ 3.0	+ 1.9	+ 3.0	+ 5.6	+ 4.6	+ 5.8	+ 4.5
. from private sources	+ 0.6	+ 0.9	+ 0.3	- 0.1	+ 0.9	+ 0.8	- 0.5	+ 0.8	- 1.0	+ 0.2
– Use of reserve-related credit facilities	+ 0.1	+ 0.5	+ 0.4	+ 0.4	+ 0.1	+ 0.1	+ 0.4	+ 0.6	+ 1.2	+ 1.1
– Other net short-term borrowing	- 0.1	+ 0.3	+ 0.9	+ 0.5	+ 0.8	+ 1.4	+ 1.6	+ 1.6	+ 1.4	+ 1.7
OTHER OIL-IMPORTING COUNTRIES										
Current account deficits[b]	+ 1.1	+ 5.6	+ 9.7	+ 8.3	+12.0	+14.7	+18.9	+27.6	+33.0	+26.4
Use of foreign exchange reserves[c]	- 2.9	- 2.4	-	- 2.7	- 2.7	- 5.0	- 3.7	- 2.8	+ 1.3	+ 4.9
Transactions not affecting net debt positions	+ 1.8	+ 1.7	+ 2.7	÷ 2.6	+ 3.6	+ 4.2	+ 6.1	+ 6.1	+ 7.3	+ 6.8
Net borrowing	+ 2.2	+ 6.3	+ 7.1	+ 8.4	+11.1	+15.5	+16.5	+24.2	+24.4	+14.8
– Net long-term borrowing[d]	+ 1.9	+ 4.2	+ 5.6	+ 6.9	+ 6.3	+10.0	+11.3	+16.6	+18.0	+14.5
. from official sources	+ 1.4	+ 1.4	+ 2.0	+ 2.3	+ 3.7	+ 3.9	+ 3.9	+ 7.9	+ 9.8	+ 7.3
. from private sources	+ 0.4	+ 2.8	+ 3.6	+ 4.6	+ 2.6	+ 6.1	+ 7.4	+ 8.7	+ 8.2	+ 7.1
– Uses of reserve-related credit facilities	+ 0.1	+ 0.3	+ 0.8	+ 1.4	+ 0.3	+ 0.8	+ 0.6	+ 0.7	+ 2.7	+ 1.6
– Other net short term borrowing	+ 0.2	+ 1.8	+ 0.6	+ 0.1	+ 4.4	+ 4.8.	+ 4.5	+ 6.9	+ 3.7	- 1.3

a Including Ecuador and Gabon, excluding Oman.
b Excluding official transfers; (-) current account surplus, (+) current account deficit.
c (-) increase in foreign exchange reserves, (+) decrease in foreign exchange reserves.
d Calculated by the IMF on the basis of balance-of-payments statistics.

Quelle: International Monetary Fund: World Economic Outlook 1983.

The International Monetary Fund therefore has special responsibility in the recycling process on two counts. For the poorest developing countries it is essential as a lender, given the stagnation or even decline in official transfers. For countries with large current account deficits, growing debt burdens and increasing financing problems, however, the Fund plays only a secondary role in terms of the volume of lending. Its real importance for them lies in the fact that it bolsters the recycling process by means of supporting measures - by influencing the economic policy of member states and providing additional funds - and acts as lender of last resort in times of crisis. The Fund is also prepared in principle to assume this function. Nevertheless, it also endeavours to exert stronger influence on the lending practices of commercial banks, which have borne the main burden of recycling up to now (see Field et al. 1983).

To sum up, it can be seen that neither a reduction in foreign exchange reserves nor recourse to official credit played a decisive role in financing current account deficits after the first and second oil crises. Official transfers have been crucial to developing countries up to now. Whether they will remain so in future is open to doubt in view of the observable trends and the restrictions being imposed on the World Bank and other multilateral development agencies.[26] This has two implications. The poorest developing countries, which cannot go to commercial banks and are reliant on official loans, will encounter increasing financial constraints which will probably be seriously exacerbated if there are further oil price rises and an associated increase in the demand for funds. The other countries will attempt to finance a large part of their oil-related current account deficits by borrowing from the commercial banking system, as they have done up to now. Recycling will continue to be carried out via the international financial markets, as national credit and capital markets cannot cope with capital flows on anything like the necessary scale. The problems that this will cause will be examined individually in the following section.

c.   Effects on the international financial markets

As we have shown, the international financial markets act as a kind of turntable between debtor and creditor countries in the recycling process. Immediately after the first oil crisis the markets performed this function more smoothly than had been expected. The involvement of the banks softened the impact of the crisis on the real economy and facilitated adjustment, although in many instances it also delayed it. After the second price shock, however, conditions in the world economy were fundamentally different and brought increased problems for large debtor countries in particular (see Morgan Guaranty 1983, p. 4), so that the risks of recycling for the banking system now began to emerge more clearly and the causes of the prevailing situation could be traced partly to developments in the wake of the first oil crisis.

The consequences of sudden increases in oil prices on the international financial system will be examined below. The risks that might jeopardise smooth recycling can be deduced from

-   the effect of rising oil prices on the growth of the international financial markets;
-   associated changes in the structure of debtors; and
-   in the structure of creditors in these markets.

The first step will be to show the link between growth in international financial markets and rising oil prices. A primary consideration in this respect is that the closer this link

is, the more secure the recycling process can be considered
to be. If in times of rising oil prices the market grows in
proportion to the borrowing requirement of deficit countries,
it can be assumed that in principle they will be able to obtain the necessary funds. However, the supposition does not
take account of the special risks for the banks in this situation.

These risks determine whether the banks will ultimately be
prepared to continue to mediate between debtors and creditors
on the necessary scale. The next step will therefore be to investigate the effects that a shift in the structure of both
debtors and creditors as a result of rising oil prices has on
the banking system.

(1) Effects on market growth

Nothing has yet been proven conclusively about the factors determining the growth of the Euro-currency markets, and on the
theoretical plane there are considerable differences of opinion whether these markets should be regarded as a largely autonomous international phenomenon or as geographically separate parts of a single market owing to the strong interdependence between the individual Euro-currency markets and national money markets.[27] The latter argument is aimed mainly at management of the supply side of these markets and is based on
the assumption that the supply of, say, Euro-dollars dpends
on the development of the overall money supply in the USA.
It therefore denies that the Euro-currency markets have the
ability to create money themselves. This can be explained
with the help of Chart 8.

It is assumed that a certain portion of, say, the US money
supply is held in the form of Euro-dollars and that the growth
of the Euro-dollar market is therefore dependent on the devel-

Chart 8: THE EURO-DOLLAR MARKET AS A PART OF THE OVERALL
US MONEY MARKET[a]

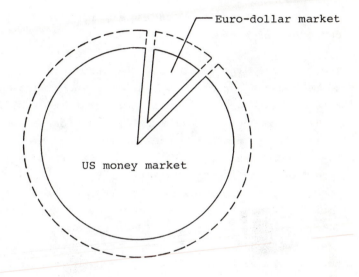

Euro-dollar market

US money market

a The chart is taken from I.H. GIDDY, F. DUFEY: The International
Money Market, Englewood Cliffs 1978, p. 129.

opment of the national money supply. Assuming that other determining factors remain unchanged, the Euro-dollar market
then grows at the same rate as the overall US money supply.
This is portrayed by the broken line in Diagram 2. Note, however, that we have yet to explain the size of the Euro-dollar market's share in the total market and the factors that
bring about changes in this share, in other words, an autonomous contraction or expansion in the Euro-dollar market independent of changes in the US money supply.

The opposite hypothesis that the Euro-currency markets are
to be regarded as more or less independent international markets is based on the special characteristics of these markets,
their large degree of freedom from national supervision, their
institutional framework and the resultant high efficiency of
the markets. The special financial instruments that have developed there and the system's ability to cope with even very
large capital flows should also be mentioned. Provided it is
not suggested that the Euro-currency markets create money in-
dependently, there is no fundamental contradiction between
these two arguments, as the second hypothesis simply explains
the factors enabling a Euro-currency market to exist at all.

The degree of international financial interdependence has increased generally as a result of the trend in oil prices and
the ensuing debtor and creditor positions. These developments
had a primary effect on the growth of the international markets owing to the fact that the OPEC countries - unlike the
original income recipients (particularly private households) -
invested a large part of the surpluses in the Euro-markets
rather than in the financial markets of the USA or other countries. However, whether this induces a permanent expansion in
the international markets depends solely on the behaviour of
the banks operating there.

The decision whether the proceeds of an OPEC investment are
to remain in the Euro-markets or to flow directly into individual countries is taken by the institution accepting
the investment. Regardless of the identity of the original
investor, this decision is based on the banks' earnings expectations and risk considerations, with the banks compar-
ing the terms available to them in national and international markets (cf. Mayer 1979). For example, if increased demand for money causes interest rates in the USA to rise so
that the banks expect earnings to be higher there than in
the Euro-dollar market, they will transfer part of their
dollar holdings to the domestic market (cf. Cohen 1981, p. 46).
Liquidity will increase in the US market but decline in the
Euro-dollar market. As a consequence, the interest rate differential between the two markets will narrow again. Conversely, liquidity will generally tend to increase in the
international markets if the demand for money eases in national markets (cf. also Wirtschaftswoche 1981, p. 73).

However, national and international markets are competing
for OPEC funds not only on the basis of earnings but also
that of risk. For example, if the creditworthiness of potential borrowers in the Euro-currency markets is considered to be lower than that of debtors in national markets, the
liquidity of the various markets will again be affected.
This does not influence the fact that countries with different credit ratings - for example, industrialised and developing countries - are competing for the available funds in
the international markets too.

It follows from these remarks that in overall terms no
close, direct link need exist between OPEC surpluses and
the growth of the international financial markets.[28]

An inflow of funds from OPEC countries can be offset by capital outflows into national markets if conditions are favourable. Two phases in the growth of the Euro-markets and in the share of OPEC funds in these markets can be distinguished to date: between 1973 and 1977 the growth of the Euro-markets was clearly determined by the fact that oil-importing surplus countries and oil-importing deficit countries turned to the markets simultaneously. Between 1977 and 1981 this tendency was occasionally overlaid by other factors, such as the current account trend in the USA and the resultant increase in international liquidity.[29]

The question remains as to the extent to which in these circumstances recycling can be considered to be assured in the event of future rises in oil prices. Whether increasing demand from deficit countries will be fully satisfied by the banks depends on risk considerations and the creditworthiness of potential borrowers in various markets. Up to now, there has generally been a tendency for continuing growth in the demand for finance, owing to several factors. First, industrial countries are showing a growing readiness to finance their budgets and current account deficits via the international financial markets. This might create strong competition for less creditworthy countries such as heavily-indebted developing countries. Secondly, some developing countries have virtually no alternative, as the support available from international institutions must be regarded as far from adequate by comparison with these countries' financing problems. Moreover, if oil prices again increase and cause or exacerbate economic disequilibria in industrial countries, the budgets of these countries will show increasing deficits which, if they are financed in national markets, will crowd out private borrowers, some of whom will also turn to the Euro-markets (cf. Trouvain 1980). Finally, the Euro-markets will continue to hold certain attractions for OPEC countries, banks and borrowers because of the difference in yields between the national and international markets. The extent to which the banks will be prepared to lend to deficit countries will depend on the willingness of the institutions to accept risks and the creditworthiness of the potential debtor countries. The increasing preparedness of borrowers from industrial countries to take up funds on the international markets creates the danger that developing countries will be squeezed out owing to their being higher-risk debtors. Hence the prerequisite for smooth recycling in the future would be an expansion in the international financial markets that accomodated the credit demand from both industrialised and developing countries. The probability of this ocurring depends, however, on risk and earning conditions in national and international markets, and is therefore to be regarded as slight, as will be demonstrated below. If the banks' willingness to lend declines, this will mean that future market growth will be lower than required for smooth recycling. The future financing of oil-related current account deficits via the international markets cannot therefore be regarded as assured in general terms, and even less so in individual cases subject to special risks. The following section will examine the extent to which such risks are attributable to a change in the debtor structure of these markets as a result of rising oil prices.

(2) Changes in the structure of debtors

Loans to non-oil developing countries have accounted for an ever-increasing share of bank loan portfolios since the first oil crisis. Table 3.10 shows the borrowing of industrial and developing countries in international capital markets from 1973 onwards. Industrial countries financed a substantial

Table 3.10: BORROWING IN INTERNATIONAL CAPITAL
             MARKETS BY INDUSTRIAL AND DEVELOP-
             ING COUNTRIES, 1973 - 1981
             - in billions of US dollars-

	1973	1974
TOTAL INDUSTRIAL COUNTRIES	17.67	23.64
- foreign and international bonds	6,03	6.37
- Euro-currency credits	11.64	17.27
USA	2.34	1.54
- foreign and international bonds	1.33	0.19
- Euro-currency credits	1.01	1.35
JAPAN	0.20	0.57
- foreign and international bonds	0.05	0.25
- Euro-currency credits	0.15	0.33
FEDERAL REPUBLIC OF GERMANY	0.06	0.14
- foreign and international bonds	0.06	0.13
- Euro-currency credits	-	0.01
FRANCE	0.15	4.00
- foreign and international bonds	0.10	0.67
- Euro-currency credits	0.05	3.33
UNITED KINGDOM	4.72	6.03
- foreign and international bonds	1.32	0.31
- Euro-currency credits	3.40	5.72
ITALY	4.74	2.44
- foreign and international bonds	0.03	0.05
- Euro-currency credits	4.71	2.39
TOTAL DEVELOPING COUNTRIES	9.13	10.08
- foreign and international bonds	0.86	0.37
- Euro-currency credits	8.27	9.71

a Second quarter of 1981

Table 3.10 (continued)

1975	1976	1977	1978	1979	1980	1981[a]
21.34	30.57	33.85	53.74	42.85	56.19	15.66
16.27	23.13	22.79	22.40	24.04	26.32	8.12
5.07	7.44	11.06	31.34	18.81	29.87	7.54
1.00	0.84	2.37	4.13	6.56	12.00	2.00
0.46	0.43	1.52	1.67	2.73	4.51	1.30
0.55	0.41	0.85	2.46	3.83	7.49	0.70
1.98	2.38	2.00	2.88	3.87	3.96	1.26
1.65	2.01	1.93	2.79	3.87	3.70	1.26
0.33	0.37	0.07	0.09	-	0.26	-
0.23	0.37	0.29	0.34	0.63	0.16	0.14
0.23	0.37	0.29	0.34	0.48	0.16	0.11
-	-	-	-	0.15	0.00	0.03
2.31	3.55	3.77	3.78	4.78	4.33	2.54
1.80	2.82	1.91	1.30	2.05	2.37	0.75
0.51	0.73	1.86	2.48	2.74	1.96	1.79
1.30	3.42	4.11	6.20	2.61	2.74	0.35
0.70	1.24	1.64	1.48	1.24	0.96	0.23
0.60	2.18	2.48	4.72	1.38	1.78	0.12
0.18	0.11	1.08	3.03	3.74	7.06	2.07
0.06	0.09	0.30	0.23	0.32	0.88	0.19
0.12	0.02	0.78	2.81	3.41	6.18	1.88
13.23	20.47	24.90	44.37	46.37	41.03	11.97
0,76	2.34	4.76	6.09	4.01	2.90	1.35
12.46	18.13	20.14	38.28	42.36	38.13	10.62

Source: World Bank: Borrowing in International Capital
Markets, various years.

part of their requirement by means of foreign and international loans, a possibility that was open to very few developing countries (cf. Maynard, Davies 1982, p. 165). On the other hand, the volume of Euro-credits raised by industrial countries barely increased during the period under review. Developing countries resorted predominantly to this form of financing, so that the volume of Euro-credits to these countries increased substantially. As was already apparent in Table 3.9, Euro-credits were concentrated essentially on a small number of countries, whereas low-income countries, for example, scarcely had access to such credit. Hence bank lending to certain countries with a poor credit rating constitutes a particularly large proportion of their portfolios and is a cause of concern.

Every foreign loan entails special risks for the lending bank, with the country risk being particularly important. This arises if the borrower is prevented from meeting his payment obligations by government intervention for reasons for which he is not responsible or if the state in question is itself a borrower and is not willing or able to redeem its debt.

Such a situation can arise as a result of higher oil prices if a country suffers a setback in its economic development and is no longer able to generate the sums required for debt service payments.

Assessment of this risk depends on a multitude of factors that differ from one country to another and for which there are no uniform criteria. As assessment is usually made on the basis of the country's balance-of-payments situation, its total external indebtedness, economic growth, the ratio of debt to debt service commitments and the ratio of

interest payments to exports. Qualitative factors are also
sometimes taken into account in deciding whether to grant
credit.[30]

Table 3.11 summarises some of these criteria for the group
of developing countries under examination for the years from
1973 to 1982. The first point to note is the absolute increase in the external debt of developing countries as a
whole, with the exporters of industrial goods and the other
oil-importing countries accounting for a particularly large
share. In themselves, these absolute figures do not tell us
much. If external debts are set in relation to the countries'
exports, the difference between the coefficients for the two
years is far less marked. The change in the ratio of external indebtedness to gross domestic product is also far less
dramatic, although a clear increase can be discerned.

The assessments for individual country groups differ, however, depending on the kind of debt criteria used. If the
absolute level of foreign debt is considered, the countries
exporting industrial goods are very badly placed. If the
ratios of foreign debt to exports form the basis of comparison, the low-income countries are to be regarded as particularly doubtful borrowers, as are net oil-exporters in terms
of the ratios of foreign debt to GDP. The use of these ratios
is based on the notion that they permit a rough estimate of
the performance of an economy in relation to its debts. They
indicate the percentage of exports or GDP that would have to
be applied to repayments if the country's entire outstanding
foreign debt fell due at one time.

Table 3.11: THE DEBT SITUATION OF NON-OPEC DEVELOPING COUNTRIES[a], 1973 AND 1982

	Total foreign debt			Debt service ratios as % of exports		
	in US$ bn	as % of exports	as % of GDP	Total debt servicing	Interest payments	Redemption
1973						
All developing countries	130.1	115.4	22.4	15.9	6.1	9.8
Net oil-exporters	20.4	154.7	26.2	29.0	8.8	20.1
Major exporters of manufactured goods	40.8	91.7	20.2	14.5	5.6	8.9
Low-income countries	25.4	227.9	20.1	14.6	6.1	8.5
Other oil-importing countries	25.2	96.9	26.2	12.7	5.4	7.2
1982						
All developing countries	612.4	143.3	34.7	23.9	13.2	10.7
Net oil-exporters	108.1	179.5	44.7	37.9	21.8	16.1
Major exporters of manufactured goods	184.3	116.2	33.2	23.7	12.8	10.9
Low-income countries	80.1	254.1	26.2	11.8	4.6	7.2
Other oil-importing countries	127.1	138.0	35.8	20.5	12.4	8.1

a Including Ecuador and Gabon, excluding Oman.

Source: International Monetary Fund: World Economic Outlook, Washington, D.C. 1983.

As this is not a very realistic assumption, assessments are
often based on debt service obligations, in other words re-
demptions plus interest payments. Here too, the difference
between 1973 and 1982 do not appear to be so large at first
sight, although it is noticeable that interest payments account for an ever larger share, except in the case of low-
income countries. It is a point to consider, however, that
in 1982 the net oil-exporters among the developing countries,
for example, had to devote almost 40 % of their export earnings to debt servicing and that this portion of their receipts
from abroad was therefore no longer available for pressing
ahead with economic development, which is the only factor
that can give them the ability to repay debts in future.

The risks facing the banks differ from those in domestic lending in that it is not so much a question of having to write
off outstanding debts entirely owing to the insolvency of the
client. Whereas a domestic enterprise that goes bankrupt usually ceases to exist and its payment obligations are also ex-
tinguished, in the case of a sovereign borrower this is obviously not the case, so that its liabilities are not generally cancelled despite temporary insolvency. Instead, its
debts are usually restructured for longer repayment periods
or debt servicing is temporarily suspended. Hence in external lending the main danger for the banks lies less in insolvency than in a freezing of claims that can lead to temporary
illiquidity and may also mean forgoing a more lucrative deployment of funds elsewhere (cf. Mayer 1978, p. 5). It should
also be borne in mind that the banks can incur book losses
if they write down the value of non-performing loans on
risk grounds.

A bank can guard against these dangers by ensuring that its
average interest rate spreads are wide enough to permit the
creation of additional reserves that can be used to make
good any liquidity shortfalls and losses in earnings (cf.
Mayer 1978, p. 7). However, the development of interest rate
spreads on the Euro-markets, particularly after 1977, suggest that the banks either paid insufficient heed to the
danger described above or had no opportunity to obtain wider spreads in the market (see Table 3.13). We shall return
later to the background to this development.

The observance of traditional banking rules also offers some
protection against such risks. These include keeping external claims within responsible limits as a proportion of the
consolidated balance sheet and ensuring that capital resources
provide an adequate cushion. Table 3.12 shows changes in the
capital resources of banks as a percentage of their balance
sheets in countries with major capital markets. From this it
is clear that, except in the case of British and Swiss banks,
the ratio has fallen slightly despite increasing risks in
banking business up to 1980 and that the decline is particularly marked in the case of the ten largest banks in the USA
and Germany. These include precisely those banks that are
particularly prominent in external business.

The risks are further increased by the fact that lending in
the Euro-markets has been concentrated chiefly on a small
number of countries in recent years. Greater political and
geo-economic diversification in bank lending might attenuate
the existing risks.[31] Furthermore, an increasing number of
loans are being granted by international syndicates, thereby spreading any possible loss over several banks. If the
earnings position and liquidity provisions of all the banks
are poor, this may create an additional danger of chain re-

Table 3.12: CAPITAL-ASSET RATIOS OF BANKS IN COUNTRIES WITH MAJOR CAPITAL MARKETS 1972 - 1980[a]

- percentages -

	1972-1973	1974	1975	1976	1977	1978	1979	1980
Federal Republic of Germany								
– 10 largest banks	3.09	3.00	2.82	2.87	2.82	2.72	–	–
– all banks	3.45	3.46	3.38	3.47	3.45	3.36	3.32	3.27
France	–	2.92	2.76	2.45	2.36	2.08	2.43	2.22
United Kingdom								
– 4 largest banks	–	–	5.40	5.40	5.90	6.30	6.10	5.80
– all banks	–	–	6.00	5.20	5.20	5.20	5.10	5.00
Japan								
– 10 largest banks	3.13	3.76	3.38	3.05	3.08	3.51	–	–
– all banks	–	5.91	5.65	5.40	5.28	5.12	5.13	5.28
Canada	–	–	3.56	3.51	3.40	3.27	3.16	2.99
Switzerland								
– 3 largest banks	–	5.54	5.53	6.11	6.10	6.23	6.09	6.04
– all banks	–	6.26	6.24	6.63	6.59	6.68	5.63	6.13
USA								
– 10 largest banks	–	3.67	3.86	4.18	4.15	3.98	3.85	3.89
– all banks	–	3.94	4.15	4.49	4.35	4.15	4.00	4.13

a The data should be interpreted with caution owing to differences in definitions in the various countries and problems of aggregation. See in this regard the footnotes in: International Monetary Fund: International Capital Markets 1981, Table 3, p. 13.

Source: International Monetary Fund: International Capital Markets 1980, 1981.

actions and multiple collapse. The formation of syndicates
is no substitute for balances loan diversification, as is
often supposed.

In general, it can be seen that the risks in the banks' external business have steadily increased on the debtor side
since 1973. At the same time, they were also faced with growing risks on the creditor side.

(3)   Shifts in the structure of creditors

Up to now, oil price increases have also been associated
with a shift in the structure of creditors in the international capital markets. This was particularly true of the
period after the first oil crisis; for example, between 1973
and 1974 the banks' Euro-currency liabilities towards OPEC
countries rose from $ 10 to 29.1 billion, thereby increasing
from less than 8 % to more than 16 % of the market's total
liabilities (cf. Maynard, Davies 1982, p. 171). In June 1982
this component stood at about $ 95 billion, or around 14 %
of the total (see Bank for International Settlements 1982,
Table 7).

The shift in the creditor structure towards OPEC states means
that a larger proportion of bank deposits is held by a group
of investors whose behaviour may differ from that of conven-
tial investors and is therefore less predictable. At the same
time, the number of investors has decreased. For these reasons the banks face the danger that very large sums might be
withdrawn suddenly on economic or political grounds.[32] This
danger is all the greater as a large part of the Arab states'
deposits are at short term. The scale of their deposits also
gives these investors a kind of monopoly position that enables
them in certain circumstances to influence the terms on which
they invest their funds.

To what extent can the withdrawal of OPEC deposits from a particular bank or group of banks represent a serious danger for the institutions concerned? This undoubtedly applies only above a certain level of withdrawal and then generally only in the short term, for it has been shown that with funds on this scale the OPEC countries have little choice but to reinvest their resources with other Euro-banks or in the USA, in other words to leave them in the banking system as a whole. Hence it can be expected that the system as a whole will not encounter difficulties. Reinvestment of the funds in the USA simply means that interest rates on the Euro-markets, where there will then be increased additional demand, must rise against those in the USA until sufficient capital flows back into these markets.

For the banks concerned, however, the withdrawal of deposits does cause a short-term liquidity problem that can jeopardise their survival if they cannot tide themselves over that short period, as the banks lend mainly at long term but only raise funds at short term. The main cause of concern is the possible scale of the withdrawals, but provided the system as a whole does not boycott the banks concerned they will manage sooner or later to obtain the funds they need, although their refinancing costs may increase.

(4) Changed market conditions and the consequences for future recycling

The recycling process therefore exposes the international capital markets to risks from the creditor side as well as from a shift in the structure of debtors. In both cases banks run the risk of short-term liquidity shortages and losses of income. A general impression of the situation can be gained from Table 3.13, which shows developments in important characteristics of the Euro-credit markets after 1973. It can be seen that there was no fundamental change in the conditions on these markets until after 1977, which suggests that oil price movements were not an important influence.

Table 3.13 shows that conditions for the banks have been much less favourable in recent years than in the period after 1973. For example, after 1977 the average size of individual credits rose substantially, thereby increasing the risk associated with each loan. Moreover, in recent years lending terms have lengthened progressively whereas interest rate margins have narrowed overall and the difference in the conditions offered to OECD and non-OECD countries, for example, have slowly diminished. This is an indication that conditions have been determined less and less by the country risk associated with the granting of a loan. The true cause of the deterioration in the situation on the Euro-markets after 1977 is to be found not so much in oil price developments as in the temporary increase in the markets' liquidity as a result of the serious worsening of the US current account that year and a loss of international confidence in the dollar, which lasted until 1980 and led to extremely high outflows of American capital in spite of rising US interest rates. The outflows reflected falling demand for credit in the USA itself, which was further accentuated by the weakness of economic activity in that country (cf. Mayer 1978, p. 1). This prompted American banks increasingly to look for profitable opportunities in the Euro-markets, even if they entailed greater risk. The result was heightened competition among the banks, which translated into very

Table 3.13:   CHARACTERISTICS OF THE MEDIUM-TERM EURO-CREDIT MARKET, 1976, 1977, 1978 AND 1979

	1976 I.	1976 II.	1976 III.	1976 IV.	1977 I.	1977 II.	1977 III.	1977 IV.	1978 I.	1978 II.	1978 III.	1978 IV.	1979 I.	1979 II.	1979 III.	1979 IV.
New loans (US$ bn)	24.3		32.5		33.8	26.2	31.4	43.7	55.0	64.9	64.2	79.4	57.1	66.0	107.7	81.9
Average size of individual loans (US$ mn)	65		78		90	70	62	75	108	112	100	94	86	74	119	90
Longest maturity (years)[a]	8		10		8	10	10	10	12	12	12	15	18	15	15	15
Average maturity (years/months)[a]	5/8		5/10	5/8	6/8	6/6	6/5	7/10	7/9	8/4	8/5	8/11	8/6	9/4	7/9	9/3
Lowest spread[a]	$1\frac{1}{16}$		$1\frac{1}{4}$	$\frac{1}{8}$	$\frac{15}{16}$	$\frac{15}{16}$	$\frac{7}{8}$	$\frac{5}{8}$	$\frac{5}{8}$	$\frac{5}{8}$	$\frac{1}{4}-\frac{3}{8}$	$\frac{1}{2}$	$\frac{1}{2}$	$\frac{3}{8}-\frac{1}{2}$	$\frac{3}{8}-\frac{1}{2}$	$\frac{1}{4}-\frac{3}{8}$
Average spread[b]	1.50		1.55	1.45	1.25	1.20	1.10	1.17	1.05	1.10	0.90	0.87	0.87	0.76	0.73	0.64
- OECD countries[c]								0.84	0.82	0.80	0.72	0.69	0.65	0.62	0.67	0.49
- CMEA								1.05	0.97	0.70	0.74	0.73	0.90	0.63	0.61	0.57
- other non-OECD countries[d]								1.46	1.22	1.26	1.15	1.03	0.95	0.87	0.76	0.74
. Argentina											1.29	0.92	0.79	0.88	0.78	0.76
. Brazil											1.34	1.26	1.17	0.99	0.86	0.72
. Chile											1.75	1.10	-	0.96	0.85	0.92
. Korea											1.00	0.91	0.73	0.40	0.70	0.69
. Philippines											1.02	1.20	0.85	0.93	1.01	0.92
. Thailand											0.97	1.10	-	-	0.64	-

137

Table 3.13 continued:

	1980				1981				1982		
	I.	II.	III.	IV.	I.	II.	III.	IV.	I.	II.	III.
New loans (US$ bn)	63.2	61.6	80.4	106.7	68.5	105.3	272.5	134.9	86.1	124.4	91.7
Average size of individual loans (US$ mn)	88	88	81	102	87	102	238	105	86	116	93
Longest maturity (years)[a]	15.5	15	12	12	14	14	15	15	15	15	15
Average maturity (years/months)[a]	8/9	7/8	7/6	7/7	8/4	7/9	7/10	6/7	7/10	6/10	7/11
Lowest spread[a]	$\frac{3}{8} - \frac{1}{2}$	$\frac{3}{8} - \frac{1}{2}$	$\frac{1}{4} - \frac{1}{2}$	$\frac{1}{4} - \frac{3}{8}$	$\frac{1}{4} - \frac{3}{8}$	$\frac{1}{4}$	$\frac{1}{4} - \frac{1}{2}$	$\frac{1}{4} - \frac{3}{8}$	$\frac{1}{4} - \frac{3}{8}$	$\frac{1}{4}$	0.3
Average spread[b]	0.67	0.69	0.63	0.75	0.70	0.77	0.69	0.69	0.68	0.81	0.81
- OECD countries[c]	0.56	0.57	0.54	0.56	0.54	0.47	0.46	0.46	0.56	0.54	0.57
- CMEA	0.58	0.73	1.17	0.96	n.a.	n.a.	n.a.	n.a.	n.a.	n.a.	n.a.
- other non-OECD countries[d]	0.78	0.84	0.82	1.03	0.82[e]	1.12[e]	0.94[e]	0.90[e]	0.85[e]	1.10[e]	1.19[e]
. Argentina	0.56	0.63									
. Brazil	0.79	0.98									
. Chile	0.95	1.12									
. Korea	0.78	0.81									
. Philippines	0.79	0.88									
. Thailand	0.77	-									

a Loans of $50 million and above.
b Weighted average of spreads for loans of $ 50 million and above with a maturity of at least 3 years.
c Excluding Turkey.
d Excluding the People's Republic of China.
e Including CMEA.

Source: ECD: Financial Market Trends, various years; World Bank: Annual Report, various years.

favourable terms for borrowers, such as longer maturities
and lower interest rates. The narrowing of the interest
margins again forced the banks increasingly to accept OPEC
funds in whatever quantity they could in order to on-lend
them to high-risk borrowers, as it was now only the sheer
number of transactions that generated the necessary earnings. This inflated the volume of the Euro-markets, which
also tended to be favoured by another factor. The dollar's
decline caused other Western industrial countries to intervene in the foreign exchange markets, sometimes on a massive
scale, resulting in substantial increases in foreign exchange
reserves and an underlying acceleration in national money
creation in these countries (cf. Mayer 1979, pp. 17 ff). The
liquidity of the Euro-markets therefore also increased indirectly owing to the greater inflow of non-dollar currencies. From 1981 onwards this trend was reversed, producing
an improvement in Euro-market terms, albeit a slight one.

Hence it is clear that oil prices had their clearest impact
on events in the Euro-markets between 1974 and 1976-77. Subsequently, the predominant factor was the heavy reliance of
these markets on events in the US money market and on US monetary, economic and trade policies. This second phase should
be regarded as an exception, however. The fact that the high
liquidity of the markets after 1977 also allowed less creditworthy borrowers to finance their currenct account deficits
from this source should not lead us to conclude that the same
might be possible in future and that the size of the international financial markets will expand to match the growing need
for finance and investment opportunities brought about by rising oil prices. Increasing demand for credit in industrial
countries, for example, would mean higher and more secure earnings for the banks in national markets and might cause a greater volume of capital to flow there so that correspondingly less

credit would be granted in international markets. A marked
relative narrowing of the markets has already become apparent of late,[33] reflecting primarily an increasing awareness
of risk on the part of banks in the light of the current debt
problems. Such a contraction will have two consequences in
the event of future oil price increases: first, it will lead
to a stricter selection of borrowers, which means that fewer
countries will be able to raise funds in this way. The countries worst affected will be developing countries with a
low credit rating. Secondly, it will be possible to finance
oil-related current account deficits in these markets only
at increased cost, if at all. This will further exacerbate
the debt service problems of certain countries. Particularly
where these countries are concerned, financial recycling will
therefore increasingly approach the limits in the event of a
further oil price increase, so that adjustment of the real
economy will then become unavoidable (cf. also Dicken 1980,
p. 1146).

2. Proposals for solving the recycling and debt problems

The smooth operation of the recycling mechanism can be assured in the case of an eventual new round of oil price increases only if the risks it creates for the international capital markets are reduced. This means above all that a solution to the present debt crisis must be found in order to maintain the ability of the financial system to cope with future requirements. Over the longer term, steps must be taken to ensure that a debt crisis cannot recur. However, it is not only the debtor risks currently at the forefront of attention that must be taken into consideration but also the problems that can arise on the creditor side.

This might be achieved in several ways. First, the burden on the international capital markets could be eased by intensifying multinational co-operation and involving addditional official intermediaries, thereby spreading risks more widely. Another possibility under discussion would be to introduce various measures and arrangements to strengthen the private banking system itself and thus to protect it better against the risks of recycling. Finally, consideration is also being given to extending the control of the international financial markets as a way of limiting the risks.

a. Multinational co-operation

Among the proposals for increased multinational co-operation it is those aimed at overcoming the present debt crisis that have been at the centre of public interest of late. Although the crisis can be blamed only partly on the past trend in oil prices,[34] any future recycling problem can only be dealt with successfully if the functional capability of the international financial system can be maintained.

In 1982 and 1983 the scale of the debt problem became apparent
for the first time when heavily-indebted developing countries
such as Argentina, Brazil and Mexico found themselves temporarily unable to meet their payment obligations. Since then
ever more countries have suspended their debt service payments and the extent of rescheduling has increased dramatically.[35] For example, in 1981 loans worth $ 2.6 billion were
officially rescheduled, whereas in 1983 the figure was estimated at about $ 90 billion (cf. Cline 1983, p. 10).

Hitherto, politicians and international institutions have not
worked out a uniform procedure to be followed if a country
cannot meet its payment obligations. In practice, they have
confined themselves to participation in emergency "rescue
operations" in which short-term official bridging loans have
paved the way for rescheduling and further lending by the
banks and at the same time programmes for longer-term economic adjustment by the debtor country have been worked out
jointly by all the parties involved (see Cline 1983, pp. 40 ff).

There are several disadvantages in proceeding in this manner.
First, there is a fundamental danger that agreement will not
be reached quickly enough or at all in an emergency and that
grave consequences will ensue for the international financial
system. Secondly, given the divergent interests of debtors,
commercial banks, official institutions and governments, there
is no guarantee that the rescheduling negotiations will actually find a way out of the crisis - in other words a solution the debtor country can apply rather than a palliative -
and that the country will not again be faced with payments
problems within a very short space of time (cf. Garten 1982
pp. 281 ff). Hence closer co-ordination among all the parties
involved on the general handling of debt problems would be
desirable.

In the past there have been many proposals aimed at limiting debtor risks for the banks and at the same time continuing to ensure the necessary flow of finance to developing countries.[36] There is broad agreement that the terms of existing foreign loans should be prolonged to give countries greater scope for making repayments and introducing economic adjustment measures and that at the same time interest rates should be reduced to ease the burden of debt servicing. For example, a proposal by Rohatyn (cf. Rohatyn 1983) suggests debt rescheduling in order to lengthen credit maturities for developing countries to between 15 and 30 years and to reduce interest rates to about 6 %. The repayment calender would be so arranged that a country's total debt service payments would not amount to more than 25-30 % of its annual exports. The proposals of Kenen and Shumer (cf. Cline 1983, pp. 114 f) and the approach adopted by Meyer-Preschany (cf. Meyer-Preschany 1983) also tend in the same direction. The latter suggests dividing a country's total outstanding loans into three parts and giving them staggered maturities of a minimum of 2-4 years, 10 years and a maximum of 25-30 years.

Where such a radical rearrangement of debt is contemplated, the proposals usually provide for the conversion of bank loans into bonds or some other kind of security. Some schemes assume that the central banks of debtor countries will have responsibility for issuing these securities. One example is the proposal made by Bailay, who suggests that loans to developing countries be replaced by a new financing instrument, the "exchange participation note". This security, which would be issued through the central bank of the debtor country, constitutes a claim on the country's current and future foreign exchange earnings. The central bank would then be ultimately liable for the payment of outstanding debts (cf. Bailey 1983). Other plans require the involvement of international organisations such as the IMF, the World Bank or, as in Kenen's proposal, a new institution as intermediary between the various parties to the rescheduling process or even as lender of last resort in this connection.

Criticism of such proposals is directed primarily at is cost for the banks, the states involved and international organisations, which raises doubts about its feasibility (cf. The Economist, 2.4.1983). For example, if an international institution takes over the bank loans at a discount and pays the banks in long-term bonds issued by itself, as in the Kenen and Rohatyn proposals, the banks have to bear a loss, albeit a limited and predictable one. Rohatyn's proposal provides for dividing this loss among holders of bank shares, taxpayers and governments. It is doubtful, however, that the present debt crisis is a sufficient spur to persuade the parties involved to commit themselves to a long-term formal arrangement of this kind.

This raises the question how one should interpret the underlying assessment of the debt crisis on which these proposals are based. The advocates of the schemes described here assume implicitly that the crisis reflects not a temporary shortage of liquidity but the insolvency of certain debtor countries and that a complete long-term rearrangement of debt is therefore required. This view is not universally accepted, however (cf. Cline 1983, p. 117). It is expected in many quarters that an economic upswing in the Western industrial countries, a fall in US interest rates or progress in developing countries in adjusting to changed external conditions and other factors will have a positive effect on the future solvency of debtor countries (cf. also Morgan Guaranty 1983, pp. 10 ff). If that were so, however, the present situation would signify a liquidity problem and not a solvency problem, so that a radical restructuring of general indebtedness such as has been proposed would seem neither necessary nor desirable, given the costs involved and the difficulties in carrying it out. Instead, central banks and official institutions should strive for closer co-ordination so that they are still better prepared to intervene in individual cases of emergency, as in the past. Attempts at fundamental reform should be directed less at overcoming the existing debt crisis than at preventing a recurrence.

A further question in this context relates to the contribution that closer multinational co-operation can make to safeguarding the recycling process over the longer term. Here it is a question of ensuring that deficit countries' unavoidable borrowing requirements caused by rising oil prices will be met but at the same time preventing the portfolios of commercial banks from becoming overburdened with loans to debtor countries with a low credit rating. It is also important to ensure that sufficient resources are available to finance oil-related current account deficits; in other words, attention should be paid to the problems that can arise on the creditor side in the recycling process as well as the debt aspects.

As we have shown, in times of rising oil prices it is primarily the borrowing requirement of developing countries with a fairly long-term need of funds that is not assured. Two groups of countries should be distinguished in this respect. Alternative forms of finance will have to be found for those countries that cannot turn to the capital markets. There are other countries, however, whose creditworthiness is limited but which in times of high liquidity in the international markets have managed to obtain loans from commercial banks, in some cases on a substantial scale. With the banks growing more risk conscious, there is no guarantee that this will be possible on a similar scale in future, nor can it be regarded as desirable. It is to be feared that some countries will ignore the need to adjust their real economy to changed circumstances if unconditional finance is readily accessible.

There is therefore a need for resources that can be placed at the disposal of weak debtor countries for a fairly long period until real adjustment measures begin to bite, and it is probably almost impossible to waive the setting of conditions that will ensure true adjustment. This raises the problem of conditionality, which we have already mentioned. As neither a substantial increase in national development aid nor an appreciable stepping-up of direct recycling can be expected in future, the question arises who should provide and grant the necessary funds. Most of the proposals along these lines allocate this function to existing international institutions or organisations, such as the IMF, the World Bank, the EC or OPEC.[37]

Apart from the possibility of a new allocation of special drawing rights mentioned above,[38] the Interntional Monetary Fund could follow previous practice by establishing additional special facilities to meet financial shortfalls among member countries in the event of future oil price increases.[39] There have been demands that the World Bank should review its capital regulations whereby total lending must be fully covered by total capitalisation.[40] This 1:1 ratio is widely held to be highly conservative and unnecessary.[41]

Realisation of these proposals is impeded primarily by the financial constraints to which the IMF and the World Bank will be subject even if their operations are expanded (cf. Financial Times, 14.3. 1984). As already mentioned, the willingness of member states to pay higher contributions is low and there are serious doubts about the institutions themselves turning to the international capital markets on a large scale to finance their lending.

For this reason it might make sense to turn to the OPEC surplus countries for the resources that will be needed to finance oil-related current account deficits. One suche proposal has come from the European Community,[42] which has suggested issuing Community loans that could be subscribed by OPEC states. However, most of the funds raised in this way would go to EC member countries and only small amounts would be passed on to developing countries.

In principle, issuing loans for subscription by surplus countries is also a suitable method for international institutions to solve their financing problems. On the other hand, the analysis of the OPEC countries' strategies and investment objectives showed that they often prefer to commit their capital surpluses for short periods and that where they make longer-term investments they attach decisive importance to safeguarding the value of their assets and obtaining adequate remuneration. Proposals for procuring funds for recycling through multinational official channels therefore focus mainly on the form the loans should take in order to persuade the OPEC countries to invest more of their capital surpluses at long term.

The remarks that follow concentrate on describing the common features of the various schemes without going into individual details. Some of the proposals also attempt to combine the interests of various country groups (cf. Koopmann, Scharrer 1981, pp. 88 ff). These include not only the special investment objectives of the OPEC countries and the borrowing requirements

of the deficit countries but also, for example, the desire of
oil-consuming countries to secure their oil supplies and avoid
sharp price increases. The last aspect might persuade the industrial countries, above all, to accept solutions that entail
disadvantages and costs for them.

In order to accomodate the surplus countries' wish to safeguard
the value of their assets and obtain adequate remuneration it
is often proposed that investment income be linked to a price
index and/or to a basket of currencies.[43] Gutowski and Roth,
for example, propose that in return the surplus countries would
undertake to invest certain minimum amounts for long contractually agreed periods. The resources raised would then be invested in the free market or on-lent to developing countries
on concessional terms.

If revenues are to be tied to a price index, the question of
the reference variable arises. The Gutowski-Roth proposal, for
example, provides that the rate of interest would equal the
annual oil price increases (which would also have to be agreed
by treaty) plus an inflation adjustment based on the rise in
the UN index of export prices.[44] Such an arrangement would give
oil-consuming countries the advantage of a predictable oil-
price progression, provided it could be ensured that the oil-
exporting countries felt bound by the agreement. On the other
hand, set rates of price increase could prove detrimental to
oil consumers in times of an oversupply on the oil markets
that would allow even temporary price reductions. Moreover,
there would always be the danger that the surplus countries
might borrow funds on the open market and reinvest them under such an agreement as soon as market interest rates fell
below the index-linked contractual rates, so that in the
final analysis the oil-consuming countries would merely incur costs but there would be no overall addition to resources.

The Gutowski-Roth plan avoids the first disadvantage by making the agreed oil price a maximum price and providing that OPEC countries would respond to price movements by adjusting production. It attempts to counter the second disadvantage by limiting the OPEC countries' investments to a maximum of SDR 40 billion a year.

In principle, the OPEC countries would welcome an assured real rate of interest, but it must be asked whether they would long consider the agreed oil price rises (and hence also the guaranteed minimum rate of interest) as adequate in times of high excess demand in the oil markets and whether the export price index accurately reflects their import demand structure and hence allows a true adjustment for inflation. Moreover, their willingness to abide by such an agreement will always be low if the contractually agreed interest rates are lower than comparable market rates.

Similar arguments also apply to investments in currency units. One possibility might be to follow the plans to establish a substitution account in the International Monetary Fund into which dollar reserves would be paid in exchange for interest-bearing claims in special drawing rights.[45] Increased long-term investment in instruments denominated in currency units would reduce the danger of destabilising portfolio switches and make the investment behaviour of surplus countries more transparent. Discussion about the substitution account has shown that in principle the OPEC countries also welcome such forms of investment. Nevertheless, it must be asked here too how durable this attitude will be, whether the weighting of the currencies in the SDR, for example, matches the structure of these countries' currency preferences[46] and whether a different currency structure and combination would not offer higher earnings for the same or less risk over the long term. Experience with the special drawing right in its present form is insufficient to allow a final judgement to be made in this regard. However, one obstacle to the greater use of SDRs hitherto is the fact that the market in them is very narrow and still in its infancy, so that the liquidity of such investments is rather limited.

Taking an overall view, it must therefore be doubted whether the schemes described above can mobilise resources on a sufficiently large scale to permit substantial official multinational participation in the recycling process and thus truly relieve the pressure on the international capital markets. It would therefore appear that the international commercial banking system will have to continue to bear the main burden in the future. We must therefore inquire into the possible ways of protecting the banks against the risks described. This question will be examined in the section that follows.

b.   Strengthening the commercial banking system

Commercial banks find themselves exposed to three basic types of risk in the recycling process. The first is a debtor risk arising out of the low creditworthiness of some countries with oil-related borrowing requirements; it is made manifest in the temporary suspension of capital and/or interest payments and in possible book losses incurred by the banks. The second is the danger of a sudden withdrawal of deposits, either because depositors have lost confidence in their bank or in the banking system as a whole[47] or for non-economic motives, a possibility indicated in the analysis of the investment strategies and objectives of OPEC surplus countries. Thirdly, the banks run an increased liquidity risk. If deposits are withdrawn on a large scale or if a debtor becomes temporarily insolvent the bank may be unable to meet its own immediate payment ob-

150

ligations. The proposals discussed in this section are concerned with arrangements to protect the commercial banking
system against such risks, either with or without the assistance of official institutions.

One way of reducing the risks to which the banking system
is exposed would be to strengthen the co-operation between
banks and official international institutions in the granting of credit, in other words to build upon the existing
co-financing schemes. Joint financing projects involving
commercial private banks have been carried out mainly by
the World Bank up to now.[48] In addition, a kind of de facto
co-financing has long been practiced between the IMF and the
banks, for in some cases the latter grant external loans only if the country concerned has agreed a stand-by arrangement with the IMF subject to appropriate conditions.

Co-financing reduces primarily the debtor risk for the banks.[49]
The banks' diversification costs fall, that is to say the cost
of obtaining information on individual debtor countries, as
the international institutions themselves already have a
large part of the necessary data; co-financing therefore encourages the banks to diversify and to spread their risks.
Moreover, the payments discipline of debtor countries will
be improved by the involvement of official institutions on
which they are crucially reliant for finance in times of
crisis. Hence the risk to the banks' liquidity is also reduced. The danger of withdrawals of deposits, on the other
hand, could be diminished at best in the long term if this
form of finance became more common and hence depositors'
confidence in the banking system was strengthened. In any
event, co-financing has no effect on withdrawals for non-
economic reasons.

The advantage of co-financing for official institutions is that a larger number of projects can be implemented for a given input of capital or more resources can be mobilised. At the same time, however, it becomes clear that the contribution to be paid by the institutions imposes limitations on this form of finance. Apart from a string of individual problems, such as the setting of interest rates or co-ordination of the different needs of official institutions and commercial banks as regards lending conditions, co-financing will also play a minor role in future recycling in view of the limited financial resources of the institutions themselves. Another point to consider is that co-financing has been used hitherto mainly to provide funds for special projects in particular countries. To enhance the importance of co-financing in the recycling process this project link would have to be discontinued, in other words the World Bank would have to become much more active than hitherto in programm aid.

A completely different proposal for reducing the risks described above suggests that banks operating internationally should act largely as intermediaries or brokers for loans in future (cf. International Currency Review 1981, p. 47). Finance would not be provided by banking consortia but by the placing of loans with non-banks; the banks would undertake no more than the preparations, the conduct of negotiations and the launch of the loans.

This proposal seeks to circumvent debtor risks directly. It would relieve the burden on bank portfolios and a liquidity risk could not arise, at least not as a result of the debtors' payment behaviour. It is questionable, however, whether this approach would, in fact, make a substantial contribution to solving the recycling problem and whether investors from OPEC countries would show an interest in such private placings. They are unlikely to be willing to assume the risk associated with lending to debtor countries with a poor credit rating. Such an arrangement would be tantamount to direct recycling, which it has been shown stands little chance on a large scale.

The insurance of certain banking operations has long been discussed as one way of reducing risks.[50] There are essentially three options here:

- the insurance of individual loans;

- the insurance of particular bank assets; and

- the insurance of particular deposits.

The insurance of individual loans guards against the debtor risks described above. However, it would also make bad debtors appear more attractive, even if their poor creditworthiness were reflected in the level of the insurance premium, as these costs could no doubt be passed on to the borrower. Such an arrangement would therefore encourage the banks to neglect the risk aspects of lending more than they have hitherto (cf. Basagni 1981, p. 166).

Similar arguments apply to the insurance of particular bank assets. For example, the insurance cover might be related to a given percentage of the bank's portfolio of loans to developing countries, so that the bank's debtor risk and its liquidity risk would be reduced. Nonetheless, problems always arise when insurers are called upon to assess the different situations of banks, such as the different quality of their portfolios. Moreover, this type of insurance cover also creates an incentive to neglect risk considerations.

In the case of the insurance of particular deposits a distinction has to be made between protection of the depositor and protection of the bank. If the depositor is insured, the bank is essentially protected against a flight of money owing to a loss of confidence, but not from withdrawals for non-economic reasons, so that some degree of risk remains. In general, it is safeguarded against the withdrawal of deposits and the accompanying liquidity risk only if the deposit itself is insured and the bank is the policy holder. Here too there is the problem of how the situation of the individual bank and the deposits are to be evaluated for insurance purposes and the criteria that should be applied in determining the premiums.[51] In certain circumstances even the bank involved can have great difficulty assessing deposits; the development of universal standards is all the more problematic.

Like the other two forms of insurance, deposits insurance suffers the defect that it lulls the banks into paying less attention to the risks of recycling described above. In the end, the risks are not reduced but only shifted onto another party or even increased. In the case of deposits insurance, for example, this occurs in that it conflicts with efforts to achieve the necessary diversification of creditors. Such an arrangement would therefore be advantageous to the individual bank but would not lead to a solution of the problem for the system as a whole.

A proposal by Wilfried Guth for a "safety net" that would be organised and funded by the banks themselves has aroused particular interest.[52] This would swing into action whenever a solvent bank encountered serious liquidity difficulties in the international credit markets. Co-operation with the central banks is not ruled out, but the initiative would have to come from the banks. A safety net of this kind therefore aims to reduce the liquidity risk directly, irrespective of the causes of temporary illiquidity.

Details with regard to implementation of the proposal have not been discussed so far. The main problems will be encountered in establishing guidelines on the circumstances in which a bank can invoke the arrangement and on what criteria. Only when such guidelines have been drafted will it be clear how a system of this kind should be judged. One objection that has already been raised in connection with the insurance of banking activities also applies here: every institutionalised form of financial assistance for use in crises encourages the banking system to attach less importance to the risk aspects of lending to the extent to which it no longer has to bear these risks. For that reason the institutionalisation of financial assistance should be avoided as a rule. Moreover, this proposal should be seen primarily as an attempt by the banks to deflect official moves to strengthen the supervision of the international financial markets (cf. Handelsblatt, 9.6.1980).

It must therefore be concluded that the proposals examined hitherto for strengthening the commercial banking system can hardly reduce the dangers associated with recycling because their contribution in this respect is too small or that they would actually magnify the existing risks in certain circumstances. Hence the most promising scheme appears to be one that the IMF and the World Bank have been promoting for some time in conjunction with the Bank for International Settlements and which aims to improve the state of information on debtor countries and thus bring greater clarity to the international financial markets.[53] The initiative by the "Ditchley" group of commercial banks that set up the Institute of International Finance in January 1983 to centralize data on debtor countries[54] is a step in the same direction. Certainly some of the risks can be avoided only if lenders are better informed about the debt situation of individual countries, as in this way the banks become more aware of

the possible dangers. This aspect is particularly important
for small banks, whose ability to gather information is severely limited. Rapid and inexpensive access to information
will also enable them to diversify their portfolios more
widely.

These efforts aim only at reducing debtor risks, however.
Nor do they ensure that the banks will actually be more risk
conscious in their behaviour. Hence for these reasons they
cannot be considered adequate in themselves. The following
section will therefore examine the possibilities open to official institutions, and especially central banks, to counter the risks through stricter control of the international
financial markets.

c.   Control of the international financial markets

Various schemes for controlling the international activities
of banks have been under discussion for a long time and some
have already been implemented at national level.[55] However,
not all of them are designed to help solve the problems described here, so that we must first inquire into the objectives that can be associated with moves to establish tighter
control.

There are essentially two main motives for wanting stricter
control of the international capital markets: risk policy objectives, which relate directly to the problems of concern
here, and efforts to improve the scope for national monetary
management.[56] The growth of the Euro-markets in recent years
and the accompanying increase in the international mobility
of capital are generally regarded as a destabilising influence on national economic developments and on the impact of
monetary and other economic measures, mainly on account of

the wide fluctuations in interest and exchange rates (cf. Versluysen 1981, p. 247). In addition, the interdependence of national money and capital markets owing to the international interest rate link has a detrimental effect on the management of the domestic money supply. Insofar as it is not possible to control domestic liquidity, the danger of inflation increases.

This circumstance explains the desire of national economic policy-makers to control and curb international liquidity in order to prevent it impeding domestic monetary policy. However, this monetary control aspect is not central to the recycling problem. Indeed, attempts to exercise control directed at reducing the international mobility of capital may even conflict with the solutions required in this context.

Hence the schemes for controlling the international capital markets considered below are primarily those that are designed to contain risks (prudential controls). They aim essentially at safeguarding the stability of the banking system and hence the continuity of international lending. Their objective is therefore to limit the banks' risks arising from their external commitments without undermining the efficiency of the international financial system, which will continue to be an indispensable element in the recycling process.

Two sets of questions must be answered when considering possible schemes for controlling the international capital markets. What should be controlled, and by whom?

The instruments for influencing the international operations
of banks comprise essentially the following (cf. OECD 1981,
Vol. 1, p. 8):

- exchange controls,

- interest rate controls,

- minimum reserve requirements,

- tax regulations and

- banking supervision (prudential controls).

The first four possibilities of intervention aim principally
at curbing and controlling international capital flows in general and hence at improving the management of domestic liquidity, but the purpose of banking supervision is to contain the
risks associated with banking operations. The last category
therefore seems best suited to make a contribution towards
solving the problems described here.[57]

Banking supervision is torn between the desire to minimise
the risks stemming from the banks' external operations and
the need to avoid restricting the workings of the financial
system to such an extent that the necessary flow of credit
can no longer be maintained. This conflict again came to prominence in 1983 in a dispute between central banks and commercial banks at the height of the debt crisis (cf. Financial
Times, 22.4.1983). The banks tried to curtail their interbank
lending to banks in the major debtor countries, which was exposed to extremely high risks in this exceptional situation,
and the central banks of the Western countries exerted considerable pressure to prevent them from doing so. Whereas previously the central banks had expressed the view that the
banks should grant less risky loans, the interests of banks and
central banks had apparently undergone a sudden reversal. However,
in this exceptional situation the central banks attached para-

mount importance to maintaining the necessary lending in the short term. It was feared that an abrupt restriction of interbank credit might have triggered a liquidity crisis that would have threatened the stability of the system (cf. Financial Times, 9.5.1983).

As this example shows, banking supervisory authorities must basically weigh a reduction in risk against maintenance of the necessary level of lending. From the supervisory point of view it would be desirable to concentrate on three aspects of the banks' conduct: the observance of balance-sheet- ratios that enable the banks to cope with temporary liquidity shortages and losses of income, due appreciation of country risks and the problem of maturity transformation. Various kinds of arrangement are conceivable in this respect, such as the establishment of general capital and liquidity rules, authorisation requirements and limits on the permissible size of certain transactions. However, difficulties always arise even at national level when the supervisory authorities attempt to increase market transparency and improve the information at their disposal, for example by requiring the production of consolidated balance sheets.[58] The situation is far more complicated if, as in the case under consideration here, banking supervision is to extend beyond national borders and therefore to impinge upon different national jurisdictions.

Of all the measures discussed, the adjustment of capital and liquidity rules to suit the special situation of the banks' external operations appears to be the one most capable of implementation. By contrast, monitoring the risks associated with individual transactions and the establishment of guidelines on the diversification of lending according to countries promises to be far more difficult. Here it is mainly a question of ensuring that the banks use appropriate proce-

dures to assess the creditworthiness of a country and have all
the information needed for this purpose. There is broad agreement that decisions on the actual level and composition of
loans and the setting of internal limits fall within the com-
petence of the banks and that the authorities should assume no
responsibility in this regard (cf. IMF 1981, p. 15). Accordingly, official efforts are being concentrated mainly on improving the level of information of the supervisory authorities.

In countries in which the authorities pay attention to the diversification of lending, they have generally required the
banks hitherto to provide information only on particular commitments and individual countries.[59] They are equally cautious
in their monitoring of maturity transformation in the financing of lending, if they do so at all (cf. IMF 1981, p. 16).
The system of banking supervision in the USA is an exception in this regard; the new regulations that came into
force at the beginning of 1983 have far-reaching consequences for the banks, which are required to give the US
supervisory authorities detailed information each quarter
on certain aspects that are not evident from the balance sheet,
such as overdue loans, agreed payments moratoria, adavances
sensitive to interest rate changes, reserves and the like (cf.
Börsen-Zeitung, 9.10.1982). For example, they are obliged to
treat loans more than 90 days in arrears as non-performing.
In practice this leads debtor countries to give priority to
paying US bank loans that are in danger of reaching this limit (cf. Financial Times, 7.11.1983), thereby exacerbating the
problems facing banks in other countries that are not subject
to such strict supervision. This shows that unco-ordinated
supervisory measures by individual national authorities do not
reduce the risks facing the banking system as a whole.

Even more far-reaching prudential measures have been discussed in the USA of late.[60] These aim to:

- tighten up present practices in the examination and assessment of country risks;

- introduce a system of special reserves for loans to countries that do not meet their payment obligations punctually;

- establish guidelines on the spreading of bank fees over the lifetime of a foreign loan;

- increase the reporting frequency and the amount of information on the banks' country exposures; and finally to

- improve co-operation with supervisory authorities abroad via the International Monetary Fund.

Hence in the USA, as in other Western countries, it is unanimously agreed that in the final analysis co-ordination of the activities of national supervisory authorities is indispensable to the efficient supervision of banks' international operations. This was acknowledged as early as 1975, when a committee of the banking supervisory authorities from the Group of Ten and Switzerland (the Cooke Committee)[61] was set up to further the exchange of information and develop guidelines for co-ordinated banking supervision. The principles on which the Committee has agreed are contained in the so-called "concordat"[62] concluded in 1975, which was concerned primarily with the division of responsibility between the various national authorities.

The concordat was revised in May 1983.[63] The guidelines it contains may be summarised as follows. Distinctions are drawn between three aspects of the supervision of banks' foreign establishments: solvency, liquidity and foreign exchange operations and positions. Responsibility for supervising the solvency of an institution depends upon the type of establishment involved; in the case of branches it lies chiefly with the parent authority, in that of subsidiaries it is shared jointly by the parent and host authorities and in the case of joint ventures it rests principally with the authorities in the country of incorporation.

Responsibility for monitoring liquidity is also apportioned according to the type of establishment; basically, the host authority is responsible for supervising the institution in its own country, while the parent authority monitors the liquidity of the banking group as a whole. There is provision for various forms of co-operation between host and parent authorities, depending on the type of establishment involved. Finally, the task of supervising the banks' foreign exchange operations and positions is shared equally between host and parent authorities.

The revised concordat lays particular stress on the need for co-operation between host country and parent country and sets out at some length which authorities have jurisdiction in which circumstances. An underlying principle here is the exchange of information among countries; it provides in particular for host and parent authorities to notify one another immediately in the event of "serious" problems. The revised edition differs from the original concordat mainly in the greater stress it lays on the fact that efficient banking supervision is possible only on the basis of the consolidation of worldwide banking operations.

Like the first agreement, the new concordat does not adopt a position with regard to individual measures. It should therefore be seen mainly as a first step in the right direction and as an encouragement to the exchange of information. The Cooke Committee does not see itself in any case as a forum in which details concerning the co-ordination of national prudential controls can be decided (cf. Cooke 1981, p.239). However, in the final analysis, the main problem will be seen to lie in the practical arrangements for such co-operation, given the different national interests and legal and institutional conditions in the various countries.

To sum up, it is quite conceivable to limit the risks deriving from the banks' foreign operations and hence help safeguard the recycling process by strengthening control over the international capital markets, provided, however, that such control is confined to prudential banking supervision. Co-ordinated action is ultimately unavoidable in this field. At the same time, however, there is the danger that excessive supervisory measures will restrict the banks' lending ability too severely and thus hamper recycling. In its efforts to achieve maximum security, policy should not disregard the need to leave the banks sufficient scope to recycle resources. In setting the scope available to them, the sole concern should be to ensure the smooth financing of current account deficits that are unavoidable in the short term but not to absolve debtor countries from responsibility for internal and external economic adjustment. The requirements and problems associated with such an adjustment are examined in the following chapters.

Footnotes to Chapter 3

1   This information relates only to the years after the first oil crisis
    owing to the lack of data on Iran and Iraq.

2   Cf. Syrie et Monde Arabe 1981, pp. 19 ff. See Salacuse 1980 with re-
    gard to the development of new financial institutions after 1973. Cf.
    also Shihata 1982 on OPEC development aid in general.

3   Cf. Handelsblatt, 11.9.1980. In March 1981 Saudia Arabia agreed to
    lend the Fund a total of about $ 10 billion after negotiations last-
    ing about a year. See also Neue Zürcher Zeitung, 31.3.1981.

4   The basic alternatives open to the surplus countries in all the in-
    vestment decisions discussed below are therefore either to accumu-
    late cash surpluses, safeguard them and invest them at sufficiently
    high yield, or to leave the oil in the ground. Cf. also Keran, Al-
    Malik 1982, p. 113.

5   The Bank of England indicates that the investment preferences of OPEC
    countries as a group differs fundamentally from those of other coun-
    try groups, at least as far as currency composition is concerned. Cf.
    Bank of England 1981, p. 496. For example, it is shown that OPEC coun-
    tries hold a smaller proportion of their official reserves in dollars
    and a higher proportion in Deutsche Mark than the industrial countries.

6   See, for example, International Herald Tribune, 14./15.3.1981. It ap-
    pears that hitherto the surplus countries have modified the currency
    composition of their investments mainly by investing new cash sur-
    pluses in accordance with their new criteria but not by transferring
    capital that is already invested. Cf. Wallich 1981.

7   The most recent example of this is the agreement with the IMF in the
    spring of 1983 on the association of Saudi Arabia with the Group of
    Ten's General Arrangements to Borrow as soon as the 1984 enlargement
    and revision come into force. Cf. also IMF 1983, pp. 254 ff and
    Deutsche Bundesbank: Geschäftsbericht 1982, p. 48.

8   This also applies in part to the Federal Republic of Germany. Cf. for
    example Wirtschaftswoche 1980, pp. 32 ff.

9   For example, Japan liberalised its foreign exchange law in 1980. Cf.
    Handelsblatt, 8.10.1980. A particular aspect of this has been high-
    lighted by Volcker, among others, namely that with the visible trend
    towards the increased direct investment of OPEC surpluses in indus-
    trial countries these countries are increasingly playing a de facto
    role as financial intermediaries in the recycling process. Cf. Vol-
    cker 1980, p. 4.

10 This was the case in both oil shocks. Cf. also Schäfer 1982,
   p. 3.

11 See Bank of England 1980, p. 159 in this connection and in rela-
   rion to the remarks that follow.

12 The newly industrialising countries are Brazil, Greece, Hong Kong,
   Mexico, Portugal, Singapore, South Korea, Spain, Taiwan and Yugoslavia. Cf. OECD Observer 1981, p. 12, footnote 1.

13 Cf. Chapter 2, section 2.

14 Cf., for example, Matthöfer 1980, p. 14.

15 Cf. Frankfurter Allgemeine Zeitung, 16.1.1981. The banks try dis-
   creetly to ward off OPEC countries if their deposits seem to account for too large a share of the total. See Wallich 1981, p. 773.

16 This raises a particular problem for developing countries in times
   of rising interest rates. As bank loans are usually granted at variable interest rates, an increase in rates raises the cost of debt
   servicing for these countries. As a result, the debtor risk increases
   further, so that the banks will demand still higher risk premiums
   for new loans. Cf. also Gotur 1983, p. 34.

17 An example of the increased activities of such institutions in recent years can be seen in the fact that the World Bank's annual lending programme rose from $ 2 billion in 1973 to $ 11.2 billion in the
   1983 financial year. See Yohai 1983 in this connection and also with
   regard to possible options for still greater World Bank involvement
   in future. Regional institutions, such as the Arab development funds,
   are also important in this connection, even though their contribution
   has been small hitherto. For example, between 1978 and 1980 the aid
   granted by the most important Arab funds – the Abu Dhabi Fund for
   Arab Economic Development, the Kuwait Fund for Arab Economic Development and the Saudi Fund for Development – totalled only about $ 2
   billion. Cf. in this connection and regarding the activities of the
   Arab funds in general Syrie et Monde Arabe 1981, pp. 25 ff.

18 Loans could be obtained from the Trust Fund until 30th April 1981.
   Since that date only profits from sales of IMF holdings of gold have
   been distributed from this Fund. On 31st December 1981 the proceeds
   of gold sales totalled around SDR 1 billion. Cf. IMF 1982a.

19 The eligibility conditions were based on those laid down by the International Development Association for financial assistance. Cf. IMF 1982a,
   p. VII.

20 Industrial countries borrowed from the Fund chiefly after the first oil crisis, and then only on a small scale. Italy and the United Kingdom were exceptions. See the following table:

USE OF FUND CREDIT BY INDUSTRIAL COUNTRIES[a]

- in billions of US dollars -

	Industrial countries as a group	United Kingdom	Italy
1974	1,78	–	1,66
1975	2,21	–	1,34
1976	2,77	1,96	–0,14
1977	0,86	1,92	–1,02
1978	–2,94	–1,92	–0,88
1979	–3,16	–1,28	–1,14
1980	–0,81	–0,33	–
1981	–0,59	–0,30	–
1982[b]	–0,46	–0,29	–

a End-year values, changes in relation to previous year.

b Changes in relation to fourth quarter of 1982.

Source: International Monetary Fund: International Financial Statistics, various years; calculations by the authors.

21 For an example of this often held opinion see Schäfer 1980, pp. 227 ff.

22 Regarding the increase in quotas see International Monetary Fund 1983, pp. 50 f.

23 On the factors that determine the Fund's actual financing ability see also Morgan Guaranty 1980, pp. 11 f.

24 On that occasion Saudi Arabia granted the IMF credit lines of SDR 4 billion (about $ 10 billion) for each of two years and indicated its willingness in principle to support the Fund on the same scale for a third year. Cf. Neue Zürcher Zeitung, 31.3.1981.

25 Regarding the Fund's role so far in crises see also Cline 1983, pp. 40 ff.

26 At the time of writing, the institutions' members were discussing not an increase in contributions but a reduction on budgetary grounds. Cf. OECD Observer 1983a, p. 17.

27 Johnston 1981 reviews the various theories to explain the growth in the Euro-currency markets.

28 The view that only a weak link of this kind is present is also to be found in Bacha, Alejandro 1982, pp. 81 f.

29 This is to be seen, for example, in the fact that despite a sharp expansion in the markets after 1977 the proportion of OPEC deposits remained virtually constant.

30 A more detailed treatment of the various methods banks employ to assess country risks cannot be given here; a summary is to be found in Angelini et al. 1979, pp. 122 ff. Cf. also Committee on Banking Regulations and Supervisory Practices 1982.

31 The reasons why this has happened on only a limited scale so far are to be found in factors such as the associated high cost of information for the individual bank. The more accessible the information, the more willing will banks be to diversify more widely. Cf. Eaton, Gersovitz 1981, p. 15.

32 Even in the absence of spectacular events, banks see very short-term OPEC deposits as a problem, as unlike other deposits they can fluctuate widely in direct proportion to the depositors' export earnings. Cf. Group of Thirty 1981, pp. 16 f.

33 Cf. Bank of England 1983, p. 489.

34 On the causes of the crisis see also Cline 1983, pp. 13 ff.

35 Cf. also Süddeutsche Zeiutng, 17.1.1984.

36 Regarding the individual proposals see also Cline 1983, pp. 114 ff and Euromoney, July 1983.

37 A review of various proposals for greater multinational participation in recycling is to be found in Europäisches Parlament 1983b, pp. 55 ff.

38 Cf. p. 27.

39 The proposal that the IMF should establish a special facility to compensate for interest rate fluctuations similar to the facility for compensating fluctuations in export earnings aims in the same direction. Cf. The Economist, 2.4.1983.

40 Cf. North-South Commission 1980, p. 248.

41 Cf. also Financial Times, 14.3.1983.

42 Cf. Europäisches Parlament 1983b, p. 55.

43 Cf. for example Gutowski, Roth 1980, Europäisches Parlament 1983b.

44 Cf. Gutowski, Roth 1980. A critique of this proposal is contained
    in Schlecht 1980.

45 This plan was originally supposed to help avoid an international
    dollar "glut", but the Western industrial countries were unable to
    agree among themselves owing to numerous unsolved problems that its
    implementation would have caused. Cf. for example Laney 1980, pp.
    127 ff.

46 A factor militating against this, for example, is the large dollar
    component in the SDR, as the surplus countries are also seeking al-
    ternatives to investments in dollars. Cf.Europäisches Parlament 1983a,
    p. 23.

47 Dean and Giddy distinguish between "local" and "global" shocks for
    the banks in this context. Cf. Dean, Giddy 1981, pp. 19f.

48 For further details see World Bank 1983d.

49 In general it should be noted that the banks' willingness to engage
    in co-financing falters in times of rising oil prices. Immediately
    after an oil crisis it is very low. Only as market liquidity subsides
    in the course of time and international lending risks increase are
    the banks more inclined to collaborate with official institutions.
    This circumstance also illustrates the need for control over the in-
    ternational capital markets that could stabilise the banks' conduct
    and provide a permanent safeguard against risk.

50 Regarding the various possibilities see International Currency Re-
    view 1981, pp. 45 ff.

51 Regarding the problem whether fixed or variable premiums should be
    charged, see for example Dean, Giddy 1981, pp. 23 ff.

52 This proposal is described in International Herald Tribune, 16.6.
    1980.

53 Cf. Finanzierung und Entwicklung 1983, p. 30.

54 Cf. Frankfurter Allgemeine Zeitung, 13.1.1983.

55 For a review of national regulations affecting banks' international
    operations see OECD 1981.

56 The additional objectives of increasing the efficiency of national
    and international markets mentioned by Swoboda and the attempt to
    treat different groups of financial intermediaries in the same man-
    ner can also be classified under the two objectives named. Cf. Swo-
    boda 1980, p. 30.

57 Cf. the banks' own assessment of the various control instruments in Group of Thirty 1982, pp. 17 ff.

58 This problem has been mentioned again recently in Köhler 1983.

59 The fact that this is not taken for granted can be seen from the stir caused in September 1980 when the Deutsche Bundesbank required German banks to give disaggregated information on their external lending in twelve countries. Cf. Börsen-Zeitung, 30.9.1980.

60 For details see Partee 1983, pp. 2 ff.

61 Regarding the establishment and the activities of this and other bodies see Muller 1982.

62 The text of the concordat is reprinted in IMF 1981, Annex, pp. 29-32. On the works of the Committee see also Cooke 1981.

63 The text of the revised concordat is reprinted in Bank for International Settlements 1983.

PART II - INTERNAL AND EXTERNAL ADJUSTMENT TO REAL OIL PRICE
            INCREASES

Chapter 4:   The problem of stability

1.   The effects of real oil price increases on energy and raw
     material prices

a.   Prices of petroleum products and other sources of energy

Real oil price increases cause the costs of oil refining to
increase by more than the general rate of inflation. Crude
oil is now the largest item in the industry's cost account.
For example, in 1981 crude oil costs represented more than
50 % of overall costs for oil refineries in Western Europe.
By contrast, in 1973, immediately before the first oil crisis,
they accounted just for 22 % of total costs and in 1978, before the second oil shock, their share stood at 41 %, still a
substantially smaller proportion than in 1981 (for details cf.
Shell 1983, p. 11). Changes in the cost of crude oil are
therefore the main determinant of oil product prices.

At the same time, the prices of petroleum products are also
determined by the market structure und by the behaviour of
suppliers in the oil industry. This is strongly influenced
worldwide by the oligopoly of the "seven sisters", which
are, in descending order by size of turnover in 1981, Exxon,
Mobil, Texaco, Shell, Socal (Chevron), BP and Gulf. Their
joint turnover in 1981 came to almost $500 billion, approx-
imately equivalent to the gross national product of the United Kingdom. The corporations employ more than 800,000 people
throughout the world and their sales of petroleum products
totalled about 1 billion tonnes in 1981, about one-third of
world oil requirements (Schiffer 1982, p. 94).

Nonetheless, competition is often keen in the individual sectors of the oil market, owing partly to strong oligopolistic rivalry but also partly to significant outside competition from suppliers who do not have their own refineries. In the Federal Republic of Germany, for example, the latter were "clearly able to prevent ploys to restrict competition both during the phase of expansion up to 1973 and in the more recent phase of stagnation or concentration" so that here "the prices of petroleum products are not obtained by adding up the individual cost elements but are set in accordance with supply and demand in individual product markets" (Schürmann 1982, p. 142).

Hence the extent to which increases in crude oil costs are passed on in higher product prices depends partly on the behaviour of demand. The income and price elasticity of the demand for oil products are important measures in this respect. The income elasticity indicates how the demand for oil products behaves irrespective of changes in relative prices if, for example, disposable incomes are reduced by real oil price rises. Table 4.1, which takes Germany as an example, shows that petroleum products as a group have a high and above-average income elasticity: the coefficient for the period from 1973 to 1981 comes to 1.2, whereas the comparable measure for all sources of energy is only 0.9.[1] The demand for petrol and diesel oil is particularly responsive to changes in income, while the opposite is true of heavy heating oil. However, with real incomes remaining constant, the demand for heating oil reacts more strongly to price changes than do fuels; if the price of heating oil rises by 1 % in real terms, demand for this commodity falls by 0.4 %, but the price elasticities of petrol and diesel fuel are significantly lower: 0.2 and 0.1 respectively. As a group, petroleum products show a higher price elasticity than all sources of energy (see Table 4.1).

Table 4.1: PRICE AND INCOME ELASTICITY OF THE DEMAND FOR ENERGY IN THE FEDERAL REPUBLIC OF GERMANY, 1973-1981[a]

	Price elasticity		Income elasticity		Coefficient of determination (R^2)
	Coefficent	t value	Coefficient	t value	
Petroleum products	-0.44	-3.5	1.21	2.8	0.68
Heavy heating oil	-0.37	-4.1	-0.74	-1.8	0.91
Light heating oil	-0.44	-3.2	1.03	1.5	0.71
Diesel oil	-0.05	-5.9	1.50	7.9	0.95
Petrol	-0.24	-2.0	1.57	6.3	0.89
Coal	-0.60	-1.2	0.23	2.4	0.31
Hard coal	-0.65	-1.8	0.29	0.3	0.54
Coke oven coke	-0.34	-0.8	-0.55	-0.8	0.23
Brown coal	-1.08	-1.3	1.29	1.2	0.24
Coal briquettes	-1.31	-1.5	-0.33	-0.2	0.64
Gas	0.01	0.1	1.75	10.9	0.98
Natural gas	0.18	1.6	1.23	17.8	0.99
Town gas	0.10	1.2	2.20	8.2	0.97
Electricity[b]	-0.48	-3.5	-0.26	-0.7	0.86
Total energy	-0.32	-4.8	0.89	6.3	0.87

a Calculations of the equation $\ln EC = a + b \ln EP + c \ln GNP + u$ by the least squares method, where EC stands for energy consumption, EP the real price of energy (nominal price of energy adjusted by the GNP deflator); the coefficients b and c express the respective price and income elasticities, a is the constant and u represents random fluctuations.

b 1974-1981.

Source: Statistisches Bundesamt; Arbeitsgemeinschaft Energiebilanzen: Energiebilanzen der Bundesrepublik Deutschland; calculations by the authors.

The influence of price and income elasticity on the oil companies' pricing policies calls for detailed examination. For present purposes, however, it is sufficient to illustrate the link between the prices of crude oil and oil products, irrespective of the strength of the various influences on the supply and demand sides. The OECD uses a simple measurement formula for this which correlates the observed rates of change in the prices of oil products and crude oil. If one takes the seven largest OECD countries as an example, one finds that between 1970 and 1980 the prices of petroleum products paid by industry and households followed closely the movements in crude oil prices: a 1 % increase in crude oil prices was associated with rises in the prices of oil products of 0.8 and 0.7 % respectively in these two sectors. The link was much weaker in the case of the transport sector: 0.4 % (see Table 4.2). This chiefly reflects the fact that the proportion of tax is particularly high here, duties are generally levied on a volume basis, and taxes have not been raised in accordance with oil prices.[2]

A general rise in the coefficients can be observed as time proceeds. Viewed from this perspective too, households and industry differ from the transport sector; in the first two sectors the spread has narrowed much more than in transport (see Table A-5).

The prices of other sources of energy in competition with oil products have also risen in real terms as a result of the oil price increases. This is particularly true of gas prices; those charged to industrial users rose on average by almost as much as the prices of oil products between 1970 and 1980. The "sympathetic movement" was much weaker in the case of coal and electricity; over the same period the price increases for these energy products was only 75 and 63 % of that in petroleum products (IEA 1982a, p. 85).

Table 4.2:   THE RELATIONSHIP BETWEEN THE PRICES OF CRUDE OIL AND PETROLEUM PRODUCTS IN THE SEVEN LARGEST OECD COUNTRIES BY SECTORS, 1970-1980[a]

	Industry	Households and small consumers	Transport
USA	0.83	0.79	0.44
Canada	0.67	0.47	0.29
Japan	0.71	0.54	0.44
Fed. Rep. of Germany	0.60	0.70	0.33
France	0.76	0.74	0.46
United Kingdom	0.78	0.72	0.51
Italy	0.74	0.79	0.52
Total	0.76	0.71	0.43

a   Increase in the prices of petroleum products if crude oil prices rise by 1 %.

Source: IEA: World Energy Outlook, Paris 1982, p. 81.

Table 4.3 shows that in the Federal Republic of Germany the rise in real gas prices between 1973 and 1981 was 10 %, exactly the same as the real price increase for petroleum products. Coal prices, on the other hand, rose only half as fast in real terms. The contrast between coal and its main substitute - heavy heating oil - is considerably greater, as the latter recorded a real increase of 16 % a year. The smallest rise was in electricity prices, which rose by just under 2 % a year in real terms.

Table 4.3: CHANGES IN REAL PRICE INDICES FOR SELECTED ENERGY PRODUCTS IN THE FEDERAL REPUBLIC OF GERMANY, 1965-1981[a]

- average annual rates of change -

Energy products	65-73	73-78	78-81	73-81
Crude oil	-2.0	15.9	32.8	22.0
Petroleum products	1.3	4.3	20.0	10.0
Heavy heating oil	-1.3	9.4	26.7	15.6
Light heating oil	2.1	4.5	29.7	13.3
Diesel oil	0.0	-0.2	15.7	5.5
Petrol	-0.1	0.4	15.2	5.7
Coal and coal products	1.1	6.4	5.1	5.9
Hard coal	0.5	9.0	2.9	6.7
Coke oven coke	2.5	4.9	4.3	4.7
Brown coal	-0.2	4.7	3.4	4.2
Coal briquettes	-0.4	4.2	6.7	5.1
Gas	-2.6	7.6	14.1	10.0
Town gas	-5.4[c]	4.5	14.1	8.0
Natural gas	-4.1[c]	10.1	14.7	11.8
Electricity	-1.8	1.7	1.3	1.6
All energy products[b]	-1.1	3.5	12.2	6.7

a Adjusted for inflation by the GNP deflator.

b Obtained from the price indices for the individual energy products, weighted according to their share in final energy consumption.

c 1968-73.

Sources: Statistisches Bundesamt and calculations by the authors.

Over the same period a marked "decoupling" of other energy prices from the prices of oil products can be discerned. Whereas prices moved closely in step until 1978 - for example, the real prices of hard coal and natural gas rose by 9 and 10 % a year respectively while that of heavy heating oil went up by 9.4 % - in subsequent years the rise in the price of coal and, to a lesser extent, that of gas was considerably smaller than that in competing petroleum products.

The pattern of price movements is similar in the other major industrialised countries. For example, in the industrial sector of the seven leading countries the "elasticity" of gas prices in relation to the prices of petroleum products rose steadily until 1978, when the coefficient even went above unity, but fell back sharply in later years (see Table A-6). Similar price relationships are to be seen in the households' and small consumers' sector (see Table A-7).

Other energy products must enjoy price advantages over mineral oil if they are to take its place and the differences must be sufficiently large to offset possible non-price factors that impede substitution, such as high conversion costs, increased expenditure on environmental protection or disadvantages from the point of view of handling and transportation. In the final analysis it is not market prices for energy but effective cost prices - and administrative regulations - that determine whether consumers decide to convert. The classic example of this is coal, whose loss of market share in the last few decades can also be attributed to non-price factors of the kind described.

A key role in the development of energy prices and energy price relationships is played by the state, which influences prices in a variety of ways, both direct and indirect. In some cases the state owes its strong position to the high capital stake it holds in enterprises in the energy sector; examples are to be found primarily in France, the United Kingdom and Italy. The legal status of such enterprises is of less consequence, however, than the interventions in the name of energy policy (Matthies 1983, p. 90). The governments of the industrial countries are now broadly in agreement that national energy prices should reflect those obtaining on the world market.

The prices and price relationships that are formed in the market under conditions of competition can nevertheless deviate substantially from the optimum for the economy as a whole. This must take account of not only the long-term marginal cost of energy production - including a depletion premium - but also the social costs incurred on account of such things as environmental damage or supply uncertainty. Actual market prices should be adjusted accordingly by means of taxes, import duties and the like.

The criteria for an optimum energy price policy are far easier to deduce in theory than to apply in practice. Difficult problems of definition, information and measurement arise. What is to be understood by the long run in concrete terms? How high is the trend rate of production costs for the various energy products? What is the basis for measuring the depletion rate? How can one ascertain the environmental costs and assess (and influence) technological developments that affect the environmental acceptability of particular forms of energy? A way must then be found to overcome political opposition aroused by differentiated (those affected would say discriminatory) state intervention in the price mechanism on energy markets. In addition, the impact of state energy price adjustments on international competitiveness, the price level, income distribution and other objectives of economic policy must be considered and, where necessary, strategies must be developed that take these side effects into account.

It is therefore extremely difficult to formulate a conclusive and practicable concept for an energy price policy appropriate to the economy as a whole. Nevertheless, such a policy is an essential part of an overall strategy for improving the conditions for growth, particularly as it has a decisive influence on price expectations and hence on energy saving and substitution.

b.   Commodity prices

The oil price shocks we have experienced so far have been accompanied by price rises for other commodities that do not belong to the energy sector. This was particularly pronounced in the first oil crisis, when the price index for commodities (excluding energy) doubled, whereas the export unit value of industrial products rose by "only" about 40 % (Koopmann, Scharrer 1981, p. 2). In the second oil crisis the effect was weaker. After an initial sharp rise, commodity prices came under strong downward pressure, owing mainly to the long period of stagnation or recession in Western industrial countries, which was itself attributable in no small measure to the increase in energy prices, so that by 1982 commodity prices had fallen back almost to their 1978 level.[3] In real terms they were about 40 % below their 1974 peak (Financial Times, 23.2.1983a). It remains to be determined whether there is a long-term connection between energy prices and

179

commodity prices, in which direction it operates and what importance should be attributed to it.

Oil and other hydrocarbons or energy sources are very important direct and indirect cost factors in some commodity sectors, so that real oil price rises can substantially alter
supply conditions. An example of direct increases in costs
would be aluminium, the production of which requires an unusually high consumption of electricity. Increased energy
prices also exert strong cost pressure on other minerals,
particularly where extraction entails the large-scale use
of energy-intensive plant. In agricultural products energy
cost increases are predominantly indirect, e.g. via the use
of oil-based fertilisers.

The prices of raw materials are also affected by oil-induced increases in the cost of industrial substitutes for raw
materials. The majority of these are produced from hydrocarbons, and the production process itself is energy-intensive.
The energy requirement of natural raw materials is small by
comparison (Roze 1981, pp. 51 ff). Hence in the case of
the latter there is scope for price increases and improved
competitiveness vis-à-vis synthetic substitutes. One example
ist natural rubber.

Here the oil and energy requirement is far smaller than in
the production of synthetic rubber, where costs have risen
dramatically owing to the increase in the price of energy.[4]
As a consequence, there was a fundamental reversal in the
price trend. Whereas the price of synthetic rubber had fallen steadily in both real and nominal terms until 1973
owing to both declining crude oil prices and technological
innovations, since then it has risen sharply. To a high
degree, prices have moved in step with crude oil price rises. The suppliers of natural rubber took adavantage of this

180

development to raise their prices by far more than the increase in costs, thereby greatly improving the financial parameters for an expansion in production facilities and an increase in their production efficiency and in their ability to compete on grounds of quality. In these circumstances natural rubber might once again greatly increase its overall market share, which has shrunk to 30 %, the more so as the potential for innovation and productivity gains in the manufacture of synthetic products seems to have been largely exhausted.[5] At the same time there is room for further price increases, the upper limit being set by the development of oil and energy prices and the prices of synthetic substitutes that follow in their train.

Increases in oil and energy prices also reinforce attempts to impose higher commodity prices against the wishes of the market. Such attempts have derived considerable impetus from the partial success of OPEC. Their objective is generally to reverse the negative trend in the terms of trade of many primary producing countries. A special aspect of this is the possibility of offsetting at least part of the external payments burden resulting from the rise in energy prices by raising commodity prices in real terms.

However, the chances that the primary producing countries can get away with overpricing their commodities in the long run must be considered slight. Even the OPEC cartel is suffering repeated setbacks in its efforts to find a common denominator in the disparate interests of its members in order to derive the maximum cartel profit. Where most other commodities of importance for the economy as a whole are concerned, the conditions for pursuing a price policy that runs counter to market forces are much less favourable. In most cases the number of actual and potential suppliers is far

greater and even with today's extraction techniques the lifetime of non-renewable natural resources has lengthened spec-
tacularly since the Club of Rome examined the subject. For
example, in 1972 the lifetime of aluminium reserves was put
at 31 years, but by 1981 it had already grown to 253 years.
Over the same period the lifetime of copper reserves increased from 21 to 70 years, of lead reserves from 21 to 43, of
tin reserves from 14 to 41 and iron deposits from 93 to 184
years (Die Zeit, 7.5.1982). At the same time, there has been
a geographic diversification of deposits, with an increasing
predominance of reserves being located in politically more
stable countries.[6] A broad range of possible substitutes is
also available; for example, in the telephone industry copper wire is being increasingly replaced by optical fibres,
for which the raw material is in abundant supply, tin is being substituted by aluminium and there is a general movement
from heavy to light metals.

In summary, it can be concluded that as a general rule rising
oil prices are not expected to exert lasting upward pressure
on the prices of other raw materials. However, real oil
price rises do improve the competitiveness of natural raw
materials that are threatened by substitutes.

2. Repercussions on the general price level

In theory, changes in relative prices need not necessarily
raise the overall price level, even if they are as profound
as the oil price shocks of 1973-74 and 1978-81. In actual
fact, however, experience to date has taught that real oil
price rises can hardly be said to have no effect on prices,
as a swift examination of the statistical series will indicate.

a. Price rises on a broad front

When the price of crude oil rose dramatically at the end of
1973, the general rate of price increases in the Western
industrial countries had already accelerated considerably
in the course of strong monetary expansion. The average
rate of inflation, measured in terms of the consumer price
index, had shot up from 4.6 % in 1972 to 7.7 % in 1973. The
following year, however, it practically doubled again to
13.2 % in spite of a sharp reduction in economic growth -
in the OECD the rate of growth of GDP fell from 6 % in 1973
to 0.8 % in 1974. In the period between the two oil shocks
the rate of inflation dropped back in stages to 7.2 % in
1978, only to rise markedly again at the time of the second
oil price rise. The peak was reached in 1980 with a rate of
12 %. Since then, with the price of crude falling and growth
decidedly weak, there has been a process of disinflation
(see Chart 9).

In the oil-importing developing countries the break in the
consumer price trend had actually come before the first oil
shock. The rate of inflation in this group of countries rose
from 13 to 21 % between 1972 and 1973, owing mainly to the
steep rise in food prices that preceded the oil price in-

Chart 9: DEVELOPMENT OF CONSUMER PRICES IN THE WORLD AND IN INDIVIDUAL COUNTRY GROUPS, 1970-1982[a]

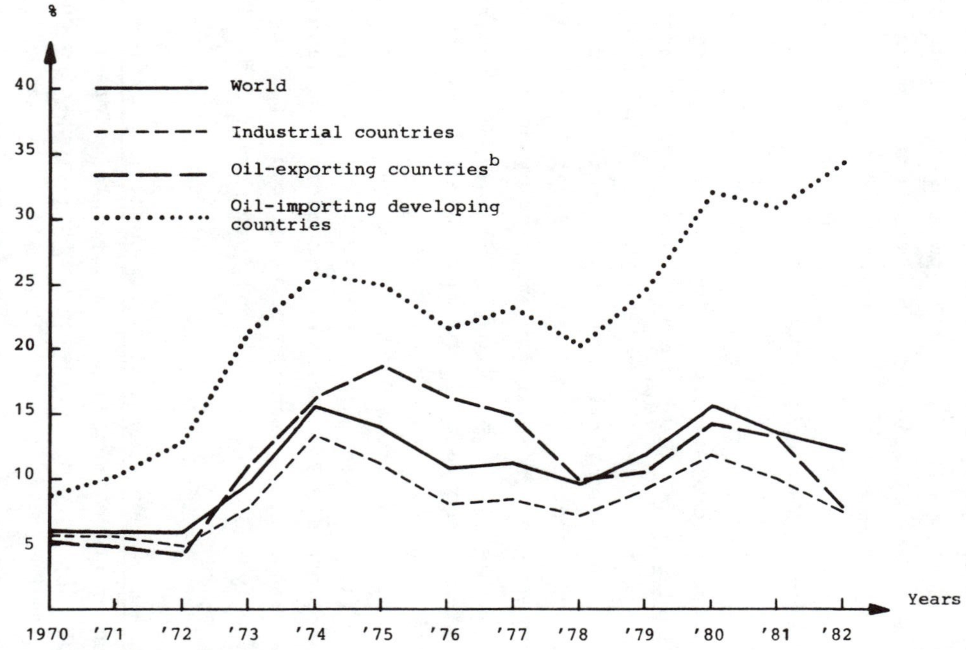

World

Industrial countries

Oil-exporting countries[b]

Oil-importing developing
countries

a Average annual rate of increase.
b OPEC countries (excluding Gabon and Ecuador) and Oman.
Source: IMF: International Financial Statistics.

184

crease. However, dearer oil caused a further acceleration in prices despite slower demand growth, so that in 1974 the rate of inflation stood at 26 %. It remained at a high level between the two oil shocks (between 1974 and 1978 the prices of consumer goods rose by 22 % a year) before again moving upwards during the second crisis to an average of 29 % between 1978 and 1981. Even in 1982, when crude oil prices were falling, inflation continued unabated at 34 % in the oil-importing developing countries. The increase in the pace of inflation during the second oil crisis and in 1982 is all the more conspicuous as the prices for developing countries' raw materials other than oil rose much less strongly than in 1972-74 (for details see preceding section, p. 9).

In the oil-producing countries, too, inflation gained strong impetus in the years after 1972. The index figures show that the rise in prices followed a similar time pattern to that in industrial countries but that it was substantially less than in the oil-importing developing countries. Moreover, there was a conspicuous sharp slowdown in inflation in 1982, when it came to only 8 %, little more than half the figure for the previous year (14 %).

Regression estimates for individual OECD countries confirm the suspected link between oil price rises and inflation.[7] The rates of change in import prices of crude oil and the increase in the money supply over and above the real rate of GDP growth constitute the independent variables. The regression equation to be calculated is therefore as follows:

$$gCP = a_0 + a_1 \; gOP + a_2 \; (gM - gGDP_r) + e$$

where the symbols have the folowing meanings:

g $\quad$ = $\quad$ rate of growth

CP $\quad$ = $\quad$ consumer price index

OP $\quad$ = $\quad$ unit value for crude oil imports

M $\quad$ = $\quad$ money supply (M_1)

GDP_r $\quad$ = $\quad$ real gross domestic product

a_0 $\quad$ = $\quad$ constant

a_1, a_2 = $\quad$ regression coefficients

e $\quad$ = $\quad$ random fluctuations.

Table 4.4 gives the results of the time series calculated for sixteen countries for the years from 1966 to 1981. It shows that all the regression coefficients bear the expected positive sign. Moreover, in the majority of countries the influence of oil prices is statistically significant at the 0.01 level (Sweden, Japan, Denmark, Belgium, Austria, Greece, Italy, the Netherlands, Germany) or at the 0.025 level (France, Ireland, Switzerland, Portugal). Only the USA and Spain fail to meet this criterion.[8]

A simple correlation estimate on the basis of IMF data on the rise in energy prices and in the general price level from the first quarter of 1973 to the final quarter of 1980 in the seven principal Western industrial countries points to the same conclusion. If the change in energy prices borne by households and enterprises is compared with the change in the general price index, the correlation coefficient across the seven countries comes to 0.7.[9]

b. $\quad$ Marked divergences between countries

The real increases in oil prices nevertheless triggered inflationary impulses of widely differing strength in individ-

Table 4.4: REGRESSION ESTIMATES ON THE INFLATIONARY EFFECTS OF THE RISE IN OIL PRICES[a]

	Influence of oil prices		Influence of the money supply		Coefficient of determination (R^2)
	a_1	t value	a_2	t value	
USA	1.3	1.4	9.3	3.9	0.67
Japan	5.2	5.6	1.8	1.6	0.74
Belgium	4.1	3.9	3.4	3.2	0.63
Federal Rep. of Germany	2.3	2.6	1.1	1.2	0.37
Denmark	4.6	4.7	2.0	1.7	0.64
France	2.8	2.3	3.6	2.5	0.57
United Kingdom	5.5	2.2	5.4	2.8	0.48
Italy	1.1	3.0	4.4	1.5	0.47
Netherlands	2.6	3.0	2.6	3.6	0.56
Austria	2.9	3.7	2.7	3.5	0.63
Sweden	1.1	8.7	2.4	3.5	0.55
Switzerland	3.7	2.2	6.4	5.9	0.33
Ireland	4.2	2.3	3.9	2.2	0.42
Greece	1.1	3.0	3.6	1.3	0.58
Portugal	8.8	2.1	1.2	6.8	0.39
Spain	2.5	1.1	7.8	3.5	0.53

a The regression equation is given in the text.

Sources: OECD: Statistics of Foreign Trade; OECD: National Accounts; IMF: International Financial Statistics; calculations by the authors.

ual countries. This holds true for each of the three country groups distinguished here. However, only the oil-importing developing countries and more especially the Western industrialised countries will be considered below, since the
data available on the oil-producing countries are very incomplete.

In the oil-importing developing countries the dispersion of
inflation rates increased substantially after the first oil
crisis, as can be seen from the standard deviation and the
coefficients of variation for changes in consumer prices
(see Table 4.5).

The reasons for this cannot be examined in detail here owing
to the great diversity of this group of countries. However,
preliminary clues can be found by dividing inflation rates
into imported and "home-grown" components for the years from
1972 to 1979. The results of these calculations, which have
been made for twelve developing countries, are reproduced in
Table 4.6.[10]

It can be seen first that in all the countries "home-grown"
inflation was by far the larger component even during the
years of the oil crisis. Secondly, the share of imported inflation in the overall rise in prices increased sharply in
most of the countries in 1974 and 1979, reflecting the direct
impact of oil price rises. Thirdly, the increase in imported
inflation was much more uniform than the "home-grown" price
increase; the standard deviations for the increase in imported inflation in 1974 and 1979 work out at 2.7 and 2.2 respectively. The primary or "unavoidable" price effect of the oil
shock - the "impact effect" - did not therefore vary much
from one country to another. By contrast, the standard deviation is more than twice as large (6.0) in the case of

Table 4.5:   INFLATION DIFFERENTIALS AMONG DEVELOPING
              COUNTRIES, 1970 - 1982[a]

	Average value[b]	Standard deviation	Coefficient of variation[c]
1970	5.5	5.9	1.1
1971	5.9	6.7	1.1
1972	10.2	15.1	1.5
1973	20.3	43.7	2.2
1974	29.3	60.7	2.1
1975	24.7	49.2	2.0
1976	20.9	58.7	2.8
1977	19.4	27.3	1.4
1978	15.8	23.8	1.5
1979	21.0	25.1	1.2
1980	24.0	24.3	1.0
1981	22.2	25.6	1.2
1982	20.5	29.8	1.5

a   The countries in question are listed in Appendix 1.

b   Unweighted arithmetic mean of annual rates of change in consumer
    prices.

c   Quotient obtained from the standard deviation and the average
    value.

Source: IMF: International Financial Statistics; calcu-
           lations by the authors.

Table 4.6: IMPORTED AND HOME-GROWN INFLATION IN OIL-IMPORTING DEVELOPING COUNTRIES, 1972 - 1979[a]

- percentages rates -

	Imported inflation								Home-grown inflation							
	1972	1973	1974	1975	1976	1977	1978	1979	1972	1973	1974	1975	1976	1977	1978	1979
Greece	1.0	0.5	4.3	-1.1	-0.8	-1.4	-0.7	-0.2	5.0	19.4	20.9	12.3	15.4	13.0	12.9	18.7
Portugal	0.4	-0.4	7.3	-0.2	-0.7	0.7	0.6	3.2	7.8	9.5	18.9	16.2	16.3	26.4	20.9	22.0
Spain	-0.9	-0.2	4.1	-1.4	-0.4	-0.1	-1.6	-1.1	8.7	11.8	16.6	16.7	16.7	22.8	20.0	16.7
Turkey	-0.9	-1.5	5.0	-0.1	-1.3	0.2	0.4	3.1	16.4	21.9	27.8	16.4	17.0	25.0	43.7	69.2
Brazil	0.3	2.1	4.4	-1.1	-0.6	-0.2	-0.3	2.5	17.3	20.6	31.4	32.8	41.9	42.1	41.9	55.6
Paraguay	0.1	-0.6	0.6	4.1	-1.9	0.3	-0.7	-0.2	8.7	20.9	23.7	6.6	5.0	9.2	10.4	20.5
Hong Kong	-1.9	3.6	8.8	0.9	-1.7	1.8	0.5	1.8	7.8	12.8	12.2	2.4	7.8	4.1	5.7	14.2
Korea	0.1	3.0	3.8	-0.2	-4.5	-3.0	-3.3	5.0	15.4	13.1	29.7	24.4	17.9	16.5	20.8	19.0
Pakistan	8.3	3.3	4.1	-2.7	-1.3	-0.1	-0.5	1.7	15.6	23.0	25.2	12.4	9.2	7.8	7.1	11.4
Philippines	-0.5	1.0	1.2	0.3	-0.3	-0.7	-0.2	-0.3	7.0	17.8	31.9	7.9	9.5	8.8	8.9	16.9
Thailand	-0.7	-3.3	-0.7	1.0	-1.8	-0.8	-0.2	1.3	9.1	19.4	19.6	4.8	4.7	8.5	8.6	11.6
Kenya	1.2	2.3	6.8	3.0	-1.0	-2.2	0.8	0.0	6.7	7.9	13.7	13.6	19.0	16.8	2.9	7.2

a With regard to the method of calculation, see footnote 10.

Source: OECD: National Accounts (for Greece, Portugal, Spain and Turkey); UN: Yearbook of National Accounts Statistics (for the remaining countries); calculations by the authors.

"home-grown" inflation, measured as the difference between
the average annual rates of the GDP deflator in the periods
1973-79 and 1965-73; this figure approximates to the "longer-run effect" of the first oil price rise on the level of
prices.[11] The great divergence in inflation rates in the
non-oil developing countries therefore seems to be more the
result of different degrees of success in the adjustment
process and different economic policy reactions to the rise
in oil prices than a reflection of different degrees of
"derangement" caused by real oil price increases.

In the Western industrial countries rates of inflation have
also diverged more strongly since the first oil price shock
(see Tables 4.7 and 4.8). It might be possible to explain the
divergence in terms of structural factors. First, it is conceivable
that the impact of real oil price increases on industrial producer prices is all the stronger, the greater the size of
energy-intensive sectors in relation to a country's industrial structure. However, this hypothesis does not stand up to
empirical examination, as shown by a simple cross-section calculation for eleven countries, in which for each country the
difference between the rates of change in industrial producer prices in the periods 1973-80 and 1967-73 is set against
the share of energy-intensive industrial sectors in total
production by manufacturing industry in 1973.[12] The outcome
is a negative value (-0.3) instead of the expected positive
correlation coefficient. The correlation of price developments with the change in the structure of industry after
1973 - measured as the difference between the production
share of energy-intensive industrial sectors in 1973 and
that recorded in 1980 - also produces an unsatisfactory result, a correlation coefficient of -0.2.

Table 4.7:   INFLATION DIFFERENTIALS AMONG WESTERN
              INDUSTRIAL COUNTRIES[a] 1970 - 1982

Years	Average value[b]	Standard deviation	Coefficient of variation[c]
1970	5.4	2.0	0.37
1971	6.3	1.9	0.30
1972	6.2	1.3	0.21
1973	8.6	1.7	0.20
1974	13.2	4.3	0.33
1975	12.7	4.8	0.38
1976	10.5	4.7	0.45
1977	9.7	4.2	0.43
1978	7.2	3.2	0.44
1979	8.2	3.9	0.48
1980	11.5	4.9	0.43
1981	11.1	4.2	0.38
1982	9.5	4.1	0.43

a OECD excluding Greece, Ireland, Luxembourg, Portugal, Spain and
   Turkey.
b Unweighted arithmetic mean of annual rates of change in consumer
   prices.
c Quotient obtained from the standard deviation and the average value.

Source: IMF: International Financial Statistics; calculations
          by the authors.

Table 4.8:   INFLATION DIFFERENTIALS AMONG
              EEC COUNTRIES[a], 1970 - 1982

Years	Average value[b]	Standard deviation	Coefficient of variation[c]
1970	5.3	1.7	0.32
1971	6.4	1.9	0.30
1972	6.7	1.2	0.18
1973	8.7	1.7	0.20
1974	13.9	4.0	0.29
1975	14.1	6.2	0.44
1976	11.5	4.9	0.43
1977	10.5	4.8	0.46
1978	7.3	3.2	0.44
1979	9.3	4.5	0.48
1980	12.7	6.1	0.48
1981	11.9	5.2	0.44
1982	10.5	4.4	0.42

a Excluding Greece and Luxembourg.
b Unweighted arithmetic mean of annual rates of change in consumer
   prices.
c Quotient obtained from the standard deviation and the average value.

Source: IMF: International Financial Statistics; calculations
          by the authors.

The second point to examine would be whether the rise in the rates of inflation after 1973 was particularly strong in those countries that use oil and other energy sources on an especially large scale, be it in the corporate, household or state sectors for either energy or non-energy purposes. Energy consumption per unit of GDP (the energy coefficient) could serve as a yardstick in this respect. If this variable and the change in it between 1973 and 1980 are compared with movements in consumer prices, only a weak link can be observed, and it is in fact negative in the case of the change in the energy coefficient (see Table 4.9).

Thirdly, oil products, which rose more quickly in price than other sources of energy, account for a differing proportion of energy consumption in individual countries. However, even this cannot explain the greater spread of inflation rates since the first oil price shock, any more than different degrees of success in reducing oil's share of energy consumption (see Table 4.9).

The fourth and final question is whether differences in countries' dependence on imported oil and other energy sources can help explain price developments. The answer to that question is again negative, for neither the share of energy imports in total energy consumption, nor the proportion of oil imports in total energy imports, nor the coverage of total energy requirements by oil imports nor changes in these relationships after 1973 bear any significant correlation to changes in inflation rates in the countries under examination (see Table 4.9).

Differences in the intensity of energy-related structural characteristics cannot therefore adequately explain why the break that occured in price developments everywhere after the

Table 4.9:   RELATIONSHIP BETWEEN ENERGY (OIL) DEPENDENCY
AND INFLATION IN WESTERN INDUSTRIAL COUNTRIES[a]

	1973-75	1978-81	1973-81
Energy coefficient[b]	0.38	0.02	0.33 (-0.08)
Oil consumption as proportion of total energy consumption	0.14	0.32	0.07 (0.01)
Energy requirements covered by imports[c]	0.16	0.27	0.04 (-0.13)
Oil imports as proportion of total energy imports[d]	-0.19	-0.03	-0.26 (-0.29)
Energy requirements covered by oil imports[e]	0.45	0.23	0.03 (-0.04)

a Simple correlation of various indicators of energy (oil) dependency
for 1973 (1978) with the increase in annual inflation rates from 1973 to
1973-75 (column 1), 1978 to 1978-81 (column 2) and 1965-73 to 1973-81 (column 3). The values in parenthesis in column 3 are correlations of the
accleration in inflation after 1973 with changes in energy (oil) dependency between 1973 and 1980. Countries concerned: OECD excluding Greece,
Iceland, Luxembourg, Portugal, Spain and Turkey.

b Energy consumption per unit of GDP.

c Net energy imports as a percentage of energy consumption.

d Net oil imports as a percentage of net energy imports.

e Net oil imports as a percentage of energy consumption.

Source: OECD: Energy Balances; OECD: National Accounts; calculations by the authors.

first oil price shock differed so widely from country to country.

One reason might be that oil prices rose to differing degrees in the various countries. The range of oil price changes was indeed wide. Apart from the fact that those countries with substantial oil deposits of their own pursue different price strategies for domestic oil - for example, Canada has "uncoupled" the national oil price from world market prices, whereas the United Kingdom and the USA exercise no price controls - movements in import prices for crude oil differ considerably. This is shown by Table 4.10, which relates to the fourteen countries for which such data are available for the years from 1973 to 1981[13]. For example, oil prices in Italy in 1981 were nearly 20 times as high as before the first oil price shock, whereas in Switzerland they rose "only" sixfold. Germany and Austria also recorded a relatively small increase, whereas the United Kingdom, Ireland and the USA experienced a steep rise in the cost of oil imports. The differences in the increase in oil prices correspond closely to the differences in general price developments, the correlation coefficient being 0.95.[14]

In interpreting these results, however, it should be borne in mind that the different rates of change in oil import prices largely reflect the movements in exchange rates in the period under examination.[15] These in turn are strongly influenced by economic policy.[16]

Hence, it seems that the explanation for the wide divergences in price developments - to the extent that they are attributable to the rise in oil prices - lies less in structural differences and uneven external influences than primarily in different economic policy responses to the oil price

Table 4.10: IMPORT PRICES FOR CRUDE OIL IN INDUSTRIAL COUNTRIES, 1973-1981[a]

- 1972 = 100 -

	1973	1974	1975	1976	1977	1978	1979	1980	1981
Belgium	111.6	331.8	347.0	386.7	389.3	351.3	434.3	700.3	1020.9
Federal Rep. of Germany	114.1	310.0	308.0	338.0	338.2	293.1	386.7	630.7	857.8
Denmark	112.1	319.6	340.3	346.1	366.9	366.8	501.5	882.9	1257.6
Finland	117.4	367.0	358.5	381.5	436.9	460.5	653.3	1008.3	1291.9
France	102.8	330.8	345.9	400.5	438.8	417.3	507.8	894.3	1296.2
United Kingdom	130.7	385.2	433.0	587.5	662.6	608.0	720.4	1088.6	1414.8
Ireland	101.1	363.6	434.1	943.2	604.5	619.3	722.7	1193.2	1558.0
Italy	139.5	341.0	361.9	481.1	551.4	539.3	712.8	1249.1	1912.4
Japan	98.7	407.3	456.2	483.7	472.2	373.8	537.1	975.3	1062.1
Netherlands	107.9	313.2	327.9	373.5	367.4	327.0	430.2	711.9	988.0
Austria	117.0	327.2	295.7	321.5	319.0	283.8	384.4	608.1	836.5
Sweden	109.7	324.5	339.2	356.6	395.4	425.8	575.1	928.4	1216.3
Switzerland	119.2	298.7	269.6	271.8	278.0	218.0	298.2	478.0	648.0
USA	124.9	425.9	441.4	476.7	510.9	565.8	784.4	1289.6	1451.8

a Import unit values in national currency.

Source: OECD: Statistics of Foreign Trade; calculations by the authors.

197

shock and the different reactions of economic operators. Finally, this raises the question of the scope and limits for stabilisation policy in times of real increases in oil prices.

c.   Stabilisation policy in times of rising oil prices

Even those countries that place high priority on stability will find it almost impossible to prevent massive real increases in oil prices from having some once-for-all effect on the price level.[17] To do so, monetary policy would have to block an increase in overall nominal demand at a time of rising oil prices. At the same time, unavoidable price rises, in particular for oil products and oil substitutes, must be offset by price reductions (or reduced price increases) for other goods, especially those for which consumers reduce their demand because they are using a larger proportion of their income to acquire the goods that have become more expensive. This also means that nominal wage reductions must be possible. If the system of prices and wages does not meet this flexibility requirement, a decline in production and employment will be the inevitable result.

It can be shown empirically by examples from many industrial sectors that a weakening of demand affects prices only after a considerable time-lag, whereas cost increases caused by external shocks are immediately passed on in prices.[18] This assymmetry in pricing behaviour sets bounds to stabilisation policies. A monetary and credit policy that allowed no additional financing margin in the event of a sharp increase in the cost of oil could lead to heavy losses in production and employment without ensuring success in the search for stability. It must be asked, however, how high is the price level effect of real oil price rises that is acceptable from the point of view of stabilisation policy.

The upper limit is obviously set by the rise in the general
level of costs as a result of rising oil prices. The OECD
offers a simple formula for calculating the maximum effect:
the rise in energy prices is first multiplied by its weight
in the consumer price index. To this direct impact are then
added the indirect effects owing to increased energy input
prices being passed on in output prices. In the case of the
oil price shocks suffered so far, the OECD estimates these
at about 50 % of the direct impact of the rise in energy
costs (OECD 1980, p. 44).

Applied to the seven leading Western industrial countries,
the formula shows that between 1978 and 1981 a substantial
part of the rise in the general level of consumer prices in
these countries was an "unavoidable" consequence of the increase in the cost of energy. The proportion was highest in
the Federal Republic of Germany (21 %) and lowest in Italy
(7 %). If the changes in inflation rates between 1978 and
1981 are taken instead of the rates themselves, even higher
proportions are obtained, as was to be expected (see Table
4.11).

Such calculations must, however, be hedged round with qual-
ifications. They must not mislead one into thinking that
price rises for energy may simply be added, as exogenous inflationary impulses, to a basic rate of inflation which proceeds at a predetermined, unalterable rate. This would imply
a downward stickiness of prices and wages even in relative
terms. As the GATT Secretariat rightly states, "there is no
basis for such an assertion, which - if true - would amount
to an abdication of government responsibility in the face
of inflation" (GATT International Trade 1978/79, p. 15).

Table 4.11: THE "CONTRIBUTION" OF ENERGY PRICES TOWARDS
THE TOTAL RISE IN THE PRICES OF CONSUMER GOODS
IN WESTERN INDUSTRIAL COUNTRIES, 1978-1981[a]

in percentages

	1978	1979	1980	1981	1978-81[b]
USA	9.2	9.7	12.6	14.4	28.6
Canada	7.8	6.5	7.9	12.1	23.5
Japan	-2.6	5.9	32.5	10.2	54.5
Federal Rep. of Germany	8.0	39.0	14.5	18.6	26.5
France	7.7	15.9	19.9	14.9	30.2
United Kingdom	7.2	6.0	10.6	13.4	27.8
Italy	4.1	5.4	10.8	6.2	9.5

a See the text for an explanation of the method of calculation.

b Share of energy prices in the rise in inflation rates between 1978 and 1981.

Source: OECD: Main Economic Indicators; calculations by the authors.

Moreover, a monetary policy that merely acknowledges the rigidity of price and wage structures could arouse inflation expectations and thereby jeopardise the prime objective of stabilisation policy in times of rising oil prices, namely to prevent a price-led wage/price spiral.

A rough indicator of the general inflationary adjustment of prices and wages after an increase in the price of oil is the change in the GDP deflator. This measure does not include price increases for imported intermediate inputs nor does it reflect price changes in those imported goods, such as petrol, that are put directly to their final use in the country. Under flexible exchange rates, changes in the GDP deflator are therefore attributable mainly to domestic factors.[19] The following picture emerges for the OECD as a whole (see Table 4.12):

- during the first oil crisis domestic output rose in price by 12 % (1974), twice the rate recorded before the oil price shock (1972). In the same period "imported" inflation rose from -0.4 to 4.0 %, so that about 60 % of the additional price rise for all goods and services produced and consumed by residents was "home-grown";

- during the period between the two oil crises (1976-78) domestically generated inflationary pressure eased, aided by price-dampening effects from abroad. Nevertheless, the rise in the price of domestic production was about a third higher than in the early seventies;

- during the second oil crisis (1978-80) home-grown inflation again accelerated, again accounting for 60 % of the change in the total price rise.

Developments in the individual OECD countries differed considerably, as Table 4.12 shows for each of the seven leading members of the group. The range of "home-grown" inflation rates is reflected in the standard deviation of the GDP deflator, which rose steeply during the two oil crises and was also markedly above the pre-crisis level in the interim period (see Table 4.13).

An important cause of the acceleration in "home-grown" inflation after an increase in oil prices is the accentuation of the battle for shares of the reduced pool of real income. The development of unit wage costs can throw initial light on this.

Chart 10 shows that the rate of increase in unit labour costs in manufacturing industry in the seven largest Western industrial countries together accelerated considerably during the

Table 4.12: IMPORTED AND "HOME-GROWN" INFLATION IN THE PRINCIPAL WESTERN INDUSTRIAL COUNTRIES, 1972 - 1981[a]

- percentage rates -

	Imported inflation										Home-grown inflation									
	1972	1973	1974	1975	1976	1977	1978	1979	1980	1981	1972	1973	1974	1975	1976	1977	1978	1979	1980	1981
USA	0.2	0.8	3.0	0.1	-0.2	0.3	-0.1	0.8	1.2	-0.8	4.2	5.8	8.7	9.3	5.2	5.8	7.4	8.5	9.0	9.5
Canada	-0.4	-0.4	0.9	0.8	-1.6	1.0	1.5	0.7	1.0	0.2	5.1	9.2	15.5	10.7	9.4	7.2	6.4	10.7	10.7	10.1
Japan	-0.7	0.6	5.3	0.1	-0.1	-1.1	-1.8	2.8	3.8	-0.4	5.2	11.9	20.7	7.8	6.4	5.6	4.6	2.5	3.2	2.9
Federal Republic of Germany	-0.8	0.5	2.7	-1.1	0.3	-0.5	-1.1	1.1	1.4	1.1	5.6	6.0	6.8	6.7	3.3	3.8	3.7	3.8	4.8	4.3
France	-1.1	-0.1	5.7	-2.2	-0.2	0.3	-1.4	0.1	0.7	1.1	6.2	7.7	11.2	13.4	9.9	8.9	9.5	10.1	11.7	11.7
United Kingdom	-1.0	3.4	6.9	-2.9	1.6	0.0	-1.7	-1.6	-1.9	-1.3	8.3	7.0	15.0	26.9	14.7	14.0	10.9	15.1	18.9	12.0
Italy	-0.4	2.5	8.0	-2.1	1.3	-0.4	-2.1	0.4	0.4	2.2	6.3	11.5	18.5	17.5	18.0	19.1	13.9	15.7	20.4	17.6
Memorandum:																				
OECD	-0.4	0.6	4.0	-0.6	0.0	0.0	-0.9	0.9	1.5	0.1	5.7	7.8	11.8	11.1	7.9	8.2	8.3	9.4	11.8	10.9
EEC	-1.1	0.9	5.2	-1.8	0.4	-0.3	-1.6	0.2	0.6	0.8	6.7	7.8	11.3	13.6	9.8	9.7	8.6	9.8	12.3	10.9

a   See footnote 10 for an explanation of the method of calculation.

Source: OECD: National Accounts; calculations by the authors.

Table 4.13: DISPERSION OF IMPORTED AND "HOME-GROWN" INFLATION RATES AMONG INDUSTRIAL COUNTRIES, 1972-1981[a]

	Imported inflation			Home-grown inflation		
	Average[b]	Standard deviation	Coefficient of variation	Average[b]	Standard deviation	Coefficient of variation
1972	-1.1	0.9	-0.8	7.3	2.3	0.3
1973	0.3	1.2	4.0	9.4	2.7	0.3
1974	5.0	2.8	0.6	12.3	5.1	0.4
1975	-0.2	2.3	-11.5	12.2	6.1	0.5
1976	-0.2	1.2	- 6.0	10.4	5.2	0.5
1977	0.1	0.1	1.0	8.3	4.5	0.5
1978	-1.1	1.2	-1.1	7.6	3.0	0.4
1979	1.1	1.0	0.9	8.2	4.6	0.6
1980	1.6	1.5	0.9	9.7	5.1	0.5
1981	0.7	1.7	2.4	9.9	4.3	0.4

a OECD excluding Greece, Iceland, Portugal, Spain and Turkey. See footnote 10 with regard to the calculation of the components of inflation.

b Unweighted arithmetic mean.

Source: OECD: National Accounts; calculations by the authors.

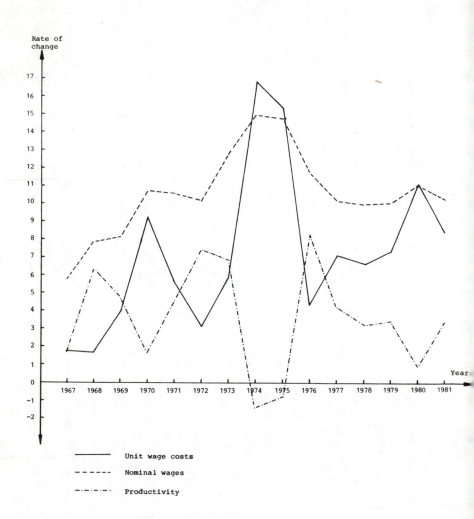

Source: OECD: Economic Outlook, Historical Statistics.

two oil crises. This development was partly the result of
steep rises in nominal wages, but it also reflects a dramatic slowdown in the rate of productivity increase. The
discrepancy between wage and productivity trends was particularly great during the first oil crisis, when a rate of
productivity increase of 7 % (1973) gave way to a decrease
of 1 % (1974). At the same time, the rate of increase in
wages accelerated from 13 to 15 %, so that in 1974 unit labour costs rose almost three times as fast as in the preceding year. In the second oil crisis wage cost pressure was
weaker, but during this phase too falling productivity growth
rates coincided with higher nominal wage increases. The developments in individual countries are presented in table 4.14.

A more accurate measure of the inflationary pressure generated internally after an increase in the price of oil can be
obtained if the movements in unit wage costs in the two oil
crises and in the interim period from 1975 to 1978 are set
in relation to the rise in the GDP deflator in a "normal"
reference period. The results calculated for the seven largest industrial countries are summarised in Table 4.15. The
period from 1968 to 1973 serves as the reference period for
the first oil shock and the years before the second. The annual rate of inflation during this period is therefore regarded as the norm to which the economy was accustomed at
that time. The "home-grown" rate of price increase between
the oil shocks is the reference figure against which changes
in unit wage costs in the second crisis are measured.

The table shows that immediately after the first jump in the
oil price unit wage costs in the seven countries together increased almost three times as fast as the GDP price deflator
during the pre-crisis period. The discrepancy was particular-

Table 4.14: MOVEMENTS IN NOMINAL WAGES, PRODUCTIVITY AND UNIT WAGE COSTS IN MANUFACTURING INDUSTRY IN THE SEVEN LARGEST INDUSTRIAL COUNTRIES, 1970-1981

- in percentages -

		1970	1971	1972	1973	1974	1975	1976	1977	1978	1979	1980	1981
USA	NW	5.1	6.3	7.0	7.1	8.3	9.0	8.1	8.8	8.7	8.5	8.7	9.8
	P	-3.0	7.6	7.5	5.5	-3.8	0.0	4.8	3.3	1.1	0.0	-1.7	2.8
	UWC	6.9	0.0	0.4	1.6	13.3	8.8	3.4	5.7	7.4	9.0	11.5	7.2
Canada	NW	7.9	9.0	7.9	8.8	13.5	15.8	13.7	10.9	7.2	8.8	10.1	12.0
	P	1.2	5.2	4.9	5.0	0.9	-1.5	3.0	3.3	1.5	0.1	-5.5	1.0
	UWC	6.1	0.5	2.6	3.7	13.4	17.1	8.4	6.7	5.0	8.3	12.8	10.7
Japan	NW	17.8	13.8	15.6	23.5	26.1	11.5	12.2	8.6	5.9	7.3	7.5	5.6
	P	15.9	5.7	10.6	9.1	-0.9	1.8	13.4	7.7	8.5	9.4	8.0	5.2
	UWC	5.3	9.1	3.8	11.0	28.1	12.6	-2.4	2.4	-1.8	-2.1	0.2	4.0
Federal Rep. of Germany	NW	12.4	13.4	8.5	9.8	12.0	9.1	5.6	7.5	4.6	5.2	6.0	5.5
	P	2.4	1.7	5.0	6.2	1.1	0.7	9.0	2.9	1.5	4.1	0.1	1.4
	UWC	14.3	7.8	4.0	6.4	9.1	6.8	0.6	5.3	5.0	2.4	7.1	4.7
France	NW	10.5	11.2	11.3	14.6	19.3	17.3	14.1	12.7	12.9	13.0	15.1	14.5
	P	6.5	5.2	5.3	4.9	2.3	0.7	8.2	4.2	4.8	4.4	1.2	0.6
	UWC	6.7	6.1	5.4	8.2	15.5	15.4	5.5	8.2	6.6	8.5	14.7	14.7
United Kingdom	NW	10.1	12.5	13.8	12.9	17.1	30.0	19.8	4.7	18.2	15.0	17.2	9.7
	P	0.6	2.4	6.0	8.5	-1.7	-2.2	5.4	1.2	1.1	1.3	-4.2	5.6
	UWC	13.0	10.2	5.0	5.0	24.0	32.6	12.6	10.9	12.8	15.0	22.9	9.7
Italy	NW	21.7	13.5	10.4	24.2	22.4	26.7	20.9	27.9	16.2	19.0	22.5	23.7
	P	5.5	0.0	5.7	9.8	3.3	-10.2	13.0	4.4	2.9	6.7	4.6	0.7
	UWC	14.3	11.9	5.7	12.9	18.9	34.8	10.4	17.6	11.2	9.6	12.1	18.2
Together	NW	10.8	10.6	10.2	12.9	15.0	14.8	11.8	10.2	10.0	10.1	11.1	10.3
	P	1.7	4.6	7.5	6.9	-1.3	-0.8	8.3	4.3	3.3	3.5	1.0	3.4
	UWC	9.3	5.7	3.2	5.9	16.9	15.4	4.4	7.2	6.7	7.4	11.2	8.5

NW = nominal wages (basic rates), P = productivity (real value added per person employed), UWC = unit wage costs.

Source: OECD: Economic Outlook, Historical Statistics.

Table 4.15: INFLATIONARY PRESSURE FROM UNIT WAGE COSTS, 1974 - 1981[a]

- in percentages -

	1974	1975	1976	1977	1978	1979	1980	1981
USA	255.8	169.2	65.4	109.6	142.3	140.6	179.7	112.5
Canada	252.8	322.6	158.5	126.4	94.3	107.8	166.2	139.0
Japan	407.2	182.6	-34.8	34.8	-26.1	-38.9	- 3.7	74.1
Federal Rep. of Germany	146.8	109.7	9.7	85.5	80.6	63.2	186.8	123.7
France	242.2	240.6	85.9	128.1	103.1	90.4	156.4	156.4
United Kingdom	320.0	434.7	168.0	145.3	170.7	113.6	173.5	73.5
Italy	262.5	483.3	144.4	244.4	155.6	56.5	71.2	107.1
Together	291.4	265.5	75.9	124.1	115.5	100.0	151.4	114.9

a See the text for an explanation of the method of calculation.

Source: OECD: Economic Outlook, Historical Statistics; calculations by the authors.

207

ly pronounced in Japan, whereas in Germany developments still came closest to meeting the stability requirement.

In 1975 the wage cost pressure continued practically unabated despite a slower rise in energy prices. From this it must be concluded that it was high rates of price increase of the previous year rather than the "historical" rate of inflation that had the decisive influence on wage settlements. This appears to be particularly true of Italy and the United Kingdom. In these two countries unit wage costs rose far faster than was consistent with stability even in the remaining years of the interim period. In some countries, by contrast, and particularly in Japan, inflationary pressure subsided considerably during this phase.

In the second oil crisis the movement in unit wage costs was again totally at odds with stability, far exceeding the average rise of the GDP deflator in the period from 1975 to 1978. It is conspicuous that on this occasion, in contrast to the first oil crisis, Germany experienced a strong wage push but in Japan it was weak.

In view of such developments, the task of stabilisation policy at times of real oil price increases consists primarily in making employers and trade unions more acutely aware that the adverse real income effect of a rise in the price of oil cannot be avoided. From the point of view of incomes policy this means a clear rejection of wage indexation mechanisms tied to changes in consumer prices. Moreover, monetary policy must make it credible that the acceptance of a nonrecurring price surge does not mean the fundamental abandonment of a policy oriented towards stability, for in fact inflation does not solve the problems, it only makes them worse. Renunciation of recessionary pressure at the outset could be bought only

at the cost of possibly much more severe stabilisation measures later. Moreover, inflationary price increases have un-
controllable effects on income distribution and, if exchange
rate adjustment is insufficient, impair the country's international competitiveness. In addition, there is a danger of
distortions in resource allocation, since in times of high
inflation domestic price relations do not correctly reflect
the changed economic circumstances. The real adjustment to
dearer oil can therefore be seriously delayed.

3. Implications for the German monetary and exchange rate
   policy

After the first oil crisis the exchange rate aspect had initially little or no importance for monetary policy in the
Federal Republic of Germany. There were many reasons for
this. Firstly, the Deutsche Mark showed a persistently strong
tendency to appreciate after the beginning of floating in
spring 1973. With large balance of payments surpluses on current account in spite of rising oil prices, even the temporary dip in the exchange rate did not arouse lasting expectation of depreciation and was therefore no cause for concern.
Secondly, the Deutsche Mark was not yet an international investment and reserve currency to the extent that it would
later become. As a result, monetary policy was largely free
from exchange rate constraints and could concentrate on the
problem of how to counter the imported inflation and the danger to general price stability caused by the oil price rise.
The first point to investigate concerns the limitations to
which monetary policy is generally subject in such a situation owing to the country's domestic economic circumstances.

Although the primary responsibility of the Deutsche Bundesbank is to safeguard the value of the currency, it must also take account of the impact of oil price increases on national income and employment and the effect of its policy
on domestic economic policy.[20] Past experience has shown
that this can very easily lead to a conflict of aims. Curbing an acceleration in the rate of inflation basically requires a restrictive monetary policy, in other words a slowdown in money supply growth. On the other hand, if the Bundesbank wishes to counteract a fall in the general level of
demand and the associated risk of a decline in employment
caused by oil price increases and to engineer a gradual ad-

justment of the economy to changed circumstances, it would
have to expand the money supply in order to bring down interest rates and thus offer an incentive for increasing
production and new investment, even at the risk that the additional liquidity would also provide scope for further
price rises.

Thus, in times of rising oil prices, monetary policy is faced with the following controversial questions:

- should it only combat "home-made" price increases or
  imported inflation due to rising oil prices as well?
- should it continue to guide the money supply along its
  potential path as in the past, or should it deviate from
  it at least temporarily in order to enable the economy
  to adjust gradually to changed circumstances?

As will be shown, the answer to these questions depends on
the economic and policy conditions facing the central bank;
it is differences in the assessment of these initial conditions and of the scope for monetary action they afford that
give rise to the current disagreements on the "right" monetary policy course in times of rising oil prices.

The Bundesbank gave priority to the fight against inflation
after both oil crises.[21] In both instances it was faced with
the problem that the rate of price increase at home had already accelerated before the onset of the crisis (see Emminger 1980, pp. 118 f). The Bank therefore justified its restrictive policy primarily with the argument that it wished
to combat "home-made" inflation, to give as little scope as
possible for passing on oil price rises and hence to limit
their indirect influence on domestic prices.[22] It was aware

of the danger of adverse employment effects associated with such a policy, but held the view that a less restrictive monetary policy could not prevent but only postpone such effects, pointing repeatedly to the experience of other industrial countries, particularly after the first oil crisis.[23] It feared that toleration of higher rates of price increases would set a wage/price spiral in motion which would cause corporate profits to contract, undermine confidence in the value of the currency and increase both unemployment and inflation. In 1974 these fears did not appear unjustified, in view of the relatively high inflation rate of 7 %, large budget deficits and wage claims of between 15 and 18 % (see Gutowski,Härtel, Scharrer 1981, pp. 61 ff.).

This attitude is not without its critics, however. After the first oil crisis the Bundesbank was blamed in various circles for having brought on the recession, which was already looming in 1974, or having at least accentuated it by being too slow and hesitant in reversing its monetary policy.[24] This accusation should be assessed in the light of the special economic policy situation in which Germany found itself from spring 1973 to the end of 1974,[25] and especially of the effects that a more expansionary monetary policy would have had on inflationary expectations in such circumstances (see Schlesinger 1978, p. 19).

In spring 1973 the German economy was already suffering a cyclical bout of inflation and various domestic and external factors were contributing to increased inflationary expectations. First, the prevailing rate of inflation was felt to be unusually high in comparison with previous years, so that practically no one expected it to fall in the immediate future. Until spring 1973 the strong upward tendency of the Deutsche Mark and the central bank's consequent obligation

to intervene in the foreign exchange market tied the Bundesbank's hands in the fight against inflation, so that a sta-
bility-oriented monetary policy lacked credibility. Secondly, the Government's expansionary fiscal policy, the large
budget deficit and aggressive wage claims by the unions suggested that inflation was likely to rise further. Inflationary expectations were boosted further by the increase in oil
prices in autumn 1973. In such a situation, the Bundesbank
had practically no alternative but to begin by breaking these
expectations by means of shock therapy, in other words by
persevering with the decidedly restrictive monetary course
upon which it had already embarked.

Had the economic policy climate been different, a more expansionary monetary policy might have been conceivable. An important question in this regard is whether inflationary expectations already exist before a rise in oil prices and, if
this is not the case, whether an expansion in the money supply will itself give rise to such expectations. The latter
will occur particularly in conditions of full employment. In
an underemployed economy with spare production capacity, on
the other hand, a moderately expansionary monetary policy
can also be seen as a signal that the central bank wishes to
contribute to an economic recovery and is preparing the necessary monetary conditions. The concomitant reduction of interest rates will stimulate private demand and give firms an
incentive to expand production and make new investment (see
Pohl 1980, p. 57). In these circumstances, inflationary expectations do not arise until employment and the capacity
utilisation rate increase. In this situation it would therefore make sense to allow the money supply to rise initially
when oil prices increase so that the economy has room to adjust smoothly to the changed circumstances, and only later

to reduce money supply growth gradually in order to counteract inflationary expectations and price rises as they develop.

How far and how long the Bundesbank should tolerate the effects of rising oil prices on the domestic price level therefore depends on the economic and policy conditions prevailing before the oil price rise. These include the capacity
utilisation rate in industry and the employment situation
as well as the existence of inflationary expectations, the
trade unions' incomes policy and the level of the budget
deficit, in other words the government's claim on the gross
national product.

In addition, the Bundesbank must pay regard to exchange rate
considerations, which determine whether and on what conditions its chosen monetary strategy can be implemented. Its
freedom of action is now circumscribed by two factors.
First, membership of the European Monetary System obliges
the Bundesbank to maintain the exchange rate of the Deutsche
Mark within narrow margins of fluctuation against other member currencies by means of market intervention. Secondly,
the Deutsche Mark has gained increasing importance as an
international investment and reserve currency in recent
years.[26]

The enhanced importance of the Mark in international financial markets has led to an increase in the degree of capital mobility and, more and more, domestic and foreign securities can be regarded as close substitutes. This means
that the link with interest rates abroad has grown closer,
particularly with regard to US interest rates.[27] Hence interest rate changes at home or abroad trigger international
capital movements and corresponding shifts in exchange

rates on a far larger scale than in earlier years. This increasingly restricts the Bundesbank's freedom of action. For example, if it attempts to reduce domestic interest rates by expanding the money supply while interest rates abroad remain unchanged, it encourages capital outflows that cause the exchange rate of the Mark to decline. If it does not wish to allow this exchange rate movement, it must buy its own currency in exchange market interventions. However, this tends to neutralise the desired money supply effect, so that domestic interest rates either do not decrease at all or fall by less than intended.

International asset holders do not reach their investment decisions on the basis of absolute interest rate differentials but the differential adjusted for the difference between the prevailing exchange rate and that expected in future. If the spread of international interest rates is narrow, the Bundesbank has, in principle, two options if it wishes to maintain a degree of latitude for domestic monetary policy. It can tolerate the change in the exchange rate, which is caused by the international capital movements and which eliminates the adjusted interest rate differential. However, if it also wishes to hold the exchange rate of the Mark constant, it can attempt to exert a positive influence on exchange rate expectations. If private investors assume that the Mark exchange rate will rise in future, they will purchase DM securities in Germany despite lower interest rates provided they expect the future rise in the exchange rate to be larger than the interest rate differential, in other words if the appreciation gain exceeds the foregone interest.[28] Hence, strong expectations of an appreciating Mark broaden the Bundesbank's scope for reducing interest rates.

After the second oil crisis exchange rate aspects shifted
increasingly to the forefront of monetary policy considerations in Germany. The economic policy conditions facing
the Bundesbank were quite different from those experienced
at the time of the first crisis. Domestic inflation posed
less of a threat, as there was little evidence of rising
inflationary expectations, a situation for which budgetary
and incomes policies were responsible in equal measure.[29]
Whereas in the wake of the first oil price rise monetary
policy gave priority to curbing the high rate of "home-
grown" inflation, after the second oil crisis its chief concern was to prevent oil price increases from being passed
on. For this purpose a less restrictive course of action
than in 1974 would have been feasible. However, the Bundesbank's room for manoeuvre was severely restricted by the
changed external parameters, so that it was faced with an
almost permanent conflict between domestic and external
requirements.

The main exchange rate constraint stemmed from the persistent depreciation of the Mark against the dollar, which was
attributable essentially to two factors. First, Germany's
current account showed a large deficit for the first time
after the second oil price shock; this had a lasting effect
on DM exchange rate expectations and constituted an incentive for capital outflows. However, such an incentive was
also created by high interest rates in the USA, which came
about as a result of the switch to money-supply management
and the change of Administration.

The weakness of the Mark after the second oil crisis caused
the Bundesbank to adopt a more restrictive monetary policy
than would have been necessary in the light of domestic
requirements. In doing so it constantly stressed the need

216

to finance oil-induced current account deficits "in the market" via capital inflows. It did not consider itself in a
position to expend unlimited amounts of foreign exchange
reserves for purposes of deficit financing, but on the
other hand it was not prepared either to tolerate the threat
of a fairly substantial depreciation of the Mark that accompanied the balance of payments deficit or higher domestic inflation, as it feared the repercussions of such an exchange
rate development on the domestic price level.[30] However,
market financing of the current account deficit was unlikely, given the expectations in the foreign exchange markets
and the high level of interest rates in the USA.

The Bundesbank believed it could best counter this situation by bringing down the inflation rate at home in order
to strengthen confidence in the currency and to encourage
international investors to place increasing funds in the
Mark.[31] It therefore intended to influence private investors' expectations of future exchange rate trends and for
that purpose ascribed central importance to inflation differentials at home and abroad. As exchange rate changes tend
to equalize inflation rates in the long run, the currency
of a country with a relatively high level of price stability is generally regarded as a candidate for revaluation
provided exchange-rate-adjusted inflation differentials
persist. In this case, capital inflows occur. According to
this reasoning, it is quite clear that the Bundesbank will
initially pursue a restrictive policy in order to combat
inflation when oil prices rise, and only when this policy
produces results will it expand the money supply to stimulate economic activity.

The question nevertheless arises whether inflation differentials really determine the expectations of private inves-

tors to such an extent or whether other factors are equally important, at least in the short run, and if so, how monetary policy can influence them. Two aspects have been disregarded in the reasoning thus far. Firstly, past experience has shown that exchange rate trends do not necessarily reflect inflation differentials, even over fairly long time spans,[32] so that they have only a limited effect on exchange rate expectations. Other factors - such as economic and fiscal policies at home and abroad, balance of payments developments or cyclical trends - are equally important influences on exchange rates and hence on the formation of expectations in the period of relevance for monetary policy decisions. Secondly, expectations are strongly influenced by short-term factors such as day-to-day events on the economic and political fronts, but also by the actions of the central bank itself. For example, if the foreign exchange markets expect an easing of German monetary policy and falling interest rates in Germany, this might arouse expectations of a depreciation of the Mark that automatically constrict the scope for monetary policy.

The extent to which the Bundesbank can persuade individuals to expect an appreciation of the Mark is therefore strictly limited. If it attempts to reduce domestic interest rates in order to dampen the effects of rising oil prices on economic activity and to create the monetary conditions for a gradual adjustment to the changed situation, it might in certain circumstances have to accept that the exchange rate of the Mark will decline and lead to a further acceleration in the rate of inflation. These consequences can be avoided only if other factors, such as an economic recovery abroad accompanied by a perceivable or presumptive increase in German exports, in themselves cause a rise in the actual or expected exchange rate.

Bundesbank policy can also be constrained by membership of
the European Monetary System, which permits the Deutsche
Mark to fluctuate only within narrow margins. Hence even
if the Bundesbank decides to reduce interest rates and,
for a short time at least, to tolerate the inflationary effects of the resulting depreciation of the Mark, it is not
only the Mark/dollar exchange rate that is affected. If the
other member states of the EMS hold to their previous policy, the DM will also weaken against the other EMS currencies. If the Mark reaches the lower intervention point, the
Bundesbank is obliged to intervene.

This latter aspect has played a secondary role up to now,
however. The policies of partner countries that do not give
absolute priority to the fight against inflation tend to be
more expansionary than German monetary policy. Hence, if the
Bundesbank decides to reduce interest rates, the other countries will usually follow suit and there will be little
change in exchange rate relations within the system. Furthermore, it should be borne in mind that the Deutsche Mark en-
joys a "stability bonus" within the EMS. A devaluation of
the Mark is generally regarded as practically impossible and
any temporary weakening of the rate rarely creates expectations of a devaluation, even if the currency sinks to the
lower margin.

To summarise, it must be said that there is no clear answer
to the question of how monetary policy should generally re-
act to rising oil prices. Given the possible domestic and
external limitations on its freedom of action, the Bundesbank should steer a middle course: the direct price impact
of the rise in oil prices should largely be tolerated, but
where possible any knock-on effects on domestic costs and
prices should be prevented or at least curbed inasfar as
domestic and external conditions allow.

With an eye to influences on economic policy at home, such as
the incomes policy of the trade unions or the level of government borrowing, the Bundesbank rightly and repeatedly stresses
that economic growth and employment cannot be assured by monetary means alone during the process of adjustment to rising
oil prices[33] 'nor can it be the Bank's primary function. However, whenever the economic situation and the exchange rate
allow, it should pursue the objective of price stability only gradually and taking into account the income and employment effects stemming from its policy. With respect to inflationary and exchange rate expectations that rising oil prices
usually engender, it is vitally important that the Bank pur-
sues a clear policy at all times and makes its intentions
clear so that economic agents are not left in uncertainty
owing to ambiguity about the monetary stance. This would only further impede the process of real economic adjustment.

Footnotes to Chapter 4

1 The income elasticity of demand for petroleum products appears to have decreased after the first oil shock, however. The coefficients of elasticity calculated for the period 1960–72 and for the entire period under examination (1960–81) are considerably higher than those for the years from 1973 to 1981 both in absolute terms and in relation to the coefficients for total energy (see Tables A-3 and A-4).

2 The close overall relation between the prices of crude oil and those of oil products is confirmed by correlation estimates. A simple correlation, for example, between the price index for crude oil imports and petroleum products in the Federal Republic of Germany gives a correlation coefficient of 0.98 on the basis of data for the period from 1964 to 1981. However, there is no fixed relationship whereby crude oil price increases of a given magnitude cause changes of a given size in the prices of individual petroleum products. For the example of fuel prices, see inter alia Schmitt, Gommersbach 1982.

3 Price developments on world markets have been as follows since 1978, calculated on a dollar basis (1975 = 100):

	Raw materials excluding energy	Energy	Industrial goods
1978	114	118	125
1979	139	161	142
1980	158	266	157
1981	136	302	151
1982	118	293	147[a]

a Western industrial countries only.

Source: HWWA: Weltkonjunkturdienst; UN: Monthly Bulletin of Statistics.

4 Between 1973 and 1975 the cost of petrochemical inputs and energy more or less doubled, raising their share of total production costs to 70 % (Grilli 1981, p. 28).

5 At the same time, total demand for rubber products may be dampened by the industry's high dependence on the production of motor vehicles – more than 65 % of the entire output of rubber is used in the motor industry for tyres and other components – so that annual growth of only 1–1.5 % is expected for the next 10 to 15 years (Grilli 1981, p. 28).

6 Already half of all metallic ores is now mined in Western industrial countries, including South Africa (Die Zeit, 7.5.1982).

7 This may partly be a reciprocal relationship. M. Parkin even considers it possible that "the rapid money supply rates of the late 1960s and early 1970s were the cause both of the rise in inflation and rise in the price of oil in 1973" (Parkin 1980, p. 185). Former Chancellor Helmut Schmidt is rather more cautious when he writes that "inflation

and inflationary expectations prepared the ground for the explosive imposition of higher prices by the OPEC cartel" (Die Zeit, 25.2.83).

8   Cebula, Frewer also calculate a close link between oil prices and inflation on the basis of data for six countries (Australia, Germany, the United Kingdom, Japan, Sweden and the USA) for the period from 1956 to 1978. According to them, the increase in oil prices and the dependence on imported oil explain a large part of the rise in the general level of prices in these countries, with the exception of Sweden. (In the case of Sweden the influence of oil price rises is also significant. However, as the country's import dependence does not have the expected sign, the coefficient of determination for the overall equation works out to a low figure.) The link remains significant even if the money supply and budget deficits are taken to be additional factors (Cebula, Frewer 1980).

9   The general price index is an average of wholesale and retail prices weighted by the shares of industrial and non-industrial energy consumption in total energy consumption. With regard to the statistical basis, see IMF 1981, p. 148.

In the case of the USA an econometric analysis of the general relation between changes in relative prices and the price level even comes to the conclusion that it was the rapid increase in the cost of energy and food during the seventies that led to a significant relation between these two variables. The study states in this context: "The clear impression is that a strong relation between relative price variability and inflation ... is the result of the effects of food and energy shocks" (Fischer 1981, pp. 409 and 411).

10 The calculations are based on the modified formula proposed by Härtel and Henne for splitting the inflation rate into imported and home-grown components. According to this, an increase in import prices is only imported to the extent that it exceeds the rise in the GDP deflator. The formula is as follows:

$$gP_{FU} = gP_{GDP} + (gP_M - gP_{GDP}) \times \frac{M}{FU}$$

where g = rate of growth, P = price index, GDP = gross domestic product, M = imports, FU = final use (= GDP + M). The first expression on the right-hand side of the equation represents home-grown inflation, the second the imported component. With regard to the concept, see Härtel, Henne 1982. On the measurement of imported inflation in developing countries see also Sheehey 1979.

11 With regard to the terms "impact effect" and "longer-run effect", see Parkin 1980.

12 The eleven countries for which adequate data are available are the USA, Canada, Japan, the Federal Republic of Germany, France, the United Kingdom, Denmark, Finland, Norway, Austria and Sweden. The energy-intensive sectors (with the ISIC positions in brackets) are: paper and paper products (341), chemicals (351/2), petroleum refineries (353), petrochemicals (354), ceramics (361), glass and glass products (362), other non-metallic mineral products (369), iron and

steel (371) and non-ferrous metals (372). With regard to the statistical basis, see OECD: Economic Outlook, Historical Statistics and UN: Yearbook of Industrial Statistics.

13 The prices of crude oil imports were calculated from the relevant volume and value data in the OECD foreign trade statistics. The dollar prices per tonne of imported crude oil obtained in this way could then be converted into national currency units using the conversion factors for each year.

14 Simple correlation of the rise in oil prices between 1972 and 1981 with the difference in inflation rates between 1973-81 and 1965-73.

15 Table A-8 shows that the dollar prices of imported oil moved fairly uniformly. Deviations are due in part to differences in quality. Hence the "law of one price" seems to be broadly valid on the oil markets.

16 See also in this connection a study by the OECD, which states "the fact that the extent and timing of the unwinding of inflation after the first oil shock differed so much among OECD countries can be attributed to the large dispersion in the pattern of import price changes across countries. This in turn reflected substantial changes in exchange rates which were themselves intimately bound up with the economic policies followed by OECD countries" (OECD 1982, p. 21). M. Bruno comes to a similar conclusion: "The impact of the extreme changes in domestic import costs (with varying exchange rate changes) turns out to explain most of the variations in inflation rates in countries as widely apart as Switzerland and the United Kingdom" (Bruno 1978, p. 381).

17 However, strict monetarists deny that the oil price has any influence on the price level and blame the acceleration in inflation during the seventies entirely on money supply policy. They thus overlook the fact that large changes in relative prices can radically alter the parameters of the demand-for-money function. In this regard H.P.Gray remarks: "For a disturbance which has its origin in the real sector to be analysed within a monetary framework, it is necessary for the effect of a real disturbance on the aggregate demand-for-money function to be identified: strict monetary analyses do not do this. Processes which have their origins in the real sector may be more usefully analysed in terms of an income-expenditure-price framework because such a framework identifies directly the behavioural shifts which will take place. Then the repercussions on the monetary sector and the feedback on the real sector need to be taken into account". Gray 1981, p. 52). On the strict monetarist approach, see Parkin 1980 and de Grauwe 1981.

18 The asymmetry of pricing policy reactions to real oil price increases has various causes, which need not be analysed in detail here, particularly as they can be little influenced by economic policy, at least over the short term. In a study on the accommodation of the first oil price shock in the USA Philip Cagan states that a possible cause of the "apparent asymmetry of price response" is that "demand effects may or may not cover the entire industry, whereas supply effects

generally do, and that producers make price adjustments readily when they believe competitors are similarly affected and not otherwise" (Cagan 1980, p. 3). On the general causes and consequences of an observed decline in the flexibility of the price system in Western industrial countries, see GATT 1983.

19 However, in those oil-importing countries that have notable oil deposits and other energy sources whose prices are linked to those of oil an increase in the price of oil on the world market can have a substantial effect on the GDP price deflator via the international price system.

20 See Sections 3 and 12 of the law concerning the Deutsche Bundesbank.

21 See Deutsche Bundesbank: Geschäftsbericht 1974, p. 18, and Deutsche Bundesbank: Geschäftsbericht 1980, p. 29.

22 See Deutsche Bundesbank: Geschäftsbericht 1974, p. 16, and Deutsche Bundesbank: Geschäftsbericht 1980, p. 20.

23 See Deutsche Bundesbank: Geschäftsbericht 1974, p. 18, and Schlesinger 1978, pp. 21f.

24 See for example Pohl 1980 and Deutsche Bundesbank: Geschäftsbericht 1975, p. 5

25 In this context and the following passage see also Gutowski, Härtel, Scharrer 1981, pp. 57 ff.

26 See for example Deutsche Bundesbank 1978. With regard to the ensuing implications for German monetary policy, see also Schröder 1982. The Deutsche Mark accounted for about 15.5 % of the foreign currency liabilities of European banks in 1974, 17.3 % in 1977 and as much as 19.2 % in 1979. See Bank for International Settlements, 1980-81 Annual Report.

27 See Karl-Otto Pöhl in: Die Zeit, 1.7.1983.

28 See also Karl-Otto Pöhl in: Die Zeit, 1.7.1983.

29 See also Gutowski, Härtel, Scharrer 1981.

30 See Deutsche Bundesbank: Geschäftsbericht 1979, pp. 42 f.

31 See Leonard Gleske in: Börsen-Zeitung, 7.11.1980.

32 See for example Frenkel 1981. See also Karl-Otto Pöhl in: Die Zeit, 1.7.1983.

33 See for example Deutsche Bundesbank: Geschäftsbericht 1979, pp. 43 f.

Chapter 5:   The problem of growth and structural adjust-
             ment

1.   Are real oil price increases a brake on growth?

Do real oil price rises inevitably reduce incomes and curb
growth? Developments since the first oil shock seem to suggest that the answer to that question is an unequivocal yes.
For one thing, the terms of trade of oil-importing countries
deteriorated dramatically, as did their relative income position. For another, strong recessionary tendencies appeared
in the aftermath of both oil crises.[1] During the first oil
crisis it was primarily the Western industrial countries
that had to accept a severe slowdown in economic activity,
whereas the non-oil developing countries as a whole managed
to sustain high rates of output growth by boosting their capital imports.[2] After the sharp recession in 1974 and 1975
the industrialised economies also seemed to be entering a
new phase of growth. However, the second oil price rise
suddenly checked the upswing, which gave way to a prolonged
period of stagnation. This time the oil-importing countries
of the Third World were also seriously affected.[3]

Real oil price rises are equivalent to a redistribution of
income in favour of the oil-producing countries. Oil-importing countries also suffer a reduction in real income by the
fact that imported oil is substituted by inferior or more
expensive goods.[4] These losses of income correspond to the
social valuation of oil imports foregone (Corden 1976, p. 18).

In principle, the level of employment in an economy is unaffected by these developments. At the same time, however, one
must also take account of other income effects of rising oil

prices that have repercussions on employment. The following aspects merit special attention:

- Real oil price rises can cause a deflationary gap. For example, it is conceivable that real expenditure in the oil-importing countries will decline in the same proportion as real incomes, whereas the oil-producing countries will spend only part of their additional income. In this event production and employment will decline.

- Inflationary impulses stemming from an increase in the cost of oil can force the adoption of a restrictive monetary policy, which depresses output and employment in the short term. Over the long term, however, a consistent stabilisation policy improves the opportunities for growth and employment.

- Delay in structural adjustment to dearer oil can also reduce income and employment. If enterprises lack innovation and a willingness to take risks, the opportunities afforded by an increase in the cost of oil (the development of oil-saving products and techniques, the harnessing of new sources of energy, etc.) will not be fully exploited and the transfer of income to the oil-producing countries will be higher than it need be. If workers in the industries adversely affected by rising oil prices are not willing or able to undergo retraining or to relocate, structural unemployment will develop. In theory, it could be prevented or kept within bounds by accepting a cut in wages; this would improve the sector's price competitiveness and create an incentive to substitute labour for oil. In practice, however, sectoral wage structures are rather rigid and the scope for substitution is limited.

This section deals first with the direct income losses suffered by oil-importing countries as a result of real oil price rises; it then examines the effects of rising oil prices on overall demand and finally looks at the reactions of investors, whose behaviour is a crucial element in any structural adjustment to a rise in the cost of oil.

a.   Direct losses of income as a result of real oil price
     rises

The direct income losses suffered by oil-importing countries can be gauged approximately from the growth in nominal net oil imports (crude oil plus petroleum products), adjusted for changes in export prices. In the OECD such imports increased by 50.6 billion between 1973 and 1974, an amount equivalent to 1.5 % of the total domestic product of this group of countries in 1973 (see Table 5.1). In the case of the EC the burden was substantially higher, 2.0 %. If we look at the Group of Ten countries individually, we find that Belgium, Italy, the United Kingdom and Japan were hardest hit, while Canada was the least affected; in fact, the last country even recorded a small income gain. The Federal Republic of Germany came off relatively well, with a 1.5 % loss.

The picture changes fundamentally, however, if the entire period up to the onset of the second oil crisis is considered, in other words if the average increase in net oil imports adjusted for export prices from 1973 to 1978 is set in relation to GDP for 1973. This calculation produces equally high coefficients for the OECD and the EC (0.5 %). Germany is above the average at 0.6 % and the United Kingdom well below it with a negative value (-0.1 %). The greatest impact was felt by Japan (0.8 %).

Table 5.1: DIRECT LOSSES OF INCOME SUFFERED BY WESTERN INDUSTRIALISED COUNTRIES AS A RESULT OF REAL OIL PRICE INCREASES, 1974 – 1981[a]

	US$ bn								percentage of GDP[b]							
	1974	1975	1976	1977	1978	1979	1980	1981	1974	1975	1976	1977	1978	1979	1980	1981
USA	12.8	0.4	6.6	9.1	-0.2	15.1	14.8	0.7	1.0	0.0	0.5	0.7	0.0	0.7	0.7	0.0
Canada	-0.5	1.0	0.9	0.3	0.2	-0.8	1.4	1.0	-0.4	0.8	0.7	0.2	0.2	-0.4	0.7	0.5
Japan	11.0	-0.1	2.4	2.3	-0.2	11.8	18.9	0.8	2.7	0.0	0.6	0.6	0.0	1.2	2.0	0.1
Federal Republic of Germany	5.0	-0.6	2.1	0.7	2.6	6.6	7.1	-2.8	1.5	-0.2	0.6	0.2	0.8	1.0	1.1	-0.4
France	5.0	0.3	1.9	0.1	0.2	4.1	9.1	-1.7	2.0	0.1	0.8	0.0	0.1	0.9	1.9	-0.4
United Kingdom	4.6	-1.5	0.2	-2.7	-1.2	-2.6	-2.9	-4.8	2.6	-0.8	0.1	-1.5	-0.7	-0.8	-0.9	-1.5
Italy	4.5	-0.7	0.8	0.4	0.3	2.7	7.2	1.8	2.9	-0.5	0.5	0.3	0.2	1.0	2.7	0.7
Belgium	1.2	-0.5	0.4	0.1	0.1	0.4	1.5	0.7	2.7	-1.1	0.9	0.2	0.2	0.4	1.6	0.7
Netherlands	0.7	0.1	0.8	0.3	-0.2	1.6	1.7	-0.9	1.1	0.2	1.3	0.5	-0.3	1.2	1.2	-0.7
Sweden	1.1	0.2	0.3	0.2	-0.2	2.0	1.1	-0.7	2.1	0.4	0.6	0.4	-0.4	2.2	1.2	-0.8
Memorandum:																
OECD	50.6	-2.2	18.3	12.1	0.4	48.6	68.3	-7.4	1.5	-0.1	0.6	0.4	0.0	0.8	1.1	-0.1
EC	22.1	-3.7	6.3	-0.5	0.6	16.1	25.2	-8.3	2.0	-0.3	0.6	0.0	0.1	0.8	1.2	-0.4

a See the text with regard to the concept.
b Yardstick for 1974-78: GDP of 1973; for 1979-81: GDP of 1978.

Source: OECD: Statistics of Foreign Trade; OECD: National Accounts; calculations by the authors.

228

During the second oil crisis the OECD's direct income loss -
measured in relation to GDP for 1978 - rose from 0.8 % (1979)
to 1.1 % (1980) before giving way to a slight gain in 1981
as a result of a sharp decrease in import volumes. Developments within the EC were similar. The main sufferers among
the Group of Ten countries were Italy and Japan. Germany's
loss of income corresponded to the average. The United Kingdom, on the other hand, was among the beneficiaries of the
rise in oil prices, as it was now a large oil exporter.

The direct consequences of the oil crisis were much more serious in some oil-importing developing countries than in the
Western industrial group. Table 5.2 illustrates this point
through the example of the ten largest oil importers in the
Third World. Korea and Thailand had to accept the highest
income losses, whereas India was the least affected.

b.   Demand effects of an increase in oil prices

If they are permanent, oil price rises act like a consumption tax from which the revenue is not ultimately available
for domestic consumption. If in spite of this the level of
consumption is initially maintained or is insufficiently
curtailed, it simply means that future consumption has been
brought forward (Corden, Oppenheimer 1976, p. 32). Plausi-
ble arguments can be found to support this; for example, social or cyclical reasons can be advanced to justify postpon-
ing or spacing out the adjustment of government consumption
spending to higher oil prices. There is a danger, however,
that a wrong course will be steered and the true task of
adjustment neglected.

Consumption theory offers various hypotheses to explain the
reaction of private consumers to changes in income: the ab-

Table 5.2: DIRECT LOSSES OF INCOME SUFFERED BY NON-OIL DEVELOPING COUNTRIES AS A RESULT OF REAL OIL PRICE INCREASES, 1974 - 1978[a]

	US$ bn					percentage of 1973 GDP				
	1974	1975	1976	1977	1978	1974	1975	1976	1977	1978
Spain	1.7	0.3	0.8	0.0	0.1	2.4	0.4	1.1	0.0	0.1
Brazil	1.0	0.0	0.7	0.2	0.4	1.3	0.0	0.9	0.3	0.5
Korea	0.4	-0.3	0.3	0.4	0.3	3.2	-2.4	2.4	3.2	2.4
Turkey	0.4	0.1	0.3	0.3	-0.1	1.9	0.5	1.4	1.4	-0.5
India	0.8	0.0	0.0	0.2	0.3	1.1	0.0	0.0	0.3	0.4
Thailand	0.2	0.1	0.1	0.2	0.1	1.9	1.0	1.0	1.9	1.0
Philippines	0.2	0.1	0.1	0.1	0.0	1.9	0.9	0.9	0,9	0.0
Portugal	0.2	0.0	0.1	0.0	0.1	1.7	0.0	0.9	0.0	0.9
Pakistan	0.1	0.2	0.0	-	0.2	1.2	2.3	0.0	-	2.3
Yugoslavia	0.3	-0.1	0.1	0.1	0.2	1.4	-0.5	0.5	0.5	0.9

a   See the text with regard to the concept. The countries were selected and listed according to the level of imports from OPEC in 1981.

Source: OECD: Statistics of Foreign Trade; UN: Yearbook of International Trade Statistics; OECD: National Accounts; UN: Yearbook of National Accounts Statistics; IMF: IFS Yearbook 1982; calculations by the authors.

solute, relative and permanent income hypotheses.

If consumer behaviour is adequately described by the absolute income hypothesis, then in the event of a fall in income occasioned by an increase in oil prices consumption
will decline in accordance with the marginal propensity
to consume.

On the other hand, if the relative income hypothesis applies,
then the marginal propensity to consume will initially rise,
as consumers attempt to maintain their previous standard of
living by liquidating savings or by borrowing. Ultimately,
however, it will fall back all the more sharply the longer
the period since they achieved the income to which they
were accustomed before the oil price increase.

A third, and possibly still the most apt explanation is offered by the permanent income hypothesis, which asserts that
consumption moves in proportion to expected income. Hence,
if consumers anticipate a permanent fall in income after a
rise in oil prices they will curb consumption. The extent
to which they do this also depends on the expected impact
of real oil price increases on assets, interest rates and
other economic and non-economic factors.

As regards the influence of an increase in oil prices on investment demand, a profits squeeze due to real oil price increases impairs the capacity to invest, but at the same time
investment might be stimulated by falling real interest
rates; this is the case if financial surpluses in the oil-
producing countries increase the supply of capital worldwide, this development is not neutralised by restrictive economic measures and investment reacts flexibly
to reductions in interest rates.

The impact of rising oil prices on investors' <u>expectations</u> is of decisive importance. If expectations with regard to profit rates, sales, commodity supplies, commodity prices and so forth are predominantly pessimistic, planned investment will be shelved and firms will hesitate to launch new capital projects. This can lead to a downward spiral of contracting investment and consumer demand. The reverse is obviously the case if investors expect the economy to adjust flexibly to higher oil prices.

A key variable for developments on the demand side is the actual and expected trend in the import demand of oil-exporting countries, which influences investment decisions in the oil-importing countries and hence the demand for domestic capital goods. At the same time, it can directly offset a fall in domestic demand caused by rising oil prices.

Additional imports of goods and services by oil-producing countries can be compared with a demand boost stemming from an increase in government expenditure, which is a counterweight to the deprivation effect caused by higher taxes (in our context higher prices for imported oil). With a balanced budget, under certain assumptions this produces a positive overall demand effect equal to the additional tax receipts, as the expenditure multiplier is larger than the tax multiplier (Haavelmo theorem). The expansionary demand effects of additional imports by oil-producing countries should therefore be considerably greater than the contractionary effects of the withdrawal of purchasing power suffered by the oil-importing countries as a result of real oil prices increases.[5]

The import demand of the oil-producing countries grew strong-ly after the first oil shock, as can be seen from a simple mod-el calculation for the OPEC countries (see Table 5.3). It is based on the assumption that but for the real oil price in-crease the individual positions in the OPEC current payments balance would have remained at the 1973 levels from 1974 to 1978. All changes in OPEC's trade and payment relations with the rest of the world are therefore attributed to the rise in the price of oil. As a second stage OPEC's respending ratio is calculated,in other words OPEC's additional imports are set against the group's additional exports.

In 1974 the respending ratio was only 30 %. In the following year it jumped to almost 50 % on a cumulative basis (i.e. the changes in exports and imports calculated for 1975 in re-lation to the reference year 1973 are added to the correspond-ing figures for 1974) and continued rising until it reached almost 75 % in 1978. Hence by the beginning of the second oil price explosion the OPEC countries had respent most of their additional oil receipts on imports of goods and services and on private and official transfer payments. In the case of the "high absorbers" the respending ratio was as high as 90 %, while in that of the "low absorbers" it came to 55 %.

Table 5.3 also portrays the spending behaviour of the OPEC countries in the second oil crisis. In this instance the current account for 1978 serves as the benchmark, that is to say all changes in current account positions in subsequent years are attributed exclusively to the second oil price shock. It can be seen that by 1982 the respendig ratio had risen to almost 50 %. A striking feature is the relatively low respending ratio of the high absorbers. Nonetheless, it increased appreciably in 1980, 1981 and 1982 after having assumed a negative value in 1979, owing chiefly to the events in Iran.

Table 5.3: SPENDING BEHAVIOUR OF OPEC COUNTRIES, 1974 - 1978 AND 1979 - 1982[a]

	1974	1975	1976	1977	1978	1979	1980	1981	1982
				- in billions of dollars -					
Export growth[b]									
OPEC	74	139	229	332	436	74	232	366	437
LAC	35	68	115	169	219	40	149	251	302
HAC	39	71	114	163	217	34	82	114	134
Import growth[c]									
OPEC	22	68	129	211	318	8	54	127	201
LAC	6	21	46	79	121	14	44	84	125
HAC	16	47	83	132	197	- 7	8	39	71
Responding ratio[d]									
OPEC	30	49	56	64	73	11	23	35	46
LAC	17	31	40	47	55	35	30	33	41
HAC	41	66	73	81	91	-21	10	34	53

a OPEC plus Bahrain and Oman. See the text with regard to the measurement concept.

b Only merchandise exports.

c Merchandise imports, net imports of services and net private and official transfers.

d Import growth as a percentage of export growth.

LAC = Low-absorbing countries (Bahrain, Qatar, Kuwait, Libya, Oman, Saudi Arabia and the United Arab Emirates).

HAC = High-absorbing countries (Algeria, Ecuador, Gabon, Indonesia, Iran, Iraq, Nigeria and Venezuela).

Source: OECD: Economic Outlook; calculations by the authors.

The remaining shortfall in demand in the oil-importing countries could not be offset by expenditure financed on credit
equivalent to OPEC's capital exports, particularly as high
and at times rapidly rising real interest rates were hardly
conducive to borrowing in order to finance investment and
the acquisition of durable consumer goods. The main cause
of this development was a restrictive monetary and fiscal
policy in the leading Western industrial countries, which
opted for price stability when faced with a conflict between the fight against inflation and the revival of demand.
The yet wider deflationary gap this initially caused may
partly explain the stubborn stagnation in growth that has
been evident since the second oil price shock.

The effects of real oil price increases on growth cannot,
however, be ascertained with sufficient accuracy by means
of pure demand analysis. The supposedly flexible adjustment
of the supply side of an economy to the changed production
and demand conditions cannot be taken for granted by any
means. Moreover, demand analysis does not take account of
the direct adverse effect that an oil price increase has
on productive potential. This effect stems basically from
the fact that certain production plant become economically
obsolete prematurely. A graphic example is supplied by the
American automobile industry, which had to replace practically its entire capital stock so that it could produce
more fuel-efficient cars; the reduction in the value of the
old capital stock corresponds to the diminished resale value of the gas-guzzlers. Conventional estimates of productive capacity ignore such effects; they do not take account
of the energy factor, so that they tend to overestimate
productive capacity. The consequences can be serious. For
example, a policy of demand stimulation geared towards an

unrealistic level of potential output will fail to achieve
its objective and will solely increase the inflationary
pressure.

Whether real oil price increases merely depress the level
of potential national income or will also permanently
reduce the growth rate of incomes depends mainly on the
behaviour of investment, which is the key variable for
successful structural adjustment to higher oil prices.
Both the opening-up of new sources of oil and the development of alternative forms of energy entail increased capital expenditure. Equally, most kinds of energy conservation
and oil substitution involve investment, as does the change-
over to the manufacture of energy-saving products. Last but
not least, oil-induced terms-of-trade and productivity losses
can only be made good if more capital is made available.

c.   The impact of rising oil prices on investment

The actual investment trend since the first oil shock is in
contradiction with the increased capital requirement. This
is particularly true in the Western industrial countries,
where real gross fixed capital formation increased by less
than 1 % a year between 1973 and 1981 compared with almost
6 % a year between 1965 and 1973. At the same time, investment grew much more slowly than consumption, so that its
share of final domestic expenditure fell from 24 to 22 %
and in the EC from 23 to 20 % (see Table 5.4).

In the oil-importing developing countries the rate of
growth in investment also decreased overall after the first
oil price rise; the relatively advanced Third World coun-

Table 5.4: GROWTH IN INVESTMENT IN WESTERN INDUSTRIALISED COUNTRIES
BEFORE AND AFTER THE FIRST OIL CRISIS

	Real annual rate of growth		Percentage share of final domestic expenditure		
	1965-73	1973-81	1965	1973	1981
USA	3.6	0.4	19.1	19.3	17.9
Canada	5.2	3.4	23.9	23.0	24.0
Japan	14.4	1.8	31.0	37.0	31.3
Federal Rep. of Germany	3.2	0.5	26.8	24.9	22.1
France	6.6	0.7	23.9	24.5	20.8
United Kingdom	3.4	-1.5	18.4	23.3	16.1
Italy	5.3	0.7	19.9	21.0	20.1
Belgium	3.8	-0.6	22.5	22.2	17.4
Netherlands	4.9	-1.7	27.3	24.3	19.4
Sweden	3.2	-0.5	25.1	22.4	19.1
OECD	5.7	0.7	21.7	23.6	21.2
EC	4.6	0.0	22.8	23.2	19.8

Source: OECD: National Accounts; calculations by the authors.

ries recorded a marked slowdown, whereas the poorest developing countries more or less sustained the investment pace observed before the crisis. By contrast with the industrial countries, the share of investment in final domestic expenditure in the oil-importing developing countries continued to rise even after the first oil shock, a phenomenon that can be attributed mainly to the relatively low rate of growth in private consumption (see Table 5.5). Towards the end of the seventies, however, matters took a turn for the worse, owing not least to an increasing use of foreign credit to finance consumption and poorly productive investment (OECD Observer 1983c, p.10).

The general weakness of investment was accompanied by marked changes in the structure of investment. As early as the sixties the focus of investment had begun to shift away from the erection of entire plant to investment in machinery and equipment. This tendency intensified further after the first oil shock. The annual rate of growth in investment in machinery and equipment in the OECD declined "only" from 7.7 % (1968-73) to 2.8 % (1973-81), whereas expenditure on new factory premises fell much more sharply, namely from 4 to 0.2 % (see Table 5.6). The structural changes this reveals might be interpreted as a sign of a declining willingness among investors to take risks. As a rule, the pay-off periods on investments in machinery and equipment are relatively short, but the cost of erecting new manufacturing plant is recouped only over the long term. New plant nevertheless allow greater productivity gains to be made, for the manufacturing process is re-organised from scratch and greater account can therefore be taken of technical advances as well as changes in factor price relations and demand conditions.[6]

Table 5.5: GROWTH IN INVESTMENT, PRIVATE AND PUBLIC CONSUMPTION IN OIL-IMPORTING DEVELOPING COUNTRIES, 1965-1973 AND 1973 - 1978[a]

Country groups[b]	Investment		Private consumption		Public consumption	
	1965-73	1973-78	1965-73	1973-78	1965-73	1973-78
1.000	7.9	4.7	6.1	2.8	8.3	5.9
500 - 1.000	13.6	9.8	6.0	5.9	6.6	8.8
500	7.2	7.7	3.4	3.4	6.1	4.3
Overall	8.9	7.5	4.6	3.9	6.7	5.8

a Unweighted average of annual rates of growth.
b According to per capita income in 1977.

Source: UNCTAD: Trade and Development Report 1982.

239

Table 5.6: GROWTH IN INVESTMENT IN WESTERN INDUSTRIAL COUNTRIES ACCORDING TO SECTORS OF DEPLOYMENT[a]

	Machinery and equipment		Non-residential construction		Residential construction		Overall investment	
	68-73	73-81	68-73	73-81	68-73	73-81	68-73	73-81
USA	6.2	3.5	-0.5	-0.5	7.8	-4.4	3.9	0.4
Canada	8.3	4.5	2.9	4.3	10.0	-0.3	6.3	3.4
Japan	12.2	3.8	12.8	2.2	13.5	-0.9	12.7	2.2
Federal Rep. of Germany	8.0	2.4	4.8	0.0	4.3	-1.3	5.7	0.5
France[b]	9.8	2.8	4.2	-0.5	7.8	-0.5	6.8	1.1
United Kingdom	3.9	1.4	1.5	-2.9	-1.1	-6.9	2.3	-1.5
Italy	7.5	1.8	1.3	0.0	-0.5	-0.2	3.2	0.7
Belgium	5.4	0.8	4.4	0.4	3.1	-4.1	4.4	-0.6
Netherlands	5.2	-1.2	-2.1	-2.0	4.7	-2.1	2.4	-1.6
Sweden	6.8	1.0	2.0	-1.5	-0.9	-1.6	3.0	-0.5
OECD	7.7	2.8	3.7	0.4	6.8	-2.3	6.0	0.8
EC	7.4	1.8	3.1	-0.8	4.1	-1.9	4.9	0.0

a Real average annual rates of growth.

b 1973-1980.

Source: OECD: Economic Outlook, Historical Statistics; calculations by the authors.

The negative link between investment and real oil price increases, which can be inferred from observations made hitherto, is proven by econometric estimates. This calls for a short theoretical note by way of introduction.

An efficiently run enterprise seeking to maximise profits obviously continues to invest until the value of the marginal product of the capital input equals the capital cost calculated for the period in question.[7] (The capital cost can be regarded as directly proportional to the purchase price of the capital goods.) Hence, the following equation applies:

$$P_p \cdot MP_c = P_c$$

where P_p is the product price, MP_c the marginal product of the capital goods and P_c the periodic capital cost.

If the prices of energy products now rise, production costs increase and the net profits to be earned from the capital goods employed fall unless product prices can be raised accordingly. The enterprise can attempt to counteract this reduction in profit rates by reducing the consumption of energy. However, other conditions remaining unchanged, this means that the marginal productivity of the capital falls, as less energy is available to operate the capital goods. Whether this affects the level of the desired capital stock and hence investment activity depends on the trend of capital goods prices in relation to product prices. If the ratio P_c/P_p declines to the same extent as MP_c, the level of the desired capital stock does not alter. However, if capital goods prices move in proportion to product prices or even rise in relation to the latter, adverse investment effects must be expected.

This relationship can be portrayed diagrammatically as follows:

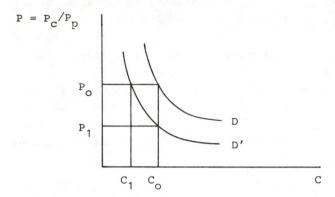

$P = P_c/P_p$

P_o

P_1

D

D'

C_1 C_o

C

An increase in the cost of energy causes the capital demand curve D to shift to the left (D'). If the ratio of capital goods prices to product prices remains unchanged, this means that the desired capital stock moves back from C_o to C_1. The rise in energy prices would have a neutral investment effect only if the price relationship between capital and output came down from P_o to P_1.

Applied to the USA, the model outlined above showed that the desired ratio of capital to labour fell by at least 9 % as a result of the first oil shock. This is a clear departure from the historical trend, which was typified by a steep rise in capital resources per worker, and has had the result that "since 1975, growth in the capital stock has barely kept pace with growth in the labour force available to the private sector" (Tatom 1979, p. 9).

The findings of another study on the USA (Uri 1980) are somewhat different, though they tend in the same direction and are based on a similar theoretical approach. The study examines the effects of energy prices on investment in two energy-intensive industries (chemicals and paper) and two that consume relatively little energy (textiles and rubber) as well as in the economy as a whole on the basis of data for the period from 1950 to 1977. It also takes into account that investment has a lagged reaction to changes in the factors that determine it.[8] The main findings of the study are:

(i)   In energy-intensive industries the price of energy is a significant negative determinant of investment. Its influence is strongest after one year in the paper industry and after two in chemicals.

(ii)   The negative investment effects of an increase in the cost of energy are not confined to one year in these sectors but extend over a fairly long period.

(iii)   In sectors with a low energy consumption investment decisions are scarcely affected by changes in energy prices.

(iv)   For the economy as a whole and the two energy-intensive industries the significance of energy prices as a determinant of investment increased substantially between the periods of 1950-72 and 1973-77.[9]

In the case of the Federal Republic of Germany, the Ifo-Institut has made an econometric study of the influence of energy prices on investment behaviour in twenty-five branches of manufacturing industry (Ifo 1983b) based on a production function of the Cobb-Douglas type expanded to include the factor energy. In the investment function derived from this, the growth in the capital stock is determined by sales expectations, the expected ratio of wage rates to capital utilisation prices and the expected ratio of energy prices to capital utilisation prices. Time-lags in adjustment are taken into account by defining temporal reaction

patterns. Most of the data used relate to the period from
1960 to 1980. The study's conclusions are broadly in line
with those relating to the USA: real increases in energy
prices dampen investment activity in most branches of industry. Positive investment effects, by contrast, stem from expectations of increased sales and a relative increase in the
cost of labour.[10]

The approaches towards ascertaining the investment effects
of an increase in energy prices described so far have been
partial models. They deal with the direct impact of individ-
dual determinants of investment but disregard the macro-
economic framework in which investment is carried out. For
example, interdependencies between industries and within
the economy as a whole are left out of account. Such reciprocal effects can only be covered in a comprehensive model
of the economy in which energy is explicitly included as
an input factor and an output variable. Hudson and Jorgenson have developed such a model for the USA; they describe
it as a "dynamic general equilibrium model of the US economy" (Hudson, Jorgenson 1979, p. 176). They have used the
model to simulate two alternative growth paths for the
US economy for the period from 1972 to 1976. The first simulation assumes current world oil prices as an exogenous
variable, whereas the alternative estimate is based on constant world oil prices (1972 prices). As all other exogenous
variables remain unchanged, discrepancies between the result
of the two model estimates can be ascribed entirely to
changes in oil prices and in the prices of other energy products that depend on them.

It emerges that the increase in energy prices has drastical-
ly reduced the desired size of the capital stock.[11] The deciding factor here was not energy-price-induced changes in

the structure of demand; in themselves, these actually had
a positive investment effect. Nor did changed factor price
relations significantly reduce the desired input of capital:
a replacement of capital in manufacturing industry, agricul-
ture, construction and transportation was almost offset by
a rise in capital utilisation in the services sector. Instead,
the main determinant was the reduction in the volume of demand caused by the rise in energy prices.

Hence theoretical considerations and empirical studies both
show that rising energy prices can be a serious obstacle to
investment and can therefore impede the growth process. To
date, the investment-inducing effects of higher energy costs
have obviously been exceeded by their dampening impact; reduced expectations of sales and profits seem to have been of
decisive importance in this respect. The third section of
this chapter will examine the ensuing consequences for economic policy. First, however, the essential structural effects
of real oil price increases will be described; this might
reveal the need for further economic measures.

2. Structural effects of an increase in oil prices

Real oil price increases and structural changes within an economy condition one another. Adjustment to much dearer oil requires substantial structural changes; if these are successful, the oil-producing countries' scope for further improving their relative income position by means of large price increases is greatly curtailed.

This section will show first how rising oil prices change the structure of demand. Such increases can cause serious problems in certain sectors; at the same time, however, they may afford opportunities for growth and employment elsewhere, although a high degree of adaptability and innovation are required if they are to be exploited to the full. The second sub-section will examine the adjustment of input structures to changes in factor price relations caused by oil prices. Energy-intensive industries, in particular, can counteract structural changes that are to their disadvantage by replacing energy by other factors of production or expensive sources of energy by cheaper ones. Above this, the reduction in energy and oil dependency is a matter of great concern for economic policy, for it plays an essential part in safeguarding growth against external disturbances.

a. Changes in the structure of demand as a result of rising oil prices

Real oil price increases cause a shift in demand to the oil-producing countries. The product composition of demand also changes to the extent that their preferences differ from those of oil-importing countries. The oil-importing countries are affected to differing degrees. From the point of view of a single country it must also be borne in mind that the oil-producing countries displace not only domestic demand but also import demand from other oil-importing countries.

246

Rising oil prices also alter the structure of <u>domestic</u> demand in the oil-importing countries. Above all, the share of energy products increases in value terms. The beneficiaries of this development are not only the oil-producing countries but also domestic energy sectors, which reap "windfall profits" and substitute domestic production for imported energy.

In the case of non-energy products demand must shift from consumer goods to capital goods if a renunciation of growth is not a possible alternative to the structural adjustment to real oil price increases. A sharp rise in oil prices also causes large structural changes <u>within</u> the two sectors.

In the capital goods sector, for example, the balance of demand shifts towards plant and machinery that permit a reduction in specific energy consumption, the conversion to cheaper sources of energy or the manufacture of new, more energy-efficient products. Individual branches of the capital goods industry also derive strong stimulus from the expansion of the energy sector, particularly as the specific capital input in that sector as a whole is much higher than in the other sectors of the economy and will probably rise significantly further in future. On the other hand, the manufacturers of capital goods that are used in contracting consumer goods industries suffer a loss of demand.

In the consumer goods field products that are inelastic to changes in income, and possibly also inferior, may gain ground. At the same time, demand concentrates more strongly on products with relatively low energy consumption figures or which help in other ways to reduce household's energy costs.

The changes in the structure of demand just described are overlaid by demand effects stemming from the different energy intensity of the various sectors of the economy. In a context of rising energy prices, differences in sectoral energy input coefficients - measured as the energy input per unit of output - cause unequal movements in supply prices and hence lead to shifts in the sectoral price pattern. Other things being equal, the shares of individual sectors in total demand therefore also change. Sectors with a low energy intensity can thus even achieve an absolute growth in income by comparison with the level that would have obtained had there been no increase in energy prices.[12] However, in energy-intensive sectors the negative price effect can be offset by positive substitution, income or preference effects. Examples of opposing price and substitution effects can be found in the plastics industry; its products have a high oil and energy content, but they are suitable for use as heat insulation or for energy-saving weight reductions in the manufacture of motor vehicles. A similar situation applies to certain aluminium products.

If the economy is sub-diveded in accordance with the three-sector model and if energy intensity is a stronger determinant of structural changes among sectors than other energy-related factors, it should be expected that real oil price rises will cause the share of the service sector to increase and that of manufacturing industry to decline. Indeed, the size of the tertiary sector has increased substantially in Western industrial countries since the first oil price shock; the only exceptions are Japan and Belgium (DIW 1983). In the case of the EC a study of the adjustment in the sectoral composition of the economy between the two oil shocks (EG 1981, pp. 126 ff) has shown that:

- only two major branches, energy and services, increased
  their shares of overall domestic product between 1973
  and 1979;

- none of the larger industrial branches could maintain
  its 1973 share of domestic product; and

- the sector for market services has been by far the greatest beneficiary of changes in the sectoral structure of
  the Community.

It would be premature, however, to conclude from these observations that real oil price increases intensify the trend
towards the post-industrial society. To test this hypothesis
it is necessary to weigh opposing forces against one another.
For example, services are unlikely to play as large a part as
industrial products in the real transfer of resources to oil-
producing countries. The tertiary sector also seems to be put
at a disadvantage by the fall in income caused by higher oil
prices in the oil-importing countries. Such effects might be
stronger than the benefits to be derived from having a lower
energy intensity.

The rough division of an economy into three sectors conceals
substantial differences in energy intensity at a lower level
of aggregation. In the services sector the transport industry
stands out on account of its high energy intensity. In the secondary sector, which will be examined more closely below, it
is branches of the basic materials and producer goods industry that have a particularly high specific energy consumption. Conversely most capital and consumer goods industries
require comparatively little energy.

The performance of energy-intensive industries can be shown
only approximately at the world level. Only index numbers

at a relatively high level of sectoral aggregation are available for the industrial production of the world as a whole and of individual regions. If developments in the sectoral structure of industry in the world before and after the 1973 oil shock are viewed on this basis, the following are apparent (see Table 5.7):

- Between 1960 and 1973 the production of manufacturing industry as a whole rose by 6.8 % a year. The driving force behind this growth came primarily from the chemicals industry and the fabrication of metal products (including mechanical engineering and transportation equipment), which achieved rates of growth of 8.8 and 8.2 % respectively. The smallest increases, by contrast, were in the clothing sector (3.8 %), textiles and food processing (4.5 % each).

- By 1982 the growth in production in manufacturing industry had fallen to 2.4 % a year. Growth slowed down in all the industrial branches examined but to widely differing degrees.

- The most pronounced slowdown in growth occurred in the chemicals industry, in basic metals industries and in the wood sector. These branches of industry, which have above-average energy intensity, suffered the largest decrease in growth rates in absolute terms. To the wood sector and basic metals industries the same applies in relative terms, too; in the wood sector the annual rate of growth in production in the period 1973-82 was only 5 % of the growth experienced between 1960 and 1973, while in basic metals industries output in 1982 was even slightly below the 1973 level, after having shown annual growth of 5.9 % in the period 1960-73.

Table 5.7: CHANGES IN THE SECTORAL STRUCTURE OF MANUFACTURING INDUSTRY WORLDWIDE BETWEEN 1960-73 AND 1973-82

| | ISIC Position | Annual rate of growth | | | | Change in annual rate of growth | | | |
| | | absolute | | % of manuf. ind. | | absolute | | % of manuf. ind. | |
		1960-73	1973-82	1960-73	1973-82	(a)	(b)	(a)	(b)
Food, beverages & tobacco	31	4.5	3.0	66.2	125.0	-1.5	0.67	34.1	191.4
Textiles	321	4.5	0.7	66.2	29.2	-3.8	0.16	86.4	45.7
Clothing & footwear	322/3/4	3.8	1.5	55.9	62.5	-2.3	0.39	52.3	111.4
Wood	33	5.8	0.3	85.3	12.5	-5.5	0.05	125.0	14.3
Paper	34	5.5	1.8	80.9	75.0	-3.7	0.33	84.1	94.3
Chemicals	35	8.8	2.6	129.4	108.3	-6.2	0.30	140.9	85.7
Non-metallic mineral products	36	6.2	1.8	91.2	75.0	-4.4	0.29	100.0	82.9
Basic metal industries	37	5.9	-0.1	86.8	-4.2	-6.0	-0.02	136.4	-5.7
Fabricated metal products	38	8.2	3.4	120.6	141.7	-4.8	0.41	109.1	117.1
Manufacturing industry	3	6.8	2.4	100.0	100.0	-4.4	0.35	100.0	100.0

(a) 1973-82 growth rate minus 1960-73 growth rate.

(b) $\dfrac{1973\text{-}82 \text{ growth rate}}{1960\text{-}73 \text{ growth rate}} \times 100$.

Source: UN: Monthly Bulletin of Statistics; calculations by the authors.

251

- The food and clothing sectors, which consume relatively little energy, recorded the best performance. In relative terms, the fabricated metals industry, which also shows a low energy coefficient, performed well, too.
  This sector thus displaced the chemical industry at the
  head of the sectoral growth league.

If industrialised, developing and centrally planned countries are viewed separately, the following picture is obtained:

- In the Western <u>industrial</u> countries the structurally weak
  sectors are not only the traditional consumer goods industries (textiles, clothing, leather and footwear) but
  also the majority of energy-intensive industries, that
  is to say the wood industry, non-metallic mineral products and basic metals industries. Rates of growth in
  these industries were already below average before the
  first oil crisis, but since then production has declined in absolute terms and the gap between their growth
  rates and average growth in the manufacturing sector
  has widened considerably. Only the chemical industry
  and the paper sector have recorded a lasting and above-
  average rise in production. In the paper sector, however,
  this might be due to a particularly good performance in
  the sub-sector printing and publishing. In the chemicals
  industry the large absolute decline in the growth rate
  is conspicuous; it was surpassed only by the basic metals
  industries (see Table A-9).

- Between 1960 and 1973 the developing countries had only
  a small lead over Western industrialised countries as
  far as industrial growth is concerned, but between 1973
  and 1982 they moved well ahead. The main engines of
  growth were not only the low-energy-consuming food and
  fabricated metal products industries but also the energy-intensive basic metals and non-metallic minerals
  industries. These two industries and above all the food
  industry also do well as compared to the preceding period, whereas the fabricated metal products industry shows
  a slowdown in growth which is much more pronounced than
  in manufacturing industry as a whole in both absolute
  and relative terms (see Table A-10).

- The opposite can be observed in the centrally-planned
  economies, where the pace of expansion in the fabricated metal products sector continued virtually unchecked.
  Moreover, this industry achieved much higher rates of
  growth than any other branch, after having been on a
  par with the chemicals industry in the period from
  1960 to 1973 (see Table A-11).

Additional information on the performance of energy-intensive industries is provided in Tables 5.8, A-12, A-13 and
A-14. Table 5.8 shows the shares of energy-intensive industries in value-added and capital formation of the manufacturing sector as a whole from 1969 onwards for individual
Western industrial countries. The developments in the USA,
Japan and Germany deserve particular attention.

In the USA the energy-intensive industries' contribution
to total manufacturing value-added declined steadily until
1972. In the following two years it rose sharply but gradu-

Table 5.8:   PERFORMANCE OF ENERGY-INTENSIVE INDUSTRIES
             IN WESTERN INDUSTRIAL COUNTRIES, 1969-1980
             - percentages of total manufacturing -

		1969	1970	1971	1972
USA	VA	26.8	26.4	25.8	24.5
	CF	41.1	42.2	40.9	35.4
Canada	VA	27.9	29.0	28.2	27.1
	CF	44.5	49.2	49.3	47.8
Japan	VA	29.6	29.1	31.2	27.8
	CF	47.3	47.2	48.9	48.2
Federal Rep. of Germany	VA	40.0[a]	40.4[a]	39.3[a]	39.1[a]
	CF	38.9	41.4	39.0	39.3
France	VA	29.7[d]	30.3[d]	29.4[d]	27.7[d]
	CF	44.0[d]	44.2[d]	45.2[d]	46.0[d]
United Kingdom	VA	n.a.	26.3	25.1	25.1
	CF	n.a.	44.7	47.9	43.1
Italy	VA	35.2	34.2	32.5	32.0
	CF	48.2	50.5	53.4	52.2

a Including ISIC positions 331, 332, 342, 355 and 356.

b Including ISIC positions 331, 332 and 342.

c Including ISIC position 290 but excluding position 354.

d Including ISIC position 220 but excluding position 354.

Table 5.8 (continued)

1973	1974	1975	1976	1977	1978	1979	1980
25.0	27.5	26.8	26.5	25.9	25.7	27.0	n.a.
35.3	40.4	46.4	46.0	42.4	38.6	38.4	n.a.
27.6	31.2	29.5	29.0	29.4	28.9	29.8	n.a.
43.8	54.6	60.6	63.7	63.7	58.8	53.3	51.9
29.0	30.5	27.4	27.1	26.9	27.3	29.2	29.3
38.1	43.3	54.8	50.6	45.3	38.0	37.9	33.6
36.1[b]	36.5[b]	36.8[b]	29.8	28.5	28.4	n.a.	n.a.
38.9	41.6	41.4	40.9	36.6	33.4	n.a.	n.a.
28.4[d]	29.8[d]	23.8[d]	27.4[c]	28.2[c]	28.9[c]	30.0[c]	28.7
43.6[d]	36.6[d]	37.2[d]	36.9[c]	35.0[c]	35.0[c]	29.6[c]	n.a.
26.3	28.0	25.8	31.4	30.4	28.9	29.5	n.a.
35.2	36.9	44.5	44.7	39.5	38.5	37.4	n.a.
33.1	34.2	31.7	31.5	30.0	29.5	31.0	n.a.
50.4	47.8	52.1	52.4	47.1	42.3	37.8	n.a.

VA = value added.
CF = gross fixed capital formation.

Energy-intensive industries = ISIC positions 341, 351/2, 353/4, 361, 362, 369, 371 and 372.

Source: UN: Yearbook of Industrial Statistics; calculations by the authors.

ally fell back until 1978; in 1979 it recorded another sudden leap. Their share of capital formation in manufacturing industry was diminishing before the oil shock, but then it began to increase rapidly. A process of relative "decapitalisation" later set in, but in 1979 their investment share was still substantially higher than in 1973 and 1974.

Events took a different turn in Japan, where the most striking feature is the sharp decline in investment in the energy-intensive industries. Whereas in 1975 these sectors still accounted for 55 % of capital formation in manufacturing industry, their share contracted in stages to 34 % in 1980, around one-third lower than in the years before the oil crisis. The structural switch from light industry to heavy industry and chemicals, which had been conducted at a forced pace mainly between 1965 and 1970, had been largely completed by the time of the oil crisis. Special emphasis had been laid on development of the chemical industry; this energy-intensive sector managed to step up its rate of growth still further after the first oil shock, whereas the equally energy-intensive steel industry dropped back into the group of stagnating sectors (Kaneko 1980, pp. 484 ff).

In Germany too the propensity to invest declined much more sharply in the energy-intensive sectors than in the other branches of manufacturing industry, so that their share in industrial capital formation contracted from about 40 % between 1969 and 1972 to one-third in 1978. International industrial statistics based on the ISIC classification system give, however, a distorted picture of changes in the value added of energy-intensive industries in Germany, so that here we must fall back on national statistics.

Table 5.9 shows first that most of the energy-intensive sectors already counted as structurally weak industries before
the first oil crisis. Only the chemical industry was a pronounced growth sector, with an annual rate of growth in value added in the region of 10 % between 1960 and 1973 compared with 5 % for manufacturing as a whole. After the increase
in oil prices this sector's lead in the growth stakes largely disappeared. In the 1974-75 recession the chemical industry even contracted more strongly than most other sectors
and in the recovery phase that began in 1975 it was not able
to take as strong a lead as it had in the past. During this
period the iron and steel industry actually recorded an absolute decline in value added, the only sector to do so. By
contrast, the pulp and paper industry achieved a considerable rate of growth in spite of its extremely high energy
intensity, although it must be said that it suffered a particularly severe setback during the recession. The same applies to the manufacture of glass and glass products.

To sum up, no clear link has been discerned so far between
sectoral energy intensity and structural change. However,
the data do show that energy-intensive industries have often
come under increased pressure to adjust. A detailed study
would have to be conducted to establish the extent to which
energy intensity was a factor in this; this would require
a finer sectoral breakdown and a theoretical approach that
encompassed the main determinants of structural change, took
account of links between industries and covered the various
and sometimes opposing effects of rising oil prices on the
composition of demand.

Table 5.9: GROWTH OF ENERGY-INTENSIVE INDUSTRIES IN THE FEDERAL REPUBLIC OF GERMANY, 1960-1980[a]

	Energy intensity[a]			Real gross production[b]				Real value added[b]			
	1960	1972	1980	60-73	73-75	75-80	73-80	60-73	73-75	75-80	73-80
Iron and steel	32.2	27.0	18.5	3.2	5.4	0.6	2.0	2.4	6.9	-0.8	1.4
Paper	-	16.1	12.6	4.7	-11.2	7.2	1.6	3.6	-10.6	6.8	1.5
Non-metallic minerals	18.5	11.2	7.8	6.4	-7.2	3.4	0.3	5.4	-6.3	2.9	0.2
Glass	14.3	9.4	7.4	5.8	-7.0	5.6	1.9	4.9	-5.8	5.2	1.9
Non-ferrous metals	9.4	7.6	7.2	5.8	12.4	1.8	4.8	5.1	9.0	2.0	3.9
Chemicals	12.2	6.7	6.2	9.4	-2.3	4.9	2.8	9.6	-3.4	5.1	2.6
Ceramics	7.8	5.8	5.8	2.7	-9.1	4.8	0.6	2.2	-9.3	4.5	0.3
Foundary products	-	4.4	5.0	2.0	-2.8	0.8	-0.2	1.5	-1.3	1.1	0.4
Manufacturing industry[c]	-	3.4	2.8	6.1	-2.4	3.6	1.9	5.2	-2.6	3.4	1.6

a Energy consumption in petajoules per million DM of gross production at 1976 prices.

b Average annual rate of growth.

c Excluding oil refining.

Source: Statistisches Bundesamt; calculations by the authors.

b.   Adjustment of the structure of inputs to changes in
     relative prices

Since the first oil shock specific energy consumption (i.e.
primary energy consumption per unit of GDP) has declined
substantially, particularly in Western industrial countries.
The decisive impulse in this direction seems to have come
from the second upsurge in oil prices, which began at the
end of 1978.   Chart 11 illustrates this development for the
three largest Western industrial countries, the EC and the
OECD as a whole. (The precise coefficients, including those
for France, the United Kingdom, Italy and Canada, are reproduced in Table A-15). The reduction was particularly marked in Japan.

Individual sectors made differing contributions to the overall energy saving. The largest reduction in specific energy
consumption occured in industry - in the seven largest Western industrial countries the saving averaged about 30 % between 1973 and 1982 - while the smallest was in the transportation sector (around 10 %). Households and small business
consumers came between the two, with a saving of about 20 %.
Changes in real energy prices follow the reverse order. In
industry they trebled, whereas the real prices that households and small business consumers had to pay for their energy requirements "only" doubled and the transportation sector's real energy prices increased by 50 % (OECD Economic
Outlook, No. 33, p. 78). The differing success of the large
energy-consuming sectors in saving energy was therefore apparently in no small part due to differences in price movements.

Chart 11: SPECIFIC ENERGY CONSUMPTION[a] IN WESTERN INDUSTRIAL COUNTRIES, 1972-1981

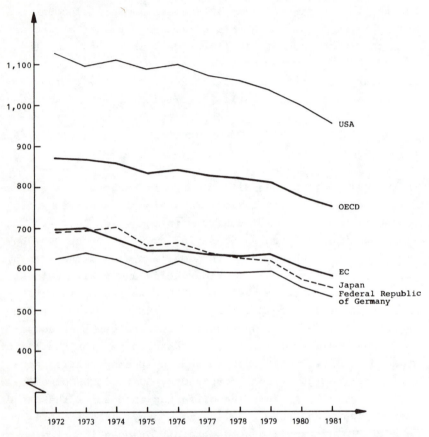

a Primary energy consumption in tonnes oil equivalent per million $ of GDP (at 1975 prices and exchange rates).

Source: OECD: Energy Balances; OECD: National Accounts; calculations by the authors.

The quotient obtained from the (negative) change in energy intensity and the changes in real energy prices provides a rough measure of the responsiveness of sectoral energy consumption to price increases. Since the first oil shock the quotient has risen substantially in each of the three sectors mentioned above. In the period 1973-78 it stood at 0.14 in industry, 0.18 in the households and small business consumers sector and even displayed a negative value of -0.15 in the transportation sector, but for the period 1978-82 it works out at 0.34 for industry and 0.32 for each of the other two sectors (OECD Economic Outlook, No. 33, p. 78).

Such calculations do not take account of structural changes within the broad sectors referred to so far. Empirical research has arrived at differing conclusions with regard to the structural component of energy-saving as against the "genuine" substitution element.

In the case of Germany only a relatively small part of the energy saving is attributed to structural change among the sectors. In a study based on data for 35 branches of manufacturing industry, the Institut für Weltwirtschaft in Kiel comes to the conclusion that the increased importance of low-energy-consuming industries accounts for only 16 % of the sector's overall energy saving (Kriegsmann, Neu 1981, pp. 63 f). The same figure is cited by the Ifo-Institut, which adds that "above all, the structural decline in the importance of the iron and steel industry and the non-metallic minerals industry was a factor" in this (Ifo 1983b, p. 25).

A more detailed study of British industry - it is based on
data for 104 branches of industry - makes the opposite finding. According to this research, structural change among the
sectors was the main cause of the decline in specific energy
consumption in British manufacturing industry in the seventies. The authors draw the conclusion that "the role of price
induced substitution as envisaged by the use of a production
function is less important than has often been assumed" (Jenne, Cattell 1983, p. 120).

A study relating to Sweden in the period from 1973 to 1978
also indicates that sectoral changes in the structure of
industry have a strong influence on energy consumption; first
of all changes in the sectoral structure of exports - such
as a relative decline in exports of paper and primary metals -
have reduced the specific energy consumption of Swedish industry (Östblom 1982).

As regards substitution as a source of energy saving, rough
indications can be drawn from a comparison of changes in energy consumption and production in energy-intensive industries. Table 5.10 shows the relevant rates of growth for four
industries - iron and steel, chemicals, non-ferrous metals,
non-metallic products - in the seven largest Western industrial countries during the period from 1972 to 1981. The index numbers for individual years are to be found in Tables
A-16, A-17, A-18, and A-19.

A reasonably uniform picture can be made out only in the
iron and steel industry, where the specific energy consumption declined markedly in all of the countries under examination. In four countries (the USA, Germany, France and the
United Kingdom) the consumption of energy declined more
strongly than production and in Japan it decreased even

Table 5.10: CHANGES IN ENERGY CONSUMPTION AND PRODUCTION IN ENERGY-INTENSIVE INDUSTRIES IN WESTERN INDUSTRIAL COUNTRIES, 1972-1981[a]

	Iron and Steel		Chemicals		Non-ferrous metals		Non-metallic products	
	EC	P	EC	P	EC	P	EC	P
USA	- 1.9 (17.0)	-0.8	14.9 (15.0)	4.5	9.0 (5.6)	0.0	24.9 (4,8)	2.3
Canada	2.0 (11.3)	3.3	- 2.6 (2.9)	4.9	0.6 (6.7)	1.6	3.8 (7.1)	0.6
Japan	- 1.8 (28.9)	1.9	- 9.9 (9.3)	4.1	4.2 (2.6)	2.9	30.7 (9.5)	1.3
Federal Rep. of Germany	- 3.6 (24.6)	-0.2	1.2 (16.9)	2.4	1.7 (3.7)	2.4	- 5.6 (8.2)	-0.2
France	- 4.5 (18.0)	-0.5	4.6 (22.1)	3.4	- 3.5 (2.7)	1.3	-13.2 (3.5)	1.5
United Kingdom	- 7.3 (17.2)	-5.0	4.8 (19.2)	1.1	- 4.4 (3.1)	-2.2	- 5.5 (8.2)	-3.0
Italy	1.1 (19.1)	3.2	- 3.3 (13.1)	0.9	1.0 (1.9)	2.4	- 6.1 (10.8)	3.2

a Average annual rates of growth; the figures in parentheses are the percentage shares of each sector in total industrial consumption of energy in the country in question in 1981.

EC = Energy consumption.

P = Production.

Source: OECD: Energy Balances; OECD: Indicators of Industrial Activity; UN: Yearbook of Industrial Statistics; calculations by the authors.

263

though production rose, while in Canada and Italy it increased much more slowly than production.

In the chemicals industry the first point to notice is that there are breaks in the trend of energy consumption in the USA (1979-80), Canada (1978-79) and Japan (1972-73) (see Table A-15); these indicate structural effects within the sector itself. However, even after adjustment there is evidence of movements in opposite directions. Production rose in all of the countries during the period under review, but in Canada, Japan and Italy energy consumption simultaneously declined whereas in the USA, France and the United Kingdom it rose more rapidly than output. It also rose in Germany, but by less than production.

In the non-ferrous metals industry the range extends from France, where energy consumption diminished considerably in spite of increased production, to the USA, where output stagnated but energy consumption rose dramatically.

The same is true of non-metallic products. The USA cuts a very bad figure, whereas France again comes out particularly well. Japan's performance as reflected in Table 5.10 appears to be strongly distorted by structural effects in 1973-74; if developments since 1974 are viewed in isolation, it can be seen that the sector's energy consumption and production have moved more or less parallel in Japan.

Overall, Germany's good performance deserves to be highlighted. Italy is the only other country that managed to reduce its specific energy consumption in all of the sectors examined.

Table 5.11 shows that the largest decrease in specific energy consumption in Germany occured in the iron and steel industry and in the non-metallic minerals industry. These branches also reacted particularly strongly to the increase in real energy prices, as the ratio of the (negative) rate of change in specific energy consumption to the rise in real branch-specific energy prices shows. In four branches - chemicals, ceramics, non-ferrous metals and glass - greater progress towards energy, conservation was made before the first oil crisis than afterwards. The explanation lies partly in the dynamic process of investment and innovation during the pre-crisis years, for investment to rationalise and modernise industry often also brought a significant reduction in the specific energy consumption. In the period that followed, this source of energy savings largely dried up, not least because of the sharp rise in the cost of energy.

This brings us to the question of the substitution relationship between energy and the "classical" factors of production capital and labour. Considerable space is devoted to this question in the literature on the rise in energy costs. Particularly controversial are the effects of rising energy prices on the ratio between inputs of energy and capital. Although engineering studies predominantly indicate wide scope for substituting capital for energy - "a number of such studies have shown that the average energy efficiency of existing plant and equipment is a small fraction (5-10 %) of the maximum possible efficiency" (Berndt, Wood 1979, p. 342) - econometric estimates have produced contradictory results.

The controversy between Berndt, Wood (1975) and Hudson, Jorgenson (1974) on the one hand and Griffin, Gregory (1976) on the other has attracted particular attention. The authors in the

Table 5.11: CHANGES IN ENERGY CONSUMPTION AND PRICES IN ENERGY-INTENSIVE INDUSTRIES IN THE FEDERAL REPUBLIC OF GERMANY AT VARIOUS PERIODS BETWEEN 1960 AND 1980

	Specific energy consumption[b]				Real energy price[c]				Ratio[d]			
	60-72	72-80	72-78	78-80	60-72	72-80	72-78	78-80	60-72	72-80	72-78	78-80
Iron and steel industry	- 1.5	- 4.6	- 5.1	- 3.0	2.4	7.9	8.0	7.6	0.63	0.58	0.64	0.39
Paper	n.a.	- 3.0	- 2.5	- 4.7	n.a.	7.0	5.9	10.4	-	0.43	0.42	0.45
Non-metallic minerals	- 4.1	- 4.4	- 4.8	- 3.0	- 0.3	9.8	8.5	13.5	-	0.45	0.56	0.22
Glass	- 3.4	- 2.9	- 2.1	- 5.5	- 1.6	9.5	8.0	13.8	-	0.31	0.26	0.40
Non-ferrous metals	- 1.8	- 0.7	- 1.5	2.3	1.8	4.1	7.1	- 4.6	1.0	0.17	0.21	0.50
Chemicals	- 4.9	- 1.0	- 1.8	1.6	3.0	5.9	5.7	6.9	1.63	0.17	0.32	-0.23
Ceramics	- 2.5	0.0	0.9	- 2.5	- 0.7	6.5	5.3	10.0	-	0.0	-	0.25
Foundary products	n.a.	1.6	4.4	- 5.5	n.a.	5.3	4.5	7.9	-	-	-	0.70
Memorandum:												
Manufacturing industry[a]	n.a.	- 2.4	- 2.5	- 2.0	n.a.	7.4	6.2	11.2	-	0.32	0.40	0.18

a Excluding oil refining.

b Annual rate of growth in energy consumption in petajoules per million DM of gross production at 1976 prices.

c Annual rate of increase in the energy price index adjusted by the producer price index.

d Negative change in specific energy consumption in relation to the change in real energy prices.

Source: Statistisches Bundesamt; calculations by the authors.

first group ascertained from time series analysis for manufacturing industry in the USA that energy and capital are
complementary; they thus assert that rising energy prices
cause not only energy consumption to decline but the capital stock as well. By contrast, the intercountry time series
study by Griffin and Gregory, which was based on industrial
data for four years and nine countries, showed a substitution relationship between the two factors.

A weakness common to these studies is that they are based
on series of data that end before the first oil shock. Moreover, a drawback of the mere time series analyses is that
they are not dynamically specified, so that they disregard
the adjustment process.

A study on Switzerland that does not suffer from these de-
fects comes to the conclusion that the scope for substitution between the factors capital, labour, energy and materials is negligible in the short term but significant in the
long term (Kugler 1982).

In the case of Germany, the Ifo-Institut detects complementarity (Ifo 1983b, pp. 12 ff), whereas the Institut für Weltwirtschaft in Kiel is of the opinion that "no evidence of
complementarity between energy and capital can be discover-
ed" (Kriegsmann, Neu 1981, p. 58).

In fact, a close complementary relationship between energy consumption and capital input should persist as long as the capital
stock remains technologically unchanged. However, capital
will be substituted for energy if capital goods based on new
technology are developed. The underlying production function

is therefore of the "putty clay" type, in other words production factors can be substituted for one another only at the
time of acquisition of plant and machinery but not in the
course of their use. According to OECD calculations that include energy as well as capital and labour among the factors
of production, such a "vintage approach" has proved realistic
for most of the seven largest OECD countries (Artus 1983).
It is also applied to this group of countries by Nordhaus in
the context of his medium-term energy policy model (Nordhaus
1980). The example of the demand for motor cars serves to illustrate the relationship. In the event of a large increase
in petrol prices that is considered to be permanent not every
car owner will immediately buy a new car with a lower specific
fuel consumption. First, the development and production of
the desired vehicles require time and secondly the age structure of the cars already on the road must be taken into consideration. Over the short term, therefore, adjustment will
consist essentially in a reduced use of existing models,
whereas over the long term their replacement by energy-saving vehicles can be expected. Similar capital theory considerations probably also apply to housing, industrial machinery
and other forms of physical capital (Winckler 1980, p. 26).

As far as the input ratio of energy and labour is concerned
there is generally found to be a high degree of substitut-
ability among the two factors of production. The substitution
relationship is to some extent a mirror image of the complementary relationship of capital and energy - in other words,
the factor labour does not replace the factor energy in isolation (which would be difficult to imagine in practice in
any case), but a "package" of capital and energy. This has
been illustrated by an example from the household sector: "The
acquisition of durable household goods such as washing ma-

chines, dishwashers and so forth has made it possible to reduce the input of labour in the home and to raise both the
average and the marginal productivity of labour. The corol-
lary is an increase in the inputs of capital and energy. If
energy prices now rise dramatically, the input of labour and
capital will be replaced again by labour. The important point
in this example is that capital and energy are used in a complementary fashion and both factors of production can replace
... the factor labour" (Winckler 1980, p. 26).

In the corporate sector such a relationship is postulated,
for example, for the industrial upswing in the USA which followed the recession brought about by the first oil shock and
which was characterised by relatively low investment and a
high use of labour: "Finally on the list of deterrents to
capital spending, there is the significantly increased cost
of building and operating new plants and equipment because
of the higher price of energy of all types. The average economist may have forgotten his microeconomics, but the average
businesman has not; he pays close attention to the relative
cost of factors of production. And over the past three years
it has become more expensive to increase capacity by adding
machinery and equipment than it has by adding workers"
(Berndt, Wood 1979, p. 351).

A number of studies examine the effects of an increase in
energy costs on the ratio of the inputs of highly skilled
and less skilled workers. The findings are contradictory.
Berndt, Morrison (1979, p. 134) detect "a compositional change
within aggregate labour favouring increased employment of blue
collar workers at the expense of white collar labourers". Ray
gives the field of recycling as an example of the increased
demand for less highly skilled labour as a result of a rise
in energy prices: "The properly organised recycling of met-

als, paper, glass and possibly other materials in quantities exceeding by many times their present level ... requires a significant amount of relatively unskilled labour" (Ray 1982, p. 226). However, research into the regional employment effects of rapidly rising energy costs in the USA comes to the opposite conclusion. Taking a region of California as an example, it shows that the rise in the cost of energy has led to a shift in consumer expenditure from labour-intensive to energy-intensive sectors. This has caused the unemployment rate to double or treble among relatively unskilled workers, mainly in the services sector (Kolk 1983).[13]

The existence of a substitution relationship between energy and labour - and the possible favouring of less well qualified workers by rising energy prices - does not, of course, mean that an increase in energy costs creates no employment problems. The income effect must be considered as well as the substitution effect. If overall demand diminishes owing to the fall in real incomes caused by higher energy prices, the demand for labour also declines. For example, the model estimates for the USA described in section 1 of this chapter show that between 1972 and 1976 the income effect was clearly stronger than the substitution effect, so that the oil price rises of 1973-74 also left their clear imprint on the labour markets (Hudson, Jorgenson 1979, p. 102).

The level of employment is also affected by the introduction of energy-saving techniques. Number of examples could be quoted to show that the installation of new, more energy-efficient plant and machinery also brings a saving in manpower.[14] Nevertheless, a large part of the energy used in manufacturing industry - roughly three-quarters of total energy consumption (Kenneth, Gassmann 1982, p. 32) - consists of process heat. Hence, increased energy productivity can be achieved here

mainly by installing improved furnaces and boilers. This
has no significant impact on the use of labour. Moreover,
the negative employment effects must be balanced against
the positive ones of increases in real incomes resulting
from modernisation; these are more likely to occur and will
be all the stronger the more flexibly enterprises and workers
respond to the demand impulses.

As well as the replacement of energy by labour and capital,
the replacement of dear energy by cheaper fuels is also an
important adjustment strategy. In practice this means mainly that oil consumption is reduced.

Table 5.12 shows that oil's share in industry's total energy consumption in the OECD diminished from 37 to 32 % between
1973 and 1981. The fact that the decline was not larger is
explained partly by a relative increase in the oil consumption of US industry from 20 to 22 %. Japan too can report
only modest success in this respect; oil's share did fall
by 9 percentage points, but in 1981 oil products still accounted for almost 50 % of total industrial energy consumption, a
much larger proportion than in any other important industrialised country. The EC countries, on the other hand, made significant progress in reducing the dependence of their industries on oil; in this group of countries oil's share contracted from 48 to 37 %.

If particularly energy-intensive industries are examined individually, it can be seen that it is chiefly in the non-metallic products industry and in the steel industry that the importance of petroleum as a source of energy has been greatly
reduced. By contrast, the share of oil used in the production
of non-ferrous metals has risen further; however, the direct
use of oil products in this industry is of secondary impor-

Table 5.12: OIL AS A PROPORTION OF THE ENERGY CONSUMPTION OF ENERGY-INTENSIVE INDUSTRIES AND OF INDUSTRY AS A WHOLE IN WESTERN INDUSTRIAL COUNTRIES IN 1973 AND 1981

- percentages -

	Iron and Steel		Chemicals		Non-ferrous metals		Non-metallic products		Industry as a whole	
	1973	1981	1973	1981	1973	1981	1973	1981	1973	1981
USA	7.4	5.6	14.3	8.4	5.5	3.3	n.a.	9.3	19.9	22.3
Canada	9.1	5.6	55.3	n.a.	16.5	6.3	37.8	31.3	38.8	25.0
Japan	22.7	8.2	65.6	67.2	n.a.	41.2	32.8	30.3	56.6	48.0
Federal Rep. of Germany	16.4	4.2	25.2	22.1	21.4	11.7	59.3	29.1	42.1	33.2
France	17.4	5.8	41.3	17.4	23.0	18.9	71.8	n.a.	51.6	41.3
United Kingdom	30.0	16.9	4.5	14.5	21.6	14.9	32.1	22.2	47.1	36.4
Italy	14.2	10.9	43.2	27.0	21.8	5.2	64.5	18.1	58.8	42.5
Netherlands	19.2	8.8	3.9	3.8	n.a.	n.a.	11.5	9.6	42.1	29.3
Sweden	42.3	29.2	47.6	42.9	16.7	25.0	86.8	62.1	52.3	38.4
OECD	16.3	8.2	34.2	20.9	10.9	14.6	53.9	25.4	37.3	32.2
EC	19.2	8.1	26.5	18.6	20.7	15.1	55.7	23.8	47.9	36.9

Source: OECD: Energy Balances; calculations by the authors.

272

tance. The main source of energy here is electricity, in the generation of which the use of oil is rapidly decreasing.

The contribution that changing the energy mix - and other adjustment strategies - makes to reducing a company's energy costs can be determined approximately using the following formula:[15]

$$gEC \approx gEP_f + gSEC - (gEP_f - gEP_a) - gPP$$

where the terms have the following meanings:

g   = growth rate

EC = incidence of energy costs (= energy expenditure as a proportion of gross production value)

EP_f = price of energy with unchanged energy mix

SEC = specific energy consumption (= energy consumption per unit of output)

EP_a = actual price of energy

PP = product price.

In the above formula the substitution effect is expressed by the term in parenthesis, in other words by the difference between the actual price of energy and the price that would have obtained had the energy mix remained unchanged. Further adjustment strategies would be to reduce specific energy consumption and to raise the final product price.

Applied to energy-intensive industries and to manufacturing industry as a whole in Germany - corresponding data for other countries are not available in a comparable form - the formula shows that changing the energy mix has contributed comparatively little so far to containing the incidence of energy costs (see Table 5.13). Reducing specific energy consumption, however, has played a much more important part, the only

Table 5.13: CHANGE IN THE ACTUAL AND IMPUTED INCIDENCE OF ENERGY COSTS IN ENERGY-INTENSIVE INDUSTRIES IN THE FEDERAL REPUBLIC OF GERMANY, 1972-1980[a]

	Incidence of energy costs		Explanatory factors		
	Actual	Imputed[c]	"Passing on"[d]	Substitution[e]	Conservation[f]
Iron and Steel	3.0	11.3	-2.8	-0.4	-4.6
Paper	1.6	13.5	-5.7	-0.4	-3.0
Non-metallic minerals	4.2	15.8	-4.5	-0.9	-4.4
Glass	4.8	15.3	-4.5	-1.0	-2.9
Non-ferrous metals	2.5	10.1	-5.4	-0.4	-0.7
Chemicals	1.0	11.8	-5.4	-0.2	-1.0
Ceramics	3.4	13.2	-5.6	-0.8	0.0
Foundry products	6.3	12.7	-6.3	-0.8	1.6
Memorandum:					
Manufacturing industry[b]	3.1	12.9	-5.3	-0.5	-2.4

a Average annual rate of growth.

b Excluding oil refining.

c Change in the energy price index assuming constant composition by sources of energy (composition of energy consumption in 1972).

d Negative rate of growth in producer price index.

e Difference between actual and imputed increase in energy prices.

f Rate of change in specific energy consumption.

Source: Statistisches Bundesamt; calculations by the authors.

exceptions being the ceramics and foundry products industry. In view of the price links among the various sources of energy and the shortages that can be expected even in important non-oil forms of energy, this relationship is unlikely to change substantially in the future.

3. Options for economic policy

The problems of growth and structural adjustment caused by
real oil price increases pose a particular challenge to economic policy in the oil-importing countries. From a general
viewpoint, its task obviously consists in ensuring that the
structure of production and consumption adjusts as flexibly
as possible to the changed scarcity conditions. In particular, it must foster a readiness to make productive investment.

The appropriate "mix" of instruments employed under such a
policy differs from one country to another. Depending on the
ideological orientation, institutional set-up and other factors specific to individual countries, either direct state
intervention and activities by the state itself are given
priority or the government influences the environment for
decisions by private households and enterprises. At the same
time, since the first oil shock broad agreement has developed,
particularly among the Western industrial countries, on the
crucial importance of correct price signals.

Scarcity prices for oil and other energy sources might conflict with the objective of stability, however. To answer
that question we have to refer back to the remarks in Chapter
3, which indicate that some rise in the general level of
prices will be inevitable if oil prices increase abruptly.
The same will occur if the rise in energy prices is held in
check by price controls, subsidies and similar measures. Experience has shown that pent-up price increases of this kind
exert an even stronger influence elsewhere or at a later
date, as may be seen in the examples of France, Italy and
Canada. By contrast, countries such as Germany that have allowed energy price movements in the world market to be fully

reflected in domestic energy prices or have accentuated the effect by raising duties on energy can point to a relatively good performance on the inflation front.[16] The reasons for this are not to be found primarily in energy price policy, however, but in monetary and fiscal policy and in the behaviour of wage negotiators.

An energy price policy consistent with scarcity conditions does also not conflict with a policy designed to safeguard the country's international competitiveness. This will be demonstrated in Chapter 6 of this study.

But is the income distribution objective jepardised? Energy price increases have a much stronger direct impact on low-wage earners than on higher income groups, as they have to use a larger proportion of their household budget for direct purchases of energy products (mainly electricity, heating oil, gas and fuels).[17]

Moreover, income distribution is indirectly affected by rising energy prices. The indirect effects stem from the fact that the prices of energy-intensive goods and services rise and that these products have different weights in the budgets of the various income categories. It has not been proven empirically whether they reinforce or soften the regressive income distribution effects of direct expenditure on energy. For example, data on Canada show that indirect energy expenditure accounts for approximately the same proportion of total expenditure for all income groups (Waverman 1979). In the USA, by contrast, both a linear (Hannon 1975) and a regressive relationship (Herendeen et al. 1979) have been detected between indirect energy expenditure and total expenditure. In either case, the net effect of direct and indirect factors is probably regressive.

The regressive distribution effects of rising energy prices on the income expenditure side could be offset by progressive effects on the income generation side, however. The latter could be expected if the rise in energy prices changed the structure of employment in favour of unskilled workers. As was shown in the second section of this Chapter, the empirical evidence in this regard is mixed. Moreover, no study has yet been able to calculate the overall effect of an energy price shock on income distribution. The only clear point seems to be the precarious situation of persons who are not gainfully employed: "In particular the retired, disabled and other people not in the labour force are unable to take advantage of progressive employment effects, and may bear the brunt of both direct and indirect regressive consumption effects" (Berndt, Morrison 1979, p. 134). In such cases the conflict between resource allocation and income distribution might, for example, be resolved by compensatory payments from general tax revenues.

What remains to be examined is the effects of non-price policy measures and the interplay of the various government measures to cope with energy scarcity. However, these aspects cannot te treated in detail here because of the multitude of actual and conceivable instruments and packages of measures.

In accordance with the dual role of economic policy in the structural adjustment to more expensive oil - namely, to strengthen the domestic energy base and to reduce the energy coefficient of the economy as a whole[18] - the present section will first discuss the role of the state in the develop-

ment of the energy sector. The question will then be asked
how the state can help reduce the dependence of economic
development on the availability of domestic or foreign energy resources (in particular oil) so that energy does not become a growth constraint in the long term.

a.   The development of the energy sector

Up to now, the energy sector has not expanded as rapidly as
expected in the oil-importing countries, as can be seen from
the low rates of growth in investment and declining investment ratios. Investment theory can provide no satisfactory
explanation for this trend. Instead, political influences appear to be of considerable importance.

The activities of the energy sector can also be of great
importance from the cyclical point of view. For example, they
may give rise to a deflationary gap. This obviously occurs
if the energy sector, whose relative income position has improved as a result of an increase in oil prices, has a lower
(marginal) propensity to spend than the rest of the economy.
According to calculations by the OECD, the resultant deflationary effect is potentially just as significant as the de-
mand-dampening effect of the transfer of purchasing power to
oil-producing countries (Llewellyn 1983, p.5).

From the point of view of structural adjustment to more expensive oil, which is the decisive aspect in this context,
it depends mainly on the capacity effect of investment in
the energy sector. No comprehensive data on this aspect are
available on which to base an international comparison. The
following information therefore relates only to energy investment in the EC and specifically in the Federal Republic
of Germany.

In the European Community - excluding Denmark, Greece and
Luxembourg - energy investment only increased from 7 % of
gross fixed capital formation in 1970 to 8.4 % in 1980. Ad-
mittedly, an acceleration in the overall pace of investment
can be detected within this time span - the annual rate of
growth rose from 3.1 % in 1970-73 to 3.4 % in 1973-77 and
4.9 % in 1977-80 - but these figures conceal marked disparities between countries. Only France and Italy showed a steady
upward trend.[19] The weak overall investment performance of
the energy sector is also reflected in its investment ratio.
Immediately after the first oil shock energy companies in
the Community of Six stepped up investment much faster than
output, so that the investment ratio jumped from 33.2 % in
1973 to 38.9 % in 1975. However, it then declined steadily,
so that in 1979 it stood at 32 %, below the 1973 level. The
decline in the investment ratio in other sectors of the economy, such as manufacturing industry and the private services
sector, was much smaller by comparison.[20]

Germany's energy sector experienced an investment boom that
began in the late sixties and continued until 1975. The annual rate of growth in the volume of investment between 1968
and 1975 was 8.1 % in the energy sector, many times higher
than in the economy as a whole (1.8 %). The main force behind this dynamic growth was the electricity industry, whose
share of total energy investment rose from 60.7 to 68.1 %.
The trend was reversed after 1975. The volume of investment
in the energy sector declined by 2.1 % a year until 1980 -
compared with an increase of 4.7 % a year in overall investment - and the electricity industry's share sank to 58.9 %.
Investment was intensified only in hard-coal mining.[21]

The conventional theory of investment cannot adequately explain the investment trends in the energy sector. Calculations by the DIW with regard to Germany show that there is only a weak link between changes in the relative prices of capital and energy goods on the one hand and changes in gross fixed capital formation in the various energy industries on the other (DIW 1982b, p. 361). This suggests that political influences tipped the balance, such as the often mentioned legal and administrative obstacles to the construction of major energy production plant.

The future trend of energy investment is difficult to predict. Investment decisions will be based mainly on expected oil price developments. Numerous investment projects that had been planned after the second oil shock in anticipation of a persistent increase in the cost of oil have now been abandoned or shelved, as oil price expectations have been revised substantially downwards owing to the actual decline in oil prices.[22] However, investments that are regarded as economically sound despite the modified expectations have also been affected (IEA 1983, p. 56).

In market economies it is the task of economic policy to ensure that such projects that are viable over the long term can be put into effect and operated by private initiative. The deciding factor here is the stability of the economic framework provided. This includes a clear conception of future energy supply systems (shares drawn from each energy source, degree of decentralisation of the energy supply, the relative importance of major projects and smaller units, etc.), transparency in tax and expenditure policies and unambiguous criteria for encouraging the development of new energy technologies.[23] Economic policy must also determine the trade-off between economy and security of energy supply and decide how the resulting costs are to be distributed.

281

For example, if domestic energy companies that are not competitive at the international level are to be protected
against foreign competition in order to ensure supplies, import controls and prices that are excessive by international
standards do not seem particularly well suited because of
their negative effects on resource allocation. Compensatory
payments that could be financed out of general tax revenues
would be preferable in this case. Special duties would also
be conceivable, however, such as a levy on oil imports or oil
consumption of the kind discussed in the EC but eventually
rejected.

The development of the energy sector in the oil-importing
countries is not only a problem of domestic policy for each
country but also a fundamental issue in international relations. The spill-over effects of energy projects, the scale
of individual schemes, the resulting problems of finance
and the advantages of combining and concentrating scarce research and development resources are sound arguments for international co-ordination and co-operation in this field.[24]
Moreover, the energy sector would appear to be an important
area for development co-operation with the countries of the
Third World.

In the Western industrial countries several factors have ham-
pered international co-operation and co-ordination in the development of the energy sector up to now. Chief among these
are differences in energy resource endowment in individual countries, different priorities with regard to the energy mix, ideological differences and concern for national
prestige and security. It is true that broad agreement has
been reached on the underlying objectives of energy policy
and that the member countries of the IEA have declared their
willingness to submit achievements at national level to an-

nual international scrutiny in the light of commonly agreed principles and concrete targets,[25] but it is doubtful whether this "strategic" consensus will develop into detailed "operational" collaboration among a wider group of countries. The supranational energy policy sought by the EC Commission appears increasingly Utopian and, if implemented, would inevitably founder simply because of the Community's meagre financial resources. It is conceivable, however, that a small number of countries might combine to implement or finance specific energy projects on a case-by-case basis, as already occurs in energy research and development (Mohnfeld 1982, p. 160).[26] Furthermore, governments could improve the legal framework for international co-operation between firms. In the EC this would require the competition rules of the Treaty of Rome to be interpreted in a manner that fostered co-operation. The problem of a possible clash between industrial and competition policy objectives would have to be settled on the political plane.

The energy situation of the oil-importing developing countries is characterised on the one hand by high import dependency. In 1981 imported energy accounted for almost 60 % of total commercial energy consumption in this group of countries, a proportion that had barely altered since 1973 (cf. Table A-22). In the middle-income developing countries (those with a per capita income of at least $ 410 in 1981) energy consumption rose at an annual rate of 4.9 % between 1974 and 1980, considerably faster than energy production (3.7 %). The disparity between consumption and production therefore widened further; between 1960 and 1974 energy production had increased by 7.8 % a year and consumption by 8.7 %. In the low-income countries (excluding China and India, where energy consumption and production grew in step) domestic energy production was expanded much more strongly than con-

sumption; the annual growth rates for the period from 1974
to 1980 work out at 6.5 and 2.0 % respectively, following
rates of 14.7 and 9.0 % respectively between 1960 and 1974
(World Bank 1983a, p. 188).

On the other hand, the oil-importing developing countries
have abundant energy reserves. However, the capital cost of
converting them into usable energy is enormous, particularly as the capital intensity of the investment projects -
measured in terms of the capital input per unit of energy
output - often rises sharply and in addition to the costs
of energy production itself considerable costs must be
met for such things as infrastructure (roads, harbour
works, etc.) (for details, see Polte 1983). The World Bank
estimates the volume of economically viable energy investment at nearly $ 900 billion between 1982 and 1992 at 1982
prices. Investment in electric power projects accounts for
more than half of this figure (see the columns for low-income countries and oil importers in Table 5.14). In terms
of GDP, energy investment in the developing countries (including middle-income oil exporters) would have to rise from
2-3 % in the late seventies to about 4 % in the period from
1982 to 1992 (World Bank 1983b, p. 67). The World Bank considers that most of the projected energy investments would
still be of benefit to the developing countries if the
price of oil fell to $ 25 a barrel (p.70). If it remained
unchanged in real terms, and if all the energy projects
sought by the World Bank were realised, including energy
conservation measures, the share of the developing countries' total export receipts required to pay for oil imports could be reduced from 25 % in 1980 to about 10 % in
1995 (p. 80).

Table 5.14: COMMERCIAL ENERGY INVESTMENT REQUIREMENTS IN DEVELOPING COUNTRIES,
1982 - 1992

(billions of 1982 dollars)

	Low income countries	Middle income countries		All developing countries	Annual average 1982-92
		Oil importers	Oil exporters		
Electric power					
Hydro	74.4	132.2	31.8	238.4	21.7
Nuclear	6.3	40.8	6.1	53.2	4.8
Geothermal	0.1	4.3	2.1	6.5	0.6
Thermal	43.2	75.8	39.7	158.7	14.4
Transmission and distribution	49.9	101.8	49.9	201.6	18.3
Subtotal	173.9	354.9	129.6	658.4	59.8
Oil					
Exploration	21.2	48.9	99.1	169.2	15.4
Development	43.2	32.4	195.9	271.5	24.7
Other	2.5	6.0	16.7	25.2	2.3
Subtotal	66.9	87.3	311.7	465.9	42.4
Refineries	30.8	52.8	39.7	123.3	11.2
Natural gas					
Exploration, development, transmission and maintenance	17.5	16.8	30.2	64.5	5.9
Domestic distribution	4.3	4.7	7.4	16.4	1.5
Exports	0.0	3.0	6.2	9.2	0.8
Subtotal	21.8	24.5	43.8	90.1	8.2
Coal	55.2	27.2	6.3	88.7	8.1
Total	348.6	546.7	531.1	1.426.4	129.7

Source: Reprinted from: World Bank: The Energy Transition in Developing Countries, Washington 1983, p. 68.

Financing and executing the projects raises considerable problems, however. In many cases only a small part of necessary funds can be raised from domestic savings if other equally important development projects are not to be neglected or severe restrictions placed on the population's real disposable incomes. Furthermore, in most oil-importing developing countries the capital goods industry has only limited ability to deliver the necessary equipment. There is also a lack of technical and organisational knowledge, management knowhow and similar intangible assets. The development of the energy sector therefore requires a greatly increased inflow of foreign exchange or transfer of resources. The foreign exchange content of the entire body of energy investments considered viable by the World Bank works out at about 50 %, although there are substantial differences between countries and projects (p. 69).

A substantial financial contribution will have to come from official development assistance, more of which has been directed towards the energy sector since the increase in oil prices.[27] Nevertheless, the financing of energy investments on "soft" preferential terms is increasingly running up against budgetary constraints and the competing claims of other high priority sectors,[28] so that in future an even larger portion than hitherto will have to be financed via the market. This applies primarily to the relatively advanced developing countries, whereas the poorest countries will remain heavily dependent on development aid.

Financing energy investment on commercial terms presupposes that the developing countries enjoy unhindered access to the markets of industrial countries for their manufactured goods. This will enable them both to earn part of the necessary foreign exchange directly and to improve their stand-

ing in the international credit markets (by putting up a
good export performance).

At the same time, the developing countries' access to commercial credit for energy projects can be made easier by granting official guarantees. Non-concessional loans from the
World Bank and other multilateral agencies (including OPEC)
are also helpful. Not least important, official bodies can
act as a kind of catalyst; one example in this respect is
co-financing by the World Bank and private investors, a
field in which energy projects predominate.[29]

The World Bank and other official agencies can also act as
a catalyst to private direct investment, which is especially needed in the development of the oil and gas sector. However, the international oil companies, which dispose of the
necessary technological, organisational and managerial capa-
bilities, have shown relatively little interest so far in
investing in oil-importing developing countries. This is due
partly to the preferential tax treatment of domestic oil investment in industrial countries. Such concessions could "be
revised in the interests of tax efficiency and justice" (Palmer 1983, p. 38). Other obstacles to investment are to be
found chiefly in the developing countries themselves. In
many instances the oil and gas deposits are too small by the
standards of the oil companies, which prefer to concentrate
their limited resources on major projects. However, improvements in tax arrangements could stimulate exploration for
small deposits.[30] Foreign investors are also deterred by
political risks; this is particularly true of small firms,
whereas "the large oil companies certainly welcome measures
to stabilise their relations with governments, but do not
regard political risks as a fundamental obstacle to a commitment in developing countries" (Palmer 1983, p. 38). How-

ever, they often find that domestic firms have an advantage over them in the awarding of exploration rights and that contracts can be extremely difficult to negotiate. In these instances the World Bank, for example, could act as mediator. It could similarly provide financial support for joint ventures that were in danger of failing because of the capital weakness of the indigenous partner and could participate in projects directly via the International Finance Corporation (IFC). Moreover, general investment conditions in the energy sectors of oil-importing developing countries can be improved with technical assistance from industrial countries and multilateral agencies; their prime contribution might lie in assisting with long-term energy planning, in which the role of foreign investors and the rules for their activities need to be defined in binding terms.

It also lies in the interest of the industrial countries themselves to foster the development of the energy sector in the Third World, as it eases the pressure on world energy markets and increases the security of supply. At the same time, it could be expected to generate substantial orders, particularly for capital goods and certain types of services (such as consultancy services), given the developing countries' high import requirement. Is is also in the interest of industrial countries to strengthen the competitiveness of oil-importing developing countries over the long term; such an improvement, which would be greatly aided by development of the energy sector, opens up new opportunities for the international division of labour, to the benefit of both parties.

b.   Reducing energy dependence

Severing the link between economic development and energy
consumption is a problem of structural policy, which can
come into conflict with cyclical economic policy if the latter seeks to ensure a high level of employment over the
short term. As a result, the necessary structural change is
impeded, and long-term employment and income opportunities
are lost.

Real oil price increases can, however, produce a cumulative
downturn that makes counter-cyclical measures imperative.
The deciding factor is the size of the secondary fall in
demand caused by an oil price increase. In contrast to the
primary contraction in consumption stemming from the redistribution of income in favour of oil-producing countries,
the secondary fall in demand is "unnecessary" in terms of
the economy as a whole. It comes about because the deflationary secondary effects of the decline in demand in certain sectors (the worst affected are various consumer goods
industries whose product ranges do not match changed demand
preferences and adjustment requirements and those energy-
intensive sectors that must compete primarily on price) is
not offset by expansionary second-round effects in the rest
of the economy. In this instance a compensatory fiscal policy may be required.[31]

As regards structural adjustment to increased oil prices
the state can encourage that process by a policy of "positive adjustment", which breaks down rigidities, fosters mobility and competition and removes legal and administrative
obstacles - in short, it increases the structural flexibility of an economy.[32] Special measures to encourage energy
savings and oil substitution then form part of this general
strategy.

The scope for "easy", once-only improvements in energy conservation through improved management, personnel training in maintenance and "housekeeping", relatively simple changes and improvements in existing production processes and so forth has largely been exhausted in the Western industrial countries. A further reduction in specific energy consumption therefore presupposes investment by both private households and firms.

The household sector still has considerable potential to increase its energy efficiency.[33] By exploiting it, oil-importing countries can not only greatly improve their current payments balances but also generate appreciable growth and employment effects. This has been demonstrated by a study relating to the Federal Republic of Germany (Meyer-Renschhausen, Pfaffenberger 1983), which calculates the investment requirement and energy saving that would arise in the housing sector if "the stock of old housing (buildings erected before 1978) were brought up to presentday standards of thermal insulation and the level of central heating that can now be achieved" (p. 252). The energy savings that could be achieved amount to about DM 12 billion at 1981 prices. As the energy products are mostly imported, the reduction in energy demand is reflected mainly in the current account. The deflationary effect in the domestic economy is small, and is in any case exceeded many times over by the demand-stimulating effects of increased investment in thermal insulation and boiler modernisation. The demand stimulus, which predominantly benefits domestic suppliers, is estimated at about DM 178 billion.[34] Hence there appear to be sound reasons for the state to assist households' own efforts, particularly as the positive employment effects of their activities only occur if investment expenditure is in addition to other spending, not at the expense of it.[35]

In the corporate sector considerable energy and oil-saving
effects are often obtained in investment projects in which
energy saving and oil substitution are not the main objective but a side-effect. However, such investment is impeded
by rising energy prices, as shown in section 1c. of this
Chapter. At the same time, rising energy prices give the
manufacturers of plant and equipment a strong incentive to
pay closer attention to energy efficiency and flexibility
in the sources of energy used. Moreover, with an increasing
number of investment projects the rise in energy costs is
the dominant investment motive.

These considerations suggest a kind of dual strategy:[36]

- the state ensures scarcity energy prices and price relationships so that investment to conserve energy and replace oil is worthwhile. Such projects can also be encouraged by offering financial incentives, as they promise high social benefit.[37] The means could be drawn from
  energy tax revenues;[38]

- at the same time, the state takes suitable measures to
  counteract the general weakness of investment activity
  caused by real oil price increases.

A multitude of special incentives are conceivable to stimulate investment,[39] but more important than specific measures
of this sort appears to be the general investment climate.

In this context the distribution of income between the factors capital and labour is often regarded as a crucial factor. There has been a marked shift in favour of labour since
the early seventies, as can be seen from the trend in the
real labour cost gap (see Table 5.15). It is measured as the

Table 5.15: THE REAL LABOUR COST GAP IN THE LEADING INDUSTRIAL COUNTRIES IN THE FIRST AND SECOND OIL CRISIS[a] (1972 = 100)

	First oil crisis				Second oil crisis			
	1973	1974	1975	1979	1980	1981	1982
USA	99.7	100.8	100.1	101.3	101.6	101.1	102.6
Canada	98.4	103.9	105.1	104.8	105.4	105.7	108.6
Japan	103.9	110.4	113.2	107.8	106.7	107.0	108.1
Federal Rep. of Germany	101.5	105.2	104.1	100.1	101.3	101.0	98.6
France	101.3	105.0	109.5	108.9	110.4	112.7	111.4
United Kingdom	101.1	107.0	112.0	102.4	105.3	104.1	101.0
Italy	101.5	102.4	107.2	104.2	104.2	109.1	109.9
Total	100.9	103.9	105.1	103.5	103.9	104.1	104.6

a Real labour cost gap = ratio between changes in real compensation per head of dependent employment and real national income per employed person.

Source: OECD: Economic Outlook, December 1982, p. 45; Llewellyn (1983), pp. 9 and 17.

ratio between the change in real compensation per head of
dependent employment and the change in real national income
per employed person.

It emerges that the labour cost gap widened considerably
during the first oil crisis, increasing by an average of 5 %
between 1972 and 1975 in the seven major industrial countries.
Only in the USA did changes in labour incomes have no great
effect on income distribution. In Japan, by contrast, distribution ratios shifted very markedly in favour of labour.

In the second oil crisis the reaction of wage and salary
earners was much more moderate. During this phase the real
labour cost gap changed little overall, but in 1982 it was
larger than before the first oil shock in all of the countries examined except Germany. In France, Italy, Canada and
Japan the difference between 1972 and 1982 amounted to about
10 %.

In addition, the profitability of deployed capital declined
dramatically in some countries in the second oil crisis. For
example, in the USA the gross rate of return on capital in
manufacturing fell from 17.5 % to 10 % between 1978 and 1982;
in Germany it declined from 14.6 to 11.6 % over the same period and in the United Kingdom it shrank from 7.8 to 4.3 %.[40]
These figures reflect primarily the weak productivity gains
of recent years and, closely allied to that, a substantial
increase in the macroeconomic capital coefficient i.e. the
ratio of fixed capital formation to national product.

On the one hand there therefore appears to be a need for
correction in income distribution relations, but on the
other hand the much more adverse trend in profitability
indicates that wage restraint cannot be regarded as a pan-

acea that will revitalise investment. Equally important as the price of labour are other prices such as real interest and exchange rates. Moreover, the oil price increases "have resulted in the entry of uncertainty into economic matters in a manner and depth virtually unknown in previous economic history" (Banks 1980, p. 209). This is a major obstacle to productive investment, the removal of which requires first of all a stable economic policy framework. Last not least investment behaviour is influenced by trade policies, for export-oriented industries need to have confidence in the openness of markets as a basis for investment decisions. The import of rising oil prices on trade and trade policies is dealt with in greater detail in the following chapter.

Footnotes to Chapter 5

1 Numerous studies have provided evidence of a causal relationship between the rise in oil prices and recession. For a survey of the effects of the first oil crisis in macro-economic models see, for example, Dohner 1981. With regard to the second oil shock, see Llewellyn 1983.

2 The annual average rate of growth in GDP only slowed down from 5.8
to 5.1 % in oil-importing developing countries between 1968-72 and
1973-78, but from 4.4 to 2.6 % in the OECD. Nevertheless, the performance of the various developing countries varied widely; the rate
of growth in those countries that have become important exporters of
manufactures   - Argentina, Brazil, Greece, Hong Kong, Israel, Yugoslavia, Korea, Portugal, Singapore and South Africa - slowed down
from 8.1 to 5.3 %, whereas in the developing countries in the lowest
income group - those with a per capita income of less than $ 350 in
1978 - GDP growth accelerated from 3.4 to 4.7 % (calculated from IMF
1982b, p. 144).

The importance of imports for growth is illustrated by the fact that
those oil-importing developing countries whose imports rose more rapidly between 1973 and 1976 than between 1965 and 1973 suffered a much
smaller slowdown in growth - from 4.0 % in the period 1965-73 to 3.4 %
between 1973 and 1978 - than countries with reduced import growth,
where the rise in GDP fell from 5.4 to 3 % (UNCTAD 1982, Vol. 3, p. 21).

3 The growth rate of oil-importing developing countries as a whole fell
steadily from 5.2 % in 1978 to 0.8 % in 1982 despite a continued rapid
increase in population. The trend was particularly adverse in Third
World countries heavily engaged in the export of manufactures. Here
domestic output actually declined by 0.2 % in 1981, and the increase
of the same magnitude in 1982 hardly represented appreciable growth.
In regional terms, the slowdown in growth was sharpest in Latin America, where negative growth rates of 0.1 and 1.5 % were recorded in
1981 and 1982 (IMF 1983, p. 171).

4 The substitution effect corresponds to a loss of productivity, which
is determined primarily by the elasticity of substitution. This measures the amount by which energy consumption per unit of output falls
if energy prices rise by 1 % in relation to the cost of capital and
labour. Assuming the substitution elasticity to be 1, the initial energy share to be 10 % and that there is no change in the inputs of capital and labour, an increase of 10 % in the relative price of energy
leads to a 1 % reduction in output per unit of capital and labour input.

This measure of productivity also falls if capital and labour are di-
verted from more productive uses into the energy sector, for example
to offset a decline in energy imports. Productivity declines if the
additional domestic energy production requires a higher factor input per unit of output than existing production. Denison, among others,
refers to this relationship (Denison 1979, p. 16). A similar argument

applies when the Deutsche Bundesbank attributes the slowdown in productiv ity growth after the second oil crisis primarily to falling capacity util isation but also partly to "a shift in investment towards energy-saving p jects that are not directly productive" (Deutsche Bundesbank 1981, p. 17)

5   Such an optimistic view is expressed by Fabritius, Petersen, for ex- ample: "Since the negative impact on real GDP of a $ 1 loss in the terms-of-trade is only indirect, whereas a $ 1 increase in real ex- ports affects real GDP directly as well as indirectly, 100 % respend- ing will most likely stimulate the real GDP in the industrial coun- tries, as increases in exports more than offset decreases in domestic demand" (Fabritius, Petersen 1981, p. 329). In a model calculation the authors even arrive at the conclusion that above a respending ratio of 40-45 % real oil price increases have a stimulatory effect on the GDP of the OECD (p. 235). However, this presupposes an un- changed economic policy. The considerable discrepancies between ac- tual events and the model results are explained by the fact that governments reacted to the increase in the cost of oil by introduc- ing austerity programmes in order to pursue national balance-of-pay- ments and stabilisation objectives (p. 236).

6   The GATT Annual Report for 1978-79 states in this connection that "A high proportion of equipment in total investment expenditure im- plies something of a defensive investment posture. It is character- istic of periods in which a high level of uncertainty makes large- scale, long-term commitments imprudent; firms adopt a wait-and-see attitude, content in the meantime with minor productivity improve- ments" (GATT International Trade 1978/79, p. 80).

7   The periodic capital costs, or rental price of capital goods, are "the periodic cost of the equity and debt required to finance the replace- ment cost of the asset, the value of the asset lost per period due to depreciation and taxes on the revenues from the use of the asset" (Tatom 1979, p. 2).

8   Time-lags occur because the investment need is already present be- fore it is recognised. Even once it has been recognised, a further period of time generally passes before the investment decision is actually taken, as finance must be obtained. Finally, delays are caused by the fact that the capital goods must be ordered, produced, delivered and installed (Uri 1980, p. 181).

9   With regard to the future the author concludes that "structural change has occured, implying that energy price will, in general, have a greater impact in future periods than it did have on aver- age over the period 1950-72" (Uri 1980, p. 183).

10 An exception is the non-metallic minerals industry, which is par- ticularly energy intensive. Here "the cost of energy was of greater significance than labour costs for changes in the propensity to in- vest, particularly in the seventies" (Ifo 1983b, p. 137). In other industries, by contrast, the predominant motives were "a reduction in labour costs" and "the modernisation of production facilities". However, there has been an increase in the number of industries

296

"whose investment plans are being strongly influenced from the energy side for the first time" (p. 22). It was also found that "the manufacturers of capital goods are paying increasing attention to the efficient use of energy by their machines" (p. 26).

11 At 1972 prices the desired capital stock had decreased by $ 103 billion by 1976. This figure can be compared with gross investment in 1976 which amounted to $ 165 billion, also calculated at 1972 prices (Hudson, Jorgenson 1979, p. 175).

12 Baumgarten, Herberg, for example, refer to this link: "Commodity substitution will raise demand for products that have become relatively less expensive. If, in addition, some of these products have a low income elasticity the decline in their demand due to the decline of real income will be small. The net effect may well be an increase in demand and thus in output. Moreover, if expanding industries have high, contracting industries low labour input coefficients even total employment might rise" (Baumgarten, Herberg 1982, p. 222).

13 Examples of possible employment effects of a rise in energy costs in individual sectors are also to be found in a Report of the European Parliament (Europäisches Parlament 1981). However, no conclusive overall picture can be gained.

14 In this connection see the examples in: Blick durch die Wirtschaft of 2.2.1982 and 24.2.1982.

15 On the derivation of the formula see Mously 1982.

16 In his medium-term energy policy model applied to the seven leading Western industrial countries Nordhaus deals with the inflationary effects of an energy policy that fosters the rise in energy prices. Higher energy taxes can be prevented from pushing up inflation by using the additional revenue to subsidise the prices of non-energy products. The author therefore concludes that "it would be a serious error to avoid or postpone the steep oil taxes because of fears of their inflationary impacts", for "a policy to reduce oil consumption through high oil taxation in industrial countries would be highly beneficial ... The overall economic gains that arise from the oil taxes appear to be extremely large, ranging from about $ 400 billion for the low tax to $ 1.400 billion for the high tax" (Nordhaus 1980, p. 386).

17 Empirical evidence of the regressive distribution effects of direct energy expenditure is to be found in Waverman (1975), Palmer et al. (1976), King (1978), Thurow (1978) and Meyer-Renschhausen, Pfaffenberger (1983).

18 In practice, serious contradictions can arise between the aims of "strengthening the domestic energy base" and "reducing the economy's overall energy coefficient". France is an example in this respect.

Implementation of the nuclear power programme, which is still sub-stantial despite considerable cuts in the original plans, is al-most impossible to reconcile with the objective of reducing the specific consumption of electricity. Further cuts in the nuclear expansion programme are rejected, however, on employment grounds and because the atomic power industry's leading position in the technical sphere must not be jeopardised.

19 For the basis of the data cf. EG 1982b, p. 144. The investment share of the energy sector in individual EC countries is reproduced in Table A-20.

20 For the basis of the data, cf. EG 1982c, p. 171. The investment ratios of the energy sector, manufacturing industry and the econ-omy as a whole in individual EG countries are to be found in Table A-21.

21 For the basis of the data cf. DIW 1982b.

22 A survey of postponed and abandoned energy investment projects is given in IEA 1983, p. 57.

23 For possible individual measures "which would encourage energy sup-ply investments and would not be a significant departure from the market approach" cf. IEA 1983, pp. 56 ff.

24 One example of beneficial international co-operation in the energy sector is the joint project being undertaken by the companies KHD of Germany and Sumitomo of Japan. The two firms have developed separately methods of coal gasification which are now to be incorporated into a joint pilot plant to be constructed in the grounds of a Swedish research institute (Nachrichten für Außenhandel, 1.12.1983).

25 The regular examination of national energy policies by the IEA is viewed by experts as an extremely useful exercise. "This is the only way of determining whether the same goals are being pursued and com-parable efforts being made. Member countries have to justify their national energy policies to partner countries, a fact which makes them think twice before departing from recognised principles and bans without good cause" (Mohnfeld 1982, p. 161).

26 The latest example of this is an agreement between the United King-dom and France to pool their design and development efforts on the fast breeder type of nuclear reactor (Financial Times, 8.2.1984b).

27 The proportion of energy aid in overall bilateral aid commitments of Western industrial countries rose from 4.9 % in 1978 to 8.7 % in 1981. In the case of multilateral financing institutions the energy share is far higher still (OECD Observer 1983b, p. 17).

28 This can be seen particularly clearly in the example of the World
Bank subsidiary the International Development Association (IDA),
whose aid for the energy sector has declined dramatically (OECD Observer 1983b, p. 17). The World Bank's plan to establish its own energy subsidiary is unlikely to be realised in the foreseeable future.
There also seems little scope for further increasing the energy share
of the World Bank's overall lending programme and the proposal that
additional energy resources be mobilised by raising the overall credit ceiling is meeting strong opposition (World Bank: Annual Report
1982, p. 38).

29 On the possibilities, limitations and forms of co-financing, cf. World
Bank 1983b, pp. 82 ff and Pelosky 1983.

30 The aim should be a tax structure that minimises the tax burden on
marginal deposits but is strongly progressive according to profitability (Palmer 1983, p. 38); in this way the exploration and development
of small deposits could be made attractive to smaller companies.

31 In this respect see also the remarks of the German Council of Economic Experts (Sachverständigenrat 1979, p. 156).

32 Individual aspects of a policy of positive adjustment cannot be examined in this study. See in the first instance the OECD report on positive adjustment policies (OECD 1983a).

33 Information in this regard is to be found in the various country studies carried out in the context of the Consumer Energy Conservation
Policies project at the Wissenschaftszentrum Berlin.

34 Real energy prices are assumed to be constant. If they rose, the import substitution effect would be far higher still. At the same time,
however, a contraction in demand caused by the transfer of purchasing power to other countries would have to be taken into account.

35 For an assessment of energy saving policies and programmes for pri-
vate households in eight countries (Australia, Germany, France,
Greece, the United Kingdom, the Netherlands, Sweden and the USA) see
Joerges, Müller 1983.

36 It is assumed that energy and capital are good long-run substitutes.
On the importance of this question for economic policy, see Özatalay et al.
(1979), who states that "Because a number of governmental initiatives
for energy conservation in the industrial sector are meant to accelerate the introduction of new (and presumably energy-conserving)
physical capital, the question of energy-capital complementarity or
substitution looms large. If capital and energy are actually net
complements, then such policies are misguided and even counterproduc-
tive" (p. 369).

37 On the effectiveness of measures to bring about energy conservation
    in the corporate sector, see for example Ifo 1982, which finds that
    the effects in German industry are considerable.

38 Such "recycling" of increased receipts from energy taxation is advo-
    cated by Nordhaus (1980) and others. Nordhaus also points to the
    trade-off between productivity and terms-of-trade that must be eval-
    uated by a policy designed to accentuate the rise in energy prices:
    "The slightly slower productivity growth ... results from substitut-
    ing domestic capital and labour for imported oil beyond the point
    that would be indicated by private cost minimisation alone. Such an
    "inefficient" policy is worthwhile because of the income gains from
    the improved terms-of-trade in high-tax policies" (p. 383).

39 On the effectiveness of government measures to promote investment,
    see for example DIW 1982a.

40 These data should be interpreted with the utmost caution, however,
    owing to grave problems of measurement and methodological difficul-
    ties. Cf. in this regard OECD: Economic Outlook, No. 33, 1983, pp.
    55 ff.

Chapter 6:   The problem of trade

Real oil price increases can lead to serious trade imbalances between oil-exporting and oil-importing countries. As the price elasticity of oil demand is low over the short term, oil imports increase substantially in value terms. For various reasons, however, the oil-producing countries do not immediately use all their increased revenues to import goods and services from the oil-consuming countries.

Table 6.1 shows that in the first oil crisis imports from OPEC countries jumped from 8 to 15 % of world imports. At the same time, exports to OPEC countries expanded relatively little, increasing their share of world exports from 3.9 to 4.7 %. (Exports of services are not taken into account as the relevant data are extremely incomplete, imprecise and contradictory.)

Table 6.1:   THE IMPORTANCE OF OPEC IN WORLD TRADE, 1973-1982

	Imports from OPEC		Exports to OPEC	
	$ bn	% of world imports	$ bn	% of world exports
1973	42.9	8.0	20.2	3.9
1974	118.4	15.1	36.4	4.7
1975	116.4	14.3	56.6	7.1
1976	140.3	15.1	65.0	7.1
1977	156.2	14.6	82.1	7.9
1978	151.8	12.2	95.0	7.9
1979	215.6	13.7	96.2	6.3
1980	307.5	16.0	126.7	6.8
1981	290.3	15.2	149.8	8.2
1982	239.2	13.3	144.5	8.5

Source: IMF: Direction of Trade Statistics; calculations by the authors.

The disparity narrowed between the two oil shocks; whereas imports from OPEC countries increased much more slowly than world imports, the OPEC countries took a much larger share of world exports and thereby reduced the trade gap.

The asymmetrical pattern was repeated when oil prices again soared; an erratic performance by imports from OPEC contrasted with a relatively steady growth in exports to the region. In 1982, when real oil prices declined, exports to OPEC were still rising as a proportion of world trade.

Table 6.2 shows the trade deficits of the five largest oil-importing countries with oil-producing states. Japan and the USA are by far the worst affected, the Federal Republic of Germany and Italy the least; France occupies an intermediate position.

The limited absorptive capacity of the oil-producing countries and the large temporary trade gaps can trigger a fall in demand in the oil-importing countries. This danger is obviously all the greater, the more heavily dependent a country is on oil imports and the less competitive are its enterprises in the growing markets of the oil-exporting countries.

The deflationary gap could be closed by pursuing a compensatory fiscal policy. However, this would entail the risk of reinforcing the inflationary effects of an increase in oil prices and would not resolve the underlying structural problem, which might even be made more intractable by expansionary fiscal measures. Action to overcome structural weakness is, however, undoubtedly one of the prime responsibilities of economic policy in times of rising oil prices. By adopting appropriate borrowing strategies and offering incentives for saving and investment, new processes of growth can be set in motion that both reduce the dependence on oil and exploit the opportunities that real oil price increases open up in international trade.

Table 6.2: TRADE BALANCES (NET IMPORTS) OF THE FIVE LARGEST OIL IMPORTERS WITH
THE OIL-PRODUCING COUNTRIES, 1973 - 1982[a]

	1973	1974	1978	1980	1981	1982
	- in billions of dollars -					
Japan	4.4	19.4	69.0	132.7	166.5	194.7
USA	1.2	10.9	78.7	151.7	181.6	190.7
France	2.0	9.0	31.4	55.4	66.9	75.1
Italy	2.2	9.3	23.4	37.1	43.7	50.3
Federal Rep. of Germany	1.6	6.7	6.3	18.6	20.5	18.6
	- as percentage of exports to oil-producing countries -					
Japan	164.2	240.5	133.6	159.0	156.6	151.7
USA	35.9	111.2	127.2	162.6	159.3	140.1
France	112.7	198.2	122.4	131.5	127.1	120.0
Italy	182.9	271.5	97.0	89.3	80.5	77.6
Federal Rep. of Germany	72.9	107.2	14.3	27.9	24.9	19.0

a Cumulative values with 1973 as the initial year; oil-producing countries are OPEC plus Oman but excluding Ecuador and Gabon.

Source: IMF: Direction of Trade Statistics; calculations by the authors.

This chapter focuses on the structural changes, and the consequent need for adjustment, in international trade relations resulting from the growing importance of oil-producing countries in world trade and the worldwide changeover to energy-saving and oil-saving products and production techniques. The first section deals with competition in the OPEC markets and related policy issues. The second section illustrates the effects of real oil price rises on the position of oil-producing countries in the international division of labour; particular attention will be paid to the question whether increased competition from exports of manufactures from these countries can be expected in future and how the oil-importing countries can meet such a challenge. The third and final section examines the effect of rising oil prices on the trade of oil-importing countries among themselves and related trade policy issues.

1. The struggle for markets in the oil-producing countries

Exports to OPEC countries increased every year between 1973 and 1981, with their proportion of world exports rising from 3.9 to 8.2 %. In 1982 they declined for the first time in value terms, but the value of world exports fell even more sharply (see Table 6.1). In 1983 the considerable decrease in oil revenues also greatly diminished the relative importance of OPEC as a sales outlet. This does not, however, prejudice future developments. In assessing the future, it should be borne in mind that:

- real oil prices can be expected to rise again over the long term, though not as steeply as in the past (cf. Chapter 1 of this study);

- the import capacity of oil-exporting countries will be augmented by receipts from capital investments abroad (for example, in the case of Kuwait capital income exceeded oil revenues for the first time in 1982);

- income from non-traditional exports is assuming growing importance (cf. section 2 of this Chapter);
- oil-producing countries have relatively easy access to the international credit markets.

Hence, the oil-producing countries will probably continue to account for a considerably larger slice of world exports than before the oil shock.

a.   Sectoral emphases and main competitors in OPEC markets

The OPEC countries mainly have a demand for industrial goods; in 1982 products of this kind constituted more than three-quarters of total OPEC imports but only 57 % of world imports (see Table 6.3). Hence, if the imports of OPEC countries grow more rapidly than world imports owing to rising oil prices, the structure of world imports (adjusted for price) shifts in favour of industrial goods.

Table 6.3:   IMPORTS OF MANUFACTURES AS A PROPORTION OF TOTAL IMPORTS OF VARIOUS REGIONS IN 1973, 1978, 1981 AND 1982

- percentages -

	1973	1978	1981	1982
OPEC	77.1	79.4	76.2	76.5
Other developing countries	60.3	60.0	57.3	56.5
Industrial countries	58.1	57.2	51.4	53.5
State-trading countries	67.0	65.7	58.1	58.9
World	60.5	60.5	55.6	56.9

Source: GATT: International Trade; calculations by the authors.

The composition of manufactures imported by the OPEC countries
also differs from the world structure, in some cases considerably. For example, in 1981 chemicals were much less prevalent
in OPEC's import basket than in world imports; the same goes
for office and telecommunications equipment. Conversely, machinery for specialised industries (such as metalworking and construction machinery), road motor vehicles and other machinery
and transport equipment were well above the world average (see
Table 6.4). The OPEC countries accounted for about 13 % of
world imports of these goods in 1981, whereas in 1973 their
share had been only about 5 % (cf. Table A-23).

The main beneficiaries of OPEC's import growth so far have been
the Western industrial countries. They were the best placed
"to cope with the rapid increase in the demand for industrial
commodities, particularly capital goods, and associated technology" (Nan Nguema 1983, p. 105). Those goods, whose share in
OPEC demand is considerably higher than in world demand (see
above) accounted for 48 % of total manufactured exports of
these countries in 1981 (as compared to 55 % of total OPEC imports of manufactures). In the USA and Japan the corresponding
shares were even 57 and 52 % respectively, in the EEC it came
to 45 % on average, with considerable differences between the
individual member states. The oil-importing LDCs, on the other
hand, still largely fail to meet the import requirements of
OPEC, as the major product groups referred to above represented less than 20 % of total manufactures exported by this (highly diverse) group of countries in 1981.

Even before the first oil shock the Western industrial countries held a much larger share of the OPEC markets than of the
world market as a whole. This beneficial structural effect was
magnified by a positive competitive effect until 1978: their
market share increased from 77 to 80 % and that in industrial

Table 6.4: COMPOSITION OF IMPORTS OF INDUSTRIAL GOODS BY REGION, 1981

- percentages -

	OPEC	Other developing countries	Western industrial countries	State-trading countries	World
Iron and steel	7.9	7.0	6.1	10.5	6.8
Chemicals	8.8	14.7	14.5	12.7	13.7
Other semi-manufactures	6.8	7.3	8.6	4.4	7.7
Machinery for specialised industries	18.2	16.9	10.8	28.6	14.5
Office and telecommunications equipment	2.9	5.9	6.2	3.9	5.6
Road motor vehicles	14.2	8.2	13.3	5.6	11.8
Other machinery and transport equipment	22.7	21.9	17.2	19.9	18.9
Household appliances	4.8	4.8	5.1	1.9	4.7
Textiles	4.7	6.1	4.8	5.0	5.1
Clothing	2.7	2,0	4.7	3.2	3.8
Other consumer goods	6.4	5.5	8.8	4.4	7.5
Total manufactures ($ bn)	118.0	196.1	641.9	98.7	1,090.0

Source: GATT: International Trade 1982/83; calculations by the authors.

goods from 83 to 85 % (cf. Table 6.5). Only in chemicals, road motor vehicles and household appliances were there losses of market share, and these were small (cf. Table A-24). In the years that followed, however, the Western industrial countries lost considerable ground; by 1932 their market share had fallen back to 75 % and their share of the industrial goods market to 82 % (cf. Table 6.5).

The change in the market share of non-OPEC LDCs was the mirror image of that of Western industrial countries: it contracted until 1978 but increased considerably thereafter. In 1982 it stood at 13 %, only slightly lower than their world market share (cf. Table 6.5).

The range of goods offered by non-OPEC LDCs is no longer limited to primary products and simple consumer goods but increasingly includes higher-value products. The proportion of engineering products in the total exports of these countries to OPEC rose from 17 % in 1973 to 24 % in 1981 and in exports of industrial goods from 29 to 41 %. The non-OPEC LDCs were able to increase their market shares considerably in chemicals, iron and steel products, machinery and vehicles and household appliances (see Table A-24). Firms from developing countries have also become feared competitors in the construction industry.[1]

Table 6.6 shows changes in the import market shares of the twenty largest suppliers to OPEC between 1973 and 1982, listed according to the value of their exports in 1982. It can be seen that the USA has lost its dominant position in OPEC markets and that by 1982 Japan had almost drawn level. (In 1981 the Japanese market share was even considerably higher than that of the USA.) Remarkable too is the good performance of Italian companies, which overtook their competitors

Table 6.5: IMPORT MARKET SHARES IN OPEC COUNTRIES, 1973 - 1982

- percentages -

	Total imports				Imports of industrial goods			
	1973	1978	1981	1982	1973	1978	1981	1982
Industrial countries	77.3	79.6	76.6	75.2	83.1	85.4	33.5	82.3
Non-OPEC LDCs	11.6	10.7	12.9	12.8	8.8	7.7	9.7	9.4
OPEC	1.0	1.7	2.3	2.0	0.6	1.3	1.4	1.0
State-trading countries	8.2	6.8	6.8	8.6	6.3	5.2	5.2	6.9
World ($ bn)	20.7	99.3	154.8	151.0	16.0	78.8	118.0	115.5

Source: GATT: International Trade; calculations by the authors.

Table 6.6:   MAIN COMPETITORS IN OPEC MARKETS IN
              1973, 1978, 1981 AND 1982

- percentages -

	1973	1978	1981	1982
USA	17.9	17.5	14.4	15.8
Japan	13.5	15.0	15.2	15.1
Federal Rep. of Germany	11.3	12.9	10.3	10.9
Italy	6.0	7.4	8.5	7.4
United Kingdom	8.7	8.9	7.4	7.1
France	9.1	6.8	7.3	7.1
Netherlands	2.9	2.6	2.5	2.3
Spain	1.6	1.8	2.0	2.1
South Korea	0.4	1.5	1.9	2.0
Belgium	2.3	2.3	2.0	1.6
Switzerland	1.8	2.0	1.4	1.6
Turkey	0.2	0.2	1.0	1.5
Canada	1.3	1.4	1.4	1.5
Hong Kong	1.4	1.0	1.4	1.3
Sweden	1.1	1.2	1.3	1.3
Brazil	1.2	1.0	1.6	1.3
Rumania	0.6	0.5	1.2	1.2
Saudi Arabia	0.0	0.3	1.0	1.2
Australia	1.3	0.8	1.1	1.1
Kuwait	0.6	0.8	1.3	1.0
World ($ bn)	20.2	95.0	149.8	144.5

Source: IMF: Direction of Trade Statistics; calculations by
          the authors.

from France and the United Kingdom during the period under review and considerably shortened the lead enjoyed by German industry. Among the non-OPEC LDCs, South Korea and Turkey in particular made a great leap forward.

Table 6.7 gives initial points of reference to explain the different export performances of Western industrial countries in
OPEC markets. It shows that Japan was in a rather unfavourable
position in 1973. In particular, it was relatively weak in the
engineering products that were most in demand in the years that
followed. Nevertheless, Japan flexibly adapted its export structure to suit the import priorities of OPEC countries and substantially increased its market share in important sectors,
especially mechanical engineering, vehicles and household appliances. By contrast, the EC countries, which began from a relatively favourable position, lost market shares in all sectors.
The USA also had to accept seeing its shares trimmed in most sectors; it was able to improve its position mainly in less dynamic
and quantitatively less important sectors.

Finally, if exports to OPEC countries are viewed in relation to
the overall export trend, it can be seen that Western industrial
countries geared their exports more strongly towards OPEC than
did developing and state-trading countries (for details, see
Table A-25). The differences among the industrial countries
themselves are less significant (for further information, see
Tables A-26 and A-27). Differences in their export achievements in the OPEC countries thus reflect mainly differences
in their performance in the world market as a whole.

Table 6.7: PERFORMANCE OF THE USA, THE EC AND JAPAN IN OPEC MARKETS FOR INDUSTRIAL GOODS, 1973 - 1982

- percentages -

	Import growth 73-82[a]	Sectoral structure of exports to OPEC						Market share in OPEC[b]					
		USA		EC		Japan		USA		EC		Japan	
		1973	1982	1973	1982	1973	1982	1973	1982	1973	1982	1973	1982
Iron and steel	20.4	5.3	2.9	9.6	6.2	24.5	18.0	8.7	6.0	44.0	34.9	42.0	47.6
Chemicals	21.2	10.3	9.0	13.0	10.7	5.8	3.1	17.2	18.3	62.8	58.8	10.3	7.9
Other semi-manufactures	26.3	3.7	3.9	4.0	4.8	4.3	4.5	13.6	12.0	43.9	40.2	16.7	17.8
Machinery for specialised industries	23.6	30.9	28.4	21.4	18.7	10.9	15.3	27.9	26.2	55.8	46.6	10.4	17.8
Office and tele-communications equipment	25.2	2.9	4.5	3.6	3.3	2.3	2.2	14.3	20.5	51.0	40.5	12.2	12.4
Road motor vehicles	26.4	13.6	11.5	13.4	13.8	13.2	21.9	19.3	13.7	55.0	44.2	19.9	32.9
Other machinery and transport equipment	27.0	26.3	30.3	22.7	26.4	13.6	18.4	22.7	20.8	56.4	49.1	12.4	16.0
Household appliances	24.8	2.1	1.9	2.1	1.7	7.4	8.2	10.2	8.9	30.6	20.8	38.8	48.3
Textiles	15.8	1.6	2.3	4.7	1.9	14.8	5.4	4.8	12.6	41.0	27.4	45.8	37.1
Clothing	30.7	0.4	0.5	0.9	1.2	0.4	0.3	11.1	9.0	66.7	53.0	11.1	6.0
Other consumer goods	30.5	2.5	4.7	4.4	7.5	2.3	2.7	12.0	14.2	62.0	60.9	12.0	10.3
Total manufactures (%, $ bn)	24.5	2.43	16.72	7.00	45.08	2.57	21.16	18.3	17.6	53.1	47.5	19.4	22.7

a Average annual rate of growth in OPEC imports from Western industrial countries.
b Share of Western industrial countries' total exports to OPEC countries.

Source: GATT: International Trade; calculations by the authors.

b.   Strategies to strengthen countries' competitive
     positions

Changes in market shares are determined by a multitude of
different factors which cannot be examined here in detail.
In general, it appears that non-price competition is even
more important in the markets of oil-producing countries
than in other markets of the world. An indication of this
is the good performance of German companies in OPEC member
countries after the first oil shock, notwithstanding a considerable upvaluation of the Deutsche Mark in real effective
terms. However, growing financial constraints associated
with the present oil glut may have led the oil-exporting
countries to adopt a more cautious behaviour as regards
prices. At the same time, companies are increasingly seeking to boost sales in OPEC markets by non-conventional means,
which frequently distort or restrict competition. Moreover,
competition is often not an exclusive affair of the companies directly involved but carried out by governments and
other official agencies which act on behalf of "their" firms.
What follows is a brief review of some practices applied to
gain an edge over foreign competitors on the markets of oil-
exporting countries.

Companies in which oil-producing countries have capital interests seem to have particularly good sales opportunities.
One example in this respect is the oil exploration and plant
construction firm Santa Fe International. Kuwait's sharehold-
ing in the company has meant that it has almost effortlessly
won substantial contracts not only in Kuwait itself - the
most noteworthy being the expansion of a refinery and the
construction of a petrochemical complex - but also in other
countries (mainly in oil and gas exploration and extraction),
contracts for which it would otherwise have faced stiff in-

ternational competition (Business Week, 6.9.1982).

By accepting equity capital from oil-producing countries, German companies too have been able to strengthen not only their capital base but also their competitive position in markets whose future growth will depend crucially on demand in these countries. Kuwait's purchase of a holding in Hoechst AG is a case in point. The Sheikdom considers this investment, which has been kept just below the 25 % blocking minority so far, not as a "passive financial investment" but as a decisive vehicle for promoting sales of refined products and petrochemicals and acquiring industrial knowhow. For Hoechst this means that traditional activities, such as the production of ammonia, are being terminated or at least greatly reduced (Financial Times, 3.5.1983). At the same time, however, the firm is gaining a preferential position in forward-looking fields such as the transfer of technology and plant construction[2] and markets are opening up in which it has had no more than a toehold up to now (Frankfurter Allgemeine Zeitung, 3.5.1983).[3]

Another method of doing business with the oil-producing countries is by means of barter, in which goods are supplied in exchange for goods. Compensation deals of this kind, which are common mainly in trade with the Eastern bloc, are growing in popularity in trade relations with oil exporters. The willingness to accept oil as a means of payment in order to win sales in the markets of oil producers has increased considerably. Japanese trading companies in particular appear to be distinguishing themselves in this respect. For example, in 1983 they agreed a compensation ratio of 50 % with Iran, whereby the trading companies, which handle about 80 % of Japan's petroleum imports from Iran (and re-export a substantial amount), can supply Iran with industrial goods worth half the value of Japan's long-term contractual purchases of petroleum (Frankfurter Allgemeine Zeitung, 26.4.1983). Worth mentioning is also a deal between Kobe Steel of Japan and Iran. The Japanese firm has won a steel plant contract in Iran, for which it will receive payment through a complex counter-trade agreement. Payments are to be made to Kobe from a special deposit account set up on the company's behalf by the Central Bank of Iran. Into the account will go payments for oil (lifted by a company which is half owned by Shell and half by Japanese interests) until the total reaches the contract level.[4]

Among the oil-producing countries, Algeria, Indonesia, Iran and Libya have been particularly active in compensation trade. In Algeria the nationalisation of French oil posessions in 1971 was the trigger. The Algerian authorities successfully countered the subsequent French boycott of Algerian crude by concluding a number of barter deals with American, German and Italian companies (Financial Times, 25.8.1981).

The "classical" instruments of export promotion are also used to foster exports to oil-producing countries. In this respect Germany faces subsidised competition from important competitor countries that is insufficiently restrained by the OECD Consensus on export credits. In particular, the exporters of major plant, which are about 70 % dependent on exports and win a large part of their export business in oil-producing countries,[5] point out that they are placed at a considerable disadvantage by the payment of interest rate subsidies to foreign competitors. As a result, German firms are increasingly buying components for capital projects in other countries so that they can share the financial benefits provided there.

In February 1983 the German Federal Government reacted to
the growing problems of competition encountered by German exporters by easing the conditions for granting export guarantees. At that time concessions had already been made that
would hardly have been conceivable previously. For example,
the commitment ceiling for Iraq, a nation at war and one of
Germany's most important trading partners as a result of the
increase in oil prices, was doubled in 1981 and 1982 to about
DM 10 billion (Frankfurter Allgemeine Zeitung, 26.1.1983).[6]
The Government asserts that the risk principles laid down in
1977 are still being observed, in particular those on the
covering of costs and the worldwide equalisation of risks,
but premium income is unlikely to cover probable compensation claims in full, despite the increase in insurance rates
by 40 % on average from April 1984. This would therefore be
tantamount to the payment of export credit subsidies.

Trade interests are also involved if incentives are offered
for the creation of joint ventures with companies from oil-
exporting countries. This can significantly improve the conditions for the export of other products and services that
are not produced or performed in the host country itself.[7]

Similarly, consulting firms can promote industrial exports
of a certain country. For example, a German consultant which
has won a design contract (say for a steel work) may specify
the project in a way that favours German engineering companies or may simply recommend that host countries buy goods
in Germany. Economic officials are said to regard practices
like these as an efficient means to help national firms win
orders in OPEC countries (The Economist, 4.9.1982, p. 69).

Bilateral co-operation agreements, such as those concluded
by Germany and the United Kingdom with Iraq in 1981 and by
Belgium with Algeria in 1983, are a more comprehensive instrument for shaping economic relations with oil-producing
countries by creating a legal and institutional framework
for contacts between countries in various fields. Such arrangements can influence trade in a variety of ways; for
example, they can have a direct effect through customs concessions, escape clauses, marketing assistance and similar
agreements and an indirect effect through the award of contracts as part of joint development projects.[8] One would
have to ascertain in each individual case whether the trade-
creating effects outweighed the trade-diverting effects. As
a rule, trade accords within co-operation agreements are
anything but harmless. Above all, they can encourage the
universal revival of bilateralism and a wrong perception of
reciprocity in international economic relations, thereby
jeopardising the undeniable advantages of greater efficiency inherent in a multilateral world trade order.

Bilateral trade agreements with oil-producing countries and
efforts in this direction are legion. For example, the seven
countries with which Brazil wishes to intensify trade on a
bilateral basis include five oil states: Algeria, Ecuador,
Mexico, Nigeria and Venezuela.[9] With Angola and Iran counter trade agreements are already in place. However, the benefits of such activities are contested in Brazil itself.[10]

The same is true of the agreements for the supply of natural gas that France and Italy have concluded with Algeria.
In both cases the prices are well above the world market
level. By way of compensation, French and Italian firms are
to be given favoured access to the Algerian market. France
has its sights mainly on contracts in the transportation,

housing and urban construction sector including the supply
of building materials. The intergovernmental agreement with
Algeria on co-operation in the transportation sector, for example, lays down that as a matter of principle the required
capital goods will be of French origin. Nonetheless, "the
competitiveness of French tenders will be measured in terms
of world market conditions" (Frankfurter Allgemeine Zeitung,
9.11.1982). Algeria has also offered Italian companies large
contracts for the supply of industrial goods.[11] The Algerian
Government had earlier broken off trade relations with Italy
to add weight to its demand for excessively high gas prices.[12]
Similarly, the country deliberately held back from awarding
business to French companies during the long dispute about
the prices of gas exports (MEED, 17.2.1984).

A go-it-alone approach to trade ultimately harms the interests of the oil-importing countries as a whole. The actions
of one country partly cancel out the effects of another
country's policy and countries are seduced into neglecting
energy saving and oil substitution in two ways:

- more oil and energy than necessary are imported in order
  to secure contracts; and

- disproportionate emphasis is placed on the real transfer
  of resources to oil-producing countries, which can prejudice the increased use of resources to raise the productivity of energy and oil use.

The main beneficiaries of a trade war conducted by distort-
ing competition are ultimately the oil-producing countries,
whose terms of trade improve. Trade policy towards these
countries requires closer consultation and co-ordination;
the main fora that spring to mind in this connection are
the EC, the OECD and GATT. For example, the bilateral co-

operation agreements between various member states of the European Community and oil-producing countries could be replaced or "arched over" by Community arrangements. Equally, the EC provisions for consultation on the granting of export subsidies could be tightened or applied more strictly which would be most important in the case of exports of plant to oil-producing countries, a field in which distortions of competition are particularly serious. If one is realistic, the OECD or GATT can be expected to offer little more than an improved exchange of information and technical clarification, such as on the question of bilateralism and compensation deals.

2. The oil-producing countries as competitors in the
   manufacturing sector

Initially, the rise in oil prices greatly strengthened the
traditional division of labour between oil-exporting and oil-
importing countries - petroleum in exchange for finished goods.
This development was reflected in a steep rise in crude oil's
share of world exports, which increased from 7 % in 1973 to 14 %
in 1974. It remained at this level for the next three years
before dropping back to 12 % in 1978. By 1980 it had climbed
to 15 % owing to renewed sharp price increases. After a further year at 15 %, the trend was again reversed. In 1982 and
1983 the value of crude oil exports declined much more rapidly than the value of total world exports owing to the fall in
oil prices and an appreciable weakening of demand.[13]

This course of events caused an explosive rise in the oil import bill in some oil-importing countries, as Table 6.8 shows
for the fifteen largest oil importers. In Japan, for example,
the proportion of total import expenditure spent on imported
crude has almost trebled since 1973 to stand at 37 % in 1981.
In that year Japan therefore had to earmark 4.6 % of GDP to
pay its oil bill, almost four times the proportion needed in
1973. In Korea the oil bill accounted for almost 10 % of GDP,
compared with 2.1 % in 1973, and in Brazil 47 % of expenditure on imports went on oil.

At the same time, however, the increase in oil prices had a
strong braking effect. Between 1973 and 1981 crude oil imports
declined in real terms in the majority of the countries examined, despite an increase in total imports and GDP over the
same period (cf. Table 6.9). Had it not been for the saving
and substitution effects reflected in these developments, the
oil bill would have worked out much higher, as a simple simulation illustrates. Let us assume that petroleum imports had

Table 6.8: PETROLEUM IMPORTS OF THE LARGEST IMPORTERS OF OIL IN 1973 AND 1981

	$ bn		as % of total imports		as % of GDP	
	1973	1981	1973	1981	1973	1981
USA	4.6	64.3	6.2	23.5	0.3	2.2
Japan	5.1	52.2	13.2	36.5	1.2	4.6
France	3.5	24.3	9.4	20.1	1.4	4.3
Federal Republic of Germany	3.4	21.8	6.3	13.3	1.0	3.2
Italy	3.4	22.2	12.2	24.4	2.2	6.3
Spain	1.1	10.4	10.9	32.3	1.5	5.6
Netherlands	2.6	10.6	10.4	15.8	4.0	7.6
United Kingdom	3.3	8.3	8.3	8.1	1.8	1.7
Brazil	0.9	11.3	12.2	46.9	1.1	3.9
Belgium	0.9	6.9	4.3	11.1	2.1	7.3
Canada	0.9	6.6	3.8	9.4	0.8	2.3
Korea	0.3	6.4	6.5	24.4	2.1	9.7
Sweden	0.3	3.8	2.6	13.3	0.6	3.4
Greece	0.3	1.8	9.5	20.9	2.0	4.9
India	0.3	6.0[a]	9.6	42.0[a]	0.4	3.8[a]

a 1980.

Source: OECD: Statistics of Foreign Trade; OECD: National Accounts; IMF: IFS Yearbook 1983; UN: Yearbook of International Trade Statistics; calculations by the authors.

321

Table 6.9: CHANGES IN CRUDE OIL IMPORTS, TOTAL IMPORTS AND GDP FOR THE 15 LARGEST OIL IMPORTERS, 1973 - 1981[a]

	(1) Crude oil imports	(2) Total imports	(3) GDP	(4) (1)/(2)	(5) (1)/(3)
USA	2.4	3.2	2.2	0.75	1.09
Japan	-3.2	0.5	3.7	-6.40	-0.86
France	-5.0	4.5	2.5	-1.11	-2.00
Federal Republic of Germany	-4.1	3.6	2.1	-1.14	-1.95
Italy	-0.9	1.1	2.4	-0.82	-0.38
Spain	2.7	2.8	2.5	0.96	1.08
Netherlands	-10.9	1.9	1.8	-5.74	-6.06
United Kingdom	-14.6	1.0	0.5	-14.60	-29.20
Brazil	3.3	3.4	7.1	0.97	0.47
Belgium	-3.4	2.6	1.9	-1.31	-1.79
Canada	-7.2	2.9	3.0	-2.48	-2.40
Korea	8.7	10.6	7.8	0.82	1.12
Sweden	4.2	2.2	1.6	1.91	2.63
Greece	-4.0	0.8	2.9	-5.00	1.38
India	2.1	4.6	4.1	0.46	0.51

a Average annual rate of growth. Growth in crude oil imports calculated on a volume basis; growth in total imports and GDP calculated on the basis of volume indices (1975 = 100); data for Brazil and Korea: 1973-1980; for India: 1973-1978 and for Spain: 1973-1979.

Source: OECD: Energy Balances; OECD: National Accounts; IMF: IFS Yearbook 1982; UN: Yearbook of World Energy Statistics 1980; calculations by the authors.

increased in step with GDP after the first oil shock and that the rate of growth in GDP and the trends in other imports and in crude oil prices had remained unchanged. In these circumstances Japan, for example, would have had to spend about 75 % more for oil imports than was actually the case and the burden on the country's import bill and on domestic output would have been twice as high (cf. Table A-28).

Calculated on the basis of data for 1973 and 1981, Japan's price elasticity for crude oil imports thus works out at -0.25; in other words, for every real increase of 1 % in the import price of crude oil, the volume of crude oil imported per unit of GDP (the income elasticity is therefore set at 1) decreases by 0.25 %. The coefficients of elasticity for the sub-periods 1973-1978 and 1978-81 also work out approximately the same. In actual fact, however, the price elasticity must have increased considerably, for the reactions to the second oil crisis had just set in in 1981. In any case, they were much stronger than the immediate reactions to the first oil crisis, which are reflected in the price elasticity for the period 1973-74. The same applies to the other countries examined (cf. Table 6.10). There are therefore strong and growing forces acting against an expansion in traditional trade links between oil-exporting and oil-importing countries in the event of real oil price increases.

At the same time, the division of labour is taking on new forms, as the oil-producing countries are using part of their receipts from oil exports to diversify their domestic production base in order to reduce the heavy dependence of foreign exchange receipts and the entire trend of incomes on exports of a single, and moreover non-renewable commodity.

Table 6.10:   PRICE ELASTICITY OF CRUDE OIL IMPORTS
              IN OECD COUNTRIES,
              1973-81, 1973-74, 1973-78 AND 1978-81[a]

	73-81	73-74	73-78	78-81
USA	0.01	0.03	0.28	-0.41
Japan	-0.25	-0.01	-0.25	-0.24
Belgium	-0.21	-0.12	-0.32	-0.14
Federal Rep. of Germany	-0.25	-0.05	-0.32	-0.20
Denmark	-0.38	-0.03	-0.40	-0.34
France	-0.28	-0.04	-0.29	-0.28
Greece	-0.30	-0.02	-0.18	-0.41
United Kingdom	-0.80	-0.01	-0.61	-1.25
Ireland	-0.69	0.00	-0.26	-1.55
Italy	-0.16	0.20	0.10	-0.31
Netherlands	-0.51	-0.24	-0.78	-0.31
Finland	-0.05	-0.02	0.04	-0.13
Austria	-0.02	-0.01	0.20	-0.14
Portugal	0.15	0.20	0.25	0.05
Sweden	0.11	-0.05	0.33	-0.12
Switzerland	-0.41	-0.02	-1.09	-0.24
Spain	-0.10	0.00	-0.06	-0.18

a   Percentage changes in the specific volume of crude oil imports
    (crude oil import volume per unit of GDP) for a 1 % change in
    the real crude oil import price (deflator: GDP price index) calcu-
    lated on the basis of data for the years at the beginning and end
    of each period.

Source: OECD: Statistics of Foreign Trade; OECD: National
        Accounts; calculations by the authors.

a. Importance hitherto of non-traditional exports by oil-
    producing countries

Up to now, the oil-producing countries have hardly ranked as
serious competitors in the world markets in industrial goods.
The structure of their exports continues to be dominated by
oil.

Before the first oil crisis oil increased steadily year by
year as a proportion of total OPEC exports, rising from
75.3 % in 1961 to 88.1 % in 1973. The quadrupling of crude
oil prices in the final quarter of that year caused a jump
in the oil share, so that crude oil and (to a much smaller
extent) oil products accounted for 94.8 and 95.3 % of OPEC
exports in 1974 and 1975 respectively. In Iraq, Qatar,
Libya, Saudi Arabia and the United Arab Emirates the proportion was even approaching 100 %. Between 1976 and 1978,
when world demand for oil was weak and oil prices were falling in real terms, the oil share declined to 93.2 %. It
barely changed during the second oil shock; in 1981 it stood
at 93.1 %. The effects of the sharp increases in the prices
of crude oil and oil products on the structure of exports
were therefore offset by volume decreases.[14]

The one-sided export structure of the oil-producing countries is also reflected in the small number of product groups
making up their exports (see Table 6.11). In some countries
the number of export items actually decreased during the
seventies. This was particularly marked in the case of Mexico, where the process of export diversification apparently
suffered a setback owing to the country's emergence as a
major oil exporter. By contrast, other oil producers managed to broaden their export range considerably, including
Ecuador, which like Mexico was relatively late in joining
the ranks of important oil-exporting countries.

Table 6.11: EXPORT DIVERSIFICATION IN OIL-PRODUCING COUNTRIES IN 1970, 1978 AND 1980

	Number of product groups exported[a]			Degree of concentration of exports[b]		
	1970	1978	1980	1970	1978	1980
Algeria	76	-	43	0.652	-	0.818
Ecuador	29	53	68[c]	0.495	0.440	0.499[c]
Gabon	21	-	19[c]	0.500	-	0.772[c]
Indonesia	48	97	112	0.368	0.585	0.525
Iraq	43	48	-	0.938	0.979	-
Iran	71	82[d]	-	0.742	0.906[d]	-
Qatar	1	4	3[c]	1.000	0.967	0.944[c]
Kuwait	101	-	128	0.788	-	0.689
Libya	4	4	1	0.999	0.924	1.000
Mexico	135	146	63	0.116	0.261	0.601
Nigeria	34	31	45[c]	0.583	0.895	0.945
Oman	4	3	3	0.996	0.997	0.997
Saudi Arabia	22	-	129	0.837	-	0.942
UAE	26	134	-	0.961	0.942	-
Venezuela	76	82	98	0.659	0.662	0.677

a Three-digit SITC positions with a minimum export value of $ 50,000 (1970) or $ 100,000 (1978 and 1980) or a minimum share of more than 0.3 % of total exports.

b Hirschmann index normalised to make values ranging from 0 to 1 (maximum concentration).

c 1979.

d 1977.

Source: UNCTAD: Handbook of International Trade and Development Statistics.

Among non-oil exports, the highest rates of growth were recorded by industrial goods. Manufactured exports from OPEC
countries (excluding oil products) increased by an average
of 33 % a year between 1970 and 1980. The corresponding figures for foodstuff, agricultural raw materials and ores &
metals were much lower, at 14, 20 and 19 % respectively.[15]
In 1981 and 1982, when world trade in industrial products
declined in value terms, OPEC's manufactured exports also
contracted, but their share of total non-oil exports from
this group of countries nevertheless continued to rise as
non-oil primary exports declined more sharply.[16]

The OPEC countries have sold their exported industrial products increasingly in the markets of other developing countries. Their share in total exports of manufactures by OPEC
rose from 16 % in 1973 to 34 % in 1982. Over the same period
the industrial countries' share declined from 68 to 40 %.
The state-trading countries are of no significance whatso-
ever as a market for industrial goods from OPEC.[17]

If imports of industrial goods from OPEC countries are set
in relation to the industrial and developing countries' total imports of industrial goods, they account for a mere
0.3 % in the case of Western industrial countries, unchanged
since 1973, whereas in the non-OPEC LDCs their share rose
from 0.3 to 1 % between 1973 and 1982.[18]

Closer examination of the industrial products imported by OECD
countries from OPEC shows that in 1980 imports in excess of
$ 10 million were effected in 26 product groups. In only 8
cases - tin, silver, floor coverings, radioactive and similar materials, leather, pig iron, precious stones and semi-
conductors - were imports from OPEC countries higher than
OECD exports of these goods to OPEC. In most categories ship-

ments from OPEC suppliers were also small in comparison
with total OECD imports from third countries (see Table
A-29).

Finally, if Germany's imports of industrial goods from oil-
producing countries (OPEC plus Mexico) are examined, the
most striking feature in individual product groups is the
strong concentration on particular countries. Take textiles,
which made up just under 30 % of oil-exporting countries total shipments of manufactures (excluding oil products) to
Germany in 1982; these goods come almost exclusively from
Iran, which therefore holds about 1 % of the German home
market in this sector (in the sub-group "carpets" the market share will be far higher). The second largest product
group - food products - is dominated by Indonesia, which
is also by far the most important supplier in the sectors
of clothing, wooden products and non-ferrous metals. Imports of vehicles, chemicals, electrical appliances and
toys come predominantly from Mexico, whereas Venezuela occupies the leading position in the supply of iron and steel
products to Germany. In 1982 no sector showed net German imports in trade with oil-producing countries and their market shares in the various sectors were so small that one
can still hardly speak of strong competition from the oil
states (cf. Table A-30).

b.   On the economics of oil-based industrialisation

The development strategies pursued by the oil states, and
especially their "openness" to the outside world, are of
decisive importance for shaping the "new" division of labour between oil-exporting and oil-importing countries.
Strictly speaking, an open development model requires individual projects to be assessed in accordance with inter-

national criteria of efficiency. Output and all salable inputs of a planned project must be evaluated at international competitive prices and account must also be taken of transport costs, external benefits (e.g. through integration with the rest of the economy), external costs (e.g. through environmental pollution), the transferred profits of foreign business partners, and so on (for details, see Little, Mirrlees 1974). In these circumstances (which should, however, be modified to the extent that an infant industry argument can be maintained, "learning by doing" can be expected, international competition is distorted by state intervention or private agreements and specific uncertainties overshadow international economic relations) the country in question will tend to specialise in the production of those goods and services in which it has comparative cost advantages.

Real oil price increases affect the comparative cost advantages of an oil-producing country on both the demand and supply sides. On the demand side they increase purchasing power and hence lead to expansion of the domestic market. This is important for processes in which economies of scale play a role. Economies of scale in research and development, production and marketing are considered to be significant where most durable consumer goods and many capital goods are concerned, in other words product groups that display a high income elasticity and are therefore in high demand in the oil-producing countries (MacBean 1980, p. 131). Nevertheless, the small size of the population prevents full exploitation of economies of scale in many oil states despite rapidly rising incomes. Efficient production is then possible only if manufacturing capacity is geared towards export from the outset.

Linder's concept of representative demand could also be used to help explain possible pattern of oil-exporting countries' foreign trade. This postulates strong domestic demand for particular product qualities and styles that permits the establishment of an efficient industry specialising in those products. There is also demand for them in other countries with similar demand conditions which themselves make differentiated products in the same category, in accordance with the prevalent representative demand in those countries. The intra-industry trade generated in this way is at present highly concentrated in the developed Western industrial countries; however, it is conceivable that the oil-producing countries could be drawn more strongly into exchanges of this kind and that the Linder hypothesis might serve to explain the growing trade relations among the oil producers themselves and between them and oil-importing developing countries.[19]

On the _supply side_, real oil price rises increase the importance of oil (and energy in general) as a factor of production, thereby also enhancing the availability advantages that the oil producers may derive from possession of these resources. At the same time, however, the opportunity costs of the domestic utilisation of oil and associated gas must be taken into account; to ignore them may lead to a misallocation of resources. This danger exists, for example, if oil products are subsidised from public funds, as they are on a large scale in most oil-producing countries. The international competitiveness of industries with a high hydrocarbon input so far does not derive from a locational advantage of oil-producing countries but rests on their financial ability to provide heavy subsidies for a factor of production. Similarly, it would appear problematic to provide do-

mestic industry with associated gas virtually free of charge
as long as alternative uses are conceivable, such as rein-
jection for advanced recovery or liquefaction for subsequent
export.

Real oil price rises can also greatly augment the physical
and human capital of an oil-producing country by indirect
means. For example, the increased proceeds from oil exports
can be used to improve the infrastructure and for the development of human resources, both essential prerequisites for
self-reliance and the long-term viability of increased industrialisation. At the same time, petro-dollars can help
speed up the process of industrialisation, in that machinery and equipment, turnkey plant, industrial technology,
knowhow and technical, commercial and organisational services can be purchased directly abroad.[20] The oil-producing
countries derive additional benefit from the fact that their
resource wealth substantially increases the attractiveness
of these countries for foreign investment, be it direct investment, minority interests or purely financial investments. Hence capital availability also increases indirectly
and a strong negotiating position vis-à-vis foreign investors ensures that through joint ventures with domestic enterprises, the training of indigenous technicians and man-
agers, integration between industries and other arrangements
foreign firms are better integrated into the domestic economy in accordance with the development plan than they would
be in non-oil developing countries in otherwise identical
circumstances.

Countries that benefit from real oil price rises may therefore be placed in a position in which those industrial activities that require relatively large inputs of capital,
oil and gas could be developed on internationally competi-

tive terms.[21] This is particularly true of oil producers with
small populations, as labour is in short supply and the immigration of workers from abroad is restricted for various reasons. This also affects wages and wage expectations, which are
also influenced directly by real oil price rises and the resultant improvement in the country's real income position.[22]
Hence labour-intensive processes are often unable to compete
at the international level. One-sided capital-intensive industrial development is also problematic in the oil-producing
countries with small populations, however. It rests on a non-
renewable resource and is highly dependent on the foreign man-
agers and highly-qualified technical staff required to operate
major capital-intensive projects. In the interests of balanced
industrialisation, these countries must therefore make an effort to develop a "second row" of industries in which domestic
entrepreneurial initiative can come more strongly to the fore,
simpler technologies can be applied and a broader educational
effect can be achieved. Examples cited by the World Bank are
metal fabrication, the electrical appliances industry and the
production of building materials. The growth and spread of
such industries, which are tailored more closely to the needs
of the home market, are regarded as important indicators of
the progress of capital-surplus oil exporters towards an economic structure less dependent on oil (World Bank 1981, p.
93).

A capital-intensive industrialisation model is clearly out
of the question for the densely populated oil-producing countries. Even in times of real increases in oil prices, their
main concern remains that of providing work and further training for their rapidly growing and largely unskilled reser-
voir of labour. Capital-intensive investment projects that
can be financed thanks to the proceeds from oil exports
must therefore be measured chiefly by the demands they place

on the labour force and the contribution they make to the development of the rest of the (labour-intensive) economy.[23] In
the poorer oil states there is also the question of using a
larger proportion of oil receipts for alternative purposes,
such as expanding the educational system.

The sharp increase in capital that the oil-producing countries are experiencing as a direct and indirect result of
real oil price rises therefore involves the danger of error
in the direction of development, as does the growing importance of "natural" availability advantages. Examples of the
waste of public capital can be found in all oil-producing
countries. In addition, the governments of these countries
grant private investors sometimes massive interest rate subsidies and other investment aids that greatly reduce the cost
of capital. This can lead to expensive mistakes in the country itself and to a distortion of international flows of capital and trade.

c.   Key sectors of export diversification in oil-producing
      countries

Oil refining is a "natural" focal point for industrialisation
in the oil-producing countries. Petroleum products contribute
substantially more to their exports than all other industrial
products put together. For example, in 1980 OPEC exports of
oil products to OECD countries were almost five times as
large as their exports of other industrial products to that
area (cf. Table 6.12). OPEC refineries accounted for just under one-fifth of total OECD imports in this sector, whereas
in other branches of industry imports from OPEC countries
averaged 0.4 %, a negligible share.

Table 6.12: OECD COUNTRIES' IMPORTS OF OIL PRODUCTS FROM OPEC COUNTRIES, 1975 - 1980

	1975	1976	1977	1978	1979	1980
$ million	3 403.5	3 737.6	4 049.4	6 576.3	10 582.4	15 258.8
% of crude oil imports from OPEC	4.2	3.9	3.8	6.4	7.5	7.6
% of other imports of industrial goods from OPEC	378.6	399.7	340.6	366.0	485.4	481.4
% of total OECD imports of oil products	15.5	16.8	16.1	22.0	20.5	19.0
Net imports ($ million)	2 970.4	3 254.2	3 497.9	5 863.5	9 268.0	10 319.1

Source: OECD: Statistics of Foreign Trade; calculation by the authors.

Compared with their exports of crude oil, the oil-producing countries' exports of oil products are still small, accounting for
only 8.4 % of total OPEC oil exports in 1981. However, since the
first oil price shock there has been an accelerated trend towards the substitution of exports of oil products for exports
of crude. In Algeria, for example, oil products accounted for
only 4 % of total oil exports in 1973, but 26 % in 1981. Over the
same period the proportion rose from 7 to 22 % in Kuwait, from
10 to 14 % In Ecuador and 'from 2 to 9 % in Libya (cf. Table 6.13).

These changes in the structure of oil exports reflect considerable expansion in refining capacity in OPEC countries. Between
1973 and 1981 their potential output increased from 4.2 to 6.4
million barrels a day; in terms of the worldwide capacity of the
sector, this represents an increase from 6.4 to 7.7. %.

This trend will probably continue at a faster pace in future.
For example, Kuwait will modernise and expand two of its three
oil refineries which will increase the country's oil refining
capacity to 700,000-750,000 barrels a day by 1986. As a consequence, about 60 % of Kuwait's expected medium-term oil production will be processed locally (Nachrichten für Außenhandel,
28.5.1984). In Saudi-Arabia refining capacities will expand
even stronger, to about 2 m barrels a day by 1985 (Ifo 1983c,
p. 69). Generally, Middle East oil refineries are regarded as
"better-placed to survive further major changes in the world
industry. Backed by governments and central elements of Middle
East modernisation programmes, they are unlikely to face clo-
sure during the global shake-up expected in the second half of
the 1980s. And they should be ready to capitalise on a firm
base in a sleeker, healthier and more profitable industry in
the 1990s" (MEED, 3.2.1984, p.23). For the oil-importing countries this means not only that existing plant must be further
reduced because of the general decline in demand but also that
they will come under considerable pressure from a shift in the
refinery location structure to the benefit of the oil-producing countries.[24]

Table 6.13: OPEC COUNTRIES' EXPORTS OF OIL PRODUCTS, DOMESTIC CONSUMPTION OF OIL PRODUCTS AND REFINING CAPACITY, 1973, 1980 AND 1981

| | | Exports of oil products | | | Domestic consumption | Refining capacity | |
		1 000 bpd	share in total exports of oil %	share in OPEC/world exports of oil products %	1 000 bpd	1 000 bpd	share of OPEC/world capacity %
Algeria	1973	35.5	3.5	1.8	60.4	115.8	2.8
	1980	152.8	17.6	7.7	108.1	438.0	7.0
	1981	186.5	26.3	11.0	115.8	438.0	6.9
Ecuador	1973	2.0	10.1	0.1	29.3	35.5	0.9
	1980	19.7	15.2	1.0	70.7	94.5	1.5
	1981	17.4	14.2	1.0	79.0	94.5	1.5
Gabon	1973	13.3	10.0	0.7	20.2	17.0	0.4
	1980	10.5	6.5	0.5	27.8	44.0	0.7
	1981	11.2	8.2	0.7	29.8	44.0	0.7
Indonesia	1973	154.9	13.3	7.8	182.4	381.5	9.2
	1980	162.6	13.6	8.2	397.4	471.0	7.6
	1981	140.3	11.8	8.3	442.4	471.0	7.4
Iraq	1973	7.5	0.4	0.4	81.0	183.5	4.4
	1980	35.0	1.4	1.8	191.2	305.5	4.9
	1981	-	-	-	191.2	305.5	4.8

Iran	1973	147.2	2.7	7.5	259.0	660.0	15.9
	1980	155.0	16.3	7.8	400.0	1 265.0	20.3
	1981	-	-	-	400.0	1 265.0	19.0
Kuwait	1973	205.7	7.2	10.4	16.9	541.5	13.0
	1980	343.4	20.9	17.2	44.0	594.0	9.5
	1981	229.7	22.9	13.5	46.9	594.0	9.3
Libya	1973	35.0	1.6	1.8	32.7	10.0	0.2
	1980	85.0	4.8	4.3	85.4	130.0	2.1
	1981	90.0	8.6	5.3	90.9	130.0	2.0
Nigeria	1973	15.0	0.8	0.8	48.9	57.0	1.4
	1980	73.7	3.6	3.7	171.0	247.0	4.0
	1981	43.4	3.4	2.6	235.8	247.0	3.9
Saudi Arabia	1973	331.7	4.5	16.8	68.2	676.0	16.3
	1980	406.8	4.2	20.4	474.6	178.0	18.9
	1981	481.0	5.1	28.4	576.8	178.0	18.5
Venezuela	1973	1 026.6	32.6	52.0	197.0	473.9	35.5
	1980	549.9	29.9	27.6	343.2	444.9	23.2
	1981	494.8	28.1	29.2	364.1	444.9	22.7
OPEC	1973	1 974.4	6.7	21.9	983.8	4 152.3	6.4
	1980	1 994.4	8.0	23.1	2 398.6	6 237.5	7.5
	1981	1 695.7	8.4	19.6	2 665.9	6 357.4a	7.7

a Increase over 1980 ascribable to an expansion in capacity from 15 to 135 bpd in the United Arab Emirates.

Note: bpd = barrels per day.

Source: OPEC: Annual Statistical Bulletin 1981; calculations by the authors.

Growing competition must also be expected in other industries, particularly petrochemicals, the production and initial processing of aluminium and the iron and steel industry. These sectors have a high priority in the industrial and developmental plans of oil-producing countries. A large export ratio is often built into such projects simply on account of the minimum size of plant on technical and economic grounds and the very narrow local and regional markets for some of the products concerned. Moreover, the industries mentioned have certain characteristics that make them attractive propositions for export-oriented industrialisation in countries benefiting from real oil price increases:

- they require a high input of hydrocarbons as a raw material and/or as a source of energy;

- they have a large physical capital content and do not necessarily rely on a highly developed technological and scientific base in the country itself;

- they are well advanced in the product cycle, so that products and production methods have been highly perfected ("standardized").

There is particularly strong pressure on the petrochemical industry to adjust in its traditional locations. More than 90 % of the sector's raw materials consist of crude oil and natural gas, which in the first stage of processing are converted into simple intermediate products, such as ammonia, methanol, ethylene and propylene. These "building blocks" are then used to create a large numer of more complex substances, such as plastics, artificial fibres, synthetic rubber, fertilisers and cleaning materials.

The rise in oil prices has dramatically increased petrochemical production costs in the traditional producing countries[25] and prices have also changed in relation to those of substitutes. This applies in particular to plastics, whose price advantages over conventional materials have diminished considerably in some cases. Hence real oil price increases might place an effective brake on substitution in this field.

At the same time, some oil-rich countries, and especially Saudi Arabia, are developing large-scale activities in sections of the petrochemical industry that will give them increasing shares of world markets that are likely to grow only slowly, and certainly not at the pace experienced in the decades that followed the Second World War.[26] For the oil producers this sector is a key industry whose needs match their resources in important respects. It permits an economic use of the natural gas that is automatically derived from oil production and which at present is still mainly flared off. Furthermore, much of the technology used in the sector is relatively mature (Turner 1982, p. 118), so that turnkey plant can be built for operation by the oil-producing countries themselves, possibly with the aid of foreign technical and managerial staff. Technological gaps can also be closed by setting up joint ventures with foreign firms, which on the whole have shown themselves very willing to become involved in petrochemical complexes in oil-producing countries.[27] The locational disadvantages of these countries - primarily high building costs, an inadequate infrastructure and long distances to the main markets - are therefore often offset by high capital power and an appropriate raw materials and energy base.[28]

The oil-producing countries also wish to step up their activities in the production and processing of <u>aluminium</u>.[29] Like the petrochemical industry, in the sixties and early seventies this sector was one of the structurally strong industries that managed to record substantial growth, largely at the expense of other sectors. It too now suffers from great overcapacity - out of an estimated smelting capacity of 14 million tonnes in the Western world about 4 million tonnes are lying idle - and there is broad agreement that future growth will not even approach the rates seen in the past (Financial Times, 27.10.1982).

The sector's problems do not come so much from the demand side, however; the potential for the use of aluminium appears to be far from exhausted. There is scope for aluminium to take the place of other materials mainly in the packaging industry and in motor manufacture, where relatively light aluminium products can replace heavy steel components and hence make a substantial contribution to reducing fuel consumption.[30] What gives rise to serious difficulties, is the industry's cost structure. Production of primary aluminium depends on the electrolysis of aluminium oxide obtained from bauxite, so that electricity is the dominant cost factor, accounting for up to 50 % of total costs at present.[31] The burden of electricity costs is likely to increase further in future, and by a considerable amount. Long-term contracts for the supply of cheap electricity that companies concluded before the first oil shock are gradually expiring and the electricity suppliers seem determined not to enter into such long-term commitments again and to increase tariffs dramatically. Nor can it be expected that governments will fully offset these increases in costs by paying subsidies, particularly as this would be bound to provoke demands for similar treatment from other energy-intensive industries and seems scarcely justified on the grounds of security of supply.[32]

340

As a result, the competitive conditions improve further for those production locations that have large reserves of hydro-electricity[33] (primarily Canada and Norway among the Western industrial countries) and/or can generate electricity from cheap oil or gas. In these circumstances Bahrein has already established an internationally viable aluminium industry that is still expanding.[34] In Venezuela aluminium smelting capacity has risen rapidly, from 43,400 in 1977 to 312,200 tonnes in 1981, so that the country has overtaken Italy, the Netherlands, India and Brazil and has drawn almost level with the United Kingdom (Financial Times, 27.10.1982). Indonesia is also pushing ahead rapidly with the development of the aluminium industry with the dual objective of reducing the country's still heavy reliance on imports in this field and creating an export base. Japan is providing essential technical assistance (Indonesian Commercial Newsletter, 17.5.1982). Other potential competitors in this sector are Iran, Saudi Arabia and the United Arab Emirates. However, in those countries the main objective is import substitution, not export expansion.

The steel industry, which has also suffered a dramatic decline in capacity utilisation in its traditional centres, is geared more strongly to domestic markets than the petrochemical and aluminium industries. The importance of foreign trade will probably decline further in the steel sector, particularly as the new steelworks under construction mainly in Third World countries are primarily intended for import substitution purposes. At the same time there is expected to be a polarisation in the structure of exports, whereby the sector's simplest products - crude steel and simple intermediate products - and its most sophisticated articles will both increase in importance in the export field (Gold 1982, p. 52).

Countries with large energy reserves are not the least to benefit from this trend, for exports of simple steel products are "stimulated primarily by the energy cost advantages and, to a lesser extent, by the wage cost advantages of industrialising countries" (Gold 1982, p. 58). Moreover, oil and gas-rich countries offer favourable locational conditions for small steel works, particularly if the direct reduction process is combined with electrical steel production, as this permits much greater productivity than with conventional steel-making processes at greatly reduced capital cost and greater production flexibility. The price to be paid for this is a high consumption of gas and electricity, a relatively minor inconvenience in oil-producing countries.

Hence the oil-producing countries are likely to cover an increasing part of their steel requirement with steel from their own works and to compete on world markets in certain sections of the steel industry. Until now, it has been mainly Venezuela and Mexico that have been vigorously developing a national steel industry. These countries have not only ample energy reserves but also vast iron ore deposits and substantial capacity in steel-consuming industries. The latter are lacking at present in most other oil-producing countries. However, with the trend towards smaller production units, the existence and dynamism of particularly large consumers of steel such as engineering and vehicle manufacture are no longer as essential to the establishment of a viable steel industry as they were in the fifties and sixties, when they played a decisive part in the phenomenal rise of the Japanese steel industry.

d.   Reactions and options of the oil-importing countries

The traditional manufacturing countries are faced with the
question of how they can most effectively counter the possible
trade and structural problems caused by the oil-producing
countries' efforts to diversify their exports. In itself,
the competitive potential of the oil producers should be
regarded as marginal not only in terms of the economy as
a whole but also in terms of the sector affected.[35] However, it may reinforce pressure for internal and external
adjustment that is already strong. A forward-looking economic policy must therefore take account of the development
trends indicated above within the general context of structural adjustment requirements and apportion roles between
the state and private enterprises in the adjustment process.

There is still considerable scope for a "positive" adjustment by firms to the changing competitive conditions, both
in the adaptation of existing production methods and the
development of new ones and in the modification of the production programme.

As far as production processes are concerned, the assumption
generally made in foreign trade theory that trading partners
have identical production functions is often not confirmed
in reality, even in "mature" industries. This premise might
lead one to resign oneself to the fact that process innovations ultimately bear no fruit, as they only postpone the inevitable demise of certain activities in their traditional
locations. Such a position does not seem universally tenable,
however. Firms whose international competitiveness is threatened by increases in energy and raw material costs can take
countermeasures in the form of stringent efforts to conserve
energy and find substitutes. For example, the petrochemical

industry in the USA reduced its energy consumption per unit of output by 18.2 % between 1972 and 1978, thereby saving about 360,000 barrels of oil a day. By 1985 the saving should have risen to 770,000 barrels (Holmer 1980, p. 19). In Germany the consumption of electricity per unit of chemicals produced has been steadily falling and the trend is expected to accelerate during the eighties (Bittel 1982, p. 296 f). The petrochemical industry also has room to make savings by improving its use of raw materials; in plastics processing,for instance, the input of raw materials per unit of output can still be substantially reduced. A switch can also be made from the present predominant feedstock, straight-run gasoline, to heavier fractions, coal or biomass.

There is also considerable scope for energy-saving and oil substitution in the aluminium and steel industries. One example comes from Aluminium Pechiney, a subsidiary of the metals and chemicals group Pechiney Ugine Kuhlmann. Over a period of eight years the company has reduced energy consumption per tonne of aluminium by 20 % from 3,400 thermal units in 1973 to 2,700 in 1981. Certain technical innovations that permit energy savings of this kind, such as the use of barium to purify the bauxite, where promoted by subsidies from the French agency for energ-saving (Blick durch die Wirtschaft, 5.4.1982).

The KS technology developed by the Klöckner steelworks might be taken as an example from the steel industry. The advantages of this steelmaking process are that it reduces primary energy consumption by 40 %, permits imported energy to be replaced by coal and reduces environmental pollution (Frankfurter Allgemeine Zeitung, 7.5.1982).[36]

Greater energy efficiency can also be achieved by making
changes in the production programme (although this essentially represents a separate adjustment strategy). A distinction must be drawn here between "trading-up" - a switch
of emphasis to higher-value goods and greater product dif-
ferentiation within a given product range[37] - and diversification, which entails moving into related or completely
new areas of activity. For the steel industry this might
mean greater involvement in machinery and plant fabrication, a sector where there is already considerable overcapacity, however. The aluminium industry could find opportunities for growth through recycling, for example, as
the reclamation of aluminium that has already been processed
requires only 5 % of the original input of energy.[38] The
chief fields of diversification appropriate to the petrochemical industry are the many possible applications of
biotechnology, whose potential future impact is expected
to be just as "revolutionary" as the effects of electronics
today (Teso 1982, p. 4).

The state can influence the adjustment process in the traditional producing countries in many ways. For example, it could
impose countervailing duties on imports from the oil-producing countries on the grounds of unfair competition as a result
of the payment of energy and capital subsidies. Such action
would be further facilitated by the fact that important
potential competitors - such as Mexico, Saudi Arabia and
Venezuela - are not signatories of GATT,[39] so that the GATT
code on subsidies is not applicable to trade with these
countries. Consequently, unilateral trade restrictions
could be imposed here without the need to prove "material
injury" of domestic industry, in contrast to the trade dispute between the USA and the European Community that has
now been settled but which had been triggered by the artificially low level of gas prices in the USA.

Such measures would be questionable, however. The oil-producing countries have the means of effective retaliation, given their rich resources and absorptive markets in which governments agencies are the buyers with the greatest purchasing power.[40] Moreover, most of the subsidies paid in the oil states are not granted specifically for exports but are awarded generally. One example is provided by Saudi Arabia, where the natural gas associated with oil production is supplied at low cost to all industrial plant in the country, not just the petrochemical industry (Nachrichten für Außenhandel, 19.12.1983). The importance of such assistance within the framework of economic development programmes was expressly recognised in the Tokyo Round of GATT negotiations and the suitability of the petrochemical industry as a focal point of industrialisation in oil-rich (and thinly populated) developing countries can scarcely be disputed on economic grounds.

Action to channel trade flows might become necessary, however, if imports in particular sectors rose substantially or suddenly. Trade and co-operation agreements, such as those concluded by the EC with a large number of developing countries, might be a suitable framework for resolving disputes arising in this context between oil-exporting and oil-importing countries. Until now the oil producers are not strongly represented among the countries involved.[41] European Parliament initiatives aimed at the conclusion of co-operation agreements between the Community and the Gulf States have met with little response. Various attempts to breathe new life into the European-Arab dialogue, which began immediately after the first oil shock but quickly lost momentum, have also foundered so far, mainly for political reasons.[42] Institutions, mechanisms and arrangements of this kind appear to be necessary, however, to balance the interests of oil-producing countries in export diversification and their need for technical assistance in their export-oriented industrialisation against the adjustment capacity of traditional manufacturing countries. Comprehensive arrangements of the kind mentioned also make sense in that they permit the question of the division of industrial labour to be handled in conjunction with the problem of the setting of oil prices, secure supplies of this commodity and the reinvestment of surplus oil receipts.

Besides a policy on trade and co-operation, nations may need to have an active industrial policy that promotes those processes of innovation that are insufficiently supported by private enterprise and at the same time favours the reduction in capacity in industries that are not viable over the long run.

Most examples of a successful industrial policy against the background of real oil price increases come from Japan.[43] For example, the construction of new plant by the Japanese petrochemical industry was largely halted at an early date on the instigation of the Government, whereas in Western Europe the authorities mostly proved incapable of mastering the investment boom in this sector triggered by the rapid growth in demand before the crisis (Turner 1982, p. 125).

In contrast to Germany and other producers placed at a disadvantage by the energy situation, Japan has slashed smelting capacity in the aluminium industry from 1.6 million tonnes in 1977 to 0.7 million tonnes at the end of 1982 (Financial Times, 9.2.1983). Further closures are foreseen under the Government's five-year programme for the industry. Indeed, Japan is regarded as the only OECD-country that has considered it necessary to define an overall policy with the specific aim of restructuring its aluminium industry. What is more, "the need to make drastic reductions in the industry's capacity in Japan was the result of passing on the increases in generating costs in power prices paid by aluminium producers" (OECD 1983b, p. 11).

In the iron and steel industry Japan is again in a fundamentally better position than other countries that are also being squeezed by new competition. Despite capacity utilisation rates as low as in Western Europe and the USA, Japanese steelmakers are continuing to make large profits, mainly as a result of far-reaching measures to save energy and automate production. The sale of steel technology and steelmaking plant to developing countries also constitutes a growing source of income. The Japanese steel industry regards this as a part of their diversification strategy, whereas steel producers in other industrial countries are chiefly worried about the boomerang effect of such activities (Woolcock 1982, p. 114).

The methods of achieving Japan's industrial policy, which may also partly explain the successful adjustment of the Japanese steel industry, cannot be simply transposed to other countries. They must find their own ways of overcoming structural problems of adjustment stemming from real oil price rises and the consequent increase in competition from the oil-producing countries; a detailed examination of those methods cannot be undertaken in this study.

3. Consequences for trade between oil-importing countries

The emergence of a deficit in an oil-importing country's
trade account with oil-producing countries does not necessarily mean a deterioration in its overall trade position.
An example in this regard is provided by Germany in the first
oil crisis.[44] Germany's deficit on trade with the OPEC countries increased from DM 4.2 billion in 1973 to DM 12.8 billion in the following year. Over the same period net exports
to non-OPEC LDCs increased by DM 3.9 billion, to Western industrial countries by DM 18.9 billion and to state-trading
countries by DM 3.3 billion, so that the surplus on the overall trade account increased from DM 33.0 to 50.8 billion.

This development was largely due to cyclical disparities
among major trading partners. In France and Italy total demand (and hence imports from Germany) expanded relatively
strongly in 1974 (by 3.2 and 4.1 % respectively), whereas
only slight growth of 0.7 % was recorded in Germany. At the
same time, Germany's terms of trade with other oil-importing
countries improved,[45] so that part of the price increases imposed by OPEC could be "passed on" to other trading partners.[46]
This can also be seen in the substantial rate of "exported"
inflation, portrayed by the difference between the price rise
for total demand for goods and services on the one hand (GNP
plus imports) and the increase in prices for domestic demand
on the other (cf. Table A-31).

The reverse was the case in the second oil crisis. Not only
was there a serious deterioration in Germany's trade balance
with OPEC - the bilateral trade surplus of DM 5.1 billion recorded in 1978 turned into a deficit of DM 7.8 billion in
1979 and was followed by a shortfall of DM 14.6 billion in
1980 - but net exports to other countries also declined,

falling by DM 8.2 billion in trade with Western industrial
countries (although in fact the oil-producing countries Norway and the United Kingdom alone accounted for 7.6 billion
of this), by DM 1.8 billion with non-OPEC LDCs and by
DM 3.2 billion with state-trading countries. Worldwide there
was therefore a negative swing of DM 32.9 billion.

The terms of trade can provide little by way of explanation
for this turn of events.[47] Furthermore, export prices were
not to be outdone by the rate of increase in domestic prices
- indeed, there was even a small rate of exported inflation
in 1979 (cf. Table A-31). The growth differential had gone
into reverse, however: in 1979 and 1980 growth in Germany
was distinctly faster than in the country's major trading
partners, especially France, the United Kingdom, the USA
and the Netherlands. The result was a strong wave of imports.
At the same time, doubts began to be expressed about the international competitiveness of German industry.[48]

The following sections will examine the way in which real
oil price rises influence competitive conditions in trade
among oil-importing countries. Rising oil prices have differing effects on the level of costs in industries exposed
to international competition. At the same time they cause
changes in the structure of demand, which may offset cost
disadvantages. Not least, international competitiveness is
determined by the flexibility with which a country adjusts
to changed cost and demand conditions.

a.   The influence of rising energy costs on international
      competitiveness

Countries in which energy-intensive goods account for a relatively large proportion of total exports can find themselves at a competitive disadvantage in international trade.

Their exports grow more slowly than world exports unless offsetting changes in preferences occur and unless demand for
energy-intensive goods is inelastic to changes in price.

Table 6.14 shows that in some cases the proportion of total
exports that consists of products with a high energy content
differs considerably among the leading Western industrial
countries. Canada has a particularly high ratio - 28 % in
1980 - whereas energy-intensive products make up a particularly small part of the exports of the United Kingdom (10 %).
Germany is relatively badly placed, as is France, where also
the structure of exports, contrary to the general trend,
shifted considerably towards energy-intensive products between 1973 and 1980. On the other hand, such products declined substantially as a proportion of Japan's exports.

At first sight, the differences in the structure and trend
of these countries' exports measured in terms of the energy
intensity criterion seem to fit remarkably well with the
trend of export market shares (see Table 6.14). This might
be the result of pure chance, however, as a multitude of
factors determine competitiveness as expressed in export
market shares.

If the examination is confined to energy-intensive sectors
in Western industrial countries, it emerges that the burden
of energy costs has evolved differently in each country. In
public debate the blame for this is laid mainly on international differences in the prices of fuels and in the ratios
of those prices one to another.[49] However, differences in energy prices do not seem to have had a serious influence on
the international competitiveness of energy-intensive industries overall.[50] In _individual_ manufacturing sectors in which
energy is the most important cost factor this might very well

Table 6.14: IMPORTANCE OF ENERGY-INTENSIVE PRODUCTS IN THE TRADE OF WESTERN INDUSTRIAL COUNTRIES AND THE EXPORT MARKET SHARES OF THESE COUNTRIES IN 1973 AND 1980

	Exports of energy-intensive products in millions of dollars		%		Export market shares[b]	
	1973	1980	1973	1980	1973	1980
USA	7,721	25,677	11.0	12.1	17.7	17.2
Canada	6,987	17,971	27.7	28.5	6.4	5.1
Japan	7,012	19,080	19.1	14.7	9.3	10.5
Federal Rep. of Germany	11,204	31,481	16.6	16.4	17.0	15.5
France	5,193	17,229	14.1	15.5	8.9	9.0
United Kingdom	3,801	11,392	12.4	10.0	7.7	9.3
Italy	2,670	8,789	12.0	11.2	5.6	6.4
Memorandum:						
OECD	68,563	198,943	17.3	16.1	100	100
EC	34,378	101,256	16.4	15.4	53.0	53.3

a See Appendix 2 for a list of energy-intensive products.

b Exports of the country or region as a precentage of total OECD exports.

Source: OECD: Statistics of Foreign Trade; calculations by the authors.

be the case, however. The question is therefore whether economic measures should be taken in such cases.

Justification for policy action would still be strongest if
price differences were due to subsidies and similar measures,
but even then one would first have to establish whether the
damage to trading partners caused by state aid was substantial. In this context it is also well to reflect that despite
their short-term disadavantages "realistic" energy prices can
raise the level of competitiveness in the long run by the fact
that the necessary changes in production processes and programmes are made earlier than in other countries where energy
prices are kept artificially low.[51]

Nevertheless, in certain circumstances distortions of competition arising from energy price subsidies might justify corrective measures by the state. A guideline in this respect
could be the subsidy code agreed in the Tokyo Round of GATT
negotiations which partly reinterprets GATT Articles 6 (an-
ti-dumping and countervailing duties), 16 (subsidies) and 23
(safeguarding of concessions) and expressly includes general
subsidies, not just those on exports. In practice, however,
it has been found that the subsidy code still leaves too
much room for differences of interpretation, as was seen
for example in the steel dispute between the European Community and the USA.

The situation takes on a different complexion if different
energy prices in various countries primarily reflect differences in natural locational conditions. This applies, for
example, if country A has substantial hydroelectric potential
and can therefore generate electricity cheaply, whereas country B is forced to produce electricity from the now much more
expensive fossil fuels. If the government of country B decid-

ed to establish equality of competition by subsidising electricity prices, there is a danger that it would have an adverse effect on resource allocation. If relative costs change abruptly, general subsidies might be granted (on a temporary reducing basis) in order to prevent collapse, but it is essential that necessary changes in the structure of production should not be impeded and that economically desirable adjustment strategies by the firms concerned be encouraged.

The need for structural adjustment also arises if energy price differences between countries are a manifestation of different energy policy priorities and preferences. For example, if a country gives atomic energy a small role in energy supply or no role at all even though electricity from nuclear power stations would be cheaper, or if environmental measures greatly increase the cost of electricity from coal-fired power stations, it follows that power-intensive processes will be under increased pressure to adjust.

b. The international division of labour in energy-sensitive goods and services

Apart from energy costs, other supply factors influenced by real oil price rises determine the competitiveness of a country in trade with oil-importing countries. Those countries that develop products (including services) for use in exploiting new sources of energy (energy-producing goods) or in conserving energy (energy-saving goods) are most likely to increase their trade.

Examples of energy-producing goods would be plant and equipment for offshore activities (where there is a trend from stationary to moveable production platforms), small hydroelectric works for developing countries, components for nuclear reactors, coal liquefaction plant or the know-how for

extracting fuels from biomass. Brazil, where a substantial
and rapidly growing proportion of motor vehicles are fuelled
by alcohol,[52] ist striving to develop exports of alcohol engines and the associated technology into a substantial source
of foreign exchange. A co-operation agreement along these
lines has already been signed with Paraguay, and other Latin American countries have also shown interest.[53] In the coal
conversion field the Federal Republic of Germany has built
up a technological lead that is to be exploited more fully
to generate exports.[54]

Where energy-saving goods are concerned, devices, plant and
systems that reduce the energy used in production or permit
a conversion to cheaper sources of energy must be distinguished from consumer goods that save energy or help replace
expensive fuels. For example, competitive advantages can be
achieved by developing systems to regulate temperatures or
boilers that consume less energy or can burn a variety of
fuels or by combining conventional forms of heating with
new techniques (e.g. heat pumps).[55] The same applies to new
developments in motor car technology that reduce specific
fuel consumption without having an offsetting negative effect on other factors that determine the demand for cars,
such as purchase price, safety, quality of workmanship, benefits of use, etc.

The scale and potential of the markets for energy-producing
and energy-saving goods and related services and the ratio
of one to the other are controversial. On the one hand it
is claimed that there is a vast market worldwide for energy-saving technology, whereas "the highly sophisticated technologies, such as nuclear technology, have only a comparatively ... small sales potential" (Deutscher Bundestag 1982,
p. 10/91).[56] The response from the opposing faction is that

"the markets described in theory ... simply do not exist in practice", since there is "a very wide gulf ... between the intellectual awareness of the need to save energy and actual ... consumer behaviour, both here and abroad" (Deutscher Bundestag 1982, p. 10/137). Hence it is claimed that the number of firms that can sell energy-saving devices abroad is far smaller than the section of industry that "is locked into other sectors by supply contracts and whose own export potential is also being stunted by the hold-up in the erection of energy supply plant" (Deutscher Bundestag 1982, p. 10/98).

This raises a further point of controversy, namely the link between the international competitiveness of sub-contractors of energy supply plant, such as firms in the general engineering or equipment industries, and the existence of a sufficient number of initial domestic buyers. The theory goes that only this can generate increases in output and hence export opportunities, particularly as substantial development work is often required (Deutscher Bundestag 1982, p. 10/97). Whether this is true would have to be investigated empirically.[57] A priori, the proposition is hardly tenable, however, as it underestimates the opportunities for the international division of labour.

The precondition for the international division of labour to occur in energy conservation, oil substitution and energy extraction is that domestic markets are also open to foreign suppliers. In practice this is by no means always the case, however. For example, the French Government subsidies the conversion from oil or gas to coal only if equipment manufactured in France is used (Nachrichten für Außenhandel, 3.12. 1982). The markets in offshore equipment are also under strong protectionist pressure. As a result, the emergence of efficient patterns of production is impeded.

Not only trade policy but also energy and industrial policies determine the development of international specialisation in the sectors in question. The measures applied here include research promotion, investment grants and similar activities in favour of the energy sector and energy-related activities.

It will be almost impossible to avoid distortions of international competition in this context, particularly as governmental agreements on energy and industrial policy have proved extremely difficult to achieve even at the regional level, such as that of the European Community. However, distortions of competitive conditions in this case appear less serious than, say, cut-throat competition among oil-importing countries on the OPEC markets. Whereas the latter chiefly benefits the OPEC countries, action by individual states to hasten adjustment of the patterns of production to an increase in the cost of energy improves the income position of oil-importing countries as a whole vis-à-vis the oil-producing countries. The trade gains of the successful countries are therefore not nullified by losses sustained by the other oil-importing countries, as in a zero-sum game.

c.   Real oil price increases threatening an open trading
     system

Open markets and competitive patterns of trade can make a major contribution towards solving problems caused by real oil price increases not only in regard to energy-sensitive goods and services but also in the economy in general. In actual fact, however, the oil price rises were accompanied by growing protectionism in the oil-importing countries, occasioned by persistent current account deficits and the rapid gains made by foreign suppliers in certain sectors.

The main cause of increasing protectionism is the slowdown in growth, itself caused in large measure by the rise in the cost of oil. As growth slows down, competition in international markets grows more acute and the chances of finding new jobs or sources of income are viewed less optimistically. The instruments of protectionism include the distortion of competition by means of export promotion measures as well as import restrictions.

Under a system of floating exchange rates, trade restrictions are difficult to justify as a means of solving balance-of-payments problems. However, the changeover to flexible currency relationships in the seventies was unable to prevent the emergence of substantial foreign trade disequilibria; developments in the oil markets were clearly a crucial factor in this.

In such cases, Article 12 of the GATT permits import restrictions in order to protect foreign exchange reserves, subject to certain conditions. However, tariff measures would be a lesser evil than the volume restrictions for which the GATT provides, as the price mechanism would then continue to operate as a control instrument. Examples in this regard are the special import duties imposed by the United Kingdom in 1964 and the USA in 1971 and the various cash deposit schemes by which Italy attempted to restore balance-of-payments equilibrium in 1974, 1976 and 1981. Experience has shown, however, that the problems are rarely resolved in this manner; indeed, they are more likely to be exacerbated, as the almost inevitable devaluation comes too late.[58]

Countries beset with sudden and serious trade problems in individual sectors can invoke Article 19 of the GATT. In practice, this provision is rarely used, however, for injured trading partners have a right to compensation and, more important, the safeguard clause is not to be used selectively against individual countries. Instead, in recent years numerous bi-

lateral safeguard arrangements have been concluded that by-
pass and ultimately undermine the GATT.

After the first oil shock the Federal Republic of Germany
and Japan, in particular, had to endure the not altogether
convincing complaint that their foreign economic policies
were harming their trading partners.[59] In the second oil crisis criticism was directed mainly against Japan.

Japan has a particularly heavy reliance on imported oil -
net oil imports accounted for an average of just under 70 %
of total energy consumption between 1978 and 1981, compared
with only 20 % in the USA and about 45 % in the EC countries
- so that during and after the second oil crisis it had to
cope with rapidly growing deficits in trade with the oil-
producing countries. Between 1979 and 1982 the cumulative
shortfall came to $ 124 billion, equivalent to 162.1 % of Ja-
pan's exports to this group of countries (cf. Table 6.15).
By running up trade surpluses against other oil-importing
countries, however, Japan was able to eliminate all but
$ 2.6 billion of the oil deficits. The worst affected by
this policy were the USA and the EC, whose cumulative net
imports from Japan each amounted to about one-third of Japan's deficits with the oil-producing countries. The European Community's problems were further exacerbated by the
fact that its trade deficit with the USA was also rising
rapidly; in relation to exports to the USA, it increased
from 23.8 % in 1978 to 35.6 % and 64.3 % in the two following years before declining to 33 % in 1981 and 22.8 % in
1982.

This led to the apparent paradox of a dramatic rise in net
imports from oil-producing countries but a halving of the
ratio between the oil deficit and the total foreign trade

Table 6.15: TRADE BALANCES (NET IMPORTS) OF OIL-IMPORTING INDUSTRIAL AND DEVELOPING
            COUNTRIES WITH OIL-PRODUCING COUNTRIES, 1973 - 1982

	1973	1974	1975	1976	1977	1978	1979	1980	1981	1982
					- in billions of dollars -					
USA	1.2	9.7	9.5	16.9	24.3	18.9	32.8	40.2	29.9	8.3
Japan	4.4	15.0	11.6	13.3	13.3	11.4	24.1	39.6	33.8	26.5
Fed. Rep. of Germany	1.6	5.0	1.3	-1.5	-0.6	-2.6	4.2	8.2	1.8	-2.2
France	2.0	7.1	4.7	6.4	5.9	5.3	9.0	15.1	11.5	8.2
Italy	2.2	7.2	4.1	3.8	3.2	3.0	5.9	7.8	6.6	6.6
Brazil	0.7	2.4	2.4	3.3	3.2	3.5	5.7	7.6	7.3	7.0
Korea	0.3	1.0	1.0	1.1	1.1	1.2	2.1	3.6	3.2	n.a.
Spain	0.9	3.1	2.7	3.7	3.4	3.2	4.3	7.5	6.7	5.4
memo: EC	10.5	32.4	18.1	20.6	14.6	8.7	27.3	41.6	24.2	15.2
				- as percentage of exports to oil-producing countries -						
USA	35.9	151.6	91.6	138.6	180.1	118.2	226.8	237.1	144.0	36.5
Japan	164.1	278.8	140.9	144.6	112.0	80.1	181.8	213.3	147.5	121.7
Fed. Rep. of Germany	72.9	126.1	19.2	17.9	-5.6	-21.2	40.2	65.4	12.0	-13.7
France	112.6	250.4	102.4	136.7	106.3	84.8	125.7	160.7	109.6	80.6
Italy	182.8	318.7	110.1	90.5	54.1	43.3	76.1	80.4	51.9	62.4
Brazil	300.8	437.2	364.6	594.7	408.5	384.2	713.8	521.9	505.5	391.6
Korea	417.9	569.0	294.0	154.6	86.1	87.8	124.5	160.5	120.2	n.a.
Spain	252.3	634.6	338.4	447.1	288.1	196.4	218.4	282.7	228.3	174.3
memo: EC	129.8	238.3	78.7	78.3	43.1	21.9	70.0	81.6	41.0	28.1
				- as percentage of net imports from the world -						
USA	55.0	102.3	-425.8	98.7	62.1	44.8	81.4	111.1	75.4	26.3
Japan	323.6	228.3	547.4	-548.4	-136.3	-61.7	319.4	365.4	-392.0	-371.3
Fed. Rep. of Germany	-12.8	-25.7	-8.6	10.6	3.6	12.4	-34.5	-167.9	-15.1	10.1
France	182.8	106.8	537.1	88.8	107.5	219.1	142.3	80.0	79.2	35.6
Italy	39.2	67.5	114.6	62.2	113.0	771.8	103.2	35.8	41.9	53.0
Brazil	84.5	39.3	48.9	90.0	291.7	145.3	130.4	157.9	224.2	786.4
Korea	32.1	40.0	45.1	104.7	139.7	54.1	39.2	75.4	66.1	n.a.
Spain	18.3	40.0	31.7	42.0	44.9	57.4	60.1	56.0	57.0	48.5
memo: EC	219.8	151.9	278.5	102.0	121.7	135.9	80.0	65.8	84.6	55.9

Note: The oil-producing countries comprise the members of OPEC (excluding Ecuador and Gabon) and Oman.
Source: IMF: Direction of Trade Statistics; calculations by the authors.

deficit of the EC, namely from 1.4 in 1978 to 0.7 two years later. In Japan the overall trade balance also slipped into the red in 1979 and 1980, but the corresponding ratios for these years came to 3.2 and 3.7, in other words the oil deficits amounted to several times the total deficit.

The conflicts generated by these developments have led to intensive negotiations among the countries involved. The various multilateral activities - world economic summits, GATT and OECD conferences, tripartite meetings of the trade "giants" (the EC, Japan and the USA) - seem to be less important in this context than bilateral contacts, most of which have bypassed GATT.

The bilateral consultations have a dual objective: to persuade the successful trade partner to restrict exports or curb their growth and at the same time to take concrete steps to increase imports. However, the dispute with Japan that is dominating the trade scene shows that the outcome of these efforts has been decidedly "asymmetrical" so far; whereas Japan's dynamic export growth has been curbed by self-restraint agreements and informal arrangements in "sensitive" product groups, the import situation has not noticeably changed. The various liberalisation programmes introduced or announced by Japan and tariff reductions ahead of schedule are an important step towards correction of this imbalance. However, what is most needed are increased efforts by exporting industries themselves, particularly as Japan has a relatively low level of protection, at least by normal standards.

Trade between industrial countries and non-oil developing countries is also strongly affected by real oil price rises.

These relationships typically entail large surpluses on
the part of industrial countries, reflecting the "natural"
role of capital-rich countries in a world economy based on
the division of labour.

After the first oil shock the Third World countries that
are dependent on imported oil were able to maintain or even
substantially increase their non-oil imports despite a dramatic increase in their oil bill. To a considerable extent
this was facilitated indirectly by surplus OPEC receipts,
which reached the developing countries via the international credit markets. However, as these loans were granted on
commercial terms, the borrowing countries also had to take
adjustment measures to generate or conserve foreign exchange so that they would be able to meet their repayment
obligations. However, the main debtor countries have relatively little scope for saving foreign exchange by reducing their dependence on imported oil for reasons connect-
ed essentially with the stage of industrialisation they have
already attained.

These countries therefore laid the emphasis of their adjustment efforts on the rapid development of industries producing finished goods for export, entirely in accord with the
recommendations of development advisers in the industrial
countries and international organisations. They are concentrating primarily on products that call for simple, relatively labour-intensive methods. In addition, the developing countries are competing in markets for products that
are well advanced in the product cycle, that is to say they
have reached a high level of standardisation in manufacture
and design. Some particularly dynamic Third World countries
are having growing export success with higher-value products, particularly in mechanical engineering and vehicle-

building. Shipments from manufacturing subsidiaries of foreign enterprises to group companies in other parts of the world are also becoming an increasingly important element in exports from developing countries. Finally, it deserves to be mentioned that the familiar newly industrialising countries are no longer the only competitors entering world markets; the OECD recognises that a "second generation" of dynamic exporters of finished products has now sprung up in the Third World.[60]

The ratio of exports to imports in the finished products field provides a rough measure of the competitive pressure from developing countries (see Table 6.16). It can be seen that the import cover ratio of the industrial countries as a whole has fallen since 1973. However, the average figures conceal conflicting movements in the main countries or country groups. For example, Japan was able to expand its exports to developing countries by much more than the increase in imports from that group. The opposite was true in the case of the European Community.

The industrial countries' typical reaction to the new competition has so far been to increase the mechanisation of production processes in traditional industries. This strategy is made more difficult by real oil price rises, as it often leads to an increase in energy consumption. Modified forms of adjustment are therefore needed.

Since the first oil shock, however, structural adjustment has been replaced increasingly by the protection of domestic suppliers against "cheap imports". At the same time, industrial countries have become noticeably less willing to grant trade preferences to the Third World, while the developing countries, for their part, have severely curbed their imports.

Table 6.16:   EXPORT/IMPORT RATIOS IN THE TRADE OF
              WESTERN INDUSTRIAL COUNTRIES WITH
              NON-OIL DEVELOPING COUNTRIES, 1972-1982

	Total Western industrial countries	EC	USA	Japan
	— t o t a l g o o d s —			
1972	1.16	1.08	0.95	1.48
1973	1.11	0.94	1.02	1.19
1974	1.14	1.06	1.04	1.24
1975	1.31	1.17	1.21	1.35
1976	1.05	0.96	0.95	1.21
1977	1.18	0.95	0.80	1.38
1978	1.15	1.06	0.84	1.57
1979	1.15	1.00	0.88	1.23
1980	1.13	0.96	0.96	1.35
1981	1.15	1.06	0.95	1.45
1982	1.09	1.04	0.83	1.34
	— m a n u f a c t u r e s —			
1972	2.63	3.02	1.32	6.00
1973	2.66	3.28	1.32	4.48
1974	3.26	2.64	1.52	4.43
1975	3.52	2.97	1.88	5.92
1976	2.51	2.83	1.41	5.39
1977	2.49	2.76	1.21	6.78
1978	2.46	2.65	1.11	6.12
1979	2.41	2.41	1.25	4.89
1980	2.49	2.26	1.44	6.15
1981	2.38	2.45	1.30	6.15
1982	2.13	2.43	1.06	5.60

Quelle: GATT: International Trade; GATT: Networks of World
          Trade 1955-1976, Geneva 1978; calculations by the
          authors.

Concrete steps towards liberalisation are needed if this trend, which is damaging to both sides, is to be reversed. The developing countries must be secure in the knowledge that trade concessions will not be rescinded at a later date. Liberalisation could be carried out in stages, with existing import restrictions being reduced progressively on a binding and irrevocable basis at set intervals. Such a procedure would give companies and economic policy-makers a much more certain basis on which to make their plans. In the developing countries a clear and predictable framework of trade policy is essential for the success of an export-oriented industrialisation strategy. For the industrial countries the advantage lies in the fact that the sectors affected - and the economic authorities - can prepare for the expected structural change in good time, so that the process of adjustment will be smoother. At the same time, the industrial countries can expect that with rising com-petitiveness the developing countries will open their own markets wider and increasingly subject themselves to GATT discipline. Such activities in the field of trade policy appear essential if oil-related current account deficits are to be financed and if the adjustment to more expensive oil is to be accomplished at the lowest cost to national economies and the world economy alike.

Footnotes to Chapter 6

1 For example, the rapid fall in orders received from OPEC countries
   by the German construction industry in 1982 and 1983 is blamed partly on financing problems but "not least on keen international competition from low-wage countries such as Turkey and Korea" (Nachrichten für Außenhandel, 6.4.1984).

2 In the plant construction field Hoechst is represented by its subsidiary company Uhde.

3 Kuwait's acquisition of a 10 % interest in the share capital of Metallgesellschaft in 1980 and a further 10 % in 1981 can also be seen in this
   light. Not least of Kuwait's objectives was to establish links with
   the "think tank" at Lurgi, which is a subsidiary of Metallgesellschaft
   and one of the largest engineering firms in the world, engaged mainly
   in the construction of large plant. For its part, Metallgesellschaft
   hoped for additional contracts, especially in refinery construction
   and in the petrochemical industry but also in raw material projects
   in third countries.

4 The order has also provoked accusations of a breach of licensing agreements from Korf Engineering of Germany, which accused Kobe of "licence
   cannibalism". The dispute centers on the Midrex direct reduction technology to be used in the project (Financial Times, 28.2.1984).

5 An examination of export contracts concluded by German Industry in 1981,
   most of which related to industrial plant, shows that 32 of the 56 big-
   gest contracts were signed with oil-producing countries. Libya was the
   most strongly represented, with 10 contracts, followed by Iraq with 8.
   Oil-producing countries accounted for as much as 70 % of the total contract value of DM 13.5 billion. Those with Libya alone represented 27 %
   and with Iraq 14 % (Die Zeit 28.5.1982).

6 The share of OPEC countries in total commitments is as high as around
   50 %, though declining in recent years (for details see BMWi 1984).

7 In this context mention may be made of the Saudi-German Development
   and Investment Company (SAGECO), established in Riyadh with German
   and Saudi capital and staff. The company's purpose is to facilitate
   the establishment of joint ventures between German investors and
   private Saudi firms. On the German side the federally-owned Deutsche
   Gesellschaft für wirtschaftliche Zusammenarbeit has a 43 % stake and
   the remaining shares are held by the Saudi Ministry of Finance and
   National Economy (Frankfurter Allgemeine Zeitung, 19.11.1982 and Nachrichten für Außenhandel, 1.6.1984)). By the end of 1983, a total of
   97 Saudi-German joint ventures have been established, of which 38 belong to the industrial sector (Nachrichten für Außenhandel, 3.5.1984).

8   For example, actual contracts were signed at the same time as the
    umbrella agreement on economic, technical and scientific co-opera-
    tion between Belgium and Algeria in April 1983. Belgian firms will
    supply equipment for 10 professional training centres and 7 hospi-
    tals. It is generally expected that Belgian industry will play a
    greater part in development projects in Algeria as a result of the
    agreement (Nachrichten für Außenhandel, 10.5.1983).

9   As regards payments, a variety of schemes have been proposed. For
    example, in the case of Nigeria an account with a European bank
    would be opened into which Brazil would make all its payments for
    Nigerian oil in hard currency. These funds would be useable only
    for the purchase by Nigeria of Brazilian goods or else would remain
    frozen for a two-year period (Financial Times, 25.5.1983).

10 For example, Brazil is said to have set the prices for steel prod-
    ucts supplied to Algeria below world market levels but at the same
    time to have accepted prices above the official list prices   for
    crude oil received in exchange (O Estado de São Paulo, 15.2.1983).

11 Italian consumer goods and foods, some of which are already import-
    ed into Algeria (such as refrigerators, furniture, motor vehicles,
    dairy products and pasta), are given particularly good chances of
    success in exchange for gas (Nachrichten für Außenhandel, 22.10.
    1982). A contract for a gas treatment and collection plant
    (a $ 440 m project which will take 40 months to complete) has al-
    ready been awarded to Italy's Snamprogetti group, the energy equip-
    ment subsidiary of the ENI state energy company (Financial Times,
    8.2. 1984a).

12 The difference between the price paid and world prices is offset
    by subsidies raised from higher petrol taxes (Frankfurter Allgemei-
    ne Zeitung, 2.5.1983).

13 For information on the basis of the data see UN: Yearbook of Inter-
    national Trade Statistics and GATT: International Trade.

14 For details see OPEC: Annual Statistical Bulletin.

15 For information on the basis of the data see UNCTAD: Handbook of
    International Trade and Development Statistics 1983, p. 102.

16 For information on the basis of the data see GATT: International
    Trade 1982/83, Table A-22.

17 For information on the basis of the data see GATT: International
    Trade 1982/83, Table A-22.

18 For information on the basis of the data see GATT: International
    Trade 1982/83, Table A-22.

19   In this connection McBean points to the opportunities for trade re-
     sulting from the existence of similar climatic conditions (MacBean)
     1980, p. 136).

20   The oil-producing countries attach particular importance to the
     transfer of technology: "Capital goods without technology are al-
     most useless. This is the underlying reason why these countries in-
     sist on receiving technological "know-how" through technical and "on-
     the-job" training for their populations whenever a project is brought
     under contract. It is also one reason why the imported services of
     OPEC member countries have expanded so dramatically in the past. Im-
     ports of services entail the purchase of "know-how" by bringing con-
     sultant experts and technicians from outside, not only to help pro-
     ject implementation but also to assist in the training of personnel.
     This is the development of human capital which is more precious than
     that of physical capital" (Nan Nguema 1983, p. 105).

     The transfer of technology and know-how to oil-producing countries
     can also be achieved if these countries participate in technology-
     intensive firms abroad. Kuwait is vigorously pursuing such a strat-
     egy. Involvement in areas such as biotechnology, electronics and
     computer technology is intended mainly to create a "training ground
     in high technology industries for young Kuwaitis" (Financial Times,
     23.2. 1983b).

     Iraq's policy contrasts directly with the position of Kuwait. In the
     eyes of the Iraqi Government, capital investments abroad are tanta-
     mount to a misallocation of resources, as they only produce "pecuni-
     ary" income and are also exposed to high risks such as the danger of
     expropriation, whereas "domestic investment yields significant non-
     pecuniary benefits in the form of external economies" (Zainy 1981,
     p. 50).

21   Oil-producing countries may also derive locational advantages from
     an "abundant" environment. Accordingly, they may attach less impo∅r-
     tance to environmental protection than is the case in the tradition-
     al locations of oil-intensive industries in highly developed countries,
     where the environment has become a scarce good.

22   Governments attempt to counteract this effect of real oil price
     rises by increasing the supply of public goods. The World Bank's
     World Development Report 1981 states in this context: "Governments ...
     have sharply increased those types of public spending that offer
     citizens benefits in kind rather than in cash. Those have included
     more and better recreation facilities and subsidised housing. In
     addition the provision of education and health services has been
     greatly expanded with obvious long-term benefits for economic ad-
     vance" (World Bank 1981, p. 92).

23 In this connection UNCTAD points to the high import content of in-
    vestment projects in OPEC countries: "Independent evidence confirms
    that the import content of capital projects in OPEC countries is
    40-100 % higher than similar projects in OECD countries" (UNCTAD
    1982, p. 76). However, no disaggregated data for individual coun-
    tries are given.

24 The capacity utilisation rates that refineries in oil-producing coun-
    tries will achieve in future will be determined partly by the market-
    ing opportunities available to these countries. Kuwait provides an
    example of an expansionary "downstream" policy; by purchasing the
    refineries and marketing networks of the American Gulf Oil Corpora-
    tion in Scandinavia, the Benelux countries and Italy, Kuwait has
    become the first OPEC country to control the entire chain form pro-
    duction to sales for a considerable (i.e. more than one-tenth) part
    of its oil output (for details see Financial Times, 1.2.1984).

25 For example, in 1981 the production costs of high-density polyethyle-
    ne in Germany were four times as high as at the end of the sixties.
    Over the same period the proportion of raw material costs within
    overall costs increased by a factor of fifteen (Bittel 1982, p. 295).

26 An indication of the scale of the prospective supply pressure from
    the oil-producing countries is provided by the following table, which
    shows the capacity of petrochemical projects due for completion by
    1986 in the Middle East (excluding Iran and Iraq) as a percentage
    of the corresponding capacities in Western Europe (cf. Bittel 1982,
    p. 298):

Ethylene	13
Ethylene glycol	40
Polyethylene	12
Benzene	6
Ortho-xylene	8
Para-xylene	8
Styrene	17
Methanol	45

27 Nearly all of Saudi Arabia's new petrochemical plants have been
    built by 50/50 joint venture companies, with the partners including
    Mobil, Mitsubishi, Exxon and Shell (Financial Times, 29.3.1984).

28 Wealthy oil states can also overcome sales problems by buying into
    established marketing networks. For example, as already mentioned
    above, this is seen as one of the main motives for Kuwait's share-
    holding in Hoechst AG (Die Zeit, 8.10.1982).

29 For a more comprehensive analysis of structural change in the alu-
    minium industry, see OECD 1983b and World Bank 1983c.

30 According to the above-mentioned OECD study "the principal factor like-
    ly to lead to a faster increase in aluminium demand than in growth of
    GNP in the 1980s will be the expansion of outlets in the transport sec-
    tor, in particular greater recourse to the use of aluminum in the man-
    ufacture of cars so as to increase mileage" (OECD 1983b, p. 9).

31 The production of one tonne of aluminium requires twice as much energy
    as that of an equivalent quantity of copper or polyethylene and about
    five times more than that of a tonne of steel (OECD 1983b, p. 7).

32 The situation facing the Governments of certain traditional producing
    countries is described as follows by the Chairman of Electricité de
    France: "If it is considered necessary to maintain aluminium produc-
    tion in Europe on strategic grounds, then aid must be given – in
    France too – for even electricity from nuclear power stations can-
    not compete with hydroelectricity in other countries. The decision
    rests with the Government, not with the electricity supply industry"
    (Frankfurter Allgemeine Zeitung, 21.4.1983).

33 Given the "non-tradeable" nature of the energy source, the opportunity
    cost of hydroelectricity generation is essentially equal to the actual
    cost. It is estimated that around 50 % of the energy consumed in alu-
    minium smelting is already derived from hydroelectric plant, 26 % from
    coal, 10 % from oil and 7 % each from natural gas and nuclear energy
    (Handelsblatt, 26.5.1982).

34 The objective is not only to diversify exports but also stimulate the
    development of manufacturing capacity in the Gulf States and hence en-
    courage import substitution in the region (Financial Times, 13.5.1983).

35 This conclusion is also supported by the results of a research project
    carried out by Battelle and the Ifo-Institut in which "archetypal"
    products – including aromatic hydrocarbons, polymerisation products
    and nitrogenous fertilisers – were examined to assess the danger to
    German industry posed by competition from newly industrialising coun-
    tries (RKW 1981).

36 A study by the UN-Economic Commission for Europe about energy use in
    the steel industry has shown that the energy performance of this sec-
    tor is still rather poor, while a wide scope for a more rational use
    of energy has been left (Nachrichten für Außenhandel, 28.12.1983).

37 Trading up to more complex products can be influenced in basically
    two ways by an increase in energy costs. Firstly, the higher-value
    products can be subject to lower energy cost pressures than simple
    products and secondly the rise in energy prices can improve demand
    conditions; for example, plastic products can be used for thermal
    insulation or in car manufacture to help reduce fuel consumption,
    in the same way as aluminium products.

38 Recycled aluminium already accounts for about 20 % of the Western
    world's total consumption of aluminium. This proportion is expect-
    ed to have risen to 26 % by 1990 (Financial Times, 27.10.1982).

39 Among the thirteen OPEC countries, only Gabon,Indonesia, Kuwait
    and Nigeria are Contracting Parties to the GATT. The GATT is also
    applied de facto in Algeria and the United Arab Emirates.

40 Attention is drawn to this aspect in a study by the Cambridge Eco-
    nomic Policy Group (Begg, Cripp, Ward 1981, p. 20), which states
    that "The Middle East's ... oil-exporting countries ... are in a
    strong position to guarantee markets for new domestic industries
    not only by restraining the growth of imports, but also ... by ob-
    liging the rest of the world to accept exports of the products of
    those industries as a quid pro quo for continued access to oil."

41 The EC concluded a co-operation agreement with Algeria in 1976
    within the framework of the "global policy" towards Mediterranean
    countries. Since 1975 there has been an agreement with Mexico on
    economic and trade co-operation that is designed to foster co-oper-
    ation in all fields both at governmental level and among private
    enterprises. Gabon and Nigeria are signatories of the Lomé Conven-
    tion.

42 On the economic arguments in favour of a dialogue between the EC
    and the Arab countries, see Franzmathes 1982.

43 An important instrument in this respect is the "Structural Improve-
    ment Law" which was passed in 1978 and renewed for a further five-
    year term in 1983. The new law enables companies in the seven areas
    of aluminium, synthetic fibres, industrial fertilisers, paper and
    board, petrochemicals, ferroalloys and electrical steel to merge and/
    or to scrap surplus capacity. The introduction of import barriers
    (import duties or quotas for certain imported goods) was consider-
    ed but rejected to forestall foreign criticism of such a measure
    (Nachrichten für Außenhandel, 24.2.1983).

44 A theoretical analysis of this situation can be found in Schmid
    (1983), where the introductory summary states that "due to a coun-
    try-specific superior technological adjustment the oil shock may
    possibly give a competitive edge to one country or a group of OECD
    countries. Then a trade diversion among trading OECD economies ben-
    efits a few of them at the expense of others and may be strong
    enough to weaken or even turn around negative output and employ-
    ment effects which originated from the real income transfer towards
    oil producers."

45 The terms of trade vis-à-vis oil-importing countries are not expli-
    citly reported by the Statistisches Bundesamt. Price ratios for finish-
    ed goods can be used as a proxy, however. In the period 1973-74 the
    terms of trade (with 1970 as the base year) improved from 106.8 to

108.3 for all such products together and from 114.1 to 117.7 for capital goods.

46 According to calculations by the RWI, between 1973 and 1979 as much as half of the total DM 13 billion burden on the German economy caused by real oil price rises could be passed on through price adjustments to foreign customers and suppliers outside the energy sector "with trade in machinery and vehicles alone producing around DM 3 billion thanks to increases in export prices that were higher than the domestic rate of price increase or increases in import prices that were below the rate of domestic inflation" (RWI 1982, p.102).

47 The terms-of-trade in finished goods changed little; the ratio of export prices to import prices (with 1976 as the base year) came to 102.4 in 1978 and 101.5 in 1980. The terms of trade on capital goods actually improved from 105.3 in 1978 to 107.2 in 1980. OECD calculations also point in the same direction and suggest that the current account deterioration between 1978 and 1980 was due in greater measure to real oil price rises than to changes in the overall terms-of-trade (cf. Table A-32). From this it may be concluded that the non-oil terms-of-trade improved.

48 In a study of oil price developments made with the help of its econometric model, the Deutsche Bundesbank comes to the conclusion that around one-third (DM 16 billion) of the negative swing in the German current account between 1978 and 1980 (DM 47 billion) was due to the rise in oil prices but that the remainder was attributable to "growing deficits on services and transfers and a general deterioration in Germany's competitive position owing to the steep real appreciation of the Deutsche Mark between 1974 and the end of 1978" (Deutsche Bundesbank 1981, p. 16).

49 Numerous examples of this are to be found in the Minutes of the Deutsche Bundestag hearing on "The competitiveness of German industry under various energy supply scenarios" (Deutscher Bundestag 1982). See also the publications of the Bundesverband der Deutschen Industrie (BDI 1983) and of the Deutscher Industrie- und Handelstag (DIHT 1983).

50 The detailed studies carried out by the Fraunhofer and Ifo Institutes on the competitiveness of energy-intensive sectors of German industry indicate a weak link between energy prices and international competitiveness (ISI 1982, Ifo 1983a). A simple examination of the trend in market shares for energy-intensive products suggests the same conclusion (cf. Table A -33).

51 The Commission of the European Communities also draws attention to this aspect when it states with regard to the increased US share of energy-intensive markets that low energy prices have not necessarily bolstered the competitive position of the United States. Probably

it was more a question that "the United States' artificial advantage in oil and gas prices prevented specialisation in sectors in which the USA has a genuine long-term comparative advantage" (EG 1982a, p. 66).

Energy price policy could also be a significant factor in relation to developing countries, as indicated, for example, in a study by Bergman, Radetzki (1979), which examines the effects of various strategies to reduce energy consumption in OECD countries. It states that: "If the strategy is based on taxation of energy consumption or the development of higher-cost domestic energy resources, the result could put energy consumers within the OECD at a disadvantage relative to consumers in the Third World. This in turn might spur relocation of some of the OECD's energy intensive industries. Richer developing countries with more flexible economies would benefit from such a relocation." (p. 31).

52 The numer of alcohol-powered cars is put at about 1 million in 1983, more than one-tenth of the total stock of cars in Brazil. The proportion will probably rise considerably in future, particularly as the Government offers large tax incentives both to suppliers of the raw material (mainly sugar cane) and to buyers and users of motor vehicles. In addition, an increasing number of diesel engines are being converted to use alcohol (Financial Times, 1.6.1983).

53 The countries involved are Costa Rica, Guyana, Haiti, Jamaica and Nicaragua. Nevertheles, exports have fallen well short of expectations so far (Financial Times, 1.6.1983).

54 The further development of coal conversion technology does require substantial subsidies (Frankfurter Allgemeine Zeitung, 9.8.1983), but in principle public funds appear to be better employed here than in, say, declining industries.

55 Another example is district heating technology, where Denmark has achieved notable export successes, mainly in the supply of equipment. Combined electricity and district heating plant in which heat can be generated from either coal or oil have attracted particular attention (Nachrichten für Außenhandel, 20.10.1981).

56 The UK Department of Energy also finds that there is enormous potential for energy-saving goods: "Conservation markets in the industrialised world are likely to be for sophisticated energy-saving systems and capital goods (possibly under leasing arrangements) as well as component parts. The potential overseas market is difficult to quantify, but certain examples indicate the scope: the United States Department of Energy estimates that about £ 5 trillion at 1972 prices will have been invested in energy-related capital stock in the US by the year 2000 ... the French government plans investment of over £ 20 billion during the next 10 years;and ... the lesser developed countries will require an increasing volume of energy-related imports involving consultancy and equipment" (British Business, 7.5.1982, p. 15).

57 See in this connection the studies on specialisation in twelve Eu-
    ropean countries, which indicate that a country is wise to base its
    choice of specialisation not primarily on relative resource wealth
    but on the dynamism of demand in individual markets. It is partic-
    ularly advantageous to move upstream or downstream within a verti-
    cally related "family" of industries, such as artificial fibres →
    textiles → clothing. The resources situation is of only secondary
    importance here, determining production techniques but not the
    choice of products (Lafay 1981; CEPII, FAST 1980).

58 On this issue see also the remarks by the Secretary-General of the
    OECD, who writes inter alia that "Import restriction by a country
    with an overvalued currency ... will only make things worse by re-
    ducing the flows of foreign exchange which would otherwise help to
    restore more appropriate exchange rates" (van Lennep 1982, p. 40).

    A modified judgement should possibly be made of the cash deposit
    scheme introduced in Italy in May 1981, for the country's foreign
    trade position in terms of the export/import ratio improved sub-
    stantially in 1981 and the recovery continued even after the me-
    chanism expired in February 1982. Nonetheless, it is difficult to
    say how much of this success was attributable to the cash deposit,
    particularly as the Government simultaneously pursued a restrictive
    policy to dampen domestic demand.

59 According to an American study (Gisselquist 1979) the largest trad-
    ing nations of the world (the USA, Japan and the Federal Republic of
    Germany) have been competing with one another for current account
    surpluses since the late sixties. The main motive on the part of
    Japan and Germany is considered to be their endeavour to increase
    their economic power in the world by investing abroad and enhancing
    their influence on the international capital markets. This rivalry
    continued even after the first oil shock. The author claims that in-
    stead of themselves bearing part of the resultant global deficit the
    "big three" shifted the foreign trade burden onto other countries,
    such as the United Kingdom, Italy, Brazil, Mexico and South Korea.
    Japan and Germany continued to pursue this "strategy" even after
    1976, when the USA had already begun to reduce its surpluses "in
    order to help other nations to reduce their deficits" (p.11). The
    USA tried in vain to persuade other countries to behave similarly
    under the pretext of the "locomotive" and "convoy" theories. Instead,
    Japan and Germany blamed the emerging US deficits mainly on the "non-
    existent" US energy policy (p. 13).

    For a critique of the argument on the distribution of burdens con-
    tained in the study, see Fest (1980), who considers that it provides
    no cure "that attacks the true real economic causes of the energy
    shortage" (p. 13).

60 The countries in question are the following: Sri Lanka, Haiti, Indonesia, Thailand, the Phillipines, Peru, Morocco, Tunisia, Mauritius, Jordan, Malaysia, Macao, Chile, Uruguay, Malta and Cyprus. The "traditional" newly industrialising countries are classified by the OECD as being Brazil, Greece, Hong Kong, Korea, Mexico, Portugal, Singapore, Spain, Taiwan and Yugoslavia. For details, see OECD: Development Co-operation, 1982 Review, pp. 123 ff.

SUMMARY AND CONCLUSIONS

1. The nominal price of petroleum is at present ten times
that prevailing before the first oil price shock in 1973-74.
In real terms, i.e. adjusted for price changes in manufactured export goods, oil prices have quintupled since then. Barring unforeseeable political events, real oil prices seem unlikely to rise before the end of the eighties. But in the
long run, the OPEC countries, which will continue to be by
far the most important suppliers in the world oil market,
may regain the ability to make fairly large increases in selling prices.

However, future increases of real oil prices would hardly
leave an impact as strong and pervasive on the world economy
as the previous price shocks did. This is mainly for two
reasons:

- the oil-importing countries have made great strides in
  their structural adjustment to higher oil prices and will
  continue to do so which reduces the real economic significance of oil;
- lessons can be drawn from the experiences of the past which
  allow a better crisis management in the future.

2. Big real oil price increases find their most visible expression in the countries' balances on current account. The
oil-importing countries as a whole record large deficits,
since oil demand is little price-elastic in the short run,
real expenditures in oil-importing countries exceed real incomes and import demand of oil-exporting countries lags behind the increase in oil revenues. Obviously, traditional
mechanisms of balance-of-payments adjustment have only limited validity between oil-exporting and oil-importing countries.

An oil-related current account surplus does not trigger automatically domestic adjustment mechanisms in the conventional sense in the oil economies, i.e. an expansion of money supply, rising prices and falling interest rates which ultimately restore external equilibrium. Nor is the exchange rate an appropriate adjustment instrument in this context. Hence oil-importing countries must borrow, directly or indirectly, on a large scale from capital-surplus oil producers.

However, real oil price increases have differing effects on the external positions of oil-importing countries. Various newly industrialising countries (NICs) of the Third World have been most severely affected, as they follow oil-intensive industrialization strategies and could participate only to a small degree in the booming oil-country markets. It is in these countries, then, where external borrowing requirements are largest after an increase in oil prices.

3. The investment behaviour of the OPEC countries so far has shown that direct recycling of oil funds to those places where they are needed is of no great overall significance. The major part of recycling is done by the international financial markets, which act as a kind of turntable between debtor and creditor countries in the recycling process.

After the first oil crisis the markets performed this function more smoothly than had been expected. The involvement of the banks softened the impact of the crisis on the real economy and facilitated adjustment, although in many instances it also delayed it.

After the second price shock, however, the risks of recycling for the banking system began to emerge more clearly. Euro-credits were concentrated essentially on a small number of

countries. As a result, lending to certain countries with
a poor credit rating now constitutes a particularly large
proportion of bank portfolios and is a cause of concern.
At the same time, banks were also faced with growing risks
on the creditor side. The shift in the creditor structure
towards OPEC states means that the number of investors has
decreased and a larger proportion of bank deposits is held
by a group of investors whose behaviour may differ from
that of conventional investors and is therefore less predictable. Moreover, it cannot be taken for granted that the
size of the international financial markets will almost automatically expand to match the growing need for finance
and investment opportunities brought about by rising oil
prices. For example, it is possible that an increasing demand
for credit in industrial countries causes a greater volume
of oil funds to flow to national markets so that correspondingly less credit would be granted in international markets.
This would lead to a stricter selection of borrowers here
as well as to increased costs of borrowing.

4. In this situation, the problem for economic policy is
to limit the banks' risks arising from their external commitments without restricting the working of the financial
system to such an extent that the necessary flow of credit
can no longer be maintained.

Various proposals have been made to strengthen the commercial banking system in the recycling process. The insurance
of certain banking operations has long been discussed as
one way of reducing risks. A "safety net" that would be organised and funded by the banks themselves has also been
proposed. However, every institutionalised form of financial assistance for use in crisis encourages the banking
system to attach less importance to the risk aspects of lend-

ing to the extent to which it no longer has to bear these risks. For that reason the institutionalisation of financial assistance should be avoided as a rule.

More promising appears to be a scheme that the IMF and the World Bank have been promoting for some time in conjunction with the Bank for International Settlements. It aims to improve the state of information on debtor countries and thus bring greater clarity to the international financial markets. The initiative by the "Ditchley" group of commercial banks that set up the Institute of International Finance to centralize data on debtor countries is a step in the same direction. These efforts aim only at reducing debtor risks, however. Nor do they ensure that the banks will actually be more risk conscious in their behaviour. Therefore, they cannot be considered adequate in themselves, but should be accompanied by "prudential controls" of the international financial markets.

Of all the measures discussed in this context, the adjustment of capital and liquidity rules to suit the special situation of the banks' external operations appears to be the one most capable of implementation. By contrast, monitoring the risks associated with individual transactions and the establishment of guidelines on the diversification of lending according to countries promises to be far more difficult. Not least, the co-ordination of the activities of national supervisory authorities raises considerable problems, given the different national interests and legal and institutional conditions in the various countries. Nevertheless, co-ordinated action is ultimately inavoidable in this field. At the same time, however, there is the danger that excessive supervisory measures will restrict the banks' lending ability too severely and thus hamper recycling. In its efforts to achieve maximum security, policy should not disregard the need to leave the banks sufficient scope for recycling resources. In setting the scope available to them, the sole concern should be to ensure the smooth financing of current account deficits that are unavoidable in the short term but not to absolve debtor countries from their responsibility for internal and external economic adjustment.

5. As compared to the private banking system, official (national and international) institutions and organisations do not participate directly to a substantial extent in the recycling process. Global approaches which aim to persuade the OPEC countries to use more of their capital surpluses for long-term investment and at the same time seek to reconcile the interests of various country groups (i.e. not only the special investment objectives of the OPEC countries and the borrowing requirements of the deficit countries but also the desire of oil-consuming countries to secure their oil supplies and avoid sharp price increases) appear to have litte prospect of success.

The possibilities of the IMF to finance current-account deficits caused by real oil price increases are also limited. Yet the IMF has special responsibility on two counts. For the poorest developing countries it is essential as a lender, given the stagnation or even decline in official transfers and the fact that access to private-sector funds is largely closed to these countries. For the more advanced LDCs the Fund plays only a secondary role in terms of the volume of lending. Instead it bolsters the recycling process by means of supporting measures - by influencing the economic policy of member states and providing additional funds - and acts as the lender of last resort in times of crisis. Commercial banks and bank consortia are increasingly making the granting of credit conditional on agreement between the debtor country and the IMF on a stabilisation programme. The IMF is thus regarded as a sort of guarantor that deficit countries follow policies which lead to external equilibrium.

381

6. External disturbances created by rising oil prices are
paralleled by serious internal imbalances. First of all,
real oil price increases cause strong inflationary pressures. What gives rise to concern in this context, is not
so much the once-for-all effect on the overall price level,
but a general inflationary adjustment of prices and wages.
In actual fact, this happened in most oil-importing countries (and, for different reasons, in the oil-exporting
countries as well), even though the surge in oil prices triggered inflationary   impulses of widely differing strength
in individual countries.

Real incomes and economic growth are also affected. Real oil
price increases are equivalent to a redistribution of income
in favour of the oil-producing countries. Equally, oil-importing countries suffer a reduction in real income by the fact
that imported oil is substituted by inferior or more expensive goods and certain production plant become economically
obsolete prematurely. At the same time, strong recessionary
tendencies appeared in the aftermath of both oil crises in
most oil-importing countries. They were due to a big deflationary gap as well as to time-lags and deficiencies in supp-
ly-side adjustment to the changed production and demand conditions.

As regards employment real oil price increases may lead to
some substitution of labour for a more expensive energy/
capital package. But positive substitution effects of this
kind have far been outweighed by negative employment effects
resulting from the overall slowdown in economic activity
caused by higher oil prices.

Finally, rising oil prices seem to have a substantial regressive net effect on income distribution. They may change

the structure of employment in favour of unskilled workers, but low-wage earners use a larger proportion of their household budget for direct purchases of energy products (and probably also for purchases of energy-intensive goods and services) than higher income groups do. Anyhow, persons who are not gainfully employed are badly affected.

7. In its effort to restore internal and external balance after an increase in real oil prices economic policy faces the general problem of trade-offs between conflicting aims. In particular, it must deal with a mismatch between micro- and macro-adjustment to rising oil prices.

For example, when policy-makers try to stimulate activities which compensate for oil-related income, growth and employment losses, they may create current-account deficits which in turn form a constraint on expansive policies. However, deficits on the current account of the balance-of-payments are not necessarily an indicator of external disequilibrium. They are less important as long as appropriate borrowing strategies are followed. They create a problem only "where borrowing is for unprofitable investment or excessively for the maintenance of consumption" (Corden, Oppenheimer, 1976, p. 34).

Economic policy would be well advised, too, not to keep energy prices artificially low in order to avoid "energy poverty". Instead, where sharp conflicts between economic efficiency (which is supported by scarcity prices) and equity (which is impaired by the same fact) arise, they might better be resolved by compensatory payments from general tax revenues.

Rising oil prices may also accentuate conflicts between stabilisation policies, on the one hand, and policies to ensure a high level of economic activity over the short term, on the other. A monetary policy that allowed no additional financing margin in the event of a sharp increase in the cost of oil could lead to heavy losses in production and employment without ensuring success in the search for stability. The upper limit of tolerable overall price increases is set by the rise in the general level of costs as a result of higher oil prices. To what degree monetary policy should permit this margin to be exhausted depends on specific internal and external conditions obtaining when oil prices surge (in particular, strength of inflationary expectations, stance of fiscal policy, trade unions' incomes policy, capacity utilisation rate in industry, expectations concerning the exchange rate), as has been shown in the case of Germany. Most important, monetary policy must prevent rising oil prices from arousing inflationary expectations. It must make it credible that the acceptance of a non-recurring price surge does not mean the fundamental abandonment of a policy oriented towards stability, for in fact inflation does not solve the problems, it only makes them worse. Real adjustment to dearer oil can be seriously delayed. Conversely, a clear policy which does not leave economic agents in uncertainty about the monetary stance may considerably improve the opportunities for growth and employment after an increase in oil prices.

In fiscal policy an expansionary stance might be required to prevent a cumulative downturn of economic activity springing from an oil-price induced deflationary gap. However, a compensatory fiscal policy of this kind, even if it succeeds in regaining overall internal balance (which is by no means assured), may turn out as a mixed blessing, as consumption is maintained at too high a level. Anyhow, the underlying structural problem remains unresolved.

9. The prime responsibility of economic policy in times of rising oil prices is to ensure that the structure of production and consumption adjusts as flexibly as possible to changing relative prices on the goods and factor markets. New processes of growth are required that reduce the dependence of economic development on the availability of domestic or foreign energy resources (in particular oil), strengthen the domestic energy base and exploit the opportunities that real oil price increases open up on national and international markets.

Essential aspects of an efficient micro-adjustment to rising oil prices include:

- reliable price signals, consistent with scarcity conditions, in the domestic economy as well as in foreign trade;

- competitive structures on national and international markets;

- transparency, predictability and reliability of economic policy;

- specific incentives, mainly to balance private and social costs and benefits;

- international co-ordination and co-operation.

10. Investment and innovation is the key variable of any structural adjustment to a rise in the cost of oil. Both the opening-up of new sources of oil and the development of alter-

native forms of energy entail increased capital expenditure. Most kinds of energy conservation and oil substitution also require investment and specific knowledge, as does the change-over to the manufacture of energy-saving products.

Activities of this kind are decidedly supported by energy price and price relationships between the various sources of energy which reflect long-term scarcity trends. Energy-related investment and innovation may also be encouraged by offering financial incentives in order to ensure that private efforts do not remain short of the "warranted" level of activities (which is, however, difficult to define).

However, actual investment trends since the first oil shock suggest that the investment-inducing effects of higher energy costs have far been exceeded by their dampening impact. Reduced expectations of sales and profits seem to be have been of decisive importance in this respect.

Economic policy should, therefore, follow a kind of dual strategy:

- it should enforce scarcity prices and provide, where necessary, financial assistance for energy projects which are viable over the long term but not carried through on private initiative alone;
- at the same time, internal and external conditions are required which cause investors to expect the economy to adjust flexibly to higher oil prices.

In this context the distribution of income between the factors capital and labour is often regarded as a crucial factor. It goes without saying that policy-makers must make employers and trade unions aware that the adverse real income effect of a rise in the price of oil cannot be avoided. Yet wage restraint alone will not revitalize investment and innovation in times of rising oil prices. Equally important as the price of labour are other prices such as real interest and exchange rates. Moreover, increased uncertainty caused by real oil price changes is a major obstacle to productive investment, the removal of which requires first of all a stable economic framework. Last not least, investment behaviour is influenced by trade policies, for export-oriented industries need to have confidence in the openness of markets as a basis for investment decisions.

11. Rising oil prices have an influence on exchange rates as well as on the "real" conditions of international trade. A distinction should be made between long-term and temporary effects on exchange rates. Over the long term, exchange rates must adjust to offset different longer-run effects of oil price increases on the external position of oil-importing countries resulting from structural differences (e.g. different importance of energy related trade) or different adjustment capacities (e.g. different ability to bring oil-price led inflationary tendencies under control). Exchange rates are also affected by oil-related capital flows, in particular the investment of oil funds by OPEC surplus countries.

Short-term exchange rate effects derive mainly from the fact that sharp oil price increases contribute to shape the expectations of operators in the foreign exchange markets. If expectations prove correct they induce a more rapid adjustment of exchange rates, but if they are wide off the mark they accentuate the divergence from a rate that accords with underlying conditions in the real economy.

The present worldwide monetary system of managed floating offers, in principle, the possibility of a flexible adjustment
of exchange rates over the long term and at the same time
permits erratic exchange rate fluctuations to be dampened by
means of official exchange market interventions and monetary
measures to soften the accompanying adverse effects on national economies. However, the study shows that real oil price increases may put additional strain on systems of fixed exchange
rates such as the European Monetary System.

12. The relationship between rising oil prices and international trade is complex. Volume effects on trade derive largely from the impact of oil prices on overall growth, but also
from defensive attitudes to international trade to which governments resort in their search for shock-absorbers.

At the same time, the commodity composition of international
trade varies, as demand preferences of oil-exporting countries
differ significantly from those of oil-importing countries.
Moreover, changes in the structure of domestic demand in oil-
importing countries caused by real oil price increases affect
chiefly goods and services which are internationally traded or
at least tradable. This holds true for most products used in
exploiting new sources of energy (energy-producing goods) or
in conserving energy (energy-saving goods) as well as for related services, but also for energy-intensive goods whose
price-competitiveness suffers from rising oil prices.

With regard to the regional structure of international trade,
the most striking feature so far has been the rapidly growing
importance that oil-producing countries have gained as a sales
outlet. This was mainly to the benefit of Western industrial
countries of which Japan and, to a somewhat lesser extent,
Italy performed particularly well. Concerning the methods
applied to gain an edge over foreign competitors, a brief re-

view of some practices (including counter-trade deals and governmental agreements as well as "classical" instruments of export promotion such as export subsidies) has shown that competition on oil country markets is often seriously distorted. However, the main beneficiaries of restrictive business practices are ultimately the oil-producing countries, whose terms-of-trade improve. Trade policies towards these countries require closer consultation and co-ordination. For example, the EEC as a whole would presumably be better off if the Community itself concluded bilateral co-operation agreements with oil-producing countries instead of allowing individual member states to do so.

13. Arrangements of this kind could also be helpful to balance the interests of oil-producing countries in export diversification and their need for technical assistance in export-oriented industrialisation against the adjustment capacity of traditional manufacturing countries.

Up to now, the oil-producing countries have hardly ranked as serious competitors in the world markets in industrial goods. Yet they are using part of their receipts from oil exports to diversify their domestic production base in order to reduce the heavy dependence of their foreign exchange receipts and the entire trend of incomes on exports of a single commodity. As a result of an increase in oil prices, they may be placed in a position in which those industrial activities that require large inputs of capital and hydrocarbons (as sources of energy as well as raw materials) could be developed on internationally competitive terms. This is particularly true of oil-producing countries with small populations, where labour is in short supply and the immigration of workers is restricted for various reasons. Nevertheless, if excessive dependence of industrialisation on non-renewable resources,

foreign management personnel and highly-qualified technical
staff from abroad is to be avoided, these countries must make
an effort to develop a "second row" of industries in which
domestic entrepreneurial initiative can come more strongly
to the fore, simpler technologies can be applied and a broader educational effect achieved. Obviously this is all the more
important for the densely populated oil-producing countries
for which a capital-intensive industrialisation model is clearly out of the question.

Key sectors of export diversification in oil-producing countries, which are examined in greater detail in the present
study, include oil refining, petrochemicals, the production
and initial processing of aluminium and, to a lesser extent
(as it is geared more strongly to domestic markets), the iron
and steel industry.

In itself, the competitive potential of the oil producers must
be regarded as marginal, even in terms of the sector affected.
It may reinforce pressure for internal and external adjustment
that is already strong in oil-importing countries. But it is
shown that there is still considerable scope for a "positive
adjustment" by firms to the changing competitive conditions,
both in the adaptation of existing production methods and
the development of new ones and in the modification of the
production programmes. Oil-importing countries might also
adopt industrial policies, as Japan most ably did, that promote those processes of innovation that are insufficiently
supported by private enterprises and at the same time favour
the reduction in capacity in industries that are not viable
over the long run. By contrast, unilateral import restrictions, in particular countervailing duties, which are demand-
ed in various oil-importing countries are highly questionable.

Not only dispose the oil-producing countries of some retalia-
tory power, but it should also be considered that most of
the subsidies paid in the oil states are granted not specifically for exports but generally. The importance of such
assistance within the framework of economic development
programmes was expressly recognised in the Tokyo Round of
GATT.

14. Finally, real oil price increases change competitive conditions in trade among oil-importing countries. They have differing effects on the level of costs in industries exposed to
international competition. Although in public debate the blame
for this is laid mainly on international differences in energy
prices, different energy prices do not generally seem to have
had a serious influence on the international competitiveness
of energy-intensive industries. Nevertheless, in individual
manufacturing sectors in which energy is the most important
cost factor, distortions of competition arising from energy
price subsidies might justify corrective measures by the
state.

The situation takes on a different complexion if different
energy prices in various countries primarily reflect differences in natural locational conditions (e.g. availability
of hydroelectric power) or different energy policy priorities
and preferences (e.g. regarding the role attached to nuclear
energy). If in these cases relative costs change abruptly,
subsidies might be granted in order to prevent collapse,
but it is essential that necessary changes in the structure
of production should not be impeded and that economically
desirable adjustment strategies by the firms concerned be
encouraged.

Those countries that develop energy-producing or energy-saving goods and services are most likely to increase their trade when oil prices rise. Yet the trade gains of the successful countries are not, as in a zero-sum game, offset by losses sustained by the other oil-importing countries, as the country group as a whole benefits from innovative action of that kind by individual member states. The precondition for an international division of labour in energy-related goods and services is, however, that domestic markets are also open to foreign supplies. In practice this is frequently not the case.

15.   Trade frictions could be reduced by means of international co-operation and co-ordination. For example, countries might jointly implement or finance specific energy projects. Governments could also improve the legal framework for international co-operation between firms. The spill-over effects of certain energy projects, the scale of individual schemes and the advantages of combining and concentrating scarce research and development resources are sound arguments for this.

Moreover, the energy sector is an important area for development co-operation with the countries of the Third World. Its development requires a greatly increased inflow of foreign exchange, since eligible projects are highly dependent on imported inputs. A substantial financial contribution will have to come from official development assistance, but the major part of energy investments must be financed on commercial terms. An important prerequisite for this is that the developing countries enjoy unhindered access to the markets of industrial countries for their manufactured goods. This will enable them both to earn part of the necessary foreign exchange directly and to improve their standing in the international credit markets.

However, since the first oil shock, oil-importing industrial countries have increasingly taken recourse to protectionist devices against "cheap imports" from non-oil developing countries. Concrete steps towards liberalisation are
needed if this trend is to be reversed. Liberalisation could
be carried out in stages, with existing import restrictions
being reduced progressively on a binding and irrevocable basis at fixed intervals. Such a procedure would give companies
and economic policy-makers in both groups of countries a more
certain basis for their planning. At the same time, the industrial countries can expect that with rising competitiveness
the developing countries will open their own markets wider
and increasingly subject themselves to GATT discipline. Such
activities in the field of trade policy are essential to secure the consistency between financing and adjustment in times
of rising oil prices.

APPENDIX 1: LIST OF OIL-IMPORTING DEVELOPING COUNTRIES

Africa

Botswana
Cameroon
Ethiopia
Gambia, The
Ghana
Ivory Coast
Kenya
Liberia
Malawi
Mauritania
Mauritius
Morocco
Niger
Ruanda
Senegal
Seychelles
Sierra Leone
Somalia
Sudan
Swaziland
Tanzania
Togo
Upper Volta
Zaire
Zambia

Asia, Oceania

Bangladesh
Burma
China
Fiji
India
Israel
Jordan
Korea
Malaysia
Nepal
Pakistan
Papua, New Guinea
Philippines
Singapore
Sri Lanka
Thailand

Europe

Cyprus
Greece
Jugoslavia
Malta
Portugal
Spain
Turkey

Latin America

Argentina
Bahamas
Barbados
Bolivia
Brazil
Chile
Colombia
Costa Rica
Dominican Republic
El Salvador
Guatemala
Guyana
Haiti
Honduras
Jamaica
Nicaragua
Panama
Paraguay
Suriname
Uruguay

APPENDIX 2: LIST OF TRADED GOODS WITH A HIGH DIRECT ENERGY CONTENT

Heading	SITC Rev.	SITC Rev. 2	
Synthetic rubber	231.2	233	
Wood, railway sleepers	243	248	
Pulp and waste paper	251	251	
Synthetic fibres	266	266	
Other man-made fibres	266	267	
Organic chemicals	512	51	
Inorganic chemicals	513, 514	52	(excluding radio-active materials)
Synth. organic dyestuffs	531	531	
Fertilizers, manufactured	56	56	
Plastic materials	58	58	
Veneers, plywood and other wood, worked	631	634	
Paper and paperboard	641	641	
Cement	661.2	661.2	
Glass	664	664	
Pig iron	671	671	
Ingots of iron and steel	672	672	
Iron and steel bars	673	673	
Plates and sheets of iron and steel	674	674	
Copper	682	682	
Nickel	683	683	
Aluminium	684	684	
Lead	685	685	
Zinc	686	686	
Tin	687	687	

APPENDIX 3:   Tables A-1 to A-33

Table A-1: INDEX OF PRICES OF CRUDE OIL, OTHER RAW MATERIALS AND EXPORTED MANUFACTURES
1972 - 1982 (1975 = 100)

| | Crude oil | Other raw materials | | | Exported manufactures | | |
	World	World	ICs	DCs	World	ICs	DCs
1972	22	55	55	56	n.a.	62	n.a.
1973	30	85	85	85	n.a.	73	n.a.
1974	100	107	103	116	n.a.	89	n.a.
1975	100	100	100	100	100	100	100
1976	106	106	102	115	n.a.	100	n.a.
1977	117	118	105	144	110	109	118
1978	117	121	115	133	125	125	124
1979	170	138	132	149	142	143	140
1980	295	157	150	172	157	158	149
1981	325	146	143	151	151	150	157
1982	311	132	133	132	n.a.	146	n.a.

ICs = Industrial countries.

DCs = Developing countries.

Source: UN: Monthly Bulletin of Statistics; IMF: International Financial Statistics, Supplement on Price Statistics, Supplement Series No. 2, Washington 1981; IMF: International Financial Statistics, July 1983; calculations by the author.

Table A-2: REAL OIL PRICES, 1975 - 1982[a]

Deflator	1975	1976	1977	1978	1979	1980	1981	1982
RAW MATERIAL PRICES[b]								
World[c]	11.02	11.22	10.97	10.73	13.77	20.07	23.98	25.31
Industrial countries	11.02	11.66	12.33	11.29	14.39	21.01	24.48	25.12
Developing countries	11.02	10.34	8.99	9.76	12.75	18.32	23.19	25.31
PRICES OF MANUFACTURES								
World[c]	11.02	11.70	11.82	10.35	13.15	19.85	23.22	22.88
Industrial countries	11.02	11.70	11.82	10.35	13.30	19.85	23.46	22.88
Developing countries	11.02	11.18	11.49	10.35	13.01	19.85	22.06	23.65
Memorandum								
Nominal price of oil	11.02	11.89	12.95	12.98	19.00	31.51	35.01	33.41

a US dollars per barrel, with 1975 as base year.
b Excluding crude oil.
c Excluding state-trading countries.

Source: UN: Monthly Bulletin of Statistics; OECD: Economic Outlook; calculations by the authors.

Table A-3: PRICE AND INCOME ELASTICITY OF THE DEMAND FOR ENERGY IN THE FEDERAL REPUBLIC OF GERMANY, 1960 – 1972[a]

	Price elasticity		Income elasticity		Coefficient of determination (R^2)
	Coefficient	t value	Coefficient	t value	
Petroleum products	-0.69	-2.8	2.37	15.6	0.98
Heavy heating oil	-0.49	-1.5	1.54	5.5	0.92
Light heating oil	0.40	6.4	4.12	4.9	0.94
Diesel oil	-0.30	-1.5	1.19	7.4	0.97
Petrol	-0.30	-1.1	1.94	7.1	0.98
Coal	-1.06	-1.8	-1.64	-9.3	0.93
Hard coal[c]	-0.38	-0.4	-1.90	-7.2	0.91
Coke oven coke	-0.66	-2.4	-0.77	-4.7	0.85
Brown coal	-0.89	-1.0	-2.10	-0.1	0.91
Coal briquettes[c]	2.63	1.6	-2.19	-9.9	0.93
Gas	1.21	1.3	2.10	3.7	0.84
Natural gas	0.08	0.5	1.77	20.1	0.10
Town gas	-3.23	-0.6	3.36	0.6	0.88
Electricity[b]	4.10	4.2	3.28	2.6	0.96
Total energy[c]	0.07	0.4	0.92	9.9	0.97

a With regard to the method of calculation, see Footnote a to Table 4.1.

b 1968-1973.

c 1962-1972.

Source: See Table 4.1.

Table A-4:   PRICE AND INCOME ELASTICITY OF THE DEMAND FOR ENERGY
             IN THE FEDERAL REPUBLIC OF GERMANY, 1960 - 1981[a]

	Price elasticity		Income elasticity		Coefficient of determination (R^2)
	Coefficient	t value	Coefficient	t value	
Petroleum products	-0.80	-9.9	2.18	26.9	0.98
Heavy heating oil	-0.75	-8.2	1.15	9.7	0.85
Light heating oil	-0.67	-6.7	2.70	1.7	0.94
Diesel oil	-0.13	-1.9	1.25	3.2	0.98
Petrol	-0.42	-5.4	1.83	3.9	0.99
Coal					
Hard coal[c]	-0.25	-1.0	-1.70	- 8.5	0.94
Coke oven coke	-0.07	-0.3	-1.90	- 8.2	0.94
Brown coal	-0.40	-2.3	-0.77	- 4.7	0.90
Brown coal	-0.36	-0.8	-2.16	- 8.1	0.91
Coal briquettes	-0.68	-1.5	-2.61	-10.0	0.94
Gas	0.25	1.7	1.90	17.3	0.94
Natural gas	-0.09	-0.9	1.70	44.7	0.10
Town gas[b]	-0.45	-1.6	5.26	8.7	0.91
Electricity[b]	-0.09	-0.4	-2.17	- 8.2	0.87
Total energy[c]	-0.23	-4.8	0.81	26.1	0.98

a For the method of calculation, see Footnote a to Table 4.1.

b 1968-1981.

c 1962-1981.

Source: See Table 4.1.

Table A-5:   RELATIONSHIP BETWEEN THE PRICES OF CRUDE OIL
              AND OIL PRODUCTS IN THE SEVEN LARGEST OECD
              COUNTRIES, BY SECTOR, 1974 - 1979[a]

Countries	1974	1975	1976	1977	1978	1979
Households and small consumers						
USA	0.69	0.72	0.87	0.94	0.98	1.11
Canada	0.18	0.25	0.36	0.41	0.46	0.34
Japan	0.19	0.24	0.29	0.32	0.39	0.37
Fed. Rep. of Germany	0.18	0.15	0.20	0.19	0.22	n.a.
France	0.37	0.40	0.43	0.47	0.58	0.63
United Kingdom	0.31	0.40	0.41	0.48	0.57	0.68
Italy	0.77	0.89	0.78	1.00	1.17	1.06
Total	0.38	0.44	0.48	0.54	0.62	0.63
Industry						
USA	1.24	1.08	0.97	1.12	0.92	0.99
Canada	0.54	0.78	0.85	0.94	1.09	0.81
Japan	0.41	0.53	0.57	0.61	0.71	0.53
Fed. Rep. of Germany	0.46	0.45	0.47	0.48	0.50	0.53
France	0.51	0.59	0.54	0.59	0.63	0.72
United Kingdom	0.62	0.70	0.60	0.71	0.76	0.84
Italy	0.37	0.79	0.87	0.86	0.86	0.84
Total	0.53	0.70	0.69	0.76	0.78	0.75
Transport						
USA	0.32	0.30	0.32	0.33	0.35	0.42
Canada	0.08	0.16	0.24	0.25	0.25	0.19
Japan	0.20	0.23	0.25	0.28	0.28	0.25
Fed. Rep. of. Germany	0.14	0.13	0.16	0.13	0.16	0.16
France	0.17	0.18	0.18	0.24	0.31	0.31
United Kingdom	0.25	0.45	0.35	0.32	0.32	0.43
Italy	0.44	0.52	0.60	0.64	0.67	0.54
Total	0.23	0.20	0.30	0.31	0.33	0.33

a   Increase in the price of oil products if crude oil prices rise by 1 %.

Source: OECD.

Table A-6:   RELATIONSHIP BETWEEN THE PRICES ON OIL
             PRODUCTS AND OTHER SOURCES OR ENERGY IN INDUS-
             TRY IN THE SEVEN LARGEST OECD COUNTRIES,
             1974 - 1979[a]

Countries	1974	1975	1976	1977	1978	1979
Coal						
USA	0.37	0.47	0.44	0.38	0.56	0.36
Canada	0.21	0.24	0.34	0.55	0.58	0.56
Japan	0.55	0.73	0.86	0.79	0.74	0.66
Fed. Rep. of Germany	0.37	0.81	0.80	0.79	1.09	0.73
France	0.41	0.51	0.57	0.53	0.61	0.49
United Kingdom	0.07	0.37	0.48	0.49	0.58	0.54
Italy	1.75	1.32	0.84	0.90	0.95	0.74
Total	0.53	0.64	0.62	0.63	0.73	0.58
Gas						
USA	0.19	0.44	0.80	1.00	1.50	1.24
Canada	0.25	0.48	0.90	0.86	0.84	0.79
Japan	0.16	0.34	0.31	0.44	0.51	0.43
Fed. Rep. of Germany	0.15	0.89	0.99	1.07	1.35	0.83
France	0.43	0.46	0.50	0.49	0.64	0.50
United Kingdom	0.21	0.40	0.63	0.74	1.02	0.91
Italy	0.00	1.02	0.83	1.25	1.70	1.30
Total	0.20	0.57	0.71	0.84	1.08	0.86
Electricity						
USA	0.25	0.41	0.49	0.49	0.72	0.48
Canada	0.01	0.13	0.22	0.27	0.28	0.30
Japan	0.55	0.58	0.61	0.77	0.86	0.72
Fed. Rep. of Germany	0.08	0.31	0.32	0.32	0.43	0.30
France	0.15	0.25	0.32	0.32	0.40	0.34
United Kingdom	0.31	0.48	0.53	0.49	0.60	0.52
Italy	0.00	0.43	0.41	0.57	0.65	0.55
Total	0.19	0.37	0.41	0.46	0.56	0.46

a Increase in non-oil energy prices if the prices of oil products increase by 1 %.

Source: OECD.

Table A-7:   RELATIONSHIP BETWEEN THE PRICES OF OIL
             PRODUCTS AND OTHER ENERGY SOURCES IN THE HOUSE-
             HOLDS' AND SMALL CONSUMERS' SECTOR IN THE SEVEN
             LARGEST OECD COUNTRIES, 1974 - 1979[a]

Countries	1974	1975	1976	1977	1978	1979
Coal						
France	0.59	1.38	1.12	1.21	1.55	1.08
United Kingdom	0.28	0.42	0.44	0.44	0.53	0.63
Japan	0.31	0.56	0.58	0.57	0.66	0.57
Fed. Rep. of Germany	0.92	0.98	0.94	1.03	1.22	0.82
Total	0.53	0.84	0.77	0.81	0.99	0.92
Gas						
USA	0.20	0.40	0.50	0.63	0.78	0.59
Canada	0.27	0.66	1.03	1.07	1.06	1.04
Japan	0.42	0.76	0.67	0.87	0.98	0.63
Fed. Rep. of Germany	0.31	0.99	0.95	1.04	1.26	0.21
France	0.25	0.42	0.40	0.39	0.41	0.34
United Kingdom	0.09	0.32	0.35	0.35	0.33	0.31
Italy	0.08	0.19	0.26	0.29	0.36	0.34
Total	0.23	0.53	0.59	0.66	0.74	0.49
Electricity						
USA	0.28	0.36	0.34	0.34	0.38	0.25
Canada	0.13	0.34	0.49	0.59	0.56	0.63
Japan	0.30	0.27	0.31	0.44	0.46	0.30
Fed. Rep. of Germany	0.30	1.13	0.90	0.93	1.16	0.41
France	0.20	0.27	0.36	0.34	0.36	0.33
United Kingdom	0.32	0.76	0.84	0.80	0.89	0.69
Italy	0.14	0.08	0.04	0.11	0.14	0.14
Total	0.24	0.46	0.47	0.51	0.56	0.39

a   Increase in non-oil energy prices if the prices of oil products rise
    by 1 %.

Source: OECD.

Table A-8: IMPORT PRICES FOR CRUDE OIL IN INDUSTRIAL COUNTRIES, 1973 – 1981[a] (1972 = 100)

Countries	1973	1974	1975	1976	1977	1978	1979	1980	1981
Belgium	126.3	375.1	416.3	442.1	478.5	492.8	653.1	1055.0	1216.7
Federal Republic of Germany	138.8	378.1	403.6	433.5	470.1	471.9	681.3	1119.6	1227.7
Denmark	128.9	364.7	411.5	399.1	425.2	464.2	663.3	1091.7	1233.0
Finland	125.7	399.1	398.6	404.1	443.1	458.7	689.0	1107.8	1225.2
France	117.7	351.8	412.7	427.7	456.8	470.9	610.4	1080.4	1223.6
United Kingdom	127.6	359.3	391.4	419.4	460.2	464.7	609.5	1006.8	1136.2
Ireland	101.4	342.7	387.3	677.3	422.3	476.8	594.1	982.7	1006.4
Italy	139.4	305.6	322.3	335.3	364.3	371.7	500.7	846.8	978.4
Japan	111.4	430.8	474.1	502.7	538.9	551.4	755.7	1320.5	1490.8
Netherlands	123.1	307.0	421.2	460.1	486.1	492.3	696.6	1162.0	1285.6
Austria	133.5	408.0	396.4	419.2	451.3	457.1	672.8	1097.8	1227.2
Sweden	120.4	350.2	397.8	395.1	425.3	455.1	647.1	1057.3	1153.3
Switzerland	143.5	382.4	398.7	415.1	443.1	467.8	684.9	1088.7	1239.7
USA	124.9	425.9	441.4	476.7	510.9	565.8	784.4	1289.6	1451.8

a Import unit values on a dollar basis.

Source: OECD: Statistics of Foreign Trade; calculations by the authors.

Tabelle A-9: CHANGES IN THE SECTORAL STRUCTURE OF MANUFACTURING INDUSTRY IN WESTERN INDUSTRIAL COUNTRIES, 1960 - 1973 AND 1973 - 1982

	ISIC	Annual rate of growth				Change in annual rate of growth			
		absolute		% of manuf. ind.		absolute		% of manuf. ind.	
		60-73	73-82	60-73	73-82	(a)	(b)	(a)	(b)
Food, beverages & tobacco	31	4.1	2.1	69.5	262.5	-2.0	0.51	39.2	364.3
Textiles	321	4.2	-1.1	71.2	-137.5	-5.3	-0.26	103.9	-185.7
Clothing & footwear	322/3/4	2.5	-0.8	42.4	-100.0	-3.3	-0.32	64.7	-228.6
Wood	33	5.2	-1.3	88.1	-162.5	-6.5	-0.25	127.5	-178.6
Paper	34	4.7	1.4	79.7	175.0	-3.3	0.30	64.7	214.3
Chemicals	35	9.0	1.6	152.5	200.0	-7.4	0.18	145.1	128.6
Non-metallic mineral products	36	5.3	-0.2	89.8	-25.0	-5.5	-0.04	107.8	-28.6
Basic metal industries	37	5.3	-2.3	89.8	-287.5	-7.6	-0.43	149.0	-307.1
Fabricated metal products	38	6.5	1.4	110.2	175.9	-5.1	0.22	100.0	157.1
Manufacturing industry	3	5.9	0.8	100.0	100.0	-5.1	0.14	100.0	100.0

(a) 1973-82 growth rate minus 1960-73 growth rate.

(b) $\frac{1973\text{-}82 \text{ growth rate}}{1960\text{-}73 \text{ growth rate}}$

Source: UN Monthly Bulletin of Statistics; calculations by the authors.

Table A-10: CHANGES IN THE SECTORAL STRUCTURE OF MANUFACTURING INDUSTRY
IN DEVELOPING COUNTRIES, 1960 - 1973 AND 1973 - 1982

| | | Annual rate of growth | | | | Change in annual rate of growth | | | |
| | | absolute | | % of manuf. ind. | | absolute | | % of manuf. ind. | |
	ISIC	60-73	73-82	60-73	73-82	(a)	(b)	(a)	(b)
Food, beverages & tobacco	31	5.3	5.7	80.3	118.8	0.4	1.08	-22.2	147.9
Textiles	321	4.1	1.9	62.1	39.6	-2.2	0.46	122.2	63.0
Clothing & footwear	322/3/4	5.6	3.4	84.8	70.8	-2.2	0.61	122.2	83.6
Wood	33	6.4	4.0	96.9	83.3	-2.4	0.63	133.3	86.3
Paper	34	8.8	3.9	133.3	81.3	-4.9	0.44	272.2	60.3
Chemicals	35	7.2	4.7	109.1	97.9	-2.5	0.65	138.9	89.0
Non-metallic mineral products	36	7.7	5.6	116.7	116.7	-2.1	0.73	116.7	100.0
Basic metal industries	37	8.0	6.4	121.2	133.3	-1.6	0.80	88.9	109.6
Fabricated metal products	38	11.0	5.7	166.7	118.8	-5.3	0.52	294.4	71.2
Manufacturing industry	3	6.6	4.8	100.0	100.0	-1.8	0.73	100.0	100.0

(a) 1973-82 growth rate minus 1960-73 growth rate.

(b) $\dfrac{1973\text{-}82 \text{ growth rate}}{1960\text{-}73 \text{ growth rate}} \times 100$

Source: UN: Monthly Bulletin of Statistics; calculations by the author.

407

Table A-11: CHANGES IN THE SECTORAL STRUCTURE OF MANUFACTURING INDUSTRY
IN STATE-TRADING COUNTRIES, 1960-1973 AND 1973-1982

| | ISIC | Annual rate of growth | | | | Change in annual rate of growth | | | |
| | | absolute | | % of manuf. ind. | | absolute | | % of manuf. ind. | |
		60-73	73-82	60-73	73-82	(a)	(b)	(a)	(b)
Food, beverages & tobacco	31	5.3	3.5	57.6	61.4	-1.8	66.0	51.4	106.5
Textiles	321	5.3	3.1	57.6	54.4	-2.2	58.5	62.9	94.4
Clothing & footwear	322/3/4	6.1	4.2	66.3	73.7	-1.9	68.9	54.3	111.1
Wood	33	6.4	4.2	69.6	73.7	-2.2	65.6	62.9	105.8
Paper	34	7.5	3.5	81.5	61.4	-4.0	46.7	114.3	75.3
Chemicals	35	11.0	4.9	119.6	86.0	-6.1	44.5	174.3	71.8
Non-metallic mineral prod.	36	8.1	4.3	88.0	75.4	-3.8	53.1	108.6	85.6
Basic metal industries	37	7.1	3.5	77.2	61.4	-3.6	49.3	102.9	79.5
Fabricated metal products	38	11.4	8.0	123.9	140.4	-3.4	70.2	97.1	113.2
Manufacturing industry	3	9.2	5.7	100.0	100.0	-3.5	62.0	100.0	100.0

(a) 1973-82 growth rate minus 1960-73 growth rate.

(b) $\dfrac{1973\text{-}82 \text{ growth rate}}{1960\text{-}73 \text{ growth rate}}$ x 100.

Source: UN: Monthly bulletin of Statistics; calculations by the authors.

Table A-12:   PERFORMANCE OF ENERGY-INTENSIVE INDUSTRIES IN DEVELOPING COUNTRIES, 1969 - 1979

		1969	1970	1971	1972	1973	1974	1975	1976	1977	1978	1979
Chile	VA	45.9	47.2	45.4	37.0	34.4	52.8	51.1	44.1	39.4	37.5	n.a.
	CF	56.1	47.9	61.9	71.1	69.6	50.0	80.4	57.7	44.9	37.6	n.a.
India	VA	31.9	35.0	n.a.	n.a.	34.8	36.7	38.0	37.9	35.8	36.0	n.a.
	CF	n.a.	n.a.	n.a.	n.a.	n.a.	n.a.	n.a.	n.a.	53.8	46.0	n.a.
Indonesia	VA	n.a.	9.0^f	9.6^f	14.1	10.9	n.a.	19.2	20.3	24.8	24.8	22.7
	CF	n.a.	5.5^f	14.5	13.3	11.1	n.a.	21.5	20.0	15.8	19.9	22.8
Yugoslavia	VA	29.9^e	24.5^e	24.3^e	22.4^e	26.6^e	29.4^e	26.5^e	21.8	22.0	21.5	23.8
	CF	n.a.	47.5	46.8	42.9^e	38.5^e	41.1^e	43.8^e	42.5	43.7	41.0	37.4
Colombia	VA	26.7	25.9	25.7	27.4	28.1	27.8	29.5	31.1	30.3	29.6	29.2
	CF	28.2	48.0	n.a.	33.0	51.6	31.4	45.0	45.3	48.5	35.0	33.9
Korea	VA	32.5	31.5	32.6	28.7	31.8	33.5	30.6	28.7	27.5	27.2	29.3
	CF	47.9	31.6	41.1	58.8	35.9	28.7	29.6	33.6	35.6	32.6	40.2
Singapore	VA	29.3	28.9	31.4	25.4	26.1	36.1	29.0	28.4	28.2	26.4	24.5
	CF	28.0	48.8	45.4	47.7	50.6	21.6	29.7	25.6	29.3	26.1	33.3
Tunisia	VA	35.4	37.9	34.0	39.3^d	38.5^c	45.0^b	37.7^a	37.0	37.2	39.0	43.2
	CF	50.5	57.2	60.7	40.9	52.5	59.7	44.4	63.5	66.8	47.0	67.3
Turkey	VA	38.7	32.0	n.a.	37.3	36.3	44.5	41.3	38.7	38.7	36.5	38.9
	CF	38.5	25.6	n.a.	n.a.	49.8	36.8	52.2	45.9	52.8	32.2	45.3
Venezuela	VA	n.a.	n.a.	n.a.	n.a.	n.a.	37.8	45.6	48.6	48.7	46.1	n.a.
	CF	n.a.	n.a.	n.a.	n.a.	n.a.	59.0	66.9	66.9	74.6	77.7	n.a.

a   Excluding ISIC position 372.
b   Excluding ISIC positions 353 and 352.
c   Excluding ISIC positions 341 and 352
d   Excluding ISIC position 352.
e   Excluding ISIC position 354.
f   Excluding ISIC positions 353 and 354.

VA = Value added; CF = Gross fixed capital formation; Energy-intensive industries = ISIC positions 341, 351/2, 353/4, 361, 362, 369, 371 and 372.

Source: UN: Yearbook of Industrial Statistics; calculations by the authors.

Table A-13: GROWTH OF ENERGY-INTENSIVE INDUSTRIES IN WESTERN INDUSTRIAL COUNTRIES, 1965 - 1973 AND 1973 - 1980[a]

	ISIC	USA		Canada		Japan		Fed. Rep. of Germany		France		United Kingdom		Italy	
		65-73	73-80	65-73	73-80	65-73	73-80	65-73	73-80	65-73	73-80	65-73	73-80	65-73	73-80
Paper and paper products	341	1.16	0.82	0.76	1.33	0.78	0.48	0.89	1.80	0.69	0.64	0.82	0.63	1.33	0.42
Industrial chemicals	351	1.95	2.15	1.26	3.07	1.11	0.35	1.74[d]	1.30[g]	1.37[f]	1.86[f]	2.61	1.55	1.35[d]	0.16[d]
Other chemical products	352	1.70	2.88	1.19	2.20	1.06	2.45	-	-	-	-	2.39	-	-	-
Oil refineries	353	0.91	0.41	1.19[b]	0.93[b]	1.22	-0.28	1.13	-0.20	1.49[b]	-1.71[b]	2.32	0.61	1.27[b]	-1.19[b]
Petrochemicals	354	1.16	0.41	-	-	1.19	0.00	-0.89	-	-	-	0.61	0.36	-	-
Ceramics	361	-	-	-	-	0.82[c]	0.24[c]	0.28	-0.80	-	-	0.71	-	-	1.00[c]
Glass	362	0.88	2.12	1.40	0.20	-	-	1.13	2.40	0.91	3.78	2.54	1.34	1.09	-
Other non-metallic products	369	0.67[e]	0.47[e]	0.70	0.47[e]	-	-	0.66	-0.10	0.57[e]	-0.07[e]	1.07	0.38	0.98[e]	-
Iron and steel	371	0.40	-2.35	0.77	1.40	1.13	0.24	0.72	-1.30	0.49	-0.29	-0.21	0.21	1.11	0.90
Non-ferrous metals	372	0.95	-1.00	0.64	0.87	1.10	0.55	0.85	2.00	0.66	0.71	0.14	0.69	0.79	0.77

a Ratio of the annual increase in the sector's output to the corresponding rate for manufacturing industry as a whole.
b Including ISIC position 354.
c Including ISIC positions 362 and 369.
d Including ISIC position 352.
e Including ISIC position 361.
f Including ISIC position 352, 355 and 356.
g Including ISIC positions 352 and 354.

Source: UN: Yearbook of Industrial Statistics; calculations by the authors.

Table A-14: GROWTH OF ENERGY-INTENSIVE INDUSTRIES IN DEVELOPING COUNTRIES, 1965 – 1973 AND 1973-1980[a]

		Chile		India		Yugoslavia		Korea		Singapore		Tunisia		Venezuela	
	ISIC	65-73	73-80	65-73	73-80	65-73	73-80	65-73	73-80	65-73	73-80	65-73	73-80	65-73	73-80
Paper and paper products	341	0.85	-	2.21	0.65	1.19	0.92	0.74	0.82	1.51	0.53	0.98	0.38	1.21	0.92
Industrial chemicals	351	-0.30	0.05	3.79	1.78	1.66	1.15	1.13	0.92	0.85	1.27	1.05[d]	1.12[d]	1.36	0.95
Other chemical products	352	3.11	-	1.66	1.00	1.96	1.39	1.15	0.98	-	1.48	-	-	1.25	1.32
Oil refineries	353	3.30[b]	-	3.35[b]	0.78[b]	1.97	1.24	1.00	0.41	1.22[b]	0.06[b]	0.41[b]	1.05	0.83	0.92[b]
Petrochemicals	354	-	-	-	-	0.35	1.51	0.70	0.74	-	-	-	-	0.96	-
Ceramics	361	1.19	-	0.35	-0.70	0.91	1.26	-0.19	1.03	0.17[f]	0.46[c]	0.84[f]	-	-	-
Glass	362	1.96	0.05	0.38	1.70	1.44	1.66	0.69	0.50	-	-	-	0.57	-	-
Other non-metallic products	369	1.56	0.50	1.76	1.25	1.29	1.24	0.67	0.54	-	0.40	-	1.78	0.96	1.33
Iron and steel	371	0.63	-	0.31	1.13	1.07	0.89	1.19	1.62	0.49[e]	1.16	-	0.87[e]	1.09	1.13
Non-ferrous metals	372	-0.74	-	3.07	0.33	1.04	0.77	0.34	1.51	-	0.33	-	-	-	-

a   Ratio of the annual increase in the sector's output to the corresponding rate for manufacturing industry as a whole.
b   Including ISIC position 354.
c   Including ISIC position 362
d   Including ISIC position 352.
e   Including ISIC position 372.
f   Including ISIC positions 362 and 369.

Source: UN: Yearbook of Industrial Statistics; calculations by the authors.

411

Table A-15: SPECIFIC ENERGY CONSUMPTION[a] IN WESTERN INDUSTRIAL COUNTRIES, 1972-1981

	1972	1973	1974	1975	1976	1977	1978	1979	1980	1981
USA	1,126	1,097	1,110	1,087	1,097	1,070	1,059	1,033	996	953
Canada	1,225	1,213	1,202	1,198	1,176	1,196	1,173	1,141	1,189	1,130
Japan	690	691	701	658	664	638	624	618	573	551
Federal Republic of Germany	625	640	622	593	616	591	589	591	554	530
France	539	556	527	496	499	489	503	503	497	493
United Kingdom	1,031	991	964	928	866	875	844	865	811	792
Italy	713	695	671	664	671	669	647	646	614	601
OECD	874	866	858	835	841	827	820	810	777	750
EC	698	699	671	644	644	633	628	634	601	582

a Primary energy consumption in tonnes oil equivalent per million $ of GDP (at 1975 prices and exchange rates).

Source: OECD: Energy Balances; OECD: National Accounts; calculations by the authors.

Table A-16: INDICES OF ENERGY CONSUMPTION AND PRODUCTION IN THE IRON AND STEEL INDUSTRY IN WESTERN INDUSTRIAL COUNTRIES, 1971 - 1981 (1975 = 100)

		1971	1972	1973	1974	1975	1976	1977	1978	1979	1980	1981[a]
USA	EC	108	115	124	120	100	100	95	99	102	94	97
	P	100	112	128	125	100	109	108	118	118	96	104
Canada	EC	81	85	93	99	100	99	94	107	116	109	102
	P	85	88	102	112	100	99	101	113	119	118	118
Japan	EC	94	97	111	109	100	100	93	86	92	91	82
	P	91	99	119	117	100	110	108	110	123	125	117
Federal Rep. of Germany	EC	100	104	117	125	100	94	86	78	85	81	75
	P	104	109	122	125	100	107	101	106	115	111	107
France	EC	106	110	116	122	100	102	99	100	91	87	73
	P	104	108	114	122	100	108	103	100	111	111	103
United Kingdom	EC	133	127	130	107	100	101	93	88	96	55	64
	P	118	117	128	115	100	104	103	101	103	67	74
Italy	EC	95	91	98	111	100	104	99	107	107	106	100
	P	86	91	102	113	100	111	111	113	116	124	121

a Production indices are estimated.

EC = Energy consumption.
P = Production.

Source: OECD: Energy Balances; OECD: Indicators of Industrial Activity; UN: Yearbook of Industrial Statistics; calculations by the authors.

413

Table A-17: INDICES OF ENERGY CONSUMPTION AND PRODUCTION IN THE CHEMICAL INDUSTRY IN WESTERN INDUSTRIAL COUNTRIES, 1971-1981[a] (1975 = 100)

		1971	1972	1973	1974	1975	1976	1977	1978	1979	1980	1981[b]
USA	EC	91	95	98	102	100	143	152	150	152	347	332
	P	86	98	106	110	100	117	127	135	146	141	146
Canada	EC	113	119	123	120	100	124	132	118	69	85	94
	P	85	91	101	106	100	106	113	123	128	133	140
Japan	EC	181	191	78	75	100	102	103	100	100	89	75
	P	93	100	113	110	100	112	117	132	144	142	143
Federeal Republic of Germany[c]	EC	100	109	125	118	100	115	111	109	126	124	121
	P	94	100	112	115	100	116	116	122	128	123	124
France	EC[d]	84	87	100	103	100	107	115	115	138	156	130
	P	92	99	113	117	100	118	122	127	137	135	134
United Kingdom	EC	85	80	96	102	100	101	103	103	108	126	122
	P	91	95	108	110	100	112	114	116	118	107	105
Italy	EC	114	119	120	116	100	104	110	108	113	101	88
	P	98	102	110	113	100	108	109	113	118	114	111

a Energy consumption including both energy and non-energy uses.
b Production indices are estimated.
c Including products of petroleum and coal (ISIC position 354).
d Including ISIC position 355 (rubber products) and 356 (plastic products).
EC = Energy consumption.
P = Production.

Source: OECD: Energy Balances; OECD: Indicators of Industrial Activity; UN: Yearbook of Industrial Statistics; calculations by the authors.

414

Table A-18: INDICES OF ENERGY CONSUMPTION AND PRODUCTION IN THE NON-FERROUS METALS INDUSTRY IN WESTERN INDUSTRIAL COUNTRIES, 1971 - 1981 (1975 = 100)

		1971	1972	1973	1974	1975	1976	1977	1978	1979	1980	1981[a]
USA	EC	92	97	102	116	100	114	137	140	148	209	211
	P	110	124	138	132	100	126	127	135	139	122	124
Canada	EC	97	97	104	110	100	87	106	110	92	95	102
	P	101	100	104	111	100	96	111	110	102	114	115
Japan	EC	84	96	102	100	100	165	174	184	194	190	139
	P	96	108	129	113	100	119	125	135	143	144	140
Federal Republic of Germany	EC	75	81	92	105	100	105	108	91	100	101	94
	P	102	104	117	115	100	120	121	126	134	134	129
France	EC	101	103	111	115	100	106	107	77	103	64	75
	P[b]	99	106	116	115	100	115	120	120	127	124	119
United Kingdom	EC	92	96	106	105	100	100	102	99	100	71	64
	P	103	105	117	113	100	106	108	107	105	97	86
Italy	EC	75	67	74	94	100	103	103	75	75	75	73
	P	93	100	111	122	100	118	122	122	121	131	124

a Production indices are estimated.

b Including non-ferrous metal mining.

EC = Energy consumption

P = Production.

Source: OECD: Energy Balances; OECD: Indicators of industrial activity; UN: Yearbook Industrial Statistics; calculations by the authors.

Table A-19: INDICES OF ENERGY CONSUMPTION AND PRODUCTION IN THE NON-METALLIC PRODUCTS INDUSTRY IN WESTERN INDUSTRIAL COUNTRIES, 1971 - 1981 (1975 = 100)

		1971	1972	1973	1974	1975	1976	1977	1978	1979	1980	1981[a]
USA	EC	91	95	99	105	100	105	111	117	280	733	702
	P	94	102	112	113	100	113	120	132	137	125	125
Canada	EC	96	102	123	114	100	103	108	105	99	146	143
	P	86	93	101	106	100	102	100	104	104	97	98
Japan	EC	13	15	24	164	100	170	166	171	182	177	167
	P	103	110	126	117	100	110	115	121	129	132	124
Federal Republic of Germany	EC	124	126	127	113	100	92	96	75	88	83	75
	P	109	115	116	109	100	107	110	113	121	121	113
France	EC	98	104	114	113	100	102	102	94	78	29	29
	P	88	97	105	111	100	105	105	107	113	118	111
United Kingdom	EC	124	112	119	110	100	90	89	91	91	80	67
	P	98	105	113	106	100	100	98	99	99	88	80
Italy	EC	102	100	106	112	100	103	93	108	115	111	57
	P	93	96	106	114	100	110	112	112	119	131	127

a Production indices are estimated.

EC = Energy consumption.
P = Production.

Source: OECD: Energy Balances; OECD: Indicators of Industrial Activity; UN: Yearbook of Industrial Statistics; calculations by the authors.

Table A-20: ENERGY INVESTMENT AS A PROPORTION OF TOTAL GROSS FIXED CAPITAL FORMATION
IN SELECTED EC MEMBER COUNTRIES, 1970 AND 1973-1980

- in percentages -

Countries	1970	1973	1974	1975	1976	1977	1978	1979	1980
Belgium	6.7	5.9	6.3	8.3	6.3	6.7	6.4	6.6	7.5
Federal Republic of Germany	5.5	7.0	8.3	9.2	8.0	7.1	6.9	6.3	6.9
France	6.3	5.7	5.8	6.4	6.8	7.1	7.9	8.4	9.2
United Kingdom	10.6	8.0	10.4	14.4	16.4	15.3	14.5	13.5	14.3
Ireland	6.6	6.7	5.2	3.3	5.6	6.2	5.0	5.4	n.a.
Italy	7.9	7.2	7.4	7.6	7.6	7.2	7.7	8.3	n.a.
Netherlands	8.2	8.2	8.4	9.9	8.5	7.1	6.4	5.7	7.2

Source: EUROSTAT: National Accounts ESA (Detailed tables by branch 1970-80); calculations by the authors.

417

Tabelle A-21: INVESTMENT RATIOS[a] IN THE ENERGY SECTOR, IN MANUFACTURING INDUSTRY AND IN THE ECONOMY AS A WHOLE IN SELECTED EC MEMBER COUNTRIES, 1970 AND 1973 - 1980

	Federal Republic of Germany			France			Italy			United Kingdom			Belgium			Netherlands		
	ES	MI	TE	ES	MI	TE	ES	MI	TE	ES	MI	TE	ES	MI	TE	ES	MI	TE
1970	26.4	17.9	27.3	32.5	17.6	23.3	30.7	14.8	21.4	50.0	13.1	18.6	30.2	19.3	22.7	40.6	21.6	25.8
1973	31.1	13.3	26.4	31.8	15.8	23.8	31.6	16.1	20.8	46.3	11.4	19.5	26.5	16.0	21.4	30.9	14.6	23.1
1974	33.5	11.9	23.6	39.0	15.6	24.3	39.1	17.2	22.4	67.2	13.6	20.3	31.9	18.2	22.7	28.8	15.6	21.8
1975	34.7	11.5	22.4	38.7	14.0	23.3	32.8	14.6	22.6	72.0	13.4	19.5	36.5	17.8	22.5	26.5	14.9	20.9
1976	29.7	11.6	22.3	43.3	14.1	23.3	34.6	12.9	20.0	71.4	12.5	19.0	28.7	14.4	22.1	19.6	13.0	19.3
1977	28.4	11.5	22.4	38.5	13.5	22.3	29.8	12.7	19.6	48.0	12.9	17.9	30.3	11.9	21.7	18.3	17.1	21.1
1978	28.1	11.1	23.0	38.7	12.7	21.4	28.8	11.5	18.7	45.2	13.4	18.0	29.2	11.3	21.6	17.3	19.0	21.3
1979	25.5	11.8	24.6	39.5	12.8	21.4	33.1	11.6	18.8	33.0	14.5	17.9	29.6	11.2	20.6	-	-	21.0
1980	28.2	12.9	25.8	46.6	13.8	21.6	-	-	19.8	-	-	17.5	33.4	13.1	21.2	-	-	20.8

a Gross fixed capital formation as a percentage of gross national product.

ES = Energy sector.
MI = Manufacturing industry.
TE = Total economy.

Source: EUROSTAT: National Accounts ESA (Detailed tables by branch, 1970-80); OECD: National Accounts; calculations by the authors.

Table A-22: DEPENDENCE OF OIL-IMPORTING INDUSTRIAL
AND DEVELOPING COUNTRIES ON IMPORTED ENERGY
1970 AND 1978 - 1980[a]

	1973	1978	1979	1980
Industrial countries[b]	37.4	40.3	40.3	37.3
Developing countries[c]	58.1	59.2	59.3	58.6
North America	13.7	20.6	19.1	14.7
Western Europe[b]	69.3	68.5	70.2	69.1
Japan	92.4	91.7	91.9	91.2
Oceania	2.7	-7.8	-7.4	-8.0

a Dependence on imported energy = net imports of energy as a percentage
   of total energy consumption.

b Excluding the United Kingdom and Norway.

c Excluding members of OPEC and other oil-exporting developing countries.

Source: UN: Yearbook of World Energy Statistics; calcula-
        tions by the authors.

Table A-23: GROWTH, COMPOSITION AND IMPORTANCE OF IMPORTS OF MANUFACTURED GOODS BY OPEC COUNTRIES, 1973 - 1981

	Annual growth rate 73-81	% of total imports of manufactures			% of world imports		
		1973	1978	1981	1973	1978	1981
Iron and steel	23.0	11.1	7.7	7.9	6.2	10.6	12.6
Chemicals	25.9	10.3	7.4	8.8	3.9	5.8	7.0
Other semi-manufactures	30.3	6.1	6.5	6.8	3.4	7.8	9.6
Machinery for specialised industries	27.7	19.1	19.2	18.2	5.8	12.9	13.6
Office and telecommunications equipment	25.8	3.4	3.7	2.9	3.2	8.7	5.7
Road motor vehicles	32.6	11.0	11.8	14.2	4.3	9.4	13.0
Other machinery and transport equipment	29.8	20.8	27.8	22.7	5.3	14.8	13.0
Household appliances	32.1	3.8	4.1	4.8	4.0	9.0	11.0
Textiles	19.9	8.2	4.2	4.7	5.6	8.1	10.2
Clothing	37.3	1.6	1.6	2.7	2.0	4.4	7.6
Other consumer goods	33.8	4.6	6.1	6.4	3.0	8.3	9.2
Total manufactures	28.4	100.0	100.0	100.0	4.6	10.0	10.8

Source: GATT: International Trade; calculations by the authors.

Table A-24: SHARES OF WESTERN INDUSTRIAL COUNTRIES AND NON-OPEC LDCs IN IMPORTS OF MANUFACTURED GOODS BY OPEC COUNTRIES, 1973 - 1981

- in percentages -

	Western industrial countries			Non-OPEC LDCs			World ($ bn)		
	1973	1978	1981	1973	1978	1981	1973	1978	1981
Iron and steel	84.8	86.7	82.3	8.5	5.8	10.2	1.77	6.05	9.30
Chemicals	88.4	87.1	84.5	6.7	6.9	9.2	1.64	5.80	10.35
Other semi-manufactures	68.0	72.5	75.8	16.5	14.7	14.3	0.97	5.10	8.05
Machinery for specialised industries	88.5	89.4	87.6	3.0	2.6	4.0	3.04	15.15	21.45
Office and telecommunications equipment	89.1	94.9	85.5	9.1	3.4	8.7	0.55	2.95	3.45
Road motor vehicles	97.7	96.2	95.8	1.1	3.2	3.6	1.75	9.30	16.70
Other machinery and transport equipment	85.2	88.6	87.1	4.5	6.2	6.7	3.31	21.90	26.75
Household appliances	80.3	79.7	75.2	14.8	14.1	20.4	0.61	3.20	5.65
Textiles	63.4	63.6	64.3	26.7	22.7	24.1	1.31	3.30	5.60
Clothing	36.0	40.0	39.7	48.0	44.0	46.0	0.25	1.25	3.15
Other consumer goods	68.5	72.9	78.0	17.8	14.6	11.3	0.73	4.80	7.50
Total manufactures	83.1	85.4	83.5	8.8	7.7	9.7	15.95	78.80	118.00

Source: GATT: International Trade; calculations by the authors.

421

Table A-25: EXPORTS TO OPEC COUNTRIES AS A PROPORTION OF THE TOTAL EXPORTS OF INDUSTRIAL, DEVELOPING AND STATE-TRADING COUNTRIES ACCORDING TO SECTOR, 1973, 1981 AND 1982

- in percentages -

	Industrial countries			Non-OPEC LDCs		State-trading countries	
	1973	1981	1982	1973	1981	1973	1981
Iron and steel	6.3	12.8	14.6	15.8	18.6	3.1	4.9
Chemicals	4.0	7.0	6.8	6.0	9.2	1.8	4.6
Other semi-manufactures	2.8	9.2	8.9	4.7	10.3	7.6	13.5
Machinery for specialised industries	6.5	14.9	15.6	11.1	16.5	2.4	6.4
Office and telecommunications equipment	3.4	6.2	7.4	3.9	3.3	0.8	3.0
Road motor vehicles	4.5	13.4	12.1	5.3	24.0	0.4	1.7
Other machinery and transport equipment	5.3	13.5	14.5	8.3	13.6	3.6	7.1
Household appliances	3.8	10.6	9.9	5.5	12.4	3.9	8.1
Textiles	4.8	9.9	9.3	8.6	10.6	5.7	9.4
Clothing	1.3	6.8	5.5	3.1	8.6	1.7	6.8
Other consumer goods	2.7	9.9	9.5	4.1	5.6	3.7	8.9
Total manufactures	4.6	11.3	11.4	6.0	10.3	2.9	6.5
Total exports	4.1	9.9	10.0	3.5	7.5	3.0	5.7

Source: GATT: International Trade; calculations by the authors.

Table A-26: EXPORTS TO OPEC COUNTRIES AS A PROPORTION OF THE TOTAL EXPORTS OF THE USA, THE EUROPEAN COMMUNITY AND JAPAN ACCORDING TO SECTOR, 1973 AND 1982

- in percentages -

	USA		EC		Japan	
	1973	1982	1973	1982	1973	1982
Iron and steel	10.0	22.1	4.8	10.0	11.9	24.4
Chemicals	4.0	6.9	3.9	6.7	6.7	8.8
Other semi-manufactures	3.8	10.3	2.2	7.1	9.5	22.5
Machinery for specialised industries	9.6	19.4	6.0	14.3	9.4	22.4
Office and telecommunications equipment	1.8	4.4	3.6	7.4	3.1	4.7
Road motor vehicles	5.5	14.3	4.6	11.6	6.9	15.6
Other machinery and transport equipment	6.0	12.8	6.2	15.1	4.4	16.0
Household appliances	4.7	11.5	2.6	6.5	4.9	10.5
Textiles	3.3	14.1	3.0	4.3	15.5	22.6
Clothing	3.7	9.1	1.2	4.2	2.7	10.9
Other consumer goods	3.1	12.0	2.6	9.5	4.1	11.0
Total manufactures	5.7	12.1	4.3	10.6	7.4	15.9
Total exports	5.0	10.7	3.8	9.3	7.4	15.7

Source: GATT: International Trade; calculations by the authors.

Table A-27: IMPORTANCE OF EXPORTS TO OPEC COUNTRIES FOR THE MANUFACTURING INDUSTRY OF THE FEDERAL REPUBLIC OF GERMANY, 1973, 1978, 1981 AND 1982

	as percentage of world exports				as percentage of world sales			
	1973	1978	1981	1982	1973	1978	1981	1982
Primary products and producer goods industry	3.1	5.6	5.8	5.7	0.6	1.4	1.5	1.6
Iron and steel	2.5	7.8	8.2	8.1	0.8	3.0	3.6	3.8
Chemicals	3.7	5.0	5.7	5.0	1.2	1.6	2.2	1.9
Capital goods industry	4.1	11.7	11.4	11.9	1.4	4.4	4.7	5.3
Structural steelwork	4.7	37.1	30.8	21.5	0.5	7.4	6.3	4.6
Mechanical engeneering	4.6	13.0	11.4	10.0	1.9	6.1	5.7	5.1
Road vehicle construction	4.3	7.9	13.3	9.8	2.0	3.0	6.0	4.8
Electrical engineering	4.4	16.7	11.2	11.8	1.0	5.2	3.6	4.2
Consumer goods industry	1.8	8.4	2.6	5.0	0.3	1.0	1.5	1.0
Foodstuffs	2.0	6.4	9.2	8.2	0.1	0.6	1.1	1.0
Total manufacturing industry	3.5	8.4	5.6	9.1	0.8	2.5	2.7	2.9

Source: Statistisches Bundesamt: Statistisches Jahrbuch; Statistisches Bundesamt: Fachserie 7, Reihe 7; calculations by the authors.

Table A-28: IMPUTED CRUDE OIL IMPORT BILL FOR THE 15 LARGEST OIL IMPORTERS
IN 1981[a]

	$ bn	As a percentage of actual imports of crude oil	As a percentage of total imports	As a percentage of GDP
USA	63.5	98.8	23.2	2.2
Japan	90.9	174.2	63.6	8.1
France	44.8	184.3	37.0	7.9
Federal Rep. of Germany	35.9	164.7	21.9	5.3
Italy	28.9	130.0	31.7	8.2
Spain	12.5	120.1	38.8	6.7
Netherlands	30.7	289.3	45.8	21.9
United Kingdom	30.4	367.1	29.8	6.1
Brazil	13.3	129.2	53.3	5.3
Belgium	10.6	153.9	17.1	11.2
Canada	15.1	230.4	21.6	5.3
Korea	5.3	94.3	23.8	9.1
Sweden	3.1	81.9	10.9	2.8
Greece	3.1	173.7	35.3	8.5
India	2.1	102.8	26.5	1.7

a On the assumption that crude oil imports rise in step with GDP between 1973 and 1981.

Source: OECD: Statistics of Foreign Trade; OECD: National Accounts; IMF: IFS Yearbook 1982;
UN: Yearbook of World Energy Statistics 1980; calculations by the authors.

Table A-29: OECD IMPORTS OF MANUFACTURED GOODS FROM OPEC COUNTRIES, 1980

Product groups	SITC position	$ million	As a percentage of SITC 5-8	As a percentage of OECD imports as a whole	from third countries	Net imports $ million
Floor coverings etc.	659	582.0	18.4	13.1	33.6	170.6
Tin	687	451.3	14.2	18.9	21.9	439.3
Silver etc.	681	419.1	13.2	3.7	10.4	393.3
Aluminium	684	291.8	9.2	2.7	22.8	-157.4
Non-electr. eng. a.motors etc. n.e.s.	714	229.6	7.2	4.3	57.8	-884.1
Radio-active materials	524	110.3	3.5	2.1	7.3	95.2
Alcohols etc.	512	86.8	2.7	2.6	16.6	-12.0
Wood manufactures	634	73.2	2.3	1.8	5.8	-63.3
Pig iron etc.	671	68.0	2.1	1.7	3.9	36.1
Pearls etc.	667	63.7	2.0	0.4	1.5	23.0
Leather	611	63.6	2.0	2.5	6.7	38.0
Semi-conductors etc.	776	63.0	2.0	0.6	1.7	1.3
Oxides etc.	522	59.3	1.9	1.2	5.4	-174.9
Measuring instruments etc.	874	50.3	1.6	0.5	11.4	-926.1
Aircraft etc.	792	45.6	1.4	0.3	9.3	-1339.6
Jewellery etc.	897	44.4	1.4	1.4	6.1	-651.2
Essential oils etc.	551	36.8	1.2	3.1	13.2	-92.5
Ingots of iron or steel	672	33.6	1.1	0.7	4.6	-565.8
Tubes etc. of iron or steel	678	24.8	0.7	0.3	3.9	-2264.0
Outer garments (women)	843	23.3	0.7	0.3	0.6	-200.4
Telecommunications etc. n.e.s.	764	22.6	0.7	0.2	1.2	-2134.1
Works of art etc.	896	17.9	0.6	0.4	1.0	-2.2
Outer garments (men)	842	16.2	0.5	0.2	0.5	-134.5
Ships etc.	793	14.0	0.4	0.3	1.4	-1251.0
Under garments	844	13.9	0.4	0.6	0.7	-59.1
Hydrocarbons n.e.s.	511	11.5	0.4	0.2	2.4	-158.3
Total manufactures	5-8	3170.0	100.0	0.4	3.1	79025.0

Quelle: OECD: Statistics of Foreign Trade, Series B; calculations by the authors.

Table A-30: THE FEDERAL REPUBLIC OF GERMANY'S IMPORTS OF MANUFACTURED GOODS FROM OIL-PRODUCING COUNTRIES[a], 1982

	Value of imports	Sectoral structure[b]	Share in relevant world imports	Share in relevant imports from developing countries	Share of domestic market[c]	Net imports
	DM million	%	%	%	%	DM million
Textiles	321.2	28.6	1.9	9.3	0.8	- 5.3
Foodstuffs	236.5	21.0	1.0	5.9	0.2	-1.410.5
Non-ferrous metals	217.5	19.3	1.7	10.3	0.8	- 225.5
Road motor vehicles	103.3	9.2	0.6	31.7	0.1	-7.740.2
Aircraft	62.4	5.5	0.5	67.2	0.4	- 137.1
Chemicals	57.2	5.1	0.2	7.3	0.1	-2.672.4
Mechanical engineering	49.8	4.4	0.3	20.2	0.1	-7.595.1
Clothing	32.0	2.8	0.3	0.8	0.1	- 55.3
Electrical appliances	26.1	2.3	0.1	1.2	0.0	-5.109.4
Wood products	24.4	2.2	0.8	4.5	0.2	- 3.1

a OPEC plus Bahrein, Oman and Mexico.
b The sector's share in total imports of manufactured goods from oil-producing countries (excluding oil products).
c Domestic market = domestic sales ÷ imports.

Source: Statistisches Bundesamt; calculations by the authors.

Table A 31: "EXPORTED" INFLATION IN WESTERN INDUSTRIAL COUNTRIES, 1970 – 1981[a]

	1970	1971	1972	1973	1974	1975	1976	1977	1978	1979	1980	1981
USA	0.02	-0.07	-0.06	0.55	1.18	0.05	-0.07	-0.15	-0.02	0.27	0.05	0.04
Canada	-0.20	-0.58	-0.18	1.08	3.37	-0.22	-1.08	-0.16	0.19	2.26	1.26	-1.16
Japan	-0.38	-0.33	-0.69	-0.47	0.80	-0.98	-0.88	-1.17	-1.03	0.33	-0.16	-0.42
Federal Rep. of Germany	-0.52	-0.62	-0.54	-0.33	1.61	-0.20	-0.10	-0.74	-0.40	0.19	-0.10	0.03
France	-0.87	-0.12	-0.77	-0.04	1.25	-1.24	-0.47	0.09	-0.49	0.02	-0.15	-0.12
United Kingdom	0.32	-0.77	-0.64	0.50	0.90	-1.01	1.78	0.47	-0.54	2.99	-1.04	-0.38
Italy	-0.03	-0.63	-0.59	0.23	1.82	-0.56	0.92	0.11	-0.98	-0.17	-0.58	-0.04
Memorandum:												
OECD	-0.07	-0.29	-0.37	0.29	1.44	-0.69	-0.17	-0.28	-0.49	0.26	-0.09	-0.24
EC	-0.12	-0.64	-0.75	-0.04	1.74	-1.94	0.05	-0.31	-0.82	0.06	-0.27	-0.06

a For the measurement concept, see Härtel, Henne 1982.

Source: OECD: National Accounts; calculations by the authors.

Table A-32: DETERMINANTS OF CHANGES IN THE CURRENT ACCOUNT BALANCES OF OECD COUNTRIES FROM 1978/79 TO 1981/82

- in billions of dollars -

| | Changes in current account balances | | | | Explanatory factors | | | | | | | |
| | | | | | Terms of trade | | | | Oil prices | | | |
	78/79	79/80	80/81	81/82	78/79	79/80	80/81	81/82	78/79	79/80	80/81	81/82
USA	14	1	3	-13	- 8	-27	7	9	-17	-33	- 8	10
Canada	0	3	- 4	7	4	1	- 2	- 1	- 1	1	0	0
Japan	-25	- 2	16	2	-12	-23	4	4	-10	-25	- 6	0
Federal Republic of Germany	-14	-11	9	10	- 7	-10	- 5	7	- 6	-13	- 3	2
France	- 3	- 9	0	- 7	- 1	- 7	- 5	2	- 5	-11	- 3	0
United Kingdom	- 6	10	9	- 5	3	4	4	1	- 2	0	1	0
Italy	- 1	-15	2	3	0	- 8	- 8	3	- 4	-10	- 3	3
memorandum:												
OECD	-36	-41	42	- 1	-29	-93	-13	29	-52	-109	-22	16

Source: OECD: Economic Outlook, various years.

429

Table A-33:   WESTERN INDUSTRIAL COUNTRIES' EXPORT
               MARKET SHARES IN ENERGY-INTENSIVE
               PRODUCTS, 1973 AND 1981[a]

	1973	1981
USA	11.3	12.9
Canada	10.2	9.0
Japan	10.2	9.6
Federal Republic of Germany	16.3	15.8
France	7.6	8.7
United Kingdom	5.5	5.7
Italy	3.9	4.4

a The energy-intensive exports of each country as a percentage of
   total OECD exports of energy-intensive products. For a list of
   energy-intensive products see the Annex.

Source: OECD: Statistics of Foreign Trade; calculations
          by the authors.

R E F E R E N C E S

MONOGRAPHS/ESSAYS

Abdullatif, Sheikh Ahmed
    (1980): A strategy for investing the OPEC surplus, in:
    Euromoney, August

Angelini, Anthonio; Maximo Eng; Francis A.Lees
    (1979): International lending, risk and the Euromarkets,
    London

Artus, Patrick
    (1983): Capital, energy and labour substitution: the
    supply block in OECD medium-term models, OECD Working
    Papers No. 2, March

Bacha, Eduar Lisboa; Carlos F. D. Alejandro
    (1982): International financial intermediation: A long
    and tropical view, Essays in International Finance, No.
    147, Princeton, May

Bailey, Norman A.
    (1983): A safety net for foreign lending, in: Business
    Week, 10 January

Bank for International Settlements
    (1982): International banking developments - second quar-
    ter 1982, Basle
    (1983): Press Review, No. 113, 14 March

Bank of England
    (1980): The surpluses of the oil exporters, in: Bank of
    England, Quarterly Bulletin, June
    (1981): Quarterly Bulletin, December
    (1983): Quarterly Bulletin, December

Banks, Ferdinand E.
    (1980): The political economy of oil, Lexington, Toronto

Basagni, Fabio
    (1981): Appproaches to the prudential supervision of in-
    ternational lending, in: Benjamin J. Cohen (ed.): Banks
    and the balance of payments, Montclair

Baumgarten, Klaus; Horst Herberg
(1982): Sectoral effects of higher costs of imported inputs, in: Jahrbuch für Nationalökonomie und Statistik, Vol. 197, No. 3

BDI (Bundesverband der Deutschen Industrie)
(1983): Energie und Wettbewerbsfähigkeit - Eine kurze Fassung, Cologne, April

Begg, Iain; Francis Cripp; Terry Ward
(1981): The European Community: problems and prospects, in: Cambridge Economic Policy Review, Vol. 7, No. 2, December

Bergman, Lars; Marian Radetzki
(1979): How will the Third World be affected by OECD energy strategies?, in: The Journal of Energy and Development, Autumn

Berndt, Ernst R.; Catherine J. Morrison
(1979): Income redistribution and employment effects of rising energy prices, in: Resources and Energy, Vol. 2, No. 2/3

Berndt, Ernst R.; David O. Wood
(1975): Technology, prices and the derived demand for energy, in: Review of Economics and Statistics, Vol. 56, August
(1979): Engineering and econometric interpretations of energy-capital complementarity, in: American Economic Review, Vol. 69, No. 3

Bittel, Alfred
(1982): Tendenzen in der petrochemischen Industrie der Bundesrepublik Deutschland, in: Chemische Industrie, Vol. 105, No. 5

BMWi (Bundesministerium für Wirtschaft)
(1984): Ausfuhrgarantien und Ausfuhrbürgschaften der Bundesrepublik Deutschland, Bericht über das Jahr 1983, Bonn, May

BP (British Petroleum)
(1984): BP Statistical Review of World Energy, London, June

British Business
(7.5.1982): Waking up to a major new market

Bruno, Michael
(1978): Exchange rates, import costs, and wage-price dynamics, in: Journal of Political Economy, Vol. 86, No. 3

Business Week
(6.9.1982): The rewards of being acquired by Kuwait
(15.8.1983): Mexico is acting like a member of OPEC

Cagan, Philip
   (1980): Imported inflation 1973-74 and the accommodation
   issue, in: Journal of Money, Credit and Banking, Vol. 12,
   No. 1, February

Cebula, Richard J.; Michael Frewer
   (1980): Oil imports and inflation: an empirical international analysis of the 'imported' inflation thesis, in:
   Kyklos, Vol. 33, Fasc. 4

CEPII, FAST
   (1980): Industrial specialization in twelve European
   countries before and after 1973, Brussels, Luxembourg

CIA (National Foreign Assessment Center of the C.I.A.)
   (1979): The world oil market in the years ahead, Supplement to OPEC Bulletin, Vol. 10, No. 39/40

Cline, William R.
   (1983): International debt and the stability of the world
   economy, Washington, D.C., September

Cohen, Benjamin J.
   (1981): Banks and the balance of payments, Montclair

Committee on Banking Regulations and Supervisory Practices
   (1982): Management of banks' international lending: country risk analysis and country exposure measurement and
   control, mimeo, March

Cooke, W.P.
   (1981): Developments in co-operation among banking supervisory authorities, in: Bank of England, Quarterly Bulletin, Vol. 21, No. 2

Corden, W.M.
   (1976): Framework for analysing the implications of the
   rise in oil prices, in: T.M. Rybczynski (ed.): The economics of the oil crisis, London and Basingstoke

Corden W.M.; Peter Oppenheimer
   (1976): Economic issues for the oil-importing countries,
   in: T.M. Rybczynski (ed.): The economics of the oil crisis, London and Basingstoke

Crocket, A.D.; D.J. Evans
   (1980): Demand for money in Middle Eastern countries,
   in: IMF-Staff Papers, Vol. 27, No. 3

Dean, James W.; Ian H. Giddy
   (1981): Averting international banking crises, New York

Denison, Edward F.
   (1979): Explanations of declining productivity growth,
   in: Survey of Current Business, Vol. 59, No. 8, Part
   II

Deutsche Bundesbank
   (1978): Die Stellung der Bundesrepublik Deutschland
   am internationalen Anleihemarkt, in: Monatsberichte der
   Deutschen Bundesbank, November
   (1981): Der Einfluß des zweiten Ölpreisschocks auf die
   Wirtschaft der Bundesrepublik Deutschland - eine öko-
   nometrische Untersuchung, in: Monatsberichte der Deutschen
   Bundesbank, April

Deutscher Bundestag
   (1982): Enquête-Kommission Zukünftige Kernenergie-Poli-
   tik, Protokolle Nr. 9 und 10 zur öffentlichen Anhörung
   vom 17. und 18. Dezember 1981, Bonn

Dicken, Engelbert
   (1980): Ölgelder-Recycling, in: Zeitschrift für das ge-
   samte Kreditwesen, No. 24

DIHT (Deutscher Industrie- und Handelstag)
   (1983): Positionspapier zur Energiepolitik, Bonn,
   27 April

DIW
   (1982a): Staatliche Investitionsförderung und private In-
   vestitionen (author: Dietmar Edler), in: DIW Wochenbericht,
   Vol. 49, No. 6
   (1982b): Der Investitionsbedarf der Energiewirtschaft in
   der Bundesrepublik Deutschland (author: Manfred Horn),
   in: DIW Wochenbericht, Vol. 49, No. 27
   (1983): Zum Wandel der volkswirtschaftlichen Produktionsstruktur im internationalen Vergleich (author:
   Fritz Franzmeyer), in: DIW Wochenbericht, Vol. 50,
   No. 6

DOE (US Department of Energy)
   (1981): Securing America's energy future - the national
   energy policy plan, Washington, D.C.

Dohner, Robert S.
   (1981): Energy prices, economic activity, and inflation:
   a survey of issues and results, in: Knuth Anton Mork (ed.):
   Energy prices, inflation, and economic activity, Cambridge, Mass.

Dornbusch, Rüdiger
    (1980): Exchange rate economics: Where do we stand?,
    in: Brookings Papers on Economic Activity, No. 1

Dunn, R.M.jr.
    (1979): Exchange rates, payments adjustment, and OPEC.
    Why oil deficits persist, Princeton

Eaton, Jonathan; Mark Gersovitz
    (1981): Poor-country borrowing in private financial mar-
    kets and the repudiation issue, Princeton Studies in In-
    ternational Finance, No. 47, Princeton, June

The Economist
    (4.9.1982): OPEC's tight fist closes on West German Engi-
    neers
    (2.4.1983): A debt partnership

EG (Europäische Gemeinschaften)
    (1981) : Jahreswirtschaftsübersicht 1981-1982, in: Eu-
    ropäische Wirtschaft, No. 10, November
    (1982a): Die Wettbewerbsfähigkeit der Industrie der Euro-
    päischen Gemeinschaft, Luxembourg
    (1982b): Jahreswirtschaftsübersicht 1982-1983, in: Euro-
    päische Wirtschaft, No. 14, November
    (1982c): Mitteilungen der Kommission an den Rat zum Inve-
    stitionsproblem, in: Europäische Wirtschaft, No. 14, No-
    vember

Emminger, Otmar
    (1980): Stabilitätspolitik heute, Rede vor dem Forum der
    Aktionsgemeinschaft Soziale Marktwirtschaft, Bonn-Bad Go-
    desberg, 3 July, reprinted in: Otmar Emminger: Vertei-
    digung der DM, Frankfurt/Main

Euromoney
    (July 1983): Those debt proposals: Radical or just wrong?,
    in: Euromoney, No. 7

Europäisches Parlament
    (1981): Bericht über die Auswirkungen der Energieproble-
    me und der technologischen Entwicklung auf den Beschäf-
    tigungsstandard in der Europäischen Gemeinschaft, in:
    Sitzungsdokumente 1981-1982, Dokument I-164/81, 15 May
    (1983a): J. Purvis: Bericht im Namen des Ausschusses für
    Wirtschaft und Währung über die Rückschleusung von Ölmilli-
    arden, in: Europäisches Parlament: Sitzungsdokumente 1982-
    1983, Dokument 1-1107/82, 15 February

(1983b): Stellungnahme des Ausschusses für Energie und
Forschung, Anlage zum Bericht Purvis im Namen des Ausschusses für Wirtschaft und Währung über die Rückschleu-
sung von Ölmilliarden, in: Europäisches Parlament:
Sitzungsdokumente 1982-1983, Dokument 1--1107/82/Anl.,
21 February

Exxon
(1980): World energy outlook, December

Fabritius, Jan F.R.; Christian E. Petersen
(1981): OPEC respending and the economic impact of an
increase in the price of oil, in: The Scandinavian Journal of Economics, Vol. 83, No. 2

Fest, Hartmut
(1980): Soll die Bundesrepublik mit Defiziten leben? in:
Wirtschaftsdienst, Vol. 60, No. 3

Field, Peter; David Shireff; William Oflard
(1983): The IMF and central banks flex their muscles, in:
Euromoney, January

Finanzierung und Entwicklung
(1983): Verschuldung: Was ist das?, September

Fischer, Stanley
(1981): Relative shocks, relative price variability, and
inflation, in: Brookings Papers on Economic Activity,
No. 2

Franzmathes, Fathi
(1982): Europäische Wirtschaft - Arabischer Markt, Han-
delsblatt-Schriftenreihe, Dusseldorf

Frenkel, Jacob A.
(1981): The collapse of purchasing power parities during
the 1970's, in: European Economic Review, Vol. 16

Frowen, Stephen F.
(1981: Why the IMF is increasing its rôle in recycling,
in: Euromoney, January

Garten, Jeffrey E.
(1982): Rescheduling sovereign debt: Is there a better approach?, in: The World Economy, Vol.5, No. 3, November

GATT
(1983): International trade in 1982 and current prospects, Press Release, No. GATT/1333, Geneva, 4 March

Gisselquist, David
(1979): Oil prices and trade deficits - U.S. conflicts with Japan and West Germany, New York

Gösele, W.
(1979): Grundzüge des Europäischen Währungssystems, in: Kredit und Kapital, No. 3

Gold, Bela
(1982): Pressures for restructuring the world steel industry in the 1980s: a case study in challenges to industrial adaptation, in: Quarterly Review of Economics and Business, Vol. 22, No. 1, Spring

Gotur, Padma
(1983): Zinssätze und Entwicklungsländer, in: Finanzierung & Entwicklung, December

Grauwe, Paul de
(1981): OECD versus the GATT on the source of inflation, in: The World Economy, Vol. 4, No. 2, June

Gray, H. Peter
(1981): Oil-push inflation: a broader examination, in: Banca Nazionale del Lavoro, Quarterly Review, No. 136, March

Griffin, James M.; Paul R. Gregory
(1976): An intercountry translog model of energy substitution responses, in: American Economic Review, Vol. 66, No. 5

Griffin, James D.; David J. Teece (eds.)
(1982): OPEC behaviour and world oil prices, London

Grilli, Enzo R.
(1981): Naturkautschuk: rosige Zukunft?, in: Finanzierung & Entwicklung, June

Group of Thirty
(1981): The outlook for international bank lending, New York
(1982): How bankers see the world financial market, New York

437

Gutowski, Armin; Wolfgang Roth
(1980): Das Vertragskonzept OPEC-Industrieländer-Entwick-
lungsländer, in: Wirtschaftsdienst, No. 12

Gutowski, Armin; Hans-Hagen Härtel; Hans-Eckart Scharrer
(1981): From shock therapy to gradualism, in: Shock therapy or gradualism? A comparative approach to anti-infla-
tion policies, Group of Thirty Occasional Papers, No. 8,
New York

Härtel, Hans-Hagen; Wolfgang Henne
(1982): Inflation - importiert oder hausgemacht?, in:
Wirtschaftsdienst, Vol. 62, No. 3

Hannon, Bruce M.
(1975): Energy, growth and altruism, in: Dennis L. Mead-
ows (ed.): Alternatives to growth-I: a search for sustain-
able futures, Cambridge, Mass.

Herendeen, R.B.; Bruce M. Hannon; C. Ford
(1979): An energy conserving tax: how large should rebates
be?, unpublished paper (Energy Research Group), Champaign-
Urbana, Il.

Holmer, Ed. C.
(1980): The challenges of the '80s from the perspective
of the US chemical industry, in: Chemistry and Industry,
5 January

Hooke, A.W.
(1983): The International Monetary Fund, Washington, D.C.

Hudson, Edward A.; Dale W. Jorgenson
(1974): U.S. energy policy and economic growth 1975-2000,
in: Bell Journal of Economics and Management Science,
Vol. 5
(1979): Energy prices and the U.S. economy, 1972-1976,
in: W.J. Mead, A.E. Utton (eds.): U.S. energy policy,
Cambridge, Mass.

IEA
(1982a): World energy outlook, Paris
(1982b): Natural gas - prospects to 2000, Paris
(1983) : Energy polices and programmes of IEA countries,
1982 Review, Paris

Ifo
    (1982): Quantitative Wirkungen der Energiesparpolitik in
    der Bundesrepublik Deutschland - Abschätzung von Energie-
    einsparungen bis 1985 (authors: H.-D. Karl et al.), ifo-
    studien zur Energiewirtschaft No. 3/1, Munich
    (1983a): Auswirkungen von Energiepreiserhöhungen auf die
    Wettbewerbsfähigkeit energieintensiver Produktionen der
    deutschen Industrie (authors: A. Gebhardt et al.), ifo-
    Studien zur Industriewirtschaft, No. 25, Munich
    (1983b): Auswirkungen von Investitionen auf den Energie-
    verbrauch in der Industrie (authors: M. Reinhard et al.),
    ifo-studien zur Energiewirtschaft, No. 4, Munich
    (1983c): Die Industrialisierung der arabischen OPEC-Län-
    der und ihre Auswirkungen auf die Industrie der Bundesre-
    publik Deutschland (authors: A. Gebhardt, W. Ochel), ifo-
    Studien zur Industriewirtschaft, No. 27, Munich

IMF (International Monetary Fund)
    (1981) : World Economic Outlook, Washington, D.C., June
    (1982a): International Financial Statistics, Supplement
    on Fund Accounts, Supplement Series No. 3, Washington,
    D.C.
    (1982b): World Economic Outlook, Washington, D.C., April
    (1983) : World Economic Outlook, Washington, D.C., May

Indonesian Commercial Newsletter
    (17.5.1982): Prospects for the aluminium industry

International Currency Review
    (1981): Insuring international bank loans: Governor
    Wallich's latest proposal, Vol. 13, No. 2, 8 May

Isard, Peter
    (1978): Exchange rate determination: a survey of popular
    views and recent models, Princeton

ISI (Institut für Systemtechnik und Innovationsforschung)
    (1982): Zur internationalen Wettbewerbsfähigkeit energie-
    intensiver Industriezweige in der Bundesrepublik Deutsch-
    land - Schlußbericht (authors: F. Garnreiter et al.),
    Karlsruhe, January

Jenne, C.A.; R.K. Cattell
    (1983): Structural change and energy efficiency in indus-
    try, in: Energy Economics, April

Jestin-Fleury, Nicole
    (1984): Les échanges énergétiques entre l'Union Sovietique
    et l'Europe occidentale, in: Problèmes économiques, No.
    1863, 29 February

Joerges, Bernward; Harald Müller
(1983): Energy conservation programs for consumers (Preprint
No. 16 of International Institute for Environment and Society,
Science Center, Berlin)

Johnston, R.B.
(1981): Theories of the growth of the Euro-currency market: A review of the Euro-currency deposit multiplier, BIS
Economic Papers, No. 4, May

Kaneko, Yukio
(1980): Changes in Japan's industrial structure since the
oil crisis, in: The Developing Economies, Vol. 18, No. 4

Kenneth, P.; H.P. Gassmann
(1982): Energy savings through information technologies,
in: OECD Observer, No. 114, January

Keran, M.W.; A.A. Al-Malik
(1982): Monetary sources of inflation in Saudi Arabia,
in: R. El Mallakh; D. El Mallakh (eds.): Saudi Arabia,
Lexington

King, Jill A.
(1978): The comprehensive human resources data system:
a model for estimating the distributional impacts of
energy policies (Paper prepared for the National Science
Foundation Conference on Microeconomic Simulation Models
for Public Analysis), Washington, March

Köhler, Claus
(1983): Bankenaufsicht verbessern, quoted from: Deutsche
Bundesbank: Auszüge aus Presseartikeln, No. 25, Frankfurt/
Main

Kolk, David X.
(1983): Regional employment impact of rapidly escalating
energy costs, in: Energy Economics

Koopmann, Georg; Hans-Eckart Scharrer
(1981): Auswirkungen der Erhöhung der Rohöl-(Rohstoff)
Preise auf das internationale Währungssystem, Hamburg

Kriegsmann, Klaus-P.; Axel D. Neu
(1981): Substitutionsbeziehungen zwischen den Produktions-
faktoren Energie, Kapital und Arbeit in der Bundesrepublik
Deutschland, in: Zeitschrift für Energiewirtschaft, No. 1

Kugler, Peter
(1982): Die Substitution zwischen Kapital, Arbeit, Energie und Material in der Schweiz: Eine empirische Analyse
1968-1980, Arbeitsbericht No. 14 of Basler Arbeitsgruppe
für Konjunkturforschung, Basle, September

Lafay, Gérard
(1981): La dynamique de spécialisation des pays euro-
péens, in: Revue économique, Vol. 32, No. 4, July

Laney, L.O.
(1980): Towards a multiple reserve system, in: Euromoney,
September

Lennep, Emile van
(1982): Protectionism vs. economic policy, in: OECD Observer, No. 115, March

Little, I.M.D.; J.A. Mirrlees
(1974): Project appraisal and planning for developing
countries, London

Llewellyn, John
(1983): Resource prices and macroeconomic policies: lessons from two oil shocks, OECD Working Papers No. 5, April

MacBean, A.I.
(1980): Identifying future comparative advantage, in:
P. Oppenheimer (ed.): Issues in international economics,
Stocksfield etc.

Matthies, Klaus
(1983): Government influence on energy prices, in: Intereconomics, Vol. 16, No. 2

Matthöfer, Hans
(1980): Ölgelder Recycling, in: Zeitschrift für das gesam-
te Kreditwesen, No. 24

Mayer, H.
(1978): Die Risiken der Banken im Auslandsgeschäft, mimeo,
October

(1979): Der Eurowährungsmarkt, seine makroökonomische Pro-
blematik und Auswirkungen, in: Außenwirtschaft, No. 1

Maynard, P.A.; P.A. Davies
(1982): Evolving problems of international financial in-
termediation, in: Donald E. Fair, François Léonard de
Juvigny (eds.): Bank management in a changing domestic
and international environment: The challenges of the eighties, The Hague

MEED (Middle East Economic Digest)
(3.2.1984): Nigel Harvey: What future for Arab refiners?
(17.2.1984): Algeria: LNG agreement brings profits for
French exporters

Meyer-Preschany, Manfred
(1983): Vor einem schmerzvollen Anpassungsprozeß, in:
Wirtschaftswoche, No. 29, 15 July

Meyer-Renschhausen, Martin; Wolfgang Pfaffenberger
(1983): Die volkswirtschaftlichen Auswirkungen von Ener-
giepreissteigerungen und -einsparungen, in: Wirtschaftsdienst, Vol. 63, No. 5

Mohnfeld, Jochen H.
(1982): European and world energy perspectives: the 1980s
and 1990s, in: Intereconomics, July/August

Morgan Guaranty
(1980): World Financial Markets, September
(1983): World Financial Markets, September

Mously, Muaffac
(1982): Auswirkungen der Energieverteuerung auf die sek-
torale Produktionsstruktur (unpublished paper), Hamburg

Muller, Huid J.
(1982): Changes in banking supervision and their consequences for banks, in: Donald E. Fair, François Léonard
de Juvigny (eds.): Bank management in a changing domestic and international environment: The challenges of the
eighties, The Hague

Nan Nguema, Marc
(1983): OPEC's trade relations with industrial countries:
past, present and future, in: OPEC-Review, Vol. 7, No. 2

Nordhaus, William D.
(1980): Oil and economic performance in industrial countries, in: Brookings Papers on Economic Activity, No. 2

North-South Commission
(1980): North-South, a programme for survival: report of
the Independent Commission on International Development
Issues, London

Odell, Peter R.
(1983): An alternative view of the outlook for the international oil market, in: Petroleum Economist, Oktober

OECD
(1980): Wages, costs and prices, in: OECD Economic Outlook, No. 27, July
(1981): Regulations affecting international banking
operations of banks and non-banks, Paris, Vols. 1 and 2
(1982): International aspects of inflation (author: Philip
Turner), in: OECD Economic Outlook - Occasional Studies,
No. 6, Paris
(1983a): Positive adjustment policies, Paris
(1983b): Aluminium industry. Energy aspects of structural change, Paris

OECD Observer
(1981): OECD and the NICs: the current trade pattern,
November
(1983a): The future of multilateral aid: new problems
for the poorest countries, January
(1983b): Support for Third-World energy, November
(1983c): Economic recovery: the North/South trade and
debt nexus, May

Östblom, Göran
(1982): Energy use and structural changes. Factors behind the fall in Sweden's energy output ratio, in: Energy
Economics, No. 1

Özatalay, Savas; Stephen Grubaugh; Thomas V. Long II
(1979): Energy substitution and national energy policy,
in: American Economic Review, Vol. 69, No. 2

Palmer, John L.; John E. Todd; Howard P. Tuckman
(1976): The distributional impact of rising energy prices:
how should the government respond?, in: Public Policy,
Vol. 24, No. 4

Palmer, Keith
(1983): Private Ölexploration in Entwicklungsländern,
in: Finanzierung & Entwicklung, March

Parkin, Michael
(1980): Oil push inflation?, in: Banca Nazionale del
Lavoro, Quarterly Review, No. 133, June

Partee
(1983): Mr. Partee discusses various issues of supervision and regulation of international lending, in:
Bank for International Settlements, Press Review, No.
106, Basle, 3 June

Pelosky, Robert J. jr.
    (1983): Private co-financing: new capital for development,
    in: EIU Multinational Business, No. 2

Pohl, Rüdiger
    (1980): Für den Abschwung nicht gerüstet, in: Wirtschafts-
    woche, No. 10, 6 March

Polak, Jacques
    (1982): Financial problems of non-oil developing countries,
    in: Norman C. Miller (ed.): International reserves, exchange
    rates, and developing country finance, Lexington

Polte, Winfried
    (1983): Energieprobleme der Entwicklungsländer (published
    by Kreditanstalt für Wiederaufbau), Frankfurt/Main

Rahmer, Bernd
    (1981): Uncertain prospects for oil, in: Petroleum Economist,
    July

Ray, G.F.
    (1982): Europe's farewell to full employment?, in: Daniel
    Yergin, Martin Hillenbrand (eds.): Global insecurity,
    Boston

RKW (Rationalisierungs-Kuratorium der Deutschen Wirtschaft)
    (1981): Strukturveränderungen der deutschen Wirtschaft,
    Eschborn

Rohatyn, F.G.
    (1983): A plan for stretching out global debt, in: Busi-
    ness Week, 28 February

Roze, Janis A.
    (1981): The competitiveness of natural resources with
    synthetic substances, in: Jorge Lozoya, Rosario Green
    (eds.): International trade, industrialization and the
    new international economic order, New York etc.

RWI (Rheinisch-Westfälisches Institut für Wirtschaftsforschung)
    (1982): Willi Lamberts: Wettbewerbsfähigkeit und Energiever-
    sorgung, in: Mitteilungen, Vol. 33

Sachverständigenrat (zur Begutachtung der gesamtwirtschaft-
lichen Entwicklung)
    (1979): Jahresgutachten 1979/80, Bonn

Salacuse, J.W.
    (1980): Arab capital and Middle Eastern development fi-
    nance, in: Journal of World Trade Law, Vol. 14, No. 4

Salop, Joanne
    (1981): The divergence indicator: a technical note, in:
    IMF-Staff Papers, Vol. 28, No. 4

Schäfer, Hans-Bernd
    (1980): Die Bereitschaftsabkommen des Internationalen
    Währungsfonds in der Kritik, in: Hans-B. Schäfer (ed.):
    Gefährdete Weltfinanzen, Bonn
    (1982): Die OPEC als Weltbankier und Kapitalanleger,
    mimeo, Hamburg

Schiffer, Hans-W.
    (1982): Die "Sieben Schwestern", in: Oel-Zeitschrift für
    die Mineralölwirtschaft, Vol. 20, No. 4

Shihata, I.F.I.
    (1982) The other face of OPEC, London

Schlecht, Otto
    (1980): Das Vertragskonzept OPEC-Industrieländer-Entwick-
    lungsländer . Eine Stellungnahme, in: Wirtschaftsdienst,
    No. 2

Schlesinger, Helmut
    (1978): Die Geldpolitik der Deutschen Bundesbank 1967-
    1977, in: Kredit und Kapital, No. 1

Schmid, Michael
    (1983): International adjustment to an oil price shock -
    the role of competitiveness, Institute for International
    Economic Studies, Seminar Paper No. 217, Stockholm, Au-
    gust

Schmitt, Dieter; Manfred Gommersbach
    (1982): Zur Frage der Auswirkungen von Rohölpreissteige-
    rungen auf die Entwicklung der Kraftstoffpreise in der
    Bundesrepublik Deutschland, in: Zeitschrift für Energie-
    wirtschaft, No. 1, March

Schröder, Wolfgang
    (1982): Das Multireservewährungssystem: Veränderte Rah-
    menbedingungen für die Politik der Deutschen Bundesbank,
    in: Werner Ehrlicher, Diethard B. Simmert (eds.): Geld-
    und Währungspolitik in der Bundesrepublik Deutschland,
    Supplement to Kredit und Kapital, No. 7, Berlin

Schürmann, Heinz J.
    (1982): Strukturwandel und Anpassungsprobleme - Eine Zwi-
    schenbilanz, in: Wirtschaftsdienst, Vol. 62, No. 3

Sheehey, Edmund J.
  (1979): On the measurement of imported inflation in developing countries, in: Weltwirtschaftliches Archiv, Vol. 115, No. 1

(Deutsche) Shell AG
  (1983): Weltenergie-Daten und Fakten (Shell Briefing Service), January

Sterling, J.
  (1980): How big is the international lending market?, in: The Banker, January

Swoboda, Alexander K.
  (1980): Credit creation in the Euromarket: alternative theories and implications for control, New York

Stewart-Gordon, T.J.
  (1983): Exaggerations, in: World Oil, March

Syrie et Monde Arabe
  (1981): Les fonds arabes de development: stratégies et moyens d'action, No. 324, 25 February

Tatom, John A.
  (1979): Energy prices and capital formation: 1972-1977, in: Federal Reserve Bank of St. Louis, Vol. 61, No. 5

Teso, Bruna
  (1982): The promise of biotechnology ... and some constraints, in: OECD Observer, No. 118, September

Thurow, Lester C.
  (1978): Prepared testimony given in hearings on the economics of the President's proposed energy policies before the Joint Economic Committee, Congress of the United States, 95th Congress, 1st Session, May 20 and May 25, 1977 (U.S. Government Printing Office, Washington, D.C.)

Trouvain, F.-J.
  (1980): Perspektiven auf den internationalen Finanzmärkten in den 80er Jahren, Lecture delivered at 34. Deutscher Betriebswirtschaftstag, Berlin

Turner, Louis
  (1982): Petrochemicals, in: Louis Turner, Neil McMullen (eds.): The newly industrializing countries: trade and adjustment, London

UNCTAD
  (1982): Trade and development report 1982 - report by the UNCTAD Secretariat, Geneva

Uri, Noel D.
    (1980): Energy as a determinant of investment behaviour,
    in: Energy Economics, Vol. 2, No. 3

Versluysen, Eugène L.
    (1981): The political economy of international finance,
    Westmead

Volcker, Paul L.
    (1980): The recycling problem revisited, in: Challenge,
    July-August

Wallich, Henry C.
    (1981): Statement to the Congress, September 23, reprint-
    ed in: Federal Reserve Bulletin, Vol. 67, No. 10

Waverman, Leonard
    (1975): The two price systems in energy: subsidies for-
    gotten, in: Canadian Public Policy, Vol. 1, No. 1
    (1979): The visible hand: the pricing of Canadian oil
    resources (Paper prepared for the Ontario Economic Coun-
    cil), August

Wetter, Wolfgang, et al.
    (1983): D-Mark-Wechselkurs und internationale Wettbewerbs-
    position der deutschen Wirtschaft, Hamburg

Weyant, John P.; David M. Kline
    (1982): OPEC and the oil glut: outlook for oil export
    revenues during the 1980s and 1990s, in: OPEC-Review,
    Vol. 6, No. 4, Winter

Wilson, Caroll L. (ed.)
    (1980): Coal - bridge to the future, Cambridge, Mass.

Winckler, G.
    (1980): Mikro- und makroökonomische Effekte der Energie-
    verteuerung, in: Wirtschaftspolitische Blätter, Vol. 27,
    No. 2

Wirtschaftswoche
    (1980): Die Multis aus dem Morgenland, No. 33, 15 August
    (1981): Verluste verstaatlichen, No. 29, 10 July

Woolcock, Stephen
    (1982): Iron and steel, in: L. Turner, N. McMullen (eds.):
    The newly industrializing countries: trade and adjustment,
    London

World Bank
  (1980): Energy in developing countries, Washington, D.C.,
  August
  (1981): World development report 1981, Washington, D.C.,
  August
  (1983a): Weltentwicklungsbericht 1983, Washington, D.C.
  (1983b): The energy transition in developing countries,
  Washington, D.C.
  (1983c): Worldwide investment analysis. The case of aluminium, World Bank Staff Working Papers, No. 603
  (1983d): Cofinancing, Washington, D.C.

Yohai, Samuel Aberto
  (1983): How the World Bank might recycle assets, in: Euromoney, January

Zainy, Muhammad Ali
  (1981): Development investment as a guide for oil production policy in OPEC countries, in: OPEC-Review, Vol. 5,
  No. 2, Summer

NEWSPAPER ARTICLES

Blick durch die Wirtschaft
  (2.2.1982): Energieersparnis für die Textilindustrie
  (24.2.1982): Neue Energieprojekte in den Niederlanden
  (5.4.1982): Energieeinsparung in der Aluminiumerzeu-
  gung

Börsen-Zeitung
  (30.9.1980): Bundesbank will Klarheit über Länderrisiken
  (7.11.1980): Gleske: Den Stabilitätsvorsprung verteidigen
  (9.10.1982): Verschärfte Kreditaufsicht für US-Banken
  (7. 1.1984): IMF erhellt internationale Verschuldung

O Estado de S. Paulo
  (15.2.1983): Os acordos bilaterais

Financial Times
  (25. 8.1981): R.C. Murphy: Libya in second OPEC oil barter
  proposal
  (20. 1.1982): Anthony Robinson: Soviet oil output down but
  gas production rises
  (27.10.1982): Ian Rodger: Growth in packaging and cars continues
  (9. 2.1983): Ian Rodger: Europe's aluminium industry: a
  year for painful choices
  (23. 2.1983a): Geoffrey Maynard: The world economy - why
  oil prices must fall more

(23.2.1983b): Kathleen Evans: When small means big in the
field of success
(14.3.1983) : Jeffrey E. Garten: Heightened role as burdens
multiply
(11.4.1983) : Roger Matthews: Saudi officials seek to end
speculation over budget policies
(22.4.1983) : BIS chief in warning on interbank lines
(3.5.1983) : Carla Rapoport: Hoechst will buy ammonia
from Kuwait
(9.5.1983) : Alan Friedman: The shock takes it toll
(13.5.1983) : Mary Frings: Kobe Steel to build aluminium
mill in Bahrain
(25.5.1983) : Andrew Whitley: Brazil seeks to recover lost
markets
(1.6.1983): Andrew Whitley: Alcohol on the road back in
Brazil
(7.11.1983): Banks fear Brazilian blot
(1.2.1984): Richard Johns: Kuwait takes up Gulf Oil's
European mantle
(8.2.1984a): Alan Friedman: Italians to build gas complex in Algeria
(8.2.1984b): David Fishlock: Britain and France to work
together on nuclear reactors
(28.2.1984): Terry Povey: Iran to pay Japanese group in
oil for disputed steel plant contract
(29.3.1984): Carla Rapoport, Hilfra Tandy: Saudi Arabia
plays an ace

Frankfurter Allgemeine Zeitung
(16. 1.1981): Eurobanken gegen zuviel OPEC-Geld
(7. 5.1982): Statt sechs nur eins. Die neue Stahltech-
nologie von Klöckner erspart Energie
(9.11.1982): Zwischen Paris und Algier eine "beispiel-
hafte Kooperation"
(19.11.1982): Engere deutsch-arabische Zusammenarbeit
(13. 1.1983): Internationale Banken schaffen Frühwarn-
system
(26. 1.1983): Klaus Broichhausen: Hermes muß streng bleiben
(21. 4.1983): Auch Strom aus Importkohle wäre zu teuer
(26. 4.1983): Japan erwartet einen Rekordexport nach
Iran
(2. 5.1983): Italien: Erdgasvertrag mit Algerien abge-
schlossen
(3. 5.1983): Trotz mancher Schwachpunkte bessere Finanz-
struktur bei Hoechst

(9. 8.1983): Benzin aus Kohle nur mit großen Subven-
tionen

Frankfurter Rundschau
    (6.4.1983): Weniger Öldollar für Moskau

Handelsblatt
    (11.9.1980): Abstimmungs-Boykott verhinderte Resolution
    gegen PLO-Beobachter
    (9.6.1980): Recycling geht nicht mehr freischwebend
    (8.10.1980): Japan - Devisengesetz wurde mit Vorbehalt
    liberalisiert
    (24./25.1.1981): Japans Yen für Saudi-Arabien
    (26.5.1982):Jürgen E. Fischer: Aluminium - ein Markt im
    Wandel: Das bestehende Innovationspotential wird auch in
    Zukunft konsequent genutzt werden

International Herald Tribune
    (16.6.1980): Guth underlines microeconomic risks for
    private banks in recycling funds
    (14./15.3.1981): Caution reigns at Saudi Central Bank

Nachrichten für Außenhandel
    (20.10.1981): Dänemark: Exporterfolg bei Fernheiztechnik
    (22.10.1982): Gaspreiseinigung mit Algerien beflügelt
    Italiens Geschäftserwartungen
    (3.12.1982): Frankreich: Höherer Absatz von Kohleheizkes-
    seln erwartet
    (24. 2.1983): Japan legt neues Rezessionsgesetz vor
    (10. 5.1983): Kooperationsabkommen Belgien-Algerien
    (1.12.1983): KHD und Sumitomo kooperieren bei Kohlever-
    gasung
    (19.12.1983): Petrochemische Industrie nicht subsidiert
    (28.12.1983): Stahlindustrie produziert zu energieinten-
    siv
    (6. 4.1984): Deutscher Auslandsbau ist nicht mehr auf Öl
    gebaut
    (3. 5.1984): Saudi-Arabien an weiterer Kooperation inter-
    essiert
    (28. 5.1984): Kuwait baut Raffineriekapazitäten aus
    (1. 6.1984): Im Blickpunkt: Investitionen in Saudi-Ara-
    bien

Neue Zürcher Zeitung
    (31.3.1981): Hoher Kredit Saudiarabiens an den IMF

Süddeutsche Zeitung
    (17.1.1984): In Ost und West schieben Länder Schulden vor
    sich her

Die Welt
    (14.4.1983): Joachim Schaufuss: Den Ausbau von Kohle- und
    Kernenergie empfohlen

Die Zeit
(7. 5.1982): Irene Mayer-List: Die Grenzen des Wachstums - Sinkende Nachfrage, fallende Preise: Die Entwicklungsländer bleiben auf ihren Rohstoffen sitzen
(28. 5.1982): Heinz-Günter Kemmer: Die eingebildeten Kranken - Je mehr Anlagen verkauft werden, desto lauter stöhnen die Exporteure
(8.10.1982): Wolfgang Gehrmann: Der Multi aus dem Morgenland - Hoechst-Beteiligung: Kuwait baut sein Öl-Imperium aus
(25. 2.1983): Helmut Schmidt: Die Weltwirtschaft ist unser Schicksal
(1. 7.1983): Die Mark wird wieder stärker